What's the Beef?

Politics, Science, and the Environment
Peter M. Haas, Sheila Jasanoff, and Gene Rochlin, editors

What's the Beef?

The Contested Governance of European Food Safety

edited by Christopher Ansell and David Vogel

The MIT Press
Cambridge, Massachusetts
London, England

Oau
© 2006 Massachusetts Institute of Technology

All rights reserved. No part of this book may be reproduced in any form by any electronic or mechanical means (including photocopying, recording, or information storage and retrieval) without permission in writing from the publisher.

MIT Press books may be purchased at special quantity discounts for business or sales promotional use. For information, please e-mail special_sales@mitpress. mit.edu or write to Special Sales Department, The MIT Press, 55 Hayward Street, Cambridge, MA 02142.

This book was set in Sabon by SNP Best-set Typesetter Ltd., Hong Kong and was printed and bound in the United States of America. Printed on recycled paper.

Library of Congress Cataloging-in-Publication Data

What's the beef? / edited by Christopher Ansell and David Vogel.
    p.   cm.—(Politics, science, and the environment)
Includes bibliographical references and index.
ISBN 0-262-01225-1 (alk. paper)—ISBN 0-262-51192-4 (pbk. : alk. paper)
1. Food service—Safety measures 2. Food handling—Safety measures. I. Ansell, Christopher K., 1957– II. Vogel, David, 1947– III. Series.
TX911.3.S3W43   2006
363.192—dc22
                                                          2005056208

10 9 8 7 6 5 4 3 2 1

Contents

Acknowledgments

This project has been a highly collaborative effort. Our primary funding came from the Institute for European Studies at the University of California, and we could like to express our appreciation for its invaluable financial support as well as for the logistical and administrative assistance of its excellent staff. Our first project meeting was held in Paris and was sponsored by Sciences Po under the direction of Renaud Dehousse. We owe a considerable debt to the participants at our preliminary meeting in Paris as well as to those who attended a similar meeting held in Berkeley for experts on European food safety in North America. They played a critical role in helping us formulate and define the basic intellectual framework for this project. Our final meeting in Berkeley was cosponsored by the Clausen Center for International Business and Policy at the Haas School of Business, directed by Sebastian Teunissen and held at the Center for Law and Society at UC Berkeley, directed by Robert Kagan.

Rahsaan Maxwell, a graduate student in the Department of Political Science at UC Berkeley, in addition to coauthoring one of the books chapters, served as the project's research assistant, helping us identify possible contributors, survey the extensive literature on European food safety, and organize each of our three meetings. We are very much in his debt.

We would also like to thank our editor at MIT Press, Clay Morgan, for his support of this project and to acknowledge the helpful advice of the three editors of the series in which this book appears, namely, Peter Haas, Sheila Jasanoff, and Gene Rochlin. The book also benefited from the constructive criticism of the three anonymous reviewers for the press.

We are especially pleased to note the number of nationalities represented in this volume. Our twenty contributors are drawn from nine countries—Canada, France, Germany, Great Britain, Italy, the Netherlands, Norway, Switzerland, and the United States—making this book a notable example of international academic collaboration.

David Vogel
Christopher Ansell
Berkeley, California
August, 2005

I

Introduction

1

The Contested Governance of European Food Safety Regulation

Christopher Ansell and David Vogel

It is now a decade and a half since the UK's Conservative minister of agriculture, John Gummer, ceremoniously fed his four-year-old daughter, Cordelia, a hamburger to demonstrate the safety of British beef. Since then, 137 British citizens have died from a variant of Creutzfeldt-Jakob disease (vCJD), presumably from eating beef infected with bovine spongiform encephalopathy (BSE), popularly known as "mad cow disease."[1] The event has become emblematic of a public policy public relations fiasco. More important, it signifies the kinds of dilemmas in the relations between science and regulation, market promotion and consumer protection, public authority and public opinion that riddle contemporary governance.

A few years later, an equally provocative symbolic action occurred across the English Channel. In the town of Millau in southwest France, an emerging farm and antiglobalization movement, led by a sheep farmer named José Bové, used tractors to destroy a McDonalds then under construction. The action of Confédération paysanne was prompted by the imposition of American import duties on French foods like roquefort cheese, mustard, truffles, and foie gras in retaliation for a European Union ban on American hormone-treated beef. Again, the action symbolized the political and social tensions surrounding the public regulation of food. Banned by the European Union (EU) as a potential health risk, the United States and Canada claimed that the EU ban on hormone-treated beef was merely disguised trade protectionism. Although the World Trade Organization (WTO) disagreed that the ban was protectionist, it ruled the ban was not scientifically supported and allowed the United States and Canada to impose trade sanctions on Europe.[2]

Most recently, President George W. Bush lambasted Europeans for contributing to hunger in Africa because of their ban on genetically modified food (GMOs). His criticism was in part an implicit reference to the earlier refusal of Zambian and Zimbabwean governments to accept U.S. food aid that contained genetically modified corn. Bush argued that Europe's five-year moratorium on the import of GM foods had undermined Africa's investment in biotech agriculture: "Our partners in Europe are impeding this effort. They have blocked all new bio-crops because of unfounded, unscientific fears. This has caused many African nations to avoid investing in biotechnologies, for fear their products will be shut out of European markets. European governments should join— not hinder—the great cause of ending hunger in Africa."[3] A week before Bush made this speech, his administration had filed a formal complaint with the WTO over the EU's regulation of GMOs.

This book is about the politics surrounding the regulation of food safety in Europe. In many respects, the issues raised by this topic are common to many types of environmental, health, and safety regulation and to many international disputes over trade. Moreover, despite the more heated attention to food safety issues in Europe in comparison with North America, the former's scientific and regulatory concerns are roughly similar to those faced by all governments. So why a book about food safety regulation? And why a book specifically about European food safety regulation?

The regulation of food safety represents a particularly important dimension of public policy for four reasons. First, few other areas of public policy so directly, personally, and continually affect the well-being of every citizen. For citizens in their roles as consumers, food safety is a highly salient and frequently emotional issue, one that affects their personal health and safety. Few other areas of policy failure, or threats or perceptions of policy failure, are as politically salient as those associated with food safety. Second, the regulation of food safety has important economic dimensions. Policy failure associated with food safety has often exacerbated the failure of markets to provide higher levels of food safety: the lack of political transparency and the inhibition of the working of economic incentives have been and are key determinants of the economic implications of those failures in Europe. Furthermore, the highly integrated nature of today's food supply chain means that economic impacts have become more severe than in the past, as repercussions are felt rapidly in domestic markets as well as across borders.[4] Third, the regulation of food safety has an important international dimension. Historically, divergent food standards have played a critical role as trade barriers. Not surprisingly, efforts to reduce the ability of national governments to use food safety standards to protect domestic populations have been a major focus of trade liberalization, both within the EU and globally (Vogel 1995). Finally, few other areas of government regulation of business have such an important cultural dimension. Both national and ethnic cultures are associated with distinctive attitudes toward food. In fact, transatlantic differences in food regulations have frequently been ascribed to distinctive European and American food cultures.

In short, food safety is an important—and often highly salient—regulatory arena, with important implications for producers, trade liberalization, and cultural attitudes and norms. Food safety is a vital concern everywhere, but nowhere else has it been brought into such sharp relief as in contemporary Europe. A series of food-related scares and disputes, most notably mad cow disease, dioxin contamination, beef hormones, and GMOs, have made European consumers unusually sensitive to food safety policies. This heightened issue saliency coincides with two major projects of institutional change—European integration and international trade liberalization—that have both produced new tensions among countries and accentuated the public's sense of a loss of control over food as a trusted commodity and cultural patrimony (Vogel 1995, Phillips and Wolfe 2001). The highly contested character of food safety regulation in Europe may represent a bellwether for conflicts that are likely to become more prominent everywhere in the next few decades as technological change and globalization reshape the way our food is produced, marketed, and distributed.

In addition to its bellwether status, the subject of European food safety regulation provides an unusually rich lens into a set of broader, interrelated contemporary political developments: (1) the growing importance of multilevel regulation, (2) the uncertain future of European integration, (3) discontent over trade globalization, (4) core disputes about risk assessment and regulatory science, (5) the evolution of frameworks for regulating novel biological technologies, (6) the shifting balance between public and private regulation, (7) the increasingly contested nature of agricultural protectionism, and finally, (8) the transatlantic divide. We discuss each of these briefly below.

Multilevel Regulation   As the vignettes that introduced this chapter suggest, food safety regulation in Europe provides a particularly illuminating example of an emerging system of multilevel regulation. UK Minister of Agriculture John Gummer represents the national level of regulation. The EU ban on hormone-treated beef and rules governing GMOs represent the European level. And the WTO-sanctioned U.S. and Canadian retaliation on French roquefort and the two countries' complaint to the WTO against the EU's restrictions on GMOs represent the international dimension of regulation. While issues associated with regulatory federalism are old ones, multilevel regulation has become an especially salient issue for two reasons. First, the creation of regulatory authority at the European level clashes with preexisting national systems of regulation. This is particularly true for food, because food safety is one of the oldest regulatory systems at the national level. Second, the extension and development of a global trade regime and the increasing density of international governance in environmental protection, human rights, and trade liberalization have created international regulatory regimes of varying importance. Multilevel systems have an appropriate role to play, as regulatory processes must operate at different scales. However, they can also lead to political tensions as different regulatory levels adopt different decision-making criteria. Among the critical issues this book addresses are the conflicts and adaptations that have resulted from the interaction of regulations at the national, European, and international levels.

The Politics of European Integration   European integration has created deep and unresolved tensions between intergovernmental and federal visions of Europe. The Single European Act (1986) moved the project of market integration significantly forward. But market integration required either the harmonization of preexisting regulatory regimes or the creation of new European regulations that overrode preexisting national policies. Food and food safety have been at the forefront of the debates over regulatory harmonization—and not least because of the importance of food as a national cultural symbol. The beef hormone, BSE, and GMO disputes have revealed tensions in the democratic character of European regulation and the organization of risk assessment and management at the European level (Majone 2000, Vos, 2000).

Trade Globalization and Its Discontents   The creation of the WTO represented a new phase in the institutionalization of trade liberalization. Most important, it established a formal process for adjudicating trade disputes that gave substantial authority to an international trade institution. Prior to the creation of the WTO, the Codex Alimentarius Commission (a joint World Health Organization and Food and Agricultural Organization standard-setting body) set voluntary food safety standards to promote agricultural trade and protect consumers.[5] But with the creation of the WTO, the Codex standards have acquired legal authority. They are now employed by WTO dispute settlement panels to help assess whether national food safety standards constitute nontariff barriers. This in turn has given food safety regulation a critical international dimension (Skogstad 2001; Josling, Roberts, and Orden 2004). Not surprisingly, the antiglobalization movement has responded by attacking globalization in general and the WTO regime in particular for undermining democratic rule and compromising stringent environmental, health, and safety standards. As Bové's actions against McDonalds (and later against GMOs) indicate, the antiglobalization movement has made food and food safety a key issue in their protest. Yet even beyond the highly visible protests of antiglobalization protesters, trade liberalization has heightened the concerns of consumers about the quality and safety of their food (Krissoff, Bohman, and Caswell 2002).

The Politicization of Science and Risk Assessment   As President Bush's statement about Europe's "unscientific" fears about genetically engineered foods suggests, the precise use and value of science and risk assessment have become deeply politicized. Of course, such disputes are well known to those who work with or study regulatory politics. Again, however, disputes over food safety suggest the outlines of a new stage or scale of politicization. Because of the three points mentioned above—multilevel regulation, European integration, and trade globalization—the stakes over the precise role and institutionalization of science and risk assessment have increased (Phillips and Wolfe 2001). The formation of European and international regulatory regimes has increased the overall importance of science and risk assessment, as they play a critical role in determining and assessing regulatory policies and standards. (Phillips and Wolfe 2001). On the one hand, science-based decision making and risk assessment have become a universal discourse shared across regulatory levels. Yet on the other hand, disputes increasingly revolve around distinctive approaches to assessing risks, as well as the weight that decision makers should attach to public attitudes and preferences. An example is the controversy surrounding the role of the precautionary principle in the disputes between the EU and its trading partners over the EU's regulatory policies toward beef hormone and the GMOs. (Noiville 2000; Löfstedt, Fischoff, and Fischoff 2002). Furthermore, the reform of existing food safety institutions following the mad cow scare has tended to accentuate rather than settle disputes over the institutional relationship between risk assessment (scientific evaluation and advice) and risk management (standard setting and enforcement).

The Regulation of Novel Biological Technologies   The Human Genome Project, animal cloning, stem cell research, and pharmaceutical and food bioengineering, among many other emerging biological technologies, seem to alternately promise startling new technological breakthroughs of great value or frightening visions of "Frankenfood," eugenics, and environmental contamination. Issues related to liability, intellectual property rights, and appropriate models of risk assessment and regulation are not yet well established. Here again, the European dispute over GM foods may establish a precedent for how societies will debate and regulate novel technologies that present complex ethical and scientific questions (Schurman and Munro 2003; Bernauer 2003).

Public versus Private Regulation   Across a range of regulatory fields, new questions are being asked about the potential for private self-regulation to serve as an alternative to costly command-and-control public regulation. In some cases, private actors have banded together to create private certifying bodies. In other cases, they have established voluntary standards (ISO 9000). In still other cases, new combinations of public and private regulation have developed. Indeed, the food industry has been a leader in experimenting with a new system of private self-regulation called hazard analysis and critical control points (HAACP) (Henson and Caswell 1999). This issue of public-private regulation is explored in this book by both van Waarden (chapter 2) and Bernauer and Caduff (chapter 4).

Contestation over Agricultural Protectionism State subsidization of agriculture in Europe and the United States has been seen as a major roadblock to freer trade and a major barrier to the economic success of developing nations. The collapse of the Cancun trade talks in 2003 represents the potential for this issue to disrupt world trade. To the extent that the role of subsidies declines, the role of food safety standards as nontariff barriers is likely to increase. Thus, food safety standards are likely to become increasingly contested as "disguised" (producer) protectionism. As more foods from developing nations are imported by developed nations—and as food chains in general become more global—concern about control and inspection of imported foods is likely to increase (Freidberg 2004). Pressures from consumers to tighten domestic food safety standards could also become more prominent. These new cleavages are likely to generate new alignments between consumers and domestic producers (sometimes called Baptist and Bootlegger coalitions; see Vogel 1995, Young 2003), as well as among producers in different countries.

The Transatlantic Divide On the one hand, Europeans appear to be more concerned and more sensitive to risks associated with food than do Americans, and these differences appear to be at the heart of trade conflicts over beef hormones and GMOs (Vogel 2003, Skogstad, forthcoming and chapter 9, this volume; Bernauer 2003). On the other hand, institutional differences between Europe and North America may accentuate, and possibly exaggerate, these differences in risk perception. Transatlantic dialogue and adjustment can also produce patterns of convergence on food safety issues (Young 2003). Whatever the precise source and status of transatlantic differences, trade disputes over food represent a critical element of the often contentious transatlantic relationship.

A Synthetic Perspective

Are disputes about European food safety regulation interesting and important merely because they touch on this important panoply of issues described above? Is there a meaning to the contentious events so emblazoned in our minds by the symbol of the "mad cow"? What are the controversies over food in Europe a "case" of: regulatory failure, risk society, trading up, multilevel governance, institutional change, policy failure, cultural divide, or something else? Each of the contributors to this book wrestled with this question. Collectively, we have searched for a synthetic perspective that would enable us to describe and identify what is distinctive about this policy area and could serve as a basis to compare it to other policy areas.

The synthetic perspective that we came to share as a group is what we call *contested governance*. The events, conflicts, and institutional reforms described in this book represent a particular syndrome of policymaking and political dispute. All governance is to a lesser or greater extent contested in the sense that policy actors pursue different interests and take different positions on policy outcomes. This kind of conflict is wholly compatible with fairly well agreed-on and legitimate institutional frameworks through which policy is typically decided and implemented. By *contested governance*, we mean to describe a more pervasive and fundamental form of conflict, one in which contestation spills beyond policy outcomes to who should make decisions and where, how, and on what basis they should be made. Contested governance is associated with a pervasive sense of distrust that challenges the legitimacy of existing institutional arrangements.

Distinguishing Contested Governance from Policy Conflict

The term *contested governance* calls attention to the pervasively contentious quality of certain public policy domains. To be sure, we are aware that all domains of public policy are subject to dispute and conflict. But the scope and depth of that conflict vary across policy domains. The term *contested governance* illuminates the particularly intense and broad-based conflict about the foundational assumptions and institutional frameworks through which a policy domain is governed. While conflict about policy outcomes is common in most political arenas, intense and broad-based conflict targeted at the fundamentals of governance is far less common (though as we suggest below, it may be becoming more common). Much policy conflict takes the institutional rules of the game for granted or merely attacks it at the margins. Of course, the day-to-day struggles of interest groups, politicians, bureaucrats, and policy experts are often battles to control the rules of the game (Moe 1990). Yet these struggles are typically constrained battles of maneuver, where wins and losses take place on the margin. Contested governance occurs when these day-to-day battles are displaced by more widespread public debate about the fundamentals of governance.[6]

The contested governance of European food safety regulation involves debates over four fundamental questions:

First, *on what basis* is food safety regulated? This question has to do with the broad criteria public officials will employ to determine food safety standards. For example, what role should scientific risk assessment play in shaping regulatory policy? What is the role of public opinion? How should the values of safety, economic efficiency, and innovation balanced? On what basis should regulation be legitimated?

Second, *who* should regulate European food safety? This question addresses the balance between private and public regulation. What are the respective roles for public authorities and of firm or industry self-regulation?

Third, *where* should food safety be regulated? This question refers to the level of government or governance responsible for setting food safety standards. Specifically, what kinds of regulation should take place at the local level, the national level, the regional (European) level, and the international level?

Fourth, *how* should food safety regulated? This question specifically addresses the establishment of authoritative bodies and procedures at each of these levels of governance. What institutional frameworks should be used to make, implement, and enforce decisions?

In the next section we outline a broad interpretative framework that illuminates some of the critical causes, general dynamics, and consequences of contested governance.

A Model of Contested Governance

Our use of the concept of contested governance is intended as an organizing device to help synthesize the major developments in food safety regulation in Europe over the past decade; it provides a useful interpretative framework for illuminating what the disputes over European food safety regulation are a "case" of, thereby providing a useful metric for illuminating the dynamics of similar cases. Our discussion focuses on three dimensions of contested governance: causes, dynamics, and outcomes.

Causes of Contestation

Triggering Events   Attention to foundational issues of political and institutional reform is typically prompted by a highly salient event or crisis that galvanizes public attention and intensive media scrutiny. This attention in turn creates windows of opportunity that may produce dramatic shifts in policy debates and coalitions (Kingdon 1995). The triggering event in the European food safety domain was quite clearly the BSE affair. As table 1.1 indicates, BSE was not the first food scare in Europe. Serious disputes about animal hormones preceded the BSE crisis and attracted considerable public attention. But the coverage and concern over BSE were far greater and more widespread. The BSE crisis created a shock to the institutional status quo, producing a collapse of trust in public authority that Jasanoff (1997) has called a "civic dislocation." Although the scandal began in Britain, it soon spread to Europe and elsewhere. The three chapters in this book on national cases (chapters 6, 7, and 8) and two of the chapters on policymaking at the EU level (chapters 10 and 11) describe the institutional crises produced by BSE.

Table 1.1
Selected recent events in European food safety

1970s: Scare over Diethylstilbestrol (DES) in French veal

1980: Four of ten EU members impose ban on beef hormones; European Commission prohibits use of several hormones.

1985: EU bans the use of growth-promoting hormones in beef production

1990: EU Council of Ministers imposes an initially temporary ban on the use of rBST in milk production; the EU legislates procedures for approval of GM crops and food.

1996: The UK government announces a connection between vCJD and BSE; EU imposes ban on British beef; U.S.-grown GMO corn and soybeans first arrive in Europe; the United States and Canada file dispute settlement requests with the WTO in regard to European ban on hormone-treated beef.

1997: EU Parliament passes a conditional censure of EU commission handling of BSE dispute.

1998: De facto European moratorium against the planting or use of GMOs is initiated.

1999: Dioxin and Coca-Cola scares in Belgium. Listeria outbreak in France. New Food Safety Agency (AFFSA) created in France. The Council of Ministers definitively bans use of rBST; EU lifts ban on British beef, but France continues ban.

2001: Major reorganization of German food safety authority; UK foot and mouth epidemic affecting cows and sheep

2002: EU adopts General Food Law, which establishes the European Food Safety Authority (EFSA); a new food safety agency (FSA) created in the UK; France lifts ban on British beef.

2003: The United States, Canada, and Argentina request WTO dispute settlement panel over the failure of EU to lift the GMO moratorium; a dispute between Finland and Italy over where to locate EFSA is finally resolved in favor of Parma, Italy.

Contested governance tends to occur in policy sectors in which mass-level attention to issues is periodic but intense—a response, for example, to brutal police behavior vividly captured on film, the horrible death of a child due to parental neglect, the siting of a landfill near a residential development, dramatic cases of espionage or corruption, a health epidemic, a fire in a crowded nightclub. These dramatic events create high issue salience because the public experiences them directly and emotionally. However, issue salience is likely to erode quickly unless the event portends or symbolizes impacts on broader publics, is seen as a pattern, or persists over time. Uncertainty about diagnosis, effects, or solutions is likely to increase the diffuse sense of the problem and heighten the issue salience. As suggested by the biotechnology dispute in Europe (see Chapter 5, this volume), media and social movement interest are probably important for maintaining and amplifying issue salience.

These triggering events disrupt taken-for-granted assumptions about how the world does or should work. They are what La Porte (1994) characterizes as "institutional surprises." Something that was assumed safe and widely used is suddenly found to be unsafe; danger and threats are suddenly discovered to have always been present where least expected. Although consumers are well aware of the possibility of food contamination, few expected to contract a brain wasting disease from eating meat. We suspect that there is something particularly disquieting about the disruption of routine assumptions that motivates future loss of trust.

These triggering events typically produce a diagnosis of prior institutional or political failure. Crises initiated by natural or uncontrollable causes are probably less likely to encourage this diagnosis than crises easily attributed to "policy disasters" (Dunleavy 1995) or "policy fiascoes" (Bovens and 't Hart 1996). Moreover, the event needs to suggest systemic, rather than merely fluke, institutional errors.[7] Looking into the future, the triggering event ought to portend future occurrences of the event. And the perceived risk of future impacts ought to be widespread. When it galvanized public attention in 1996, the mad cow "scandal" suggested systematic conflict of interest on the part of UK authorities, and the cases discovered at the time threatened to be merely the tip of the iceberg.

Finally, a powerful triggering event is likely to be societal in the scope of its consequences—for example, to transcend the boundaries between public and private and between institutional and personal. The BSE crisis, for example, was not only a crisis for public authorities, but also quite clearly a crisis for private food producers and retailers. Moreover, it was not merely a problem for these public and private institutions, but also confronted consumers with a personal choice about meat consumption. The societal scope of the crisis is implicit in the broad focus on food cultures developed by van Waarden (chapter 2) and in the comparative analysis of institutional trust developed Kjærnes, Dulsrud, and Poppe (chapter 3).

Longer-Term Trends or Tensions   The importance of a triggering event can lead analysts to discount the longer-term trends and tensions that ultimately contribute to contested governance. While the triggering event reframes interpretations of both past and future, it also reveals long-term social, political, or economic trends or institutional tensions. From this perspective, the triggering event is more like a catalyst for the crisis than a full causal explanation. We recognize the danger of such an argument. In hindsight, it is easy to interpret prior events or institutional tensions as signals of imminent crisis. Nevertheless, an overly narrow focus on the triggering event is likely to misanalyze the causes and consequences of contested governance.

While we would characterize food safety regulation prior to the BSE crisis as conflictual rather than contested, prior conflicts conditioned the public response to this particular policy failure. As suggested by Borraz, Besançon, and Clergeau (chapter 6), the French reaction to BSE was shaped by an earlier scandal that attributed responsibility for the consequences of a contaminated blood supply to the government. Hence, the French were primed to suspect government malfeasance. More generally, as table 1.1 suggests, a heightened sensitivity to food safety and health issues in Europe predates BSE. Prior debates about beef hormones reach back to the 1970s in Europe and remained controversial through the 1980s (see Skogstad, chapter 9). The United States also had a series of food scares in the 1980s and 1990s. None of these provided the same magnitude of triggering event as BSE in Europe, but even after the recent discovery of a case of BSE in the United States, which produced significant media attention and public suspicion, it appears that the "lid was put back on" the conflict. This did not occur in Europe.

The most proximate long-term change that led to the BSE crisis were changes in the technology of feeding livestock. Feeding cows meal composed of the remnants of other cows was the technology that allowed BSE to spread within Europe. Obviously the debate over biotechnology that followed on the heels of the BSE scandal was also about the changing technology of producing food. More generally, the technology of food production and marketing has become so complex and technologically sophisticated that the regulation of food has become increasingly challenging. Even before the BSE scandal, new systematic conceptions of "farm-to-fork" regulation and new strategies of regulation (e.g., HAACP) were already being developed by European regulatory agencies. As discussed by Van Waarden (chapter 2), Bernauer and Caduff (chapter 4), Borraz, Besançon, and Clergeau (chapter 6), and Steiner (chapter 8), these new strategies reflect increasing pressures for industrial self-regulation, a trend that challenges the traditional boundaries between public and private regulation.

The issue salience of BSE, as a result of the directly experienced fear and uncertainty of consumers, is an essential part of the story of the contested governance of European food safety. But attention to BSE can discourage analysts from developing a fuller appreciation of the way other contextual factors have shaped the timing and extent of the crisis. The entanglement of food issues with larger institutional and political debates has contributed to the intensity and duration of contestation. Specifically, the advancing economic and political integration of the EU and the creation of the WTO trade regime were important contextual variables that interacted with these food scares to produce contested governance in Europe.

As Hooghe and Marks (2001) argue, European integration has generated intense debate about whether the EU is the embodiment of a neoliberal or a regulated capitalism project. As detailed by Alemmano (chapter 10), food was recognized quite early in the EU's history to be a stumbling block to deeper market integration. Consequently, a significant body of European regulation has been built up around food. BSE brought this issue to a head when the continental European states banned British beef, which, according to Alemmano, brought a new appreciation of the tension between market integration and public health in EU regulation. However, the tension extends beyond even public health concerns to the way certain foods are emblematic of national cultures. The dispute around the pasteurization of French cheese is a good illustration of how food safety and cultural sovereignty have become intertwined. As suggested by Van Waarden (chapter 2), the continual chafing over the harmonization of food standards created by the European integration process and the framing of these conflicts as disputes over cultural sovereignty prepared European public opinion for its reaction to the beef hormones, BSE, and GMO disputes. He also highlights the diversity of institutional logics by which European (and other) nations regulate food; the Europeanization and internationalization of food regulation bring these different institutional logics into uneasy contact with one another.

Beyond the issue of European integration, contention surrounding the Common Agricultural Policy (CAP) has subtly shaped the contestation over food safety regulation. The BSE crisis was in part produced by the way cows were fed in Europe, a feeding regime that some have argued was indirectly encouraged by CAP (Fisher 1999). The nearly continuous controversy over the past decade around CAP reform may have also contributed to the saliency of food issues for European publics.

A third factor associated with European integration is the way that it has simultaneously and subtly affected institutional trust and the opportunity structure for the mobilization of political issues. Bernauer and Caduff (chapter 4) argue that the multilevel structure of European food safety regulation has itself discouraged the reestablishment of institutional trust in food safety regulation. The chapters by Borraz, Besançon, and Clergeau on France (chapter 6) and Rothstein on the UK (chapter 7) suggest that reform pressures from below can produce conflicts between national and European regulatory strategies.

A more subtle source of conflict is the perceived democratic deficit at the European level As Skogstad (chapter 9) argues, concern about the legitimacy of EU regulation is a source of the "political" style of its decision making. At the same time, European-level regulation has provided new opportunities for the mobilization of consumer and environmental issues and groups that may have a weaker voice at the national level, an issue explored by Ansell, Maxwell, and Sicurelli (chapter 5). In part, these new opportunities are related to the problem of a European democratic deficit. As Skogstad notes, the European Commission (EC) has encouraged the representation of European-wide consumer and environmental interests.[8]

Similar points can be made about the WTO. As the antiglobalization movement attests, the line of battle has been drawn between market liberalization and national environmental and safety regulation. Again, food has become a central symbol of consumer, producer, and cultural sovereignty, and agricultural protectionism has become a central focus of trade conflict. In addition, as described by Young and Holmes (chapter 12), the outcome of multilevel dynamics of food safety regulation among EU member states (especially "trading-up" dynamics that lead to conversence on higher regulatory standards) creates spillover conflicts for the WTO regime. Thus, the resolution of intra-EU conflicts is likely to create conflicts between the EU and its trading partners. Moreover, conflict at the international level is exacerbated because international food safety standards are more authoritative under the WTO regime than under its predecessor, the General Agreement on Tariffs and Trade. In fact, the conflict at the international level is similar to the tensions created by the need to harmonize standards at the European level. As Young and Holmes and Noiville (chapter 13) emphasize, the resolution of such conflicts will require appeals to both science and risk analysis, which typically entail contestable interpretations of both data and decision making. Noiville argues that the precautionary approach to risk adopted by the EU is not antithetical to the science-based decision making required by the WTO, but that the wide latitude for interpretation of WTO requirements is likely to contribute to political conflict. Perhaps the more general point—a theme that runs through many of our chapters—is that in the context of pervasive distrust, the resolution of interjurisdictional conflicts through scientific risk analysis is likely to exacerbate rather than mitigate conflict.

Institutional and Political Asymmetries   Contested governance is likely to emerge when policies or institutions can be perceived to have facilitated or failed to respond adequately to important public concerns. Contested governance is particularly likely to emerge when periodic but intense public scrutiny confronts an extensively institutionalized policy sector in which day-to-day routine decisions are delegated to experts or administrators with little ongoing attention or interest from the public. Buonanno's discussion (chapter 11) of the EU's "comitology" system of expert decision making provides a good example. In the face of the BSE crisis, this system for providing scientific and political advice to the European Commission was strongly criticized for its lack of transparency. We suggest three conditions that contribute to producing tension between intense public scrutiny and extensive routine administrative or expert decision making.

First, contestation is accentuated where there are sharp contrasts between demands for procedural and substantive rationality. Procedural rationality entails compliance with preestablished rules, protocols, or norms typically designed to guarantee equity, rights, accountability, or objectivity. By contrast, substantive rationality is measured according to whether outcomes themselves are regarded as true, correct, or valuable. Many of the chapters in this book suggest that conflict over food safety regulation at and between levels of governance stem from this tension between procedural standards (e.g., risk analysis) and public perceptions of risk.

Second, contestation is accentuated where public decision makers must balance multiple goals and where the costs and benefits of governance are asymmetrically distributed, such that some persons or constituency groups bear the costs while different persons or constituency groups benefit. Under these conditions, real or perceived political bias or conflict of interest is likely to contribute to the loss of legitimacy. To be sure, public decision making must often balance multiple goals or impose asymmetric costs and benefits, as exemplified by many environmental and natural resource conflicts. But public skepticism is likely to be particularly sharp where a public agency's mandate (or desire) to balance multiple goals clashes with the public's insistence on prioritization of some problems over others. The reform of food safety agencies at the national and European levels was motivated in part by the strong public perceptions that existing institutions had conflicts of interest.

Finally, contestation is accentuated where the public has limited exit options. The ability to avoid state regulation or find alternative private provision of goods will reduce the urgency of contestation. Although Kjærnes, Dulsrud, and Poppe (chapter 3) note that consumers often adopt private strategies for ensuring food safety and Borraz, Besançon, and Clergeau (chapter 6) and Steiner (chapter 8) note the importance of private quality schemes for guaranteeing the safety of food, most consumers remain highly dependent on forces well beyond their control for the provision of their food.

These factors interact with the complexity and diffuseness of problems and institutions. Where problems are complex and do not permit easy solution, they are likely to erupt periodically into public debate. Institutional complexity itself probably contributes to the contested nature of governance. Where public responsibilities are shared across multiple levels of government (multilevel or federal government) or powers are shared between different institutions (separation of powers), a structural potential is created for disputes over the relative authority and power of different institutions. Most important, contested governance will occur where specific disputes (specific to a policy sector) become entangled with more general disputes about the division of powers and responsibilities between different branches or levels of government. While the governance of space policy in the United States has been disputed since the loss of the *Columbia* space shuttle, there has been no discussion about whether the federal executive branch is the appropriate place to administer space policy. However, European and international food safety conflicts have been entangled in a much more general dispute about the regulatory authority of the EU and the WTO.

Dynamics: Spillover and Contagion

Issues of trust and institutional legitimacy are brought into stark relief during episodes of contested governance. The loss of trust in food and of institutional trust in food safety authorities following the BSE crisis, the difficulty of restoring it, and the manifold ways this loss of trust affects institutional reform and even international trade is a common theme that links all the chapters of the book. Although public and private institutions may have to work hard to maintain trust and legitimacy with their publics even under routine conditions, contested governance is typically characterized by both sudden and pervasive loss of trust and legitimacy and an uphill battle to restore it. Van Waarden (chapter 2) and Kjærnes, Dulsrud, and Poppe (chapter 3) focus in particular on the issue of the public's trust in the safety of their food. Both chapters suggest that national variation in attitudes toward food and government regulation of food make it difficult to produce European-wide solutions to the loss of trust in food safety institutions.

Confronted with a triggering event with high public saliency, public and private institutions (especially those used to low levels of public scrutiny) often try to restore the status quo ex ante by adopting public relations strategies. Such strategies often unwittingly accentuate the public's distrust because they are often interpreted as signals of business as usual or of vested interests.[9] Monsanto's attempt to manage the controversy over the introduction of bioengineered foods in Europe, as described by Ansell, Maxwell, and Sicurelli (chapter 5), provides a good example of this process.

The loss of institutional trust and legitimacy may shift the political initiative to new institutions or actors. Public opinion polls reveal that the European public exhibits considerable cynicism toward government authority and places greater trust in consumer and environmental nongovernmental organizations (NGOs; Gaskell, Allum, and Stares 2003). Moreover, the loss of trust and legitimacy is probably a critical mechanism producing a snowballing effect in which conflict begets conflict. Characteristic of contested governance, snowballing occurs either where a specific crisis initiates or encourages further sectoral disputes or where the implications of one or more crises spill over into related issue areas. For instance, while disputes over beef and milk (rBST) hormones, BSE, dioxins, and GMOs were distinct issues within the food sector, their contestation was cumulative (see table 1.1). Perhaps most dramatic, the hormone and BSE disputes spilled over to shape the public response to the growing and marketing of GMOs (see chapter 5, this volume).

Just as we argued that contested governance must be understood in terms of longer-term institutional tensions and conflicts, we observe that the dynamics of trust and legitimacy can also be understood from this broader perspective. Van Waarden (chapter 2), Kjærnes, Dulsrud, and

Poppe (chapter 3), and Bernaur and Caduff (chapter 4) suggest that restoration of trust in this case was made more difficult by the shifting institutional terrain that distributed regulatory authority across levels of governance (national, European, and international) and by the trade conflicts that have arisen with the internationalization of food markets.

Outcomes: Wholesale Institutional Reform

Long-term trends and institutional tensions are not simply risk factors for contested governance; they also shape the dynamics of crisis response and institutional reform. To respond to these trends and tensions, criticisms of existing institutional arrangements or demands or suggestions for institutional reform in a policy sector often build up over time under noncrisis conditions but lack clear political or institutional incentives to implement them. When a powerful triggering event does occur, these criticisms and reform plans will shape the diagnosis of the problem and provide blueprints (possibly contradictory) for institutional transformation. There is both a supply and demand argument here. On the demand side, the magnitude of the triggering event often leads to a search to attribute blame and obviously to diagnose the underlying problems. Criticisms or reform plans that predate the crisis events often provide elements of a both a smoking gun and a ready diagnosis of what ails the system. Contestation also provides a window of opportunity to press for reform. Often reforms stymied by vested interests or lack of political will remain waiting in the wings (March and Olsen 1989). A common theme of many of our chapters is that institutional reform trajectories evolve through interaction with peripheral issues. For instance, chapters 6 (on France) and 8 (on Germany) suggest that labeling and private quality assurance strategies, which are as much about food marketing as they are about food safety, were given a boost by reform efforts.

The combination of a sharp decline of trust and institutional legitimacy, the contagious, snowballing quality of contestation, and this window of opportunity for reform will produce the possibility of particularly large-scale institutional reform. Given the failure of earlier public relations strategies, reform itself will become a highly symbolic attempt to restore trust and legitimacy. The more trust and legitimacy are important resources for governance, as they certainly are in the case of food safety, the more we should expect reforms to dramatically signal the competence, accountability, and political independence of the new institutions. Reforms will be especially driven by the logic of attempting to restore trust and legitimacy. If successful, these institutional reforms can bring some closure to episodes of contested governance. Chapters 6 through 8 on, respectively, the UK, France, and Germany, and chapters 9 through 11 on European-level institutions all convey how the BSE scandal produced a logic of wholesale institutional reform driven by the imperative of restoring trust and legitimacy to national and European institutions. In each country case and at the European level, new or fundamentally reorganized food agencies and new, more integrated food safety legal regimes were the result.

While the institutional reforms at the national and European levels were both broad and deep, it is important not to convey the message that these reforms resolved the basic problems illuminated by regulatory failures. On the whole, the chapters on the national and EU reforms suggest guarded optimism about improvements in European food safety regulation. However, these chapters also voice cautionary notes. Most important, all the chapters note continued problems of institutional fragmentation. In the French, German, and EU cases, for instance, risk analysis functions were isolated in independent agencies, creating problematic relationships with the organization of risk management. Rothstein's chapter on the UK (chapter 7) emphasizes that developments on the EU level increase the vertical fragmentation of food safety authority. Moreover, he demonstrates that despite claims about independent and transparent scientific risk analysis, political considerations have hardly been banished from the decision-making process. Skogstad (chapter 9) makes similar observations about the EU, which she describes as having a "meditative" policy style. In addition, both Alemmano (chapter 10) and Buonanno (chapter 11) indicate that expectations for a powerful European food regulatory authority must be tempered by the reality of a small agency with highly circumscribed competencies.

Summary
To summarize, we argue that over the past decade, European food safety regulation represents a case of contested governance. We argue that the

syndrome of contested governance occurs when a highly salient triggering event interacts with long-term trends and institutional tensions to
produce a pervasive loss of institutional trust and legitimacy (causes).
Strategies for restoring trust and legitimacy are themselves contested
because they collide with institutional tensions over who, where, how,
and on what basis policy should be made and implemented. Consequently, the scope of contestation is likely to expand, become unruly, and
spill over into related issue areas (dynamics). The imperative of restoring trust and legitimacy then interacts with the expanded scope of contestation to produce wholesale institutional reforms (outcomes).

Contested Governance in Comparative Perspective

It is worth drawing out the contrast here with U.S. food safety regulation, as Skogstad (chapter 9) does in detail. Like Europe, the United
States has also suffered important episodes of food contamination, and
the U.S. food safety system has been criticized for its institutional fragmentation. Concern has also been expressed about potential conflict-
of-interest problems. However, none of these events was of the same
magnitude or salience as the BSE scandal. Nor were they tainted with
the same sense of scandal. Therefore, they have raised concerns but have
not triggered the same loss of trust and legitimacy. Of course, the United
States also faces many of the same economic, technological, and political challenges in regulating food that Europeans have confronted. But
the tensions associated with market integration or European state building are not present in the U.S. case. Moreover, the role of the U.S. federal
government in regulating food safety is hardly a matter of conflict, and
the basic institutional architecture has remained stable. In sum, U.S. food
safety regulation may be conflictual but it is not currently contested.

Although we have argued that contested governance is not politics as
usual, our analysis suggests that it may become more common in the
future. Here, we point to the features of food safety regulation shared
by many other policy domains. First, globalization of markets and the
creation (or strengthening) of international regimes to regulate them
are increasingly common across many economic sectors. International
regimes create a form of multilevel governance that can produce disputes

among different levels of authority. Second, the inherent difficulties of effective and efficient regulation of complex technological and economic processes are hardly unique to food production, processing, and marketing. These complexities often push regulation in two contrary directions: toward more centralized forms of state regulation and toward decentralized forms of private self-regulation. Many other products and services beyond food are becoming more difficult to regulate and producing similar types of tension between public and private regulation. Third, the enhanced importance of the regulatory state and the political conflicts it entails create a difficult balancing act for regulators that can easily lead to the perception of conflicts of interest. Fourth, the expanded reliance on science and risk analysis to settle policy conflicts has led to a deeper politicization of science and risk analysis. Each of these factors can lead, in the context of highly salient triggering events, to a deep questioning of the fundamental precepts of governance.

Overview of the Book

The thirteen chapters in this book are divided into six parts.

Part II addresses the social and economic context of European food safety regulation. The four chapters in this part place national food regulation in a historical and cultural context, describe public attitudes toward trust in food safety in different European countries, trace the economic structure of the European food industry, and examine the political mobilization of opposition to GMOs at the national and European levels. The central theme that underlies them is the significant challenges that the EU faces in restoring public trust in food safety in the light of long-standing cultural and national differences in standards for food safety and quality, the Europeanization and globalization of food production and consumption, variations in public confidence in food safety within the EU, and the political mobilization of European consumers.

Part III focuses on European food safety regulation at the national level, exploring political and institutional changes in food safety regulation in three critical EU member states: France, the UK, and Germany. In each of these countries, significant institutional changes have taken place in the way food is regulated. In France and the UK, new regulatory agencies have been created; in Germany, an equally important but structurally different change in regulation occurred.

Part IV examines changes in food safety regulation at the European level. These chapters place European regulatory policies and politics in a comparative context, trace the legal evolution of European food safety regulation, and examine the political factors underlying the creation of the European Food Safety Authority. Part V focuses on the international dimension of European food safety regulation, offering differing perspectives on the relationship between EU rules and those of the WTO.

Chapter 2, by Frans van Waarden, places the issue of food regulation in historical perspective, noting that compared to other aspects of public policy, food regulation has frequently been highly contested. For both cultural and economic reasons, different countries have placed values on different dimensions of food, and these have frequently clashed. Moreover, in an increasingly globalized economy, where consumers are consuming both natural and processed food from many different countries, the lack of public trust in food safety and quality has become exacerbated. It has become increasingly difficult to ensure consumers that their increasingly diverse and stringent demands with respect to food preparation and composition are being met. Some of this slack is being addressed by private firms and certification agencies, but ultimately these control mechanisms too must be backed by public authority. However, each regulatory failure has created new demands for additional private and public controls, which invariably turn out to be inadequate, thus creating pressures for still more controls.

Unni Kjærnes, Arne Dulsrud, and Christian Poppe also address the relationship between public and private authorities. The central theme of chapter 3 is the issue, problem, and challenge of trust: How can consumers be assured that the food they are consuming has been produced, processed, and distributed in ways that meet their expectations regarding both its quality and safety? The evidence cited illustrates the complexity of this problem. Notwithstanding European economic integration, consumer trust is primarily generated within a national context. Consumers in European countries exhibit markedly different degrees of trust in the food they consume. At the same time, the relationship between private and public authorities varies substantially within Europe. Both phenomena suggest the magnitude of the challenges that confront the EU's efforts to promote a European "trust regime."

Thomas Bernauer and Ladina Caduff also examine the role of institutions in fostering public trust. Their analysis in chapter 4 focuses on two dimensions: the relationship between private and public authorities and the relations between public and private systems of regulation. These are related: the growing stringency of food safety regulation at the European level, dominated by multilevel governance, has been accompanied by an increase in market concentration in food processing and distribution. Many firms have established their own food safety programs, often associated with HACCP. Although their adoption varies widely across different countries, they have become a critical strategy for many large firms seeking to enhance consumer confidence in their products. If small producers are to survive in this increasingly competitive environment, it is critical that Europe establishes a highly effective, credible, and centralized system of food regulation—a challenge that has to date proven elusive.

Christopher Ansell, Rahsaan Maxwell, and Daniela Sicurelli explore another critical dimension of the contemporary politics of food safety regulation in Europe. Chapter 5 describes the critical role that NGOs have played in mobilizing opposition to genetically modified foods in Europe at both the European and national levels. The anti-GMO movement is both broad and diverse, involving environmental groups, consumer groups, farmers, and development organizations. Collectively this movement has created a multifaceted advocacy coalition incorporating activists and supporters with a broad spectrum of interests and priorities.

Greenpeace has played a particularly important role. In both France and Italy, it had a critical role in both increasing public awareness of and mobilizing public opposition to GM foods, though the framing of this issue has varied by country. Critical to their success has been the ability of anti-GM activists to create political linkages across the member states. This has enabled them to effectively target EU institutions, while at the same time retaining an important national focus. The anti-GMO movement has built a multilevel organization capable of effective mobilization at both the national and European levels. It has had significant impacts on both national and EU regulation of this new agricultural technology and contributed to the highly contested nature of much of European food safety regulation.

Part III explores the reform of food safety systems at the national level. In chapter 6, Olivier Borraz, Julien Besançon, and Christophe Clergeau argue that the newly create French food safety agency, AFSSA (Agence française de sécurité sanitaire des aliments), has experienced considerable difficulty in establishing an independent role within the French state. Established by legislation in 1998 as a response to a series of public health policy failures in France and with the purpose of enhancing the legitimacy of public regulation, it remains a relatively weak agency. In many respects, its role in shaping food safety policy in France is both limited and undefined: the critical definition of rules and norms remains the province of authorities outside the agency. AFFSA also finds itself constrained by two important trends, which both proceed and postdate it: the increasing role of private interests in the management of food safety and the commitment of the French government to protect French agricultural interests. Nonetheless, it has managed to play an influential role in affecting specific food safety policy decisions, most notably the maintenance and the termination of the French embargo on British beef and public policies toward BSE. In both cases, the agency adopted a highly precautionary approach. Whether it will prove capable of maintaining consumer confidence in the face of future food safety crises remains problematic.

Henry Rothstein explores in chapter 7 the challenges faced by Britain's Food Standards Agency (FSA). Established in 2000 as a response to a dramatic decline in consumer confidence with the government's ability to effectively regulate food safety caused in large measure by the BSE scandal, the agency was heralded as inaugurating a new era of transparency in consumer protection. It was based on three principles: putting consumers first, openness, and independence. Rothstein critically explores the agency's performance by describing and evaluating its responses to two food safety issues: BSE in sheep and food allergies. The latter reveals a number of important limitations: a lack of coherence in regulatory decision making, its inability to give priority to the interests of consumers, the continued role played by business and economics pressures in shaping regulatory policy, the inability of policymakers to coherently and consistently make risk management decisions in cases of scientific uncertainty, the difficulty of implementing stakeholder participation, and a lack of independence. Thus, notwithstanding the political context that led to its creation, FSA continues to reflect Britain's soft regulatory style.

In chapter 8, Bodo Steiner describes the institutional changes made by the German government in response to the emergence of the first cases of BSE in Germany in 2000. The most striking change was renaming the Federal Ministry of Agriculture and Forestry as the Federal Ministry of Consumer Protection, Food and Agriculture, which took place in January 2001. This change was accompanied by a strengthening of the audit capacity of the German government as well as the establishment of a large-scale private sector quality assurance scheme. The latter shifted regulation away from publicly mandated food safety regulations toward industry-led initiatives. On balance, a number of changes in regulation, administration, and liability standards appear to have improved the effectiveness and the allocative efficiency of German food safety regulation.

The chapters in part IV explore food safety regulation at the European level. In chapter 9, Grace Skogstad places the EU's approach to regulating food safety risks in a comparative context. A nation's approach for determining and legitimating food safety regulation—or its food safety regulatory policy style—relies on a combination of three elements: science, democratic processes of representative and participatory government, and market mechanisms and incentives. These vary widely among the United States, Canada, and the EU: the first relies on state regulation of private industry, the second on state officials and the third on political officials.

Case studies of three critical areas of food safety regulation— hormone-fed beef, rBST milk, and genetically modified foods—demonstrate how differently each political system has approached the regulation of the health and other risks associated with these agricultural technologies. Underlying these differences are the centrality of democratic norms and the weaker authority of science in EU food safety regulation as compared to the United States and Canada. These differences are reinforced by both different cultural attitudes toward food produced by new technologies and a series of regulatory failures in Europe that have undermined public confidence in appeals to objective knowledge associated with regulatory science.

In chapter 10, Alberto Alemanno traces the historical evolution of food regulation by the EU. This regulation has gone through four phases. During the first phase, which began in 1962 and lasted through 1985, the European Community attempted to harmonize food law. This program met with limited success. Accordingly, from 1985 through 1997, the European Commission adopted a "new approach," which relied instead on mutual recognition of national standards and framework directives. Both approaches focused primarily on promoting intra-European trade in foodstuffs and paid relatively scant attention to safety issues. Beginning in the mid-1990s, faced with increasing public concern over food safety, the EU adopted a new set of comprehensive policies whose aim was to strengthen European food safety standards. These included the adoption of a Green Paper establishing "General Principles of Food Law" in the EU in 1997 and the establishment of a DG for consumer protection and health, which was made responsible for co-ordinating scientific risk assessments. Finally in 2002, the European Commission established the European Food Safety Authority (EFSA), making it responsible for providing scientific advice for all aspects of food safety regulation. Alemanno also notes a number of important differences between the EFSA and the U.S. Food and Drug Administration. These differences reflect both the unwillingness of European national governments to cede too much authority to a centralized regulatory authority as well as the more politicized context of risk assessment in Europe.

Laurie Buonanno focuses in chapter 11 on the factors underlying the creation of the European Food Safety Authority in 2002. This new regulatory body emerged from a complex set of developments, the most important of which was the inadequacy of the EU's comitology system to adequately address the recurrent food safety crises to which European consumers have been subject. The agency in turn both reflects and reinforces a significant change in the division of authority both within the EU and between the EU and the member states.

Chapters 12 and 13 place the regulation of European food safety in an international context. In chapter 12, Alasdair Young and Peter Holmes focus on the challenges posed by the EU's obligations under the WTO to its policy autonomy in the area of food safety. The dynamics of market integration within the EU, along with the EU's highly legalistic character and its high threshold for policy change, has made it particularly difficult for the EU to comply with adverse WTO judgments. A substantial number of EU food safety rules have been the cause of trade friction, and two have led to formal trade disputes. This reflects the fact that a number of EU rules are more risk averse than those of its trading partners.

However, detailed analysis of recent WTO jurisprudence suggests that many EU regulations are likely to pass legal scrutiny as the WTO's appellate body has repeatedly affirmed the right of the EU to choose whatever safety objectives it wishes. While conflicts may emerge with respect to regulations imposed in order to reassure the European public but with no scientific basis, the EU's new procedures for making food safety regulations will mean that its future rules are less likely to be subject to international legal challenges. Indeed, one important purpose of the new European Food Safety Authority is precisely to make EU food safety standards consistent with the provisions of the Sanitary and Phytosanitary Measures Agreement. However, in the case of already existing rules that enjoy widespread popular support, of which the hormone ban and possibly regulations governing GMOs represent important examples, the EU has found or is likely to find it difficult to adjust its policies to bring them into compliance with averse rulings. In sum, the WTO is affecting how European regulations are being made and justified, but to date it has had less impact on the substance of regulations themselves.

Christine Noiville explores a similar set of issues in chapter 13, but reaches a different conclusion. Carefully analyzing the provisions of the WTO agreement governing the permissible use of food safety and processing standards as nontariff barriers, she points to a number of ambiguities that might well pose legal challenges to highly risk-averse EU food standards. One of the most important of these has to do with the precautionary principles, a number of whose dimensions are more restrictive under WTO than under EU rules.

The final chapter by Christopher Ansell draws together many of the findings of the individual chapters around the broader theme of contested governance, with special attention to the wave of institutional reform that accompanied the debate about food safety governance. This chapter also further explores how asymmetries in risk perception, scientific expertise, and public management have accentuated political conflict around food safety.

Notes

We thank Todd La Porte, the three anonymous reviewers, and the project participants for their help in writing this introduction.

1. The links between BSE, beef consumption, and vCJD have still not been definitively established, but laboratory studies strongly support the transmission mechanism of consumption of BSE-infected beef (Andrews et al. 2003). The number of deaths from vCJD are based on December 1, 2003, figures reported by the National CJD Surveillance Unit Web site <http://www.cjd.ed.ac.uk>.

2. The ruling was appealed, and the appellate body ruled that the EU's ban was designed to protect the health of EU consumers and was not simply a form of disguised protectionism.

3. Transcript of commencement address to the U.S. Coast Guard Academy, Office of the Press Secretary, May 21, 2003.

4. For the seven most commonly ingested pathogens alone, annual illness estimates for the United States range from 3.3 to 12.3 million, with 1,900 to 3,900 annual deaths (Buzby and Roberts 1996). Medical costs and lost productivity due to the most critical four pathogens in meat and poultry alone amount to $4.0 to $4.6 billion annually (Crutchfield 2000). For Germany the annual costs were estimated to amount to at least 510 million euro in 1999 (Werber and Ammon 2000).

5. The commission is composed of member state representatives that vote on standards recommended by scientific advisory committees.

6. Our distinction between contested governance and policy conflict is similar, though not identical, to Schön and Rein's (1994) distinction between policy disagreements and policy controversies. They argue that the latter tend to be "intractable, enduring and seldom finally resolved" (4). They argue that "intractable policy controversies" require special attention because they cannot be resolved by allowing politics as usual to take its course.

7. Organizational errors can often be rationalized as "operator errors" or minimized as "one-off" events. See, for instance, Sagan (1993).

8. See the discussion on input and output legitimacy by Skogstad (2003).

9. See the discussion by Hellström and Jacob (2001) on the failure of risk communication in the BSE case.

II

The Social and Economic Context

2

Taste, Traditions, Transactions, and Trust: The Public and Private Regulation of Food

Frans van Waarden

Why is the governance of food so often contested? One reason, of course, is that the interests of producers diverge. Different countries have different food industries. Some specialize in large-scale mass production and others in smaller and more specialized high-quality niches; accordingly, their dependence on chemical additives or exclusive quality seals may differ. And thus they develop different interests with respect to food standards. Still, interests cannot be the full explanation. Differences in interests underlie conflicts in many policy fields. So why is the governance of food especially likely to be contested? A key part of the explanation is that the governance of food not only reflects different interests but also different ideas. It is associated with deeply held beliefs about what is important in life and touches on the identity of communities and societies. These ideas involve not only the substance of food regulation but also their form and organization. They engage not only what should be regulated but also how and by whom.

These cultural ideas and values form the basis of the other six "i's" that constitute institutionalization:

Institutes, that is, organizations that produce the valued food, such as a pasta or wine industry, and the organizations that service that industry, such as research and educational institutes, standardization bodies, quality control agencies, sector-specific financial institutes, and trade associations.

Interdependencies and interlinkages between the institutes, through governance mechanisms such as markets, hierarchies, networks, clans, associations, and public-private partnerships.

Information and knowledge and competencies (in personnel, patents, and publications, which provide competitive advantages), developed by the institutes, interdependencies, and interlinkages.

Interests that the institutes develop, in part based on their information and competencies (e.g., interests in their survival and growth).

Incentives. Investments in institutes and ideas motivate people to invest further in what they already have, that is, along familiar lines, to exploit their competitive knowledge advantages.

Institutions or social rule systems that help perpetuate all the former items, for example, by giving them preferential treatment over rival interests, like foreign food industries or health interests.

Together, the seven *i*'s of ideas, institutes, interlinkages, information, interests, incentives, and institutions form relatively well-established systems, clusters, or industrial communities. These help explain why some regions, once they develop a particular specialization, tend to maintain that specialization. Examples are the chemical industry along the German Rhine, the corporate legal industry of Delaware, and gambling in Las Vegas; and in food, the industries of French wine, Dutch dairy, British beef, and Swiss cheese. Their system character gives such communities resilience and resistance against threats and contributes to the contestation over food standards.

This chapter begins by exploring the cultural roots of food governance in ideas and values. This extends to the definition of risk regarding food safety; risk is in part a social and cultural construct. It then identifies and compares the variety of institutions that societies have created to reduce the risk and uncertainties involved in food transactions, both private and public. Cultures differ not only in their tastes for food but also in their "tastes" for institutions they trust to ensure them that they will get what they want. Nevertheless, one can perceive a long-term trend: in most cultures, the state becomes involved in setting minimum or graded food quality standards. These national public food standards mirror national cultural preferences. They are a major part of the clusters of seven i's in food.

The chapter then examines how these national or regional clusters, especially the food quality control institutions associated with them, are being undermined by the internationalization of food markets. It may still be feasible to enact, monitor, and enforce national food governance standards as long as food producers, consumers, and regulators come from the same society, that is, are located within the same jurisdictional boundaries. But it becomes much more difficult when this is no longer the case.

Internationalization makes it more difficult for consumers to have confidence in the food they are consuming: information asymmetries increase, the sense of risk and uncertainty becomes heightened, and trust in markets declines. On the one hand, this increases the need for national food standards, more powerful national agencies, and more effective national enforcement. But on the other hand, national regulation becomes less effective as it is less able to govern the policies of foreign producers. Thus, internationalization squeezes food regulation between increasing public demands for standards and a decline in the capacity of government to meet these demands. The most obvious solution, international food standards, is likely to be highly contested in the light of the diversity of cultures and clusters, each with different ideas and interests with respect to food.

As food quality regulation by nation-states becomes less effective, greater reliance will be placed on nonstate institutions such as quality standards and monitoring procedures by supermarket chains, commercial standardization bodies, and international trade associations. They can more easily "internationalize" than can national governments. National governments can try to export their standards, but even then, the vehicles for such diffusion are often private organizations and institutions. Thus, as long as there is no international regulatory body, greater reliance will be placed on private and semiprivate institutions. This will make regulation more inefficient as more and more agencies and institutions are required.

Food, Risk, and Culture: "De Gustibus . . . est Disputandum!"

The importance of food for social and cultural life is demonstrated by the fact that eating together almost universally symbolizes and strengthens community bonds. In most religions, communal meals are important rituals: the Holy Supper in Protestantism, the celebration of the Eucharist in Roman Catholicism, Passover in Judaism, Ramadan (not eating during the day, feasting at night) in Islam. Families typically experience and emphasize their mutual bonds by eating a daily meal together. In business, political, and diplomatic life, consultations and negotiations among strangers are lubricated by shared wining and dining.

But tastes differ. Germans love pork; Muslims will not get near it. The French relish tripe; most Americans will not touch it. Portuguese love coquilles St. Jacques; for Jews scallops are not kosher. Italians "live to eat"; the Dutch "eat to live". Some people are gluttonous debauchers; others are abstemious anorectics. Some are omnivores, others dainty gourmets. Yet people are choosy for different reasons: some insist on eating eggs produced by free-roaming chickens; vegetarians and animal liberators are horrified by the thought of gelatin. British supermarkets have lots of shelf space for frozen peas but hardly any for frozen spinach; in Germany, it is the other way around.

If anything is culture dependent, it is food. It is often a source of national pride. Germans boast about their beer brewed according to the centuries-old purity law, the British cherish their "bangers," and Italians celebrate their whole cuisine. Food can even become so important that it becomes the basis of a belief system and defines a cultural community: vegetarians, macrobiotics, Jews.

As cultures differ in what they find tasteful, so do they vary in the priority they give to different criteria, such as composition, origin, safety, healthiness, taste, freshness, nonperishability, exclusiveness, quantity, or price. This suggests that risk is not an absolute criterion but a social and cultural construct. Risk perceptions differ. For Muslims, eating pork is a much greater risk than eating rotten lamb. For them, to die is less serious than not to get in heaven. The threat is so great that an Israeli rabbi has proposed to scare Palestinian suicide bombers off with bags of pork fat hung in buses (Volkskrant 13-02-2004). The precautionary principle means something quite different for Muslims. It could mean not touching Dutch chicken filet because there is a chance that it has been "blown up" with water and pork protein to increase its weight by up to 30 percent. The French are willing to trade off the risk of contracting tuberculosis from consuming raw unpasteurized milk (though pasteurization was a French invention) in cheese production in order to enjoy the pronounced tastes of camembert or pont l'eveque. Different societies and cultures view the risks associated with eating unhealthy, or too much food, differently. The sober-living Seventh Day Adventists live on average ten years longer (Rougoor, van der Weijden, and Bol) yet there is little public interest in adopting their culinary lifestyle. Alternatively, the Atkins diet that swept the United States recently was not embraced by Europeans.

Over time, these different cultural preferences and definitions of risk have found expression in what societies regulate. Thus Muslim countries have regulated food production and distribution in line with their belief system. Unclean animals cannot be kept, slaughtered, and sold. But even in western Europe, differences can be found. Typically, the French and Italians have been more concerned with taste and quality grading, the Germans more with safety and (chemical) composition, and the Dutch more with anything that affects their exports. Americans value liberalism and contract freedom: they tend to prefer information and labeling rather than product bans.

German regulations have historically focused on composition. The best example of this tradition is the *Reinheitsgebot* (beer purity law) enacted in 1516 by Wilhelm IV, earl of Bavaria. It stated that "in the future in all cities, markets and in the country, the only ingredients used for the brewing of beer must be barley, hops and water. Whosoever knowingly disregards or transgresses upon this ordinance, shall be punished by the Court authorities' confiscating such barrels of beer, without fail." (Eden 1993). Later, when yeast was discovered as the factor behind the creation of alcohol and carbon dioxide gas, the law was amended to include yeast. However, factors that are truly crucial to the taste of beer—the quality of the ingredients, the lagering times, pasteurization, filtration, and carbonation—were not regulated.

Since then, chemical composition of food, additives, preservatives, and coloring agents has become a major issue in German food regulation. This may have to do with the paradox regarding chemistry in German culture. On the one hand, the chemical industry has been one of the strongest in Germany, responsible for many path-breaking innovations, such as aniline and all its derivatives (dyestuffs, pharmaceuticals), or synthetic rubber. On the other hand, there is a rather romantic obsession with everything "natural" and a suspicion of things artificial or synthetic. To date, Germany and Austria are among those with the strictest regulations of agricultural biotechnology.

France and Italy, by contrast, have nurtured self-images of a sophisticated cuisine and emphasized quality defined as taste. Food is important in these societies. It is a major topic of conversation in all walks of life, and much daily time is spent on lengthy lunches and dinners. The cultural importance of good food is reflected in the importance of the criterion of taste in their regulatory system. The French were the inventors of restaurant grading, and their Michelin guide and its system of stars is the most prestigious worldwide. Both countries have invested much in a well-developed regulatory system of quality grading and protection of names of origin. The system of *appellations d'origine contrôlée* (AOC) has been developed for wine, champagne, cognac, and cheese and has been extended to other products, such as olive oil, honey, pastis, biobeer, and even lavender. They certify (and grade) not only taste and quality, but also the origin of the products (*produits du terroir*). And they regulate in detail such matters as where, when, how long, under what conditions, and how precisely grapes or olives can be harvested, the maximum yield per hectare, how many days have to be waited before pressing, the minimum sugar content after fermentation, the conditions for the aging process, the date it can be marketed, and labeling standards. On top of that, final grading and certification is done by a tasting committee (Colman 2002)

Modern Dutch food regulations were created, opportunistically, with foreign trade interests in mind. Their emergence was actually a response to typical shortsighted individual commercial behavior, fraud and adulteration, perhaps typical for a nation with a long-standing merchant tradition. It is not coincidental that most of the sayings in the English language that involve the Dutch have something to do with being thrifty and cheap: "to go Dutch," "Dutch treat," "Dutch auction," "Dutch comfort," and "Dutch bargain". And indeed, the Dutch are more likely to shop for bargains than their European neighbors. Thus, while Belgian, French, German, Austrian, and Italian food advertisement stress quality and enjoyment, advertisers in the Netherlands typically appeal often to the price consciousness of consumers.

A long-standing major food regulation was the *Landbouwk-waliteitswet* (Agricultural Quality Law). It stressed purity and honesty, primarily in order to promote trade. Its origins date back to the regulations governing dairy products in the 1890s, which were established in response to the problem of adulterated butter and cheese. The invention of margarine facilitated falsification. Mixing became such a common practice that around the turn of the twentieth century, the word *Dutch butter* became a euphemism for a mixture of butter and margarine. Cheeses were tampered with as well. The new milk centrifuges made it easier to skim the fat of the milk for butter production, before the milk was used for cheese production. In this way, the same amount of milk could be used to produce both butter and cheese, although the cheese was almost completely made up of water. Hence it became known as "civil engineering works" (*waterbouwkundige kunstwerken*). The difference from good cheese was not apparent when the cheese was young. But after a couple of weeks, it collapsed. A much publicized lawsuit in England in 1903 against a Gouda cheese with only 1.6 percent fat and 57 percent water significantly harmed the international reputation of Dutch dairy products. Such adulteration was clearly harmful to Dutch producers. As the reputation of Dutch agriculture and dairy worsened, they lost their traditional export markets. Ever since, trade interests have dominated Dutch food standards.

Countries differ also in where something is regulated. And this is linked to what are considered the most important criteria for regulation. Originally, when food chains were still short, food was regulated only at the place of sale to the final consumer: the shop and restaurant. Leaders became laggards here as well. Countries that were first with food quality regulation as regards safety were also the ones that stuck longest to this concentration on the place of final sale, as did Britain until 1984 (Coates 1984).

Societies with a more sophisticated food culture, like France and Italy, which had an interest in rating quality levels, introduced regulations governing food production and processing at an early date. The area from where grapes could be harvested for a specific wine (e.g., champagne or cognac); the processes of harvesting, fermentation, and aging; and the storage conditions in the wine cellars were all prescribed in great detail. Cultures that have religious rules regarding the process of food preparation, such as the slaughter of animals, also regulate this phase of the production chain.

Where something is regulated is often linked to which government department is responsible—provided it is the government that does the regulation. If it is the department of agriculture, this may point to early state involvement (agriculture is a relatively old department) or to the importance of producer interests (e.g., export reputation). Thus, food regulation in the Netherlands has been largely the domain of the Ministry of Agriculture. Where consumer interests at the final retailing stage were regulated, this was usually the responsibility of a ministry of consumer affairs or a ministry of health.

Culture and the How of the Governance of Risk: The Diversity of Institutions of Economic Governance

Given the importance of food for life, health, identity, and culture, it is important for people to know what they are eating. But how can they be sure? Typically transactions involving food are characterized by information asymmetries. The seller knows more about the quality than the buyer does. Where, when, and under what conditions was it harvested, preserved, processed, stored, mixed? These asymmetries provide countless opportunities for fraud and deception. Food adulteration has been a practice since time immemorial. Bread has been diluted with plaster, bonemeal, or lead-white and milk with ditchwater; and beer was given a more hoplike flavor with arsenic (Rougoor, van der Weijden, and Bol 2003). Consumers who are cheated lose trust in the goods and their suppliers. Conflicts then arise between customer and supplier and between competitors, because customers may refrain from engaging in more transactions. And the market for such goods may get destroyed eventually. In a modification of Gresham's law, the bad producers drive out the good producers. This in turn provides producers with an interest in market institutions that can punish those who engage in adulteration and thus increase public trust.

Countries have differed also in their preferences for specific sources of food regulation. Today governments play a large role in food regulation; however, this was not always the case. Neither does the state have a monopoly in this area. Markets and civil society have also tried to standardize and regulate food quality. Often state regulation was preceded by societal self-regulation. However, invariably the state become involved, because private regulation turned out to have a number of disadvantages. This process has had a number of different dynamics.

Individual Strategies

Logically reduction of information asymmetries starts with the individual consumer. For some criteria and foodstuffs, sensory inspection by the consumers themselves is informative. More difficult is quality assessment–based criteria that are not immediately observable to the senses, such as the origin in space and time. Even more difficult is the evaluation of production techniques or chemical composition. Individual strategies to counter distrust and reduce uncertainty cost time and money. They are literally transaction costs, which tend to be high, because the individual cannot profit from economies of scale. Therefore, they can seriously frustrate transactions.

In order to avoid this, societies have developed institutions that serve to reduce these transaction costs. Building on typologies by Williamson (1975), Ouchi (1980), Streeck and Schmitter (1986), and Hollingsworth and Boyer 1997, several allocation and coordination principles that can perform these functions can be distinguished (table 2.1).

The Market   The market itself has provided some solutions to the problems of information asymmetry and risk and uncertainty. For example,

Table 2.1
Comparison of economic coordination principles

Coordination principle	Institutionalization	Structure	Status
Market, commercial services	Formal	Horizontal	Private
Community or clan	Informal	Horizontal	Private
Associations	Formal	Horizontal	Private
Hierarchies	Formal	Vertical	Private
Courts and case law	Formal	Vertical	Semipublic
States	Formal	Vertical	Public

registered brand names with high-quality reputations attached to them may be particularly effective in markets where transactions are frequent, such as food.

Furthermore, enterprising businesses have found market niches in selling information about and certifying the quality of the products, processes, and organization of other entrepreneurs, including in the food business, and sometimes even certifying the producer. Uncertainty reduction has become big business. Firms have specialized in the collection of information (detectives, credit registration bureaus, consultancy firms, marketing agencies), the evaluation of it (credit rating organizations), the distribution of information (advertising; consumer organizations), the certification of the truthfulness of information on behalf of transaction partners (accountants, auditors, notary publics), the drafting of contracts (lawyers and notary publics), their monitoring and enforcement (assault groups, debt collection agencies, process servers, bailiffs), or the covering of calculable risks (insurance companies, options trade).

Commercial solutions nevertheless have problems. Commercial businesses are also prone to the seductions of opportunistic and corrupt behavior. They are often paid by only one of the transaction partners and "whose bread one eats, his word one speaks". And who controls the controllers, the accountants, risk analysts, and insurers?

Furthermore, private solutions usually require the backing of an external authority. A trademark needs protection against copying by free-riding lower-quality producers, whose actions undermine its credibility. Bad products drive out good products, and bad entrepreneurs good ones. The problem is particularly serious with respect to generic products that are difficult to distinguish, a characteristic shared by many food products, such as milk, bread, and vegetables. A third shortcoming of market solutions is that while uncertainty reduction requires generally accepted standards, market competition may produce a plurality of standards, further confusing the consumer. Accordingly, efficiency requires an organization with a monopoly position on setting standards. Finally, commercial solutions still imply transaction costs. Outsourcing to specialized organizations offers economies of scale over individual uncertainty-reduction strategies. But yet other forms of uncertainty reduction, by institutions discussed below, can provide further savings.

Community, Trust, Norms, and Values   A cheaper means to save on transaction costs is trust between partners. An efficient economy runs, like society in general, largely on trust. Yet trust is not self-evident. It cannot be based on a belief in "natural" human goodness—certainly not in the case of capitalism, where competition tempts, if not forces, producers to cheat. Nor is it something that can easily be created. It is present or not. Trust is more likely found in a community with a certain identity. Ouchi (1980), Piore and Sabel (1984), Sabel (1993), Porter (1990), and Fukuyama (1995) have pointed to the importance of clan and culture for economic transactions. One strategy is to conclude transactions preferably with people whom one trusts because they belong to the same religious, ethnic, or extended family community. A Turkish consumer thus might feel safer buying meat from a Muslim butcher. Trust is enhanced by the diffuse and multiplex character of relations in such groups. The members have relations in different roles, and these offer additional channels for social control, social interdependence, and hence punishment for cheating.

Communities are also sources of social norms, which govern economic transactions. For example, observant Jews will not trade on the sabbath, while Calvinists were expected to be thrifty and not to indulge in luxuries. That too increases the predictability of the intentions and choices of transaction partners. Many cultures and religions have norms that condemn deceit, and thus mitigate mutual distrust.

Reliance on community, trust, and informal social norms has also its disadvantages. Transactions remain restricted to within a certain homogeneous social group. Thus, the scale of transactions is limited. Furthermore, cultural norms and values usually do not suffice. Agencies are needed to back them up and clarify, monitor, and enforce them. This could be a religious organization, but where the social power of such organizations is limited, others are needed.

Associations   One possibility is self-organization and self-regulation by an industrial or business sector. Groups of firms may form associations that enact and try to enforce laws, that is, internal rules. The medieval guilds were a prototype. They had elaborate quality standards and could effectively monitor and enforce them, thanks to the compulsory membership of producers, which gave them an effective sanction: expulsion meant loss of livelihood.

Most modern trade associations lack such effective sanctions. Nevertheless, many sectoral associations do try to set enforceable standards. There is an abundance of them, including the French wine *syndicats* and the Dutch dairy associations. In addition, there are also quality certificates provided by consumer associations, such as the Dutch Association of Housewives. They add to, and often compete with, standards and certificates provided by commercial standardization bodies.

Hierarchies   Entrepreneurs can also limit uncertainty through mergers and take-overs with transaction partners. Transactions that previously occurred in a market now take place in a bureaucratic organization, which becomes an allocation and coordination mechanism. Actors actually enter into transactions with themselves, and this allows them to reduce uncertainty about the intentions and possible opportunistic behavior of others. Greater size means also more market power and allows economic actors to influence or even steer the developments of markets, which reduces uncertainties for long-term investments. This has been common knowledge since the work of Williamson (1975).

Powerful firms can, however, also reduce risk and uncertainty for the final consumer by formulating, monitoring, and enforcing quality standards for their networks of suppliers that they control. In food, the concentration in retailing has had such effects. Large supermarket chains have become major quality regulators of the food chain.

The Courts and Case Law   Many economic transactions sooner or later give occasion to conflicts over the quality of the products or the observation of contracts. Such conflicts can end up before an arbitrator for settlement. The state, given its responsibility for social order, has provided such arbitrators: the judiciary, financed and employed by, but relatively independent from, the other state powers. For the enforcement of its decisions, the judiciary relies on the legitimate monopoly of the state over the exercise of force. As judges orient themselves in their decisions to earlier decisions in the interest of legal equality, these have acquired power of precedence. The accumulated decisions have produced de facto regulation: case law. Even governments that are otherwise wary of intervention in the economy have in this way become market regulators.

For the regulation of product quality, tort and liability law have acquired great importance. Consumers who feel cheated or have otherwise suffered from food products can, and do, sue producers in court. This has led to a veritable litigation industry, especially in very litigious societies, such as the United States. In continental European countries, the importance of tort litigation in also increasing, forcing producers to elaborate, strengthen, and bureaucratize their internal quality control systems.

States   In many societies and cultures, the sources of food governance already examined were not effective or efficient enough, thus forcing the state to become more directly involved.

Why the state? It has always been in the business of reducing risks and uncertainties to the life of its citizens. Many of the public goods it provides do just that. This holds first and foremost for the original and still primary task of the state: the protection of its citizens against threats to their life, liberty, and property, whether from domestic or foreign origin. Hadrian's, the Chinese, and medieval city walls created visible borders around, and thereby defined, the group to be protected. Watch towers, castles, and soldiers aided in keeping out threats, ranging from wandering dogs to foreign enemies. Today institutions such as the coast guard, airport security checks, and satellites play the same role: the police against brigands and thieves; infirmaries and hospitals against infectious diseases; and food regulators against unwholesome food and its producers: adulterers, swindlers, and crooks.

Statutory food regulations are as diverse as food markets themselves. Ancient Greece and Rome had laws against the coloring and flavoring of wine. In western Europe, laws against adulteration of food and drink arose in the later Middle Ages. Famous landmarks are the British impure food laws from 1226 (Coates 1984) and the Bavarian *Reinheitsgebot* for beer from 1516. The first modern legislation dates from the latter half of the nineteenth century: in Britain from 1860 (the Food Purity Law), extended in 1874, in Germany 1879, France 1885, Belgium 1890, and the Netherlands 1889.

Direct occasions for such intervention were usually scandals and crises, which destroyed trust in specific products and producers. History abounds with such examples: the Dutch dairy scandals around 1890; the economic crisis of the 1930s that sparked the development of the French system of *appellation d'origine controlée* (from 1935 on); and in the 1980s, the Austrian scandal of mixing antifreeze in wine (to sweeten it). The recent animal epidemics (BSE, foot and mouth disease, pig and chicken pests) led to a tightening of veterinary inspections and animal feed standards, and increased the role of European institutions in food regulation, most recently leading to the establishment of a European food regulatory agency.

These scandals reduced the trust of the public in private forms of regulation. They made it clear that private solutions to the risks and uncertainties of the market do have problems. Detectives and other reputation rating agencies threaten the privacy of economic actors; accountants, supposed to be independent and neutral, turned out to be subject to temptations of favoritism; customs and norms of clans and communities can be quite strict market-entry barriers; associations suffer from the threat of free riders and have difficulty in enforcing self-regulation; and a proliferation of competing private standards can become self-defeating as they may obfuscate markets rather than increase transparency.

Often a first reaction of the state to deficiencies of private risk and uncertainty-reducing institutions in food markets has been to support them. It does so with the basic legal infrastructure (property rights, contract law, judicial conflict resolution) without which markets, commercial risk reducers, communities, and associations could not function. Furthermore, it increases public trust in commercial risk and uncertainty reducers, such as accountants or insurance companies, by holding these to standards; it helps self-regulating associations solve collective action problems by officially recognizing them.

Eventually it supplemented or replaced private by public regulations. When the market and commercial organizations produced a proliferation of standards that threatened to make markets again intransparent, it set uniform and authoritative standards: for weights and measures, pricing units, vocational training or university degrees, and food quality certificates. And it created its own enforcement organizations, such as national, regional, or local food inspectorates.

State regulation also has its disadvantages. State agencies are further removed from the businesses and markets they are to regulate, which makes for greater principal-agent problems in the administration and enforcement of regulations. A greater distance between regulator and subject may also reduce legitimacy and hence create stronger incentives to evade or circumvent them. That forces regulators and courts (which enforce the rules) to increase the degree of specificity and detail of the regulations, which feed sentiments about the "ridiculousness", "unreasonableness" (Bardach and Kagan 1982), or inflexibility of state regulation. That gives rise to political calls for deregulation, until the next scandal sets a new cycle of (re)regulation in motion.

Public-Private Combinations These "state failures" have given rise to mixed public-private regulations and enforcement organizations in an attempt to combine the advantages of both private and of public regulation. Thus, the state provided backing for self-regulatory trade associations, for example, by giving them privileged access or statutory powers such as compulsory membership or the authority to apply disciplinary law. Examples in food markets are the French wine quality regulations, enacted and enforced by private *syndicats* of local wine growers, but recognized, authorized, and backed by the French state; or Dutch dairy quality standards, specified and enforced by a sectoral trade association, which is governed by employers' and employee associations. The latter has a status under public law and resources such as compulsory membership and the authority to regulate and tax industry, making their regulations formally equal to statutory law.

Economic Governance and Contestation Cultures and societies differ in their preferences for these various sources of food quality regulation. Commercial solutions are more readily accepted in liberal economies like the United States or the UK. Hence, not coincidentally, many of the internationally known quality rating agencies are located in these countries, like the major accountancy firms or Standard and Poor's. Reliance on community and trust depends on the distribution of trust in a society. From Fukuyama (1995) we know that societies differ in whom one trusts: family members, strangers, organizations, or the state. Chinese and Italians trust their family and local or professional community but distrust society at large, including the state. Hence they rely more on communities as sources of regulation: artisanal and professional communities, and industrial districts. Germans, Japanese, and Americans have more trust in people and agencies beyond their family, including associations and the state. Hence the state can be more important in these societies as a source of legitimate regulation. Regulation by large, abstract private firm hierarchies is also more common in these societies, whose economies are dominated by such hierarchies. Self-regulation by associations is more generally accepted in corporatist countries like the Netherlands, Austria, and Germany.

These differences in the legitimacy accorded to different sources of regulation are also sources of contestation, especially when it comes to the enactment of common international standards, as in the case of the EU or WTO.

Internationalization Trends

National public or mixed public-private regulations of food quality experience a loss in effectiveness and efficiency—and with that a loss of legitimacy—because of globalization, which breaks up the congruence between the territory of societies, markets, cultures, and regulatory states. The following internationalization trends are particularly important.

First, due to increased mobility, many Western countries have become more and more multicultural. Individualization has added to this cultural diversity. The autochthonous population harbors more and more subcultures, some of which identify themselves by the type of food they eat: vegetarianism, veganism, macrobiotics. The increase in cultural diversity means that country and culture coincide less and less. Food quality gets measured by a greater diversity of standards. And thus the information needs of the population as to how the various products score on these standards increase. It also becomes more difficult for national regulations to reflect cultural preferences.

As populations become more multicultural, they become more vocal and demanding. There is a revolution of rising expectations among ever more assertive citizens, as both voters and litigants in court, in democratic societies. They hold states responsible for providing solutions to ever more risks and uncertainties.

Second, citizens are increasingly consuming food made outside their borders. Mutual knowledge, the reputation mechanism, and norms and values can generate trust as long as the transactions take place in local communities, where partners meet regularly and where they share common cultural values. This becomes more difficult when distances increase, when parties are anonymous to one another, and when they come from different cultures. That is exactly what has happened with internationalization and thus growth of world trade. The food products we now consume come from all over the globe: apples from Australia, beef from Argentina, cod from Iceland. It has been estimated that an average good has traveled 4,000 kilometers before it reaches its final consumer. That increases information asymmetries and opportunities for deception.

Food production chains have become increasingly longer and more global. Manure from Chili gets transformed into U.S. corn, then into Belgian cows and milk, then into Dutch cheese, and a leftover, whey powder, turns into French calves and bonemeal, and then into British beef, ad infinitum. It is difficult to follow ingredients in these ever longer food chains, notwithstanding the attempts at tracking and tracing.

Contaminated food or unsafe chemicals or pharmaceuticals may spread quickly and may be difficult to trace. Where food is moved in living form, as plants or animals, it may spread pests and infectious diseases fast, in particular in the dense population concentrations typical of the bio-industry. The recent epidemics of BSE, pig and chicken pests, AIDS, and SARS illustrate this clearly.

Third, not only do ever more products come from farther away; they are composed of ever more components, whose origin may be difficult to trace. Even basic foods get decomposed, transported, and recomposed, with possible changes in the process. Fruit juice gets dehydrated at the source and transported; at the location of consumption, liquid is again added. Also additives are used as preservatives or vitamins. All this raises the suspicion of consumers. Does the fruit fiber in grapefruit juice really come from grapefruits, or from cucumbers, as the rumor goes?

Hemophiliacs use a medicine of Bayer, Factor VIII, which contains the blood plasma of more than 10,000 patients (Bogdanich and Koli 2003). Food concentrate for beef is made up of a large number of recycled and waste products, from old ground bread, to vegetable waste, rejected candies, and—before the BSE scandal—bonemeal from butchered congeners. Conversely, a slaughtered cow can end up in 50,000 different products, not only as meat and sausage, but also in glue, paper, and congeners. The number of components whose quality, safety, and reliability has to be inspected and certified has increased exponentially.

The intransparency of composed foods can pose a problem for cultures and communities that ban certain raw materials. For Muslims pork is *haram* (unclean), as is meat from other carnivorous animals. Muslims can eat only *halal* (clean) animals: beef, veal, goats, sheep, and fowl. This poses a problem for ground beef: Is it really pure ground beef? But who knows if ingredients forbidden to Muslims could also have been used in licorice, peppermint, cheese, ice cream, or cakes (*Volkskrant*, June 10, 2003)?

Muslims and Jews also have process standards, derived from their conviction that animals should not suffer unnecessarily. Muslims require that the animal must be killed by a slit of the throat by a sharp knife, a civilizing rule. However, in a time of global food chains and complicated composed foods, it becomes problematic. How is the consumer to know whether the gelatin that has been certified as coming from sheep bones is also from sheep slaughtered in such a specific humane way? While we may now have even more humane animal killing methods, religious norms are not easily updated.

Of course, risks and uncertainties are nothing new. It is arguable that at least in the West, the risks and uncertainties were much higher in the past due to the greater prevalence of diseases, poisoning, epidemics, conflict, war, and crime. What is new is that people, at least in the industrialized nations, expect ever higher levels of security. Moreover, new science and technologies have brought not only new dangers, but also more knowledge about various threats and risks, such as the carcinogenic character of certain substances and the long-term effects of smoking. This in turn has fostered a belief that it is possible to reduce all risks and uncertainties. And with new information and communication technologies, news travels instantaneously around the globe, including information about events elsewhere that could threaten our security, such as food scares and scandals, mad cow disease, and food-borne poisoning from Listeria. Such information has a direct effect: the demand for products suspected of disease becomes rapidly reduced, threatening to annihilate whole sectors. Even the news that nonpoisonous but nevertheless suspected "unnatural" foods, such as GMOs, may be included in certain products has led to consumer boycotts.

All of these factors mean that citizens expect politicians to act, ward off any imminent threats, and use all available scientific knowledge and other resources and powers of the state to do so. This is reinforced by the diffusion of information through the mass media and the internet about the reactions and demands of citizens elsewhere. A veritable race of rising expectations is the result.

Shifts in the Mix of Public and Private Regulators

The increased diversity of consumer demands with respect to food has led to a rise of new private information and quality control institutions. In shops, newspapers, and on the Internet, one is greeted by a bewildering array of quality certificates that all praise specific products and scream for attention. Food producers launch new brands that pretend to satisfy the need of consumers for certainty in safety, health, animal friendliness, and environmental responsibility and fit with specific belief systems. Commercial agencies dive into this market for information and try to build a reputation as a reliable certifier and get producers to accept (and pay) for their certificates. Consumer and sectoral producer associations try to do so as well. There are certificates from the Dutch Association of House Wives and the Dutch Association of Smoked Sausage Manufacturers, for example.

An interesting case is provided by the growing Muslim community in western Europe. The need of Muslims to identify halal food has produced over thirty private hallmark providers for halal food in the Netherlands. One of them is the Stichting Halal Voeding en Voedsel (Foundation Halal Food and Nutrition) in The Hague. It provides information and has a service that inspects the production of halal food and provides food, if approved, with the Halal Tayyib certificate. It is supervised by a council of Islamic mullahs. The fierce competition among certifiers is exemplified by the name of a competitor: Total Quality Halal Correct Certification.

Screening food on halal is time-consuming and costly; it adds to transaction costs. Someone has to foot the bill, usually the producers. Understandably this does not make the certificates popular with them. Thus competition has emerged among certifiers. Some try to gain customers by price competition, at the cost of precision of standards and monitoring. Thus, while some longer-established ones are quite precise, others certify every product that does not contain pork. Thus the bad ones drive the good ones from the market. The long-term result is a loss of trust of the Muslim community in the reliability of halal certificates, which undermines the market for commercial certifiers. This has already led, as so often in the past, to calls for government intervention. These emerge not only from the Muslim community, but also from the commercial halal certifiers, who want the government to certify their certification institutes. They want simplification of the intransparent world of Muslim certification bodies; not surprisingly, each certifier wants its certificate and criteria to become the state-authorized one. It remains to be seen how long public authorities can resist getting involved. Revealingly, the certifier of biological produce, SKAL, provider of the EKO certificate, has been backed by EU regulation since 1992.

Governments are responding to increased demands from consumers, based on the new uncertainties, produced by the globalization of the food chain and the increasing complexity of composed foods. The traditional response of nation-states to foreign threats has been to try to keep them out by erecting, maintaining, and enforcing borders—the very essence of a territorial state. This pattern continues; accordingly, the French banned British beef and the Americans Canadian beef. Furthermore, new national food regulatory agencies have been established or existing ones reformed.

This strategy of building national fortresses nevertheless becomes increasingly difficult in a globalizing world. States punish each other for protectionism, and national food regulatory agencies cannot easily regulate, let alone enforce, food standards along the long international food production chains. The internationalization of food chains gives national states an interest in extending control beyond their territory. Economically or politically powerful nations can and do impose their standards on other nations through trade relations (the "California effect," Vogel 1995) or political pressure. More frequently used, however, are less asymmetric forms: attempts to establish international standards through supranational organizations, such as the EU and WTO. Numerous kinds of harmonization measures have emerged, such as formal negotiated harmonization, soft harmonization, the open method of coordination, and mutual learning and imitation.

However, the export, harmonization, or convergence of paper regulations often does not suffice. What counts is whether and how these rules in the books are translated into rules in action. In the end, actual enforcement and compliance represent the Achilles heel of any regulation. Regulations have to be applied and enforced on the street levels, shop floors, harbors, and airfields in other countries by local authorities. Standards still discernable on products can be checked at the borders, but this is typically impossible for process standards as well as for many product standards. In such cases, countries have to trust the street-level bureaucrats in other countries and the value of the certificates and licenses that they have been given. At the end of the day, what really counts is the competence and integrity of the Thai inspector who inspects and certifies the hygiene of shrimp peeling.

Mutual trust between countries in their enforcement practices and value of certificates is complicated because the discretionary authority of street-level bureaucrats and their enforcement styles differs significantly among countries. American enforcement officers have limited discretion and apply regulations in an indiscriminating way, often making the full force of the law fall equally on all subjects of the regulations without much concern for individual circumstances. This practice is often characterized as "regulatory unreasonableness", but it also serves to maintain universalistic values: all citizens and firms are equal for the law (Bardach and Kagan 1982, Vogel 1986). British, Dutch, and Italian rule enforcers have much more discretion and are able to take account of individual circumstances in rule application. They can overlook transgressions, give exemptions, bargain with the subjects of regulation, be flexible in sanctioning, and see themselves more as educators than as police (Van Waarden 1999a, 1999b).

In the light of these national differences in enforcement styles, countries and agencies that maintain stricter enforcement procedures are hesitant to trust others that are regarded as having less strict ones. Instead, they try to control foreign controllers by directly observing the standards they consider important. They may attempt to send their own controllers and inspectors or establish international organizations with a strong reputation for inspecting inspectors. Yet external controllers of local controllers will always be at a disadvantage because they are not sufficiently familiar with local circumstances, customs, people, reputations, and networks.

In their efforts to extend food control beyond their borders, states have sought assistance from private food quality control institutions. Some of the arguments that states resorted to involving private organizations in their national regulatory systems in the past hold even more for attempts to develop international quality regulation.

Why private organizations? First, they too have an interest in maintaining consumer confidence and protecting the reputation of their industries and their brand images, in which considerable time and money may have been invested. Second, private organizations have additional channels for monitoring and enforcement of food standards. This holds in particular for international organizations with hierarchical control over their intraorganizational relations, such as multinational firms. But even national private industry organizations can enjoy influence through bargaining and contract relations with foreign suppliers. Multinationals or large supermarket chains can impose food quality standards (perhaps imposed on them by the general public or a national government) on their foreign suppliers (Havinga 2003). When British supermarket chains declared that they would guarantee their customers that their products would not contain GMOs, this was probably more effective in killing the GMO market than if it had been done through national state regulation.

International and national trade associations can also be important instruments for statutory international quality control. An interesting case is provided by the sector of animal feed, crucial for food safety. Several major recent food scandals were caused by problems in the animal food part of the meat production chain: the feeding of cows with bonemeal (making herbivores into carnivores, even cannibals) in Britain was the base of the mad cow disease problem. And Germany had problems with dioxin residues in animal feed. Here both an international and several national trade associations played a role in the operationalization, implementation, and enforcement of European regulations (Freeriks 2004).

This case also illustrates the long control chains that have developed in the food sector. The European Council for Accreditation has certified in the Netherlands the Statutory Trade Association for Animal Food, which has been entrusted by the Dutch Ministries of Agriculture and Economic Affairs to supervise private commercial certification institutes. These in turn control external accountant firms, which then control internal control departments and internal quality control laboratories that finally directly control the input, throughput, and output of animal food producers. And all this represents only one stage—albeit a crucial one—in the complex food chain. Besides these control layers there are yet the control systems of the customers, that is, the subsequent stages in the food chain: the farmers and their cooperatives, the slaughterhouses and meat packing plants, the supermarkets, and consumer associations.

Conclusion: The Control Industry a Booming Business

National food quality regulations used to reflect national cultures. However, globalization tends to disrupt the congruence among between society, culture, market, and state. States are confronted with much more diverse demands as to the criteria for food quality control as their countries become multicultural but are less able to effectively regulate food as the food chains become longer and international, and these international markets produce complex composed products.

These contradictory tendencies between which states get squeezed—greater diversity in demands for food standards from citizens, less capacity to monitor and control any such standards—are producing a proliferation of food control institutions. In reaction to food scandals, and increasing insecurity and distrust, national governments are creating more control agencies, expanding existing ones, and piling new layers of control on top of those already in place. They do so for more and more substages along an ever longer international food chain, in many countries. And they frequently are assisted by private and semipublic institutions. Here the term *multilevel* government acquires a new meaning. Insofar as states either cannot and will not cater to the increased demands for quality certificates from citizens, private organizations increasingly are filling this market niche. Food producers create their own brands, and a variety of governance institutions—commercial entrepreneurs, private foundations, consumer associations, trade associations—try to produce and popularize their own quality certificates. The proliferation that this produces, and the resultant intransparency of the world of certifications, leads to a call for certifiers of certifications—and certifiers of the certifiers of the certifiers.

Do more controls mean less uncertainty, insecurity, and fears of unsafety and deception? That is the intention. But the paradoxical reality is that the more controls we create, the more the controllers find and report that not everywhere are things 100 percent in line with often very detailed and formal criteria—if only because in practice sometimes short-cuts have to be taken. Moreover, more controls produce more information about fraud, unsafety, and poor quality, and those amplify feelings of distrust. To every new scandal or crisis, politicians react by adding one more layer of control on top of the already existing levels of controllers. Paradoxically, the more food quality inspectors and tests we have, the more we can know about our food quality, the more we want to know, and the more we feel unsafe, leading to a call for yet another layer of inspectors, controllers, and evaluators.

Thus the "control industry" has become a veritable growth industry. Distrust has become a booming business. I calculate that of the Dutch working population of 7 million, about 2 million are busy with controlling others on behalf of yet others. The decline in employment in agriculture (now only 1 percent in the Netherlands) and industry (a mere 18 percent) has luckily been offset by a growth of work in the service sector, and a large part of that is the control industry. More and more people earn their living by reducing risk and uncertainty. The more fraud—or mere threat of fraud—the more work there is. The demand is insatiable. Every higher level of control can be also distrusted (after a scandal) and produce a demand for new controllers.

3

Contestation over Food Safety: The Significance of Consumer Trust

Unni Kjærnes, Arne Dulsrud, and Christian Poppe

Trust is regarded as critical to democratic governance. Trust links citizens to the regulatory bodies that are intended to govern on their behalf, and thereby enhances the legitimacy and effectiveness of governance (Hardin 2001). But this does not imply that political distrust has opposite effects. Skepticism is assumed to have a constructive role for democracy in the sense of failing to trust until given sufficient evidence or reasons for trusting (Levi 1998). That citizens' trust is conditional seems to be fairly well accepted as a part of a legitimate democratic framework and does not necessarily contest governance. People might question the performance of politicians and governmental bodies, and a healthy skepticism is a prerequisite to democracy (Sztompka 1999). But distrust can also be subversive to governance. A more profound distrust affects the legitimacy of existing institutional arrangements, and governance itself becomes contested. Distrust becomes a problem for governance, for example, when it leads to nonproductive increase in government regulations as a means to build or regain trust (Majone 1999).

Political trust and distrust is closely associated with contested governance. Distrust not only challenges the legitimacy of existing institutional arrangements. In the case of food safety, it also involves contestation over the basis on which food safety is regulated, how legitimacy is rooted, and the role of public opinion. In particular, the reform processes of the European Union have raised the issue of political trust. Citizens in their roles as consumers are confronted with a more complex governance structure as food regulations take place on a national level and are affected by regional (i.e., European) and international policies as well. Moreover, expansion of the EU and the incorporation of five postcommunist countries make trust in regulatory institutions even more critical—and problematic.

This chapter discusses how consumer trust and distrust affects the legitimacy of European food policy. Whether trust or distrust among consumers challenges legitimacy depends in our view on two factors: the level of trust and the nature of trust and distrust. While the notion of the European citizen is still important in the discourse on food safety regulation, there have been increasing references to "the consumer" and "consumer trust." The frequent use of such concepts by the media and policymakers may indicate that consumer issues have become more important. Private and public actors are increasingly regarding consumers as relevant actors. Demands on regulatory issues from the public are frequently presented as "consumer" demands in public opinion polls, representative bodies, claims made by advocates and organizations, and even political institutions. Policy papers are explicitly referring to consumer choice and consumers' own responsibility through informed choice and labeling strategies. This may reflect a more general shift in the involvement of the public, from citizens (or an electorate) to consumers. It may also be associated with a more political focus on individual rights. Last, but not least important, it is linked to the shifting balance between the public and the private, between individuals and social institutions. As such, it may be seen as a feature of the new regulatory state.

The rise of the consumer as a critical actor in food regulatory issues is also due to more specific factors. The consumer voice is more apparent in the public space than before through debates, campaigns, and political consumption (see chapter 5, this volume) rather than as a represented interest in traditional policy decision processes. Perhaps more important is the fact that consumer demand is affected directly by regulatory practices at both a national and European level. Consumer distrust may have immediate economic costs, and regulatory reforms could be seen as a political effort to avoid a heavy and continuous drop in consumer demand. This may be one important reason that food regulation agencies and business are increasingly referring to consumers in their own decisions and strategic activities.

It is important to better understand the phenomenon of trust and the way it is influenced by both market and public arrangements. Distrust could express a healthy skepticism, but it also could represent a deeper suspicion of regulatory institutions and their role under changing conditions. This distinction is of great importance when it comes to understanding the legitimacy of governance at a national and European level.

Our main intention is to investigate the assessments of trust in food among the populations in various European countries. In particular we focus on how variations in trust can be explained. We explore associations between various measures of trust, in particular long-term and basic trust as contrasted to a more conditional trust based on institutional performance. From this, we draw some implications for the legitimacy of the regulatory process in the EU.

Explaining Variations in Trust

Previous studies have shown variations in the levels of social and political trust in general in different European countries and regions. Patterns of trust in political institutions are relatively consistent, with the Nordic and the Mediterranean countries generally representing the high and the low extremes, respectively (Kaase 1999). Similar patterns have been observed for interpersonal trust (Inglehart 1997). A recent Eurobarometer survey of consumer protection shows that several measures tend to point in the same direction in terms of high-trust versus low-trust societies, but there were also distinctive ranking orders of countries in people's evaluations depending on the type of question or issue (European Opinion Research Group 2003).

When the focus is on food and food regulatory bodies more specifically, similar variations can be observed. A Eurobarometer survey from 1998 had a special focus on food safety. It showed that while 70 to 75 percent of Finns, Spaniards, and Norwegian believed that eggs, fish, and meat are safe to eat, only a fourth of the Germans felt the same (Berg, 2000a). When it came to trust in institutions, such as supermarkets, public institutions, and consumers' organizations, similar rankings among European countries were found. In the case of food, public authorities were believed to be telling the truth by 40 to 50 percent of Dutch and Nordic respondents, while the comparable figure was below 20 percent among the French, Belgian, and Greek (Berg 2000b). Market actors were generally less trusted, with a variation between 10 and 33 percent, British and Dutch respondents being the most trusting and Portuguese and German the least. From studies on political trust, two broad theoretical types of approaches can be identified: the cultural and the institutional (Mishler and Rose 2001). They offer different perspectives on the prospects of developing trust and the stability of current trust relations. Although the two perspectives are internally very diverse, it is possible to point to distinctive differences in the social and political mechanisms from which trust is assumed to originate.

Cultural theories hypothesize that trust in institutions and politics is created outside the political sphere in a long-standing belief in other people that is rooted in cultural norms. The argument is that confidence develops only very slowly, starting out in primary socialization with the development of basic, trusting personal relations and continuing into secondary socialization processes where young people and adults engage in social networks and organizations. Trust in institutions is regarded as an extension of interpersonal trust, apprehended early in life, and projected on to political institutions and therefore conditioning the assessment of political performance (Inglehart 1997, Putnam 1993, Uslaner 1999). These ideas are typically taken in two directions. Some writers emphasize trust as a form of social capital, which is intertwined with the (unequal) distribution of social resources, thus varying in kind or degree according to social status and demography. Others see trust as intrinsically embedded in local or national cultural superstructures. In the specific case of food, social capital seems crucial, as it may both condition and enhance food-related activities. In particular, food acquisition requires that a wide range of social relations is drawn on, such as those exhibited in networks, common knowledge, and accessible skills in one's social surroundings. Moreover, over time food-procuring practices turn the individual into a skilled actor who tacitly or explicitly acquires opinions about his doings, including assertions about whether the foods potentially available are to be trusted.

Institutional theories, on the contrary, propose that trust is derived from institutional and political performance. Trust hinges on citizen evaluations of institutional performance. Institutions that perform well generate trust, while those that perform badly generate distrust and skepticism. Institutional theories seem to oppose a direct causal relationship between the development of interpersonal trust, on the one hand, and institutional or system trust, on the other. Trust in institutions is rationally based, and most contributions within this tradition seem to refer to rational choice, thus emphasizing the role of rational calculation of self-interest (Mishler and Rose 2001, Rothstein 2000). From this approach, it is expected that variations in national levels of trust are associated with the performance of those institutions, either as an aggregate output or individual experiences.

Cultural and institutional theories are often presented as mutually exclusive explanations of trust, but their opposition should not be exaggerated. Some empirical studies suggest that while cultural explanations may be important under stable conditions marked by general consensus about values and solutions, explanations related to the performance of specific institutions are needed for an understanding of trust under conditions of turbulence and social change. Social networks may also have more importance when institutional trust fails on a general basis (Guseva and Rona-Tas 2001, Völker and Flap 2001). However, it is sometimes underlined that evaluations of performance cannot be seen only as a rational consideration of self-interest, but as part of a comprehensive, dynamic process embedded in a cultural and historical setting (Rothstein 2000). Norms, resources, and skills developed within personal social networks may influence the ways in which the relationships to institutions are experienced and handled, thus being mutually reinforcing. Since institutional and cultural explanations refer to quite different mechanisms, we should therefore open up to the possibility that the cultural and institutional approaches—rather than representing competing perspectives—offer partial or complementary explanations. As we shall argue throughout this chapter, this may indeed be the case for trust in food.

Variations in Trust: The Case of Food

Our empirical analyses are based on survey data from Six European countries, including both eastern and western Germany, collected during November 2002. To illuminate our questions, we present some findings from the project TRUSTINFOOD.[1] This project includes representative surveys in six European countries (Denmark, Germany, Great Britain, Italy, Norway, and Portugal), as well as studies of institutional actors within the same countries and at the EU level. Computer-assisted telephone interviews (CATI) were conducted in November 2002 by one polling institute and its affiliates in each country. Identical standard sampling procedures, questionnaires, and instructions to interviewers were applied (for a more detailed description, see Poppe and Kjærnes 2003).[2] We describe some indicators of trust in food, which, for the most part, confirm the variations that have previously been observed. We then introduce these and other indicators into a multivariate model that is meant to explore the role of cultural versus institutional factors in explaining trust in food.

Trust expressed through trust in foods may be interpreted as referring to a generalized impression of the state of affairs in the marketplace. Various foods then represent distinct systems of provision, characterizing both performance and consumers' relations to the system. The results revealed major differences between the various food items.[3] These differences are relatively consistent among the various countries; fresh tomatoes and fresh fruits and vegetables rank highest, meats typically taking the midpositions, while sausages and burgers from fast food outlets, along with restaurant meals, were ranked lowest with regard to food safety. An additive index showed considerable variation among the countries.[4] At the top, we find British respondents, whose index for all food items is 50.8, followed by Denmark (35.8), Portugal (31.5), and Norway (31.2). At the bottom we find eastern and western Germany (20.7 and 18.8 index points, respectively) and Italy (19.4). Taken together, the figures indicate a considerable degree of uncertainty and skepticism among European consumers as to the safety of foods. The results thus confirm trust relations characteristic for each food item as well as typical features for each country in terms of high or low trust.

Institutional actors receive different evaluations, probably reflecting structurally conditioned positions and responsibilities and how they actually perform. Truth telling is one aspect that can distinguish among various actors, indicating institutional transparency as well as integrity and responsibility. The respondents were asked the following question: "Imagining that there is a food scandal concerning chicken production in your country, do you think that the following persons or institutions would tell you the whole truth, part of the truth, or would hold information back?" There is a very consistent ranking, with consumer organizations and food experts at the top, food authorities and the media in the middle, and market actors and politicians at the bottom. Yet there are distinctive features among the various countries. British respondents seem to make the least clear division between public and private actors, while Norwegians' relatively high trust in public actors is not reflected when it comes to supermarkets and industry. Germans seem to lean on experts and consumer organizations, distrusting all others. The Portuguese and Italians' sole belief in consumer organizations may seem to be a shaky basis for trust, especially when considering the rather marginal and uncertain status of such organizations within these countries. With an additive index based on these questions, Norway occupies the top position with 35.8 index points, followed by Denmark with 32.3 points, Portugal with 26.0, and Britain with 25.9 points.[5] At the bottom are Italy (24.1) and eastern and western Germany (22.6 and 23.6 index points, respectively).

In sum, the general levels of trust vary considerably among countries. British consumers express a surprisingly high degree of trust compared to earlier studies (Berg 2000a, 2000b; Frewer, Howard, and Shepherd, 1997). However, similar trends have been observed even in other studies (http://www.foodstandards.gov.uk/multimedia/pdfs/cas2002uk.pdf). Nordic consumers also find themselves relatively high on the scale, while Southern European consumers appear more skeptical, thus adhering to previous studies. In addition, trust is very differentiated with respect to where it is placed: in public institutions, industry, experts, retailers, or consumer organizations. The very parallel ranking orders may point to a consensus of diverging roles that these actors posit, with a clear and consistent distinction between third-party actors (the state and civil society) and market actors. Our main point, however, has been to point to differences regarding which actors people trust in different countries. We found that Scandinavians do not have much confidence in private actors but a lot of trust in their authorities. In Great Britain, people have a higher esteem of the retailers, whereas in Germany and Southern Europe, general distrust in food institutions as well as in marketed foods is more widespread. Trust is also differentiated concerning food repre-senting diverging system of provision, as reflected in trust in various food items. Taken together, this lends support to the anticipation that cultural disparity as well as differences in institutional settings may account for observed variations in trust.

Modeling Trust in Meats

To better understand the impact of cultural and institutional mechanisms on trust, we present two regression models. The first accounts for the cultural dimension, and the second also takes the institutional mecha-nism into account.

Since trust in food often refers to specific systems of provision, we have chosen to focus on one broad area: meat. This has been a major area of contestation in recent years in terms of food safety, but meats are impor-tant foods that are not easily left out of the diets of most Europeans. The dependent variable in the analyses is therefore Trust in Meats, which is an additive index made up of six dummy indicators of safety related to as many specific meat products, all scoring 1 if the given food item is considered very safe to eat and 0 otherwise. Each score is divided by 6 and multiplied by 100 to produce a variable that varies between 0 and 100 index points. Scoring 0 on the index means that none of the six meat items is regarded as "very safe" to eat, and a score of 100 implies that all of them are. An advantage of this scale is that it lends itself to inter-pretation in terms of percentages; for instance, scoring 20 on the index would mean that 20 percent of the items are considered to be "very safe" to eat. We also note that one food item amounts to $100/6 = 16.67$ index points. As indicated by the alpha values reported in table 3.1, the internal consistency of the index is moderate to high in all countries (Christophersen 2003).

The cultural dimension is covered by two variables: whether a person trusts most people and whether one is confident that the food that is bought and taken home is safe to eat. The former is a general indicator used throughout the trust analysis tradition and is commonly interpreted as an indicator of a basic type of trust emerging through primary social-ization (see Inglehart 1997). As compared to this, Confidence in Own

Table 3.1
Trust in six meat products, OLS regression (unstandardized coefficients)

Model	Variables	Denmark	Norway	Western Germany	Eastern Germany	Great Britain	Italy	Portugal
Model 1	Constant	24.0***	14.2***	14.1***	14.6***	36.8***	13.7***	20.8***
	Trust in Most People	3.5	8.1***	2.3	5.9***	5.8***	4.5***	13.6***
	Confidence in Own Food	15.2***	13.5***	7.0***	10.6***	5.8***	15.2***	2.3
	Adjusted R^2	.057	.089	.026	.072	.017	.069	.042
Model 2	Constant	24.4***	11.9***	17.6***	15.8***	35.3***	12.6***	22.2***
	Trust in Most People	3.3	7.3***	1.0	3.9*	4.7***	2.5*	9.6***
	Confidence in Own Food	14.7***	11.3***	5.9***	8.8***	4.4**	13.6***	1.4
	Pessimism Index	-.04	-.07*	-.2***	-.1***	-.1***	-.07***	-.2***
	Truth Telling Index	.03	.2***	.1**	.2***	.2***	.2***	.3***
	Adjusted R^2	.057	.108	.074	.123	.053	.125	.148
Index means		31.9	31.2	17.1	19.2	41.2	16.9	23.0
Cronbach's alpha		.8092	.8562	.6276	.6047	.7633	.6599	.5697

Note: $N = 932$ (Denmark), 948 (Norway), 969 (western Germany), 965 (eastern Germany), 1,437 (Great Britain), 1910 (Italy), and 973 (Portugal). *** = $p < .001$. ** = $p < .01$. * = $p < .05$.
Variable definitions: Trust in Most People: A dummy scoring 1 for "high degree," 0 otherwise. Pessimism: Additive index made up by five dummy indicators of food issues, each scoring 1 for "worse" and 0 otherwise. The indicators are (prices, taste/quality, farming methods, nutrition, and safety.) Truth Telling: Additive index made up of eight dummy indicators of institutional actors, each scoring 1 for "whole truth" and 0 otherwise. The actors in question are consumer organizations, food experts, food authorities, media, farmers, supermarket chains, politicians, and the processing industry. Trust in Meats: Additive index made up of six food item indicators, scoring 1 for "very safe" and 0 otherwise. The meat products are beef, organic beef, pork, chicken, sausages, and burgers from outlets. Index means: Calculated as the mean of the predicted average scores for each geographical area.

Food is more specifically related to food practices. The idea is that safe foods are—at least in part—obtained by using one's social and cultural capital, for example, knowledge, skills, and social networks. It follows that adequate food-procuring strategies may generate a feeling of safety with respect to the meat one actually buys, to some extent even in institutionally hazardous environments.

The institutional performance dimension is covered by two indexes: Pessimism and Truth Telling. The former is made up of five dummy indicators, each scoring 1 if the institutionally conditioned issue is considered to have deteriorated over the past twenty years and 0 otherwise. When combined to form an additive index, the variable may be interpreted as assessments about long-term institutional developments within the food area. Likewise, Truth-Telling is constructed by adding up a series of dummy indicators, reflecting how many among a total of eight institutional actors one feels will tell the whole truth in case of a food scandal like salmonella. Like the dependent variable, both indexes are standardized to produce variables that vary between 0 and 100 index points.

As indicated by the mean index values for the dependent variable in table 3.1, the countries clearly divide into high-trust and a low-trust geographical areas with respect to meat products. The highest mean scores are found in Great Britain, Denmark, and Norway. Trust is especially widespread in Great Britain, where consumers on average consider 41.2 percent of the meat products, or about 2.5 items, "very safe" to eat. The lowest averages are found in Italy and west Germany—16.9 and 17.1, respectively. East Germany and Portugal also belong to the low-trust area, with average trust levels corresponding to 19.2 percent and 23 percent of the food items, respectively.

Model I: The Cultural Dimension

Generally the results in model I indicate that cultural features have an impact on trust in meat products in all countries. However, they do so with varying magnitude and degree. For instance, the variance explained by the two variables is as low as 1.7 percent in Great Britain and 2.6 percent in west Germany. In contrast, explained variances are relatively high in Norway, east Germany, and Denmark. This leaves Portugal in a middle position. The country also distinguishes itself by being the only geographical area where confidence in one's own food does not seem to contribute to the adjusted R.[2]

Except from Denmark and west Germany, the coefficients for Trust in Most People are positive and statistically significant, estimating the mean difference between trustful and the nontrusting persons to be typically a little less than one meat product. Precisely because of its general—not to say diffuse—character, the fact that the effects are robust even when we continue to include more variables in model II suggests that we might be facing an important underlying—and probably subtly working—mechanism in the construction of trust perceptions.

The most striking results in model I are the much higher impact of interpersonal trust in Portugal and Norway. These effects appear as even more outstanding when they are compared with the outcomes for the countries that culturally, historically, and institutionally resemble them the most: Italy and Denmark, respectively. In these settings, the effects of interpersonal trust are considerably less—and even statistically insignificant in the Danish case. Given the large differences in institutional conditions in the four countries, the explanations are likely to be different too.

Norway is traditionally marked by high levels of trust in institutions and belief in social-democratic values such as social equality and public commitment to keep unemployment and poverty at a minimum (Listhaug and Wiberg 1995, Rothstein 2000). Moreover, Norway is a small-scale and only moderately urbanized society, where people typically live in closely knit communities. Compared to other countries, including those in the data set, there are relatively modest socioeconomic divisions, little poverty, and low criminal rates. Also, at the political level, Norway is characterized by a high degree of stability, little corruption, accessible politicians, and decades of steady movement toward higher standards of living and more welfare. Thus, although there are many parallel trends that do not encourage trust, the Trust in Most People variable probably sums up something like the prototype of a generalized interpersonal trust: emerging from a combination of rational routinization of everyday complexity and a corresponding lack of differentiation of trust relations, other persons are simply trusted. A certain proportion of naiveté may also be part of it: in a country where 57 percent of the population claims to trust most people, it is probably hard to develop a critical attitude to one's social and institutional environment (Poppe and Kjærnes 2003).

Many of the above characteristics may be found in the Portuguese context too. Still, it makes sense to emphasize quite different features of this setting. Politically, Portugal was a totalitarian society until recently. As we know from most other countries under authoritarian rule, such regimes do not encourage trust processes with respect to systems or other people. Following a shift to democracy and subsequently to EU membership, recent developments have been marked by rapid changes and institutional reordering. Rather than being characterized by stability and planned progress, Portugal is marked by political and social upheaval. Alongside corruption and political scandals, a major part of the population has been left to live a hand-to-mouth existence or just above the poverty thresholds, with a minimum of social security beyond their own social networks. The socioeconomic divisions in Portugal have traditionally been large, with a tangible proportion of illiterates on one end of the continuum and a small but wealthy upper class on the other. This situation still persists (Barreto 2000). Thus, although substantial improvements are currently attempted with the help of EU programs, throughout distant and recent history the Portuguese have had little reason to develop extended, generalized trust relations. Instead they have been left to rely on their personal social circles. In fact, only 14 percent of Portuguese respondents report to have trust in most people. The relatively large impact of the variable in the Portuguese setting is, in other words, referring to a distinguished minority.

The Italians and Danish represent additional sources of information especially because they historically and culturally have some common features with Norway and Portugal, respectively. Thus, the proportion of the Italian population committed to interpersonal trust is almost as modest as in Portugal: only 20 percent. Still, the Italian coefficient for that variable indicates a rather unimposing spillover effect from trust in people onto trust in meat: 4.5 index points in contrast to 13.6 in the Portuguese case. The same pattern emerges when contrasting the two Nordic countries. Although the spread of interpersonal trust is about as high, the spillover effect onto trust in foods in Denmark is less than half of what it is in Norway and even statistically insignificant. It is hard to come up with a good explanation for this. But as a starting point, it tentatively makes sense to direct attention to the fact that both Italy and Denmark are countries with elaborated food cultures and distinctive, socially and economically important food systems. Also, these are national contexts in which food is a major, recurrent topic in the public discourse. Although there is an obvious need for in-depth follow-up studies on these findings, we suggest that such features could contribute to reduce the differences between trustful and nontrusting consumers because food extensively becomes a generalized, common experience—and probably also a key element in the construction of social identities.

As for the second cultural variable, Confidence in Own Food, we generally expect that confident people are likely to be more trustful with regard to meat products in general. The anticipation is based on the fact that most of one's food is typically acquired in markets. It follows that inasmuch as one feels good about these products, the generalized assessment of the market situation as such is likely to be influenced in a positive direction. As is readily seen in table 3.1, controlling for the impact of Trust in Most People, the anticipation is supported by the data in all but one country, Portugal, where the effect is statistically insignificant. In the six remaining contexts, however, the mean difference between confident and nonconfident consumers ranges from 5.8 index points in Great Britain to 15.2 points in Italy. Several mechanisms may account for the result. In particular, since none of the countries have been subjected to anything even near a collapse in society's food supply, Confidence in Own Food is primarily about adaptations to fluctuations within a market that offers a comfortable range of choice to the consumer.[6] Thus, inasmuch as one feels content about the output of one's food-procuring practices, there are likely to be some spillover effects from one's own success onto overall assessments about the system as such.

Perhaps the most striking result associated with this variable is the difference in effect between Portugal and Italy. Both countries are traditionally considered to be marked by a strong reliance on personal networks in strategic action. Thus, we would expect that indicators reflecting this aspect of social life are important in both of these countries. But it is not: Confidence in Own Food is a relevant explanatory factor in Italy but not in Portugal. It is hard to explain why, other than suggesting that personal networks operate differently in the two countries' food institutions. It could also be a question of different success rates: in Italy, safer foods could actually be more easily obtained through stable networks, or at least result in a distinct sense of safety, as compared to Portugal.

Model II: The Institutional Dimension

The aim of model II is to identify influences from macro level mechanisms by adding two indicators of institutional performance to the model: Pessimism and Truth Telling. The new variables measure different aspects of the impact that institutional performance may have on trust in foods. Pessimism is an additive index that sums up generalized attitudes with regard to the direction of long-term developments within the food institution. The idea is that inasmuch as the performance is not believed to be up to par with previous years, consumers are likely to see the situation in the food market as less inviting and perhaps as riskier or even hazardous. Thus, we expect that people who are pessimistic about the long-term trend in institutional performance are likely to consider fewer food items as very safe to eat.

The Truth Telling variable is also an additive index summing up generalized impressions about eight different institutional actors. The kind of trust measured here is perhaps best described as honesty. Moreover, actors who are honest in case of a food scandal could typically be expected to be more honest under normal conditions. Thus, we assert that people who hold many institutional actors as truth tellers are likely to consider more food items as safe to eat.

The results strongly support both hypotheses. Both variables yield substantive and highly significant coefficients. The only exception is Denmark, where institutional performance the way we measure it does not seem to matter at all. Also, in all countries but one (Denmark), the increase in explained variance from model I to model II is substantial. This is especially the case for western Germany, Great Britain, and Portugal, where the R^2's are doubled or even tripled. The best model fits are found for Portugal, Italy, east Germany, and Norway, where 10.8 to

14.8 percent of the variance in Trust in Meat Products is explained by the four variables included in the analysis. These are also the countries where both cultural mechanisms and institutional performance have substantial effects on trust formation. The lower R^2 recorded for the three remaining geographical areas is due to the fact that the impact from the cultural or the performance dimension is weak. In western Germany and Great Britain, for instance, the impact of cultural factors is obviously modest. In Denmark, it is the other way around: cultural mechanisms are the only ones that seem to have an impact on trust formation.

The discussion presented so far suggests that trust in foods—and perhaps meat in particular—is highly sensitive to institutional performance. Starting out with Pessimism, it distinguishes itself from Trust in Most People and Confidence in Own Food by the fact that it is not a dichotomous but a continuous variable, taking on values between 0 and 100. It follows that the seemingly small coefficients imply potentials for large effects. To illustrate, even in Italy and the Scandinavian countries where the impact of Pessimism is at its lowest, the maximum difference between those who are not pessimistic about a single issue and those who believe that all five of them are subjected to negative trend could be as high as 7 index points or half a food item on average, ceteris paribus.[7] In western Germany the corresponding maximum difference is 20 index points. In absolute and substantive terms, the most pessimistic western German consumers trust 1.2 food items fewer than do their non-pessimistic counterparts.

The Truth Telling index is also a continuous variable that may take on a similar range of values. But except from Denmark, where institutional performance is unimportant, and western Germany, where the effect of Pessimism is larger than the impact of Truth Telling, the coefficients for the remaining five contexts vary between 0.2 and 0.3. This means that in Great Britain and eastern Germany, the difference between those who believe that all eight institutional actors are truth tellers and those who assess none of them to be that is about 20 index points, or 1.2 food items. In Portugal the predicted difference is even larger.

It is interesting to compare the results for western Germany and Great Britain. Both are characterized by large and competitive market situations, including those for producing and distributing foods. They also have in common the fact that they have been ridden by several severe food crises, among them BSE. And in both countries, the amount of explained variance remains low until indicators on institutional performance are included in model II. This suggests that shifts in levels of trust in meats are products of institutional rather than cultural features. For instance, the decline and subsequent rise in trust levels in Great Britain may be due to several severe food crises (poor performance) followed by visible measures to improve the situation (good performance) (Wales 2004). Correspondingly, the low trust levels recorded for western Germany could in part reflect that the many steps taken to ensure safer food in this institutional setting have been unsuccessful as trust-restoring measures (Lenz 2004). The interpretation is also supported by the results associated with the Pessimism variable; negative assessments about long-term trends seem to have a greater impact in Germany than in Great Britain. The results also strongly suggest a reflexive nature of trust-generating processes in the two market settings.

The Challenges to Multilevel Governance and Consumer Trust

From what we have seens in the previous description, each country seems to represent a distinctive combination of national traditions and compromises between public and private interests that shaped the foundation of trust in various European countries. The trust and legitimacy foundations of national food systems regulations differ considerably among countries, even among countries apparently alike and with more than forty years of common market experience together and twenty years of the Common Agricultural Policy. Their success varies considerably. This is first of all reflected in the general levels of trust. At the same time, there are also some common distinctions when it comes to the evaluation of various foods as well as food institutions.

Table 3.2 summarizes the discussion about variations among countries, considering high versus low trust, on the one hand, and the role of cultural versus institutional explanations, on the other. The diverging results for each country, as represented by unique combinations of a whole range of context-specific factors, point to distinctive dynamics of trust in food as framed here by national references. This dynamic must

Table 3.2
Trust typology

	Cultural explanations	Cultural and institutional explanations	Institutional explanations
High trust in food items	Denmark	Norway	Great Britain
Low trust in food items		Portugal	Western
		Italy	Germany
		Eastern Germany	

then be assumed to involve long-term and general as well as short-term and specific processes.

Referring to table 3.2, Danish consumers express a relatively high level of trust in food, which to a large extent could be explained by cultural factors. These findings reflect that the trust of the consumers is stable and that they are willing to tolerate temporal failures in institutional performance. Norway is also characterized by high levels of trust and significant impacts from cultural factors. However, institutional performance seems to matter in addition, thus creating more volatile trust relations. Although British consumers also appear trustful, we found their trust first and foremost depends on institutional performance. It is reasonable to interpret this trust as more conditional, positively and negatively. In the light of the recent reforms within British food policy, regulatory achievements should be regarded as relatively successful at least in the short term, as they have given consumers sufficient evidence for reestablishing trust. The potential variation of trust is also high among consumers in western Germany, but contrary to British consumers, they express a lower trust in food items. This could be explained by a lack of success among German food authorities to convince consumers of their trustworthiness. At the same time, there seems to be a potential for improvement of trust, which indicates that trust relations among west Germans express a type of healthy skepticism, which is not directed at the foundations of governance. In Portugal, Italy, and east Germany the situation is more ambiguous. Both cultural and institutional factors affect the level of trust. Institutional factors imply that there is room for escalating trust levels. Yet the generally low trust levels combined with the way cultural factors work in these countries indicate a more general suspicion of the food regulatory setup. Thus, we tentatively suggest that the legitimacy of food policy governance could be feeble and more contested in these settings. So far, none of the countries in our sample could be allocated to the low trust/cultural explanations category. Any country with such characteristics would indicate a rather dramatic situation with respect to legitimacy. It is an empirically open question whether the extension of the EU would give us this kind of observation in the future.

In our view, these findings have significant implications when it comes to understanding the relation between regulatory policies at a supranational and a national level. This implies that regulatory procedures applied by European food authorities will affect conditions trust in food in each country in a nonuniform way. Neither can we be sure that more accountability and more transparency in food policy on a EU level will have the same effect among European countries. We agree that accountability and transparency between principal and agent can strengthen the democratic legitimacy of the public food policy. Yet, seen from the point of view of citizens in various European countries, more standards and more sophisticated measures of procedural control imposed from a supranational to lower levels might have the opposite effect on consumer trust. Introducing more standards and more checks can increase complexity in terms of more procedures, more actors, more technical details, more information, and so forth. Trust in food institutions is embedded in a specific local and national social context. The process could challenge the cultural taken-for-grantedness of regulations that these contexts represent.

On the one hand, the European Food Safety Authority and its regulations, as well as the systems imposed through the major pan-European retailers, can be expected to be trusted and experienced differently across countries and different regions. On the other hand, the food scandals in Europe revealed that consumers expect that national (and regional and local) food authorities, supported by civil society actors, have a clear role in regulating actors involved in food production and distribution. Although public actors at the national level face severe problems of trust, especially in Southern Europe, there seems to be a common expectation of independent monitoring. Private actors cannot be trusted to tell the truth or give priority to consumer concerns.

Notes

1. The project Consumer Trust in Food: A European Study of the Social and Institutional Conditions for the Production of Trust (TRUSTINFOOD) (2002–2004) is supported by the European Commission, Quality of Life and Management of Living Resources Programme (QoL), Key Action 1 Food, Nutrition and Health, contract no. QLK1-CT-00291.

2. Size of samples: Denmark 1,005 eastern Germany 1,000, western Germany 1,000, Great Britain 1,862, Italy 2,006, Norway 1,002, Portugal 1,000. In these analyses, we distinguish between the eastern and the western parts of Germany, that is the *Länder* that were formerly in Deutsche Demokratische Republik and Bundesrepublik Deutschland, respectively. We have done this for theoretical reasons, wanting to explore whether cultural structures are more important in former Communist *Länder* than in the western region (Völker and Flap 2001).

3. "Do you think that the following types of food are very safe, rather safe, or not very safe to eat?" 12 foods: Eggs, chicken, pork, fresh fruits and vegetables, fresh tomatoes, canned tomatoes, organic beef, sausages, burgers from a fast-food outlet, low-fat products, restaurant meals. The figures refer to the proportions saying "very safe to eat."

4. Responses for each item added up, divided by the number of food items and multiplied by 100.

5. For each respondent, all truth-telling items are added up, including the proportions saying these actors would tell the whole truth. Next, this is divided by the number of items and multiplied by 100.

6. To illustrate, in the case of BSE one may adapt to the new situation by either turning to a safer supplier, drawing upon personal networks for safe beef provisions, or buying other types of meat but beef. None of these options were blocked in any BSE area. Cf. Kjærnes (1999).

7. For Denmark and Norway the calculation is as follows: the coefficient value $[-0.08 \times 100] = 8$ index points. For Italy the corresponding computation yields the value 7.

4

Food Safety and the Structure of the European Food Industry

Thomas Bernauer and Ladina Caduff

Although food in Europe has probably never been safer, persistent concerns of European consumers about the quality and safety of their food supply and the methods of food production are well documented in many consumer surveys (see particularly Eurostat 1998). In a recent Eurobarometer survey (2002), for example, respondents were asked to select from a list of thirteen tasks the one they considered most important for the Common Agricultural Policy (CAP). Eighty-nine percent of the respondents listed food safety, 80 percent animal welfare, and 83 percent the fight against fraud in the agricultural sector. Surveys also show that most consumers in Europe trust consumer nongovernmental organizations (NGOs) more than national governments or EU institutions when it comes to information on food safety risks (Eurostat 1998).[1]

The root causes of low consumer trust in EU food safety governance remain contested. Many scholars (Löfstedt 2004, Vos 2000, Vogel 1995) trace low consumer trust in the safety of the EU food supply and low trust in public authorities back to specific food safety problems and associated NGO campaigns. Some also point to uneven de facto food safety standards across EU member states, which has created externality problems in Europe's food market.

Clearly, a series of food safety scandals, such as abusive use of growth hormones in beef production, dioxin in Belgian chicken feed, and the mad cow disease have shattered public trust in European food safety governance and have affected public risk perceptions more broadly. Most important, successive food-related incidents have hampered the credibility of regulators (Majone and Everson 2001, Löfstedt and Vogel 2001) to the extent that they have challenged the legitimacy of the institutional status quo. As a consequence, the EU has come under strong pressure to expand its scope of influence in regulating food safety across Europe—notably also because the EU's food safety scares were in the first instance a result of failure of national and local governing bodies. Ever since, the EU's institutional reform efforts in food safety governance have been characterized by strong emphasis on increasing consumer trust. This has motivated strict forms of precautionary-type legislation (Löfstedt 2004).

The contested and unstable status quo in European food safety governance, however, cannot be attributed to exogenous food safety scares alone. It also stems from the EU's distinctive internal policy dynamics and market characteristics. This argument is laid out in reference to the United States.

Over the past decades, the United States has experienced a number of serious food safety incidents, for example, food-borne poisoning from *E. coli* 0157 and Listeria. As a consequence, food safety issues have occasionally received widespread media and public attention. As in Europe, media coverage and pressure from NGOs have in those instances influenced regulatory agencies to implement emergency measures (see also chapter 5, this volume). They have also fostered more generic institutional reforms. But in contrast to the EU, the legitimacy of U.S. food safety authorities has never been fundamentally challenged, and the U.S. food market has remained relatively buoyant. Differences across the EU and United States in market conditions and regulatory and market fragmentation help explain differences in the susceptibility to food safety crises.

As to market conditions, EU countries on average import approximately 50 percent of their total food supply from other EU countries or from outside the EU. Food import shares vary strongly across EU members. The UK, for example, imports almost 50 percent of its food supply (Food Standards Agency, 2003) but Italy only 15 percent. Particularly compared to the United States, food import shares in the EU are high: in 2001, U.S. food import shares were 11 percent for all food products and only 4.6 percent for animal products (Jerardo 2003).

Several analysts note that high levels of self-sufficiency in food production and distribution are likely to make consumers more confident in regard to the reliability and quality of supplies. The fact that around 90 percent of U.S. food consumption is produced domestically may thus be an important factor in explaining why the U.S. food market is more crisis resistant than EU markets when food safety problems arise (Caduff 2004). In this light, the slogan "Buy American" may be more than a simple marketing tool. The larger import share in the EU food supply, combined with a large heterogeneity of consumer tastes and risk perceptions, may help in explaining why European consumers react more sensitively to food safety matters. Revealingly, when food safety problems (scandals) occur, many consumers in the EU tend to switch to nationally or locally produced food supplies. In the case of BSE in Germany, for example, the share of local butcheries in fresh beef sales rose from 13 to 20 percent between March and May 1996 (Loy 1999). Opinion poll data show that these changes in the supply structure occur because local butchers are personally trusted to provide safe products of regional origin (Böcker and Hanf 2000).

In comparison to the United States, the EU's regulatory structure is much more fragmented. Despite somewhat increased centralization, its system remains a patchwork of different food safety and quality policies across Europe. Member states have relatively large leeway to use food safety regulation as a competitive tool for domestic markets. Regulatory fragmentation thus means the food market in Europe is more fragmented than the U.S. market too. It is made up of national markets in which member countries and domestic producers have incentives to draw product distinctions between country or region of origin to capture market advantages. The U.S. food market, in contrast, is largely one national market, and there is less incentive, at the state or local level, to differentiate food products by safety or geographical attributes.

Regulatory and market fragmentation has important implications for consumer food safety awareness. After all, it provides producers with the opportunity to capitalize on public saliency of food safety matters in Europe. Whenever a food safety problem in one country arises, producers in other EU member countries have at least some incentive to enhance their competitiveness by signaling to consumers, through labeling or other strategies, that their products are safer than the products of suppliers from other countries.

In summary, multilevel governance in European food safety policy, combined with high food import shares and a fragmented regulatory and market environment, has led to a marketplace that is characterized by relatively intense regulatory competition. Competitive strategies are played out between EU member states in terms of protection of national markets by means of domestic food safety regulation as well as differential administrative practices and implementation of EU and domestic regulation. Competition also takes place among sectors within the food market and between firms within particular food sectors. It is through these mechanisms that multilevel governance adds to the public saliency of food safety issues as well as to the contested, and thus unstable, status quo in European food safety policy. As a starting point for addressing the effects of multilevel governance on corporate food safety strategy, the following section illustrates changes in the marketplace with a focus on EU food processing and retailing.

Concentration in European Food Manufacturing and Retailing

The European food and drink industry, which buys and adds value to around 70 percent of all EU agricultural produce, is the largest manufacturing sector in the EU. Its production volume in 2001 was 620 billion euros, which amounted to 13 percent of total manufacturing and 13 percent of employment in manufacturing. France, Germany, Italy, the United Kingdom, and Spain accounted for 80 percent of production. The added value in 2001 was 145 billion euros (CIAA 2003a).

The European food market is very mature and saturated (in terms of volume) and faces growing competition in export markets. Retailers hold a dominant position. These conditions have provided much room for consolidation and industrial concentration. In fact, analysts have noted a consolidation of market shares, increases in profit margins, wider geographic implantation of firms, and substantial mergers and acquisitions activity (CIAA 2003a).

Despite the heavy economic weight of the food sector and rising concerns about market concentration, neither EU nor national authorities nor research institutions have systematically collected data on market concentration over a longer time period. The sketchy data available thus far suggest, however, that the EU's food market is quite concentrated, and that concentration has increased significantly in recent years. It shows that average concentration ratios in food manufacturing increased substantially between 1987 and 2000 (the latest year for which such data are available). The trend toward multinationality is strong. Moreover, the food retail sector in the EU has experienced rapid concentration over the past decade. As noted by one source:

[In 1989] the top 10 of European retailing held a market share of less than 20%, only a few companies—Metro, Aldi and Carrefour—were operating internationally at that time. . . . With the market share of the 10 largest multinational trading companies in Europe having more than doubled to 45% between 1987 and today, it is forecast that over the next 10–15 years the level of concentration throughout the European market will rise to 70–75% market share. . . . The trend towards concentration also continues unabated on the industry side. 100 groups now account for more than 45% of the sales in the total European market of approx. 882 billion Euros. The remaining 55% is shared between 18,000 small and medium sized manufacturers. The Top 25 already have a market share in excess of 30% and the trend is increasing (European Marketing Distribution 2001, 2002).

As to food retailing the same source provides market concentration figures as shown in table 4.1.

These concentration ratios are high for a sector that, particularly in Europe, is by nature geographically dispersed, fragmented, and subject to differing national and local regulation. More important, concentration has increased over time. The long-run equilibrium may be one or

Table 4.1
Market shares of top ten European and North American retailers by region, 1998

	Market share by volume (only food)
Northern Europe (Austria, Belgium, France, Germany, Great Britain, Ireland, the Netherlands, Switzerland)	32.0%
North America (Canada, United States)	22.4
Scandinavia (Denmark, Finland, Norway, Sweden)	17.4
Southern Europe (Greece, Italy, Portugal, Spain)	14.4

Sources: ACNielsen, <http://www.acnielsen.com/services/retail/>; <http://www.emd-ag.com/e/markt002.shtm>.

two major firms per country, and in larger EU countries, perhaps three to five. This point has nearly been reached in Germany, France, the UK, Austria, the Benelux countries, Sweden, and Denmark. Concentration is still growing in Greece, Italy, Spain, Finland, Ireland, and Portugal.

In summary, growing stringency of food safety regulation within the EU's multilevel governance system has coincided with increasing market concentration in food processing and distribution. Sectoral consolidation and vertical coordination provide strong incentives for industry to take more responsibility in food safety governance. Given the technological superiority notably of large and vertically integrated firms and limited state capacity in effectively controlling food safety, private sector initiatives could help improve overall food safety.

Hazard Analysis and Critical Control Point Systems

Many food processors and retailers in advanced industrialized countries have in recent years established corporate food safety systems at a cost of billions of euros (Ollinger and Ballenger 2003). They have done so in part voluntarily, in part as a result of government regulation prescribing such measures. Hazard analysis and critical control point (HACCP) systems have become the key element in most corporate food safety systems. HACCP is a process control technique based on total quality management principles. Firms use this procedure to identify and evaluate hazards that affect product safety, establish controls to prevent hazards, monitor performance of controls, and maintain records of such monitoring. The HACCP system is predicated on food producers' having an adequate system of sanitary operating procedures. It can ascertain food safety only in conjunction with good manufacturing practices and good hygiene practices. HACCP focuses on measurable indicators and may thus offer a cheaper and more timely way of controlling food safety than standard product sampling and testing. This appears most important for food-borne microbial pathogens and chemicals because these occur rarely and testing costs are high.

In December 1995, EU directive 93/43 mandating five of the seven principles of HACCP for parts of the food industry entered into force.[2] In mid-2000 the European Commission followed up with a package of five measures to update and consolidate seventeen existing hygiene directives. The introduction of HACCP in all areas of EU food production, with the exception of agriculture and retail trade, was the principal part of this package. It is likely to shift the regulator's task from direct safety inspection and enforcement to oversight of proper operation by plants of their respective HACCP systems.

Most EU countries have adopted at least some implementing measures for HACCP in meat plants, with substantial grace periods for smaller firms. However, EU plans to prescribe fully developed HACCP systems for all levels of the food supply chain are still pending, as it is seeking to combine this process standard with product performance standards and systems of certification and traceability.

Surprisingly, research on the extent to which the EU's HACCP rules have been implemented, on when and why firms are exceeding government-set standards, and on what the cost implications are for different parts of the food industry and different types of firms is still at an embryonic stage. For example, very few EU countries, with the partial exception of the UK, have carried out any systematic regulatory impact assessments of overall costs and costs for different types of food firms.[3]

HACCP Implementation

It appears that implementation of HACCP varies strongly across countries, food industry sectors, and types of firms. A working paper by the British Food Standards Agency (2001), for example, notes that the introduction of HACCP will have minimal cost implications for food businesses and consumers and poses no problem for small businesses. If this were true, one should expect high levels of implementation. Yet in implementing HACCP regulation in meat plants in 2002, most governments in the EU, including the British government, granted generous grace periods for smaller plants. And because the UK's (and other EU countries') definition of small plants was wide, around 75 percent of food firms were granted such grace periods. At the very least, these grace periods indicate potential implementation problems for small food firms.

Moreover, the few surveys that have been carried out to date show that implementation of HACCP remains highly incomplete. An Irish survey in August 2001, for example, showed that 36 percent of food businesses did not have any food safety management in place and that 52 percent had not heard of HACCP. Only 38 percent believed that they should be responsible for developing food safety management systems (Food Safety Authority of Ireland 2001).

A 2002 strategy paper by the British FSA (FSA paper 01/07/02) for achieving wider implementation of HACCP aimed at implementing documented HACCP-based controls in 30 percent of UK food businesses by mid-2004. This target, which was said to compare favorably with other EU countries, suggests that implementation of HACCP is a major problem. The FSA paper notes particular difficulties for small food businesses. In a 2000 FSA survey, 48 percent of red meat slaughterhouses and 59 percent of poultry meat slaughterhouses in England, Wales, and Scotland claimed to have full or partial HACCP systems in place. The corresponding percentage in Northern Ireland was 100 percent.

Why Firms Implement HACCP

Data on HACCP implementation are obviously scarce. But the evidence we have suggests that implementation varies across different parts of the food sector and across EU countries. Why do food firms implement or fail to implement HACCP? What role does firm size play in this context? Does HACCP promote industrial concentration by imposing higher implementation costs on smaller firms? We first outline several generic reasons that firms may want to implement HACCP. We then focus on implementation costs and effects of firm size.

In many advanced economies, and particularly in Europe, the industrialization of food production, long supply chains that cross a myriad of national boundaries and regulatory systems, periodic occurrences of food safety problems, and other factors have led to a consumer trust deficit (Unnevehr and Jensen 1999). Many food firms have sought to address this deficit by adopting business strategies that enhance trustworthiness and enable them to allocate blame and costs efficiently should one of their products turn out to be unsafe or experience declining consumer acceptance for other reasons.

Many firms have addressed trust deficits through branding, which involves a privatization of consumer trust. However, branding also involves a privatization of risk, particularly if firms move from individual brand products to turning the entire firm into a brand. In other words, branding shields food firms at least to some extent from food safety problems caused by other firms. In the best case, brand producers may even increase their market share as food safety problems with nonbrand products grow. On the downside, firms experiencing safety problems with one of their own brand products cannot externalize the costs involved to the entire food market. And they cannot free-ride on positive externalities generated by a generally safe food supply in the respective market.

This is why food firms relying on brand products tend to be more interested in stricter corporate food safety systems than nonbrand firms and are likely to be more willing to adopt strict HACCP and other food safety control measures. These systems allow firms to partition, allocate, control, and reduce risks throughout the value chain. Surveys on the beef, poultry, and dairy sectors in the United States support the proposition that brand product food firms are the leaders in HACCP implementation and overcompliance with government-set standards (Ollinger and Mueller 2003). Unfortunately, no comparable surveys exist for Europe. However, it is hard to see why empirical findings for Europe should be different from those for the United States.

In the food market, perceived safety problems are at least as important as real risks because food is a credence good: consumers are rarely able to reliably assess on their own the safety of food products. Firms may thus have an incentive to enhance their competitiveness in this market by signaling to consumers through branding and other competitive strategies that their products are safer than the products of other firms. As noted above, market and regulatory fragmentation in the EU's single market may in fact promote such behavior. However, there are also constraints on competition on food safety. Focusing on food safety as a competitive issue may backfire because it can make consumers more nervous about food safety. In addition, the firms involved may risk ending up in an expensive race to the top in food safety standards. Interestingly, the Global Food Safety Initiative and other private industry initiatives explicitly aim at limiting corporate competition on food safety issues. This indicates that at least some firms are competing on food safety standards and that such behavior is making parts of the industry nervous. Brand retailers also seem to worry that if they excessively drive up standards by competing on food safety, they may lose market shares to food discounters—as long as governments are reluctant to follow up and impose higher standards on all firms in the sector.

As noted above, sectoral consolidation has resulted in a small number of large food processors and retailers, often with global business activity. Table 4.2 shows the turnover and market shares of the fifteen largest food trade groups in western and central Europe.

Firms of this nature need to cope with multiple jurisdictions involving a plethora of food safety standards. Thus, they have strong incentives to seek private or public international food safety standards, such as HACCP, so that they can operate with the same standards in all plants and stores under their control. Several studies suggest that implementing HACCP may also produce economic efficiency gains for firms,

Table 4.2
The fifteen largest food trade groups in western and central Europe

	Trade groups (total sales in million Euro)	Turnover*	Market share
1	EMD	95,393	10.7%
2	Carrefour	58,709	6.6
3	Metro	49,856	5.6
4	EURO Group	47,342	5.3
5	Agenor	45,939	5.1
6	IRTS (Auchan-Casino)	44,585	5.0
7	NAF	40,615	4.5
8	Tesco	38,698	4.3
9	Aldi	30,007	3.4
10	Edeka	28,736	3.2
11	Leclerc	25,300	2.8
12	Sainsbury	23,224	2.6
13	Wal-Mart Europe	23,180	2.6
14	Tengelmann	14,957	1.7
15	Ahold	13,935	1.6
	Total top fifteen	580,476	64.9%

Sources: <http://www.emd-ag.com; http://www.acnielsen.com>.
*Total sales in million Euros.

notably by reducing costs of raw materials inspections, raw materials inventory and other input costs.[4]

Finally, food processor and distributor firms may use higher food safety standards (including overcompliance with government-set standards) to enhance their autonomy: adopting tougher standards may motivate governments to "leave firms alone" and not to adopt or enforce stricter public standards—in other words, firms may buy political legitimacy and public goodwill through stricter private standards. Stricter standards may also help firms in shielding themselves from vagaries associated with changing government regulation and variation in enforcement over time and jurisdictions.[5]

Firm Size and Economies of Scale

Firm size plays an important role in most of these generic explanations of variance in HACCP implementation. As indicated by substantial grace periods for smaller firms and survey results on obstacles to HACCP implementation, smaller firms appear to be less willing or able to implement full-scale HACCP systems. The available information on the marginal costs of HACCP implementation and changes in industrial structure provides additional support for this proposition.

Large firms, particularly those in concentrated markets, tend to have much more influence on their suppliers than small firms. Thus, they can impose quality standards quicker, more effectively, and at lower cost throughout their supply chain. In other words, implementation of HACCP will be easier for large firms in concentrated markets. One indication for this is that implementation of HACCP has reportedly been more difficult in the seafood industry, which is less concentrated and more disaggregated than, for example, the red meat and poultry sectors. Studies on the U.S. meat and poultry sector show, moreover, that only small plants may at times benefit from skimping on food safety efforts. Larger plants with poor quality controls have a higher probability of exiting the market (Ollinger and Ballenger 2003). In other words, large firms appear to have greater incentives and are better able to implement HACCP. Again, no comparable studies exist for the EU. But there are few reasons to assume that such studies would produce very different results than studies on the U.S. meat and poultry sector.

Moreover, several authors observe that marginal HACCP implementation costs are lower for larger than for smaller firms. As noted by
Unnevehr and Jensen (1999):

The large investments and technical skills needed for implementation have
economies of scale that favor larger firms. . . . The fixed costs of adding control
technologies and for HACCP training may be prohibitively large for small firms.
Thus its mandate may pose a greater burden on small firms, and lead to further
concentration in the processing industry. . . . HACCP regulations may also create
incentives for greater vertical coordination to control food safety throughout the
production process. . . . These incentives dovetail with other emerging forces
favoring greater coordination, such as increased demand for uniformity of
product or for specific quality characteristics to meet niche market demand. . . .
Thus HACCP regulations will reinforce these two structural trends for food
industries in industrialized countries.

A 1998 U.S. Department of Agriculture (USDA) study supports this
assertion. It suggests that HACCP cost ratios for small-to-large U.S. producers were $3:1$ in the beef sector and $10:1$ in pork production. In the
same time period, it observes growth in the number of large plants at
the expense of small plants in both sectors and large increases in margins.
In the U.S. poultry sector, where HACCP implementation cost ratios
were approximately even, we observe less market concentration and a
slower growth of margins.[6]

Again, no systematic studies on scale economies and effects of HACCP
implementation on the structure of the EU food industry exist. However,
the indirect evidence discussed here suggests that HACCP may, in principle, be promoting industrial concentration by providing larger food
processor and distributor firms with a competitive advantage. Additional
research will have to show whether larger firms might even be in a position to use HACCP as an instrument of regulatory competition.

In the United States, large food producers pushed for mandatory
HACCP standards and their phase-in in 1998, after having first supported their industry associations' resistance against mandatory public
standards. Smaller businesses resisted the Pathogen Reduction/HACCP
rule issued by the USDA's Food Safety and Inspection Service. With a
view to HACCP implementation cost ratios and changes in plant
numbers and margins, one might argue that large firms have indeed been
using stricter public HACCP standards as a strategy of gaining competitive advantage over smaller firms.

Effects of Multilevel Governance

HACCP has become a widely accepted regulatory strategy for addressing food safety problems. It focuses primarily on microbiological issues. Hence, it deals not only with credence but also experience-type characteristics of food products. Whereas in the case of credence characteristics, consumers may not be aware of or underestimate potential product deficiencies, experience-type characteristics of food products can be recognized by consumers after consumption. Microbiological food poisoning in particular has rapid and direct effects, so that the product responsible can often be identified and firms can be held accountable. Hence, compared to other types of food safety measures, market-driven incentives for investment in HACCP systems are quite strong.

How sustainable are HACCP-related corporate strategies within the EU's multilevel governance system? How much can they contribute to overall food safety in Europe? The answer depends in part on the potential for firms to appropriate market benefits through HACCP-related food safety systems and overcompliance with public standards more generally. Such benefits would include cost and technological advantages or market reputation effects for individual firms.

To start with, the EU leaves much room for local, regional, and national authorities in operationalizing, monitoring, and enforcing HACCP standards. Large food firms could, in principle, benefit from this trend (see also Bunte 2000). Their total factor productivity is higher than that of smaller firms. They operate largely out of EU countries that mandate stricter versions of HACCP. Imposing those standards throughout their value chain, in whatever country they operate, enables them to comply with any particularistic local or national food safety regulation anywhere in the EU. And their marginal costs of implementing stricter food safety standards are smaller.

Not surprisingly then, the limited surveys on HACCP implementation that exist show that large firms have, on average, implemented HACCP more quickly and more comprehensively than smaller firms. And they have exceeded minimum government-set standards more frequently than smaller firms. As exemplified by food safety governance reforms in France, Germany, and the UK (chapter 7, this volume), national food safety systems in Europe are beginning to take account of these changes by formally providing more room for industrial self-regulation.

Conversely, there is some evidence that European food safety governance in its present form may negatively affect the potential of large firms to capture market benefits by means of HACCP-related measures or overcompliance with government-set standards.

First, under the current EU food safety governance system, member states maintain a large number of nontransparent waivers and grace periods. They also provide highly uneven levels of support for smaller firms in implementing food safety controls. In some cases, compliance with national administrative practices may even involve noncompliance with the EU's HACCP standards. Formal or de facto cross-national heterogeneity of standards and administrative practices may in fact reflect national attempts to protect smaller and less efficient food firms from larger and more efficient businesses. Financial and technical support for smaller businesses at the local or national level may offset potential cost advantages of larger firms in implementing HACCP. Such cost advantages, however, are a crucial driving force for corporate food safety strategies that exceed public standards or facilitate implementation of such standards.

Second, firms engaging in strict compliance or overcompliance often find it difficult to achieve a competitive advantage by means of green marketing strategies alone. HACCP is a case in point. While HACCP aims at increasing consumer confidence in the ability of industry to supply safe food, consumers may not trust public authorities' ability to exercise effective oversight. They may also not trust industry's willingness to self-enforce adopted strategies. Moreover, in the case of HACCP no "at retail" product-specific signals are involved. Consumers may therefore fail to notice HACCP-related food safety investments. HACCP's contribution to European food safety thus crucially depends on a stable and well-performing regulatory setting.

In particular, greater centralization in European food safety governance would simplify the overall regulatory structure. Thus, it could make the lives of smaller food firms easier, particularly if they are export oriented (remember that the average import share in EU countries' food consumption is around 50 percent). More generally, further centralization in European food safety governance would provide a more stable regulatory and market environment that would benefit all types of food firms and sectors by reducing overall business uncertainty. It might also be conducive to increasing consumer trust. As a statement by the Confederation of the Food and Drink Industries (CIAA) in the EU notes: "CIAA believes that the only way to ensure that the requirements of consumer health protection are fulfilled throughout the entire food chain is by making all food businesses, regardless of their size, geographical location or point in the chain, comply with the same Community hygiene rules. CIAA agrees that the progressive implementation of the HACCP principles by all operators is the central part of the proposal. . . . Exemptions should be established at the European level in a transparent manner, as part of a risk-based approach that offers the necessary flexibility to ensure that hygiene rules are proportionate to the risk involved" (2003b).The difficulties of achieving this outcome are explored in Parts III and IV of this volume.

Notes

1. For more on consumer trust issues, see chapter 3, this volume.

2. HACCP involves seven principles. For a detailed description, see <http://www.fsis.usda.gov/OA/background/keyhaccp.htm>.

3. The most advanced research on HACCP in the EU includes a cost-benefit analysis of HACCP for twelve firms in the UK, Italy, and the Netherlands. The small number of cases, however, does not permit any generalizations with respect to the questions raised in this chapter. See J. W. van der Kamp et al. (2003). Presentations at EU workshop on Explaining Costs and Benefits of HACCP. Brussels, January 26.

4. Whether such gains are high enough to provide competitive advantages remains disputed in the relevant literature.

5. The extent to which proactive corporate strategies, particularly those relying on green marketing, can be successful in the longer term without backup from formal government regulation remains disputed.

6. Communication with James Foster and Kenneth Oye, MIT, Center for International Studies. See also Ollinger and Mueller (2003); Hooker, Nayga, and Siebert (2002); FAO (1998). The USDA/ERS has been publishing contradictory assessments on whether HACCP implementation imposes a cost disadvantage on smaller businesses.

7. Communication with James Foster, Center for International Studies, MIT.

5

Protesting Food: NGOS and Political Mobilization in Europe

Christopher Ansell, Rahsaan Maxwell, and Daniela Sicurelli

From the perspective of the debate about European food safety, 1996 was both *annus horribilis* (horrible year) and *annus mirabilis* (year of wonder) rolled into one. Five events occurred in 1996 that set off a firestorm of controversy about the character and safety of European food. First, the UK announced that a mind-wasting malady called Creutzfeldt-Jakob disease had afflicted humans and that the probable cause was consumption of beef infected with bovine spongiform encephalopathy (BSE); second, U.S.- grown genetically modified corn and soybeans began to arrive in European ports; third, Dolly the sheep, the world's first cloned mammal, was born in the UK; fourth, the United States and Canada lodged a complaint with the WTO against Europe's ban on beef raised on hormones; fifth, the U.S. biotechnology giant Monsanto took the European Commission to court for failing to approve the use of a genetically engineered hormone used to boost milk production (rBST). The wave of protest responding to these events galvanized the emergence of a powerful European social movement opposed to genetically modified organisms (GMOs). By 1998, a de facto European moratorium against the planting or use of GMOs came into effect. The ban lasted until May 2004, when the European Commission approved the import of transgenic corn in Europe and its distribution in the market on the basis of the new EU regulation on labeling and traceability of GMOs[1].

The nongovernmental organizations (NGOs) that comprise the anti-GMO movement have taken center stage in the European contestation over genetic engineering and the politics of food. Their influence has been pervasive. They have cut down GM crops grown on test sites, pressured major food retailers to go GM free, demanded the application of the precautionary principle in approving new GM crops, monitored nations and companies for compliance with the moratorium, staged media-savvy symbolic protests against the genetic patents, lobbied all levels of government in favor of a GM ban, and challenged the scientific claims of private industry and government agencies.

In this chapter, we ask how these NGOs have established themselves as critical interlocutors between public opinion and public and private organizations. We examine the organizations and coalitions that comprise the anti-GMO movement, their strategies and tactics, and the ways they have sought to frame the debate about genetic engineering. To assess the significance of this movement, we chose to examine the mobilizing tactics of the anti-GMO movement in two nations often characterized, in the European context, as less progressive environmentally: France and Italy. Our investigation takes us somewhat beyond the food safety debate into the related issues of environmental protection, farming, and globalization. This broader focus is necessary to understand the contested nature of food safety governance and the longer-term implications of this debate. In broad terms, we argue that politics of food is so visceral in Europe because of the way it links environmentalists, consumers, and small farmers together around issues of trade, corporate power, and scientific risk. Opposition to GMOs has linked these different social movement sectors together in a transnational advocacy network that flexibly mobilizes opposition and influence at multiple levels: public and private, institutional and noninstitutional, and local, national, European, and international.

The mobilization of a powerful anti-GMO movement has heightened the contested nature of European food safety. As Purdue (2000) argues, the anti-GMO movement evolved out of a network of "counter-experts" in environmental and development NGOs that were capable of challenging the scientific claims of industry and government. This capacity to marshal independent scientific expertise is a valuable contribution to public debate, but it also undoubtedly increases the politicization of science and risk assessment (Wales and Mythen 2002).[2] Most important, perhaps, the anti-GMO movement has been the strongest advocate for the adoption of precautionary approaches to risk assessment, a trend that creates significant tension in food safety regulation at the international level. To understand the relevance of this politicization, we need only to cite the findings of Eurobarometer opinion polls that indicate that the European public trusts environmental and consumer groups over universities, government agencies, or industry to provide information about the hazards of biotechnology (Gaskell, Allum, and Stares 2003).

The effectiveness of the anti-GMO movement mobilizes dissent over the actions of private corporations and government policy. The anti-GMO movement has been highly successful in channeling public opinion into effective consumer pressure on private corporations at many points along the product chain (though primarily supermarket retailers). It also operates successfully and simultaneously at multiple governmental levels, partly through an implicit division of labor between organizations operating at different levels (from GM Free Cymru [Wales] to Consumers International) and through its ability to operate simultaneously at multiple levels (especially Friends of the Earth and Greenpeace). And finally, it is able to tap into both specialized issue publics and their social networks (UK Gardeners, ChristianAid, the Danish Beekeepers' Association) and diffuse constituencies (environmental, consumer, agricultural).

Contested governance was also the context in which the anti-GMO movement mobilized. We argue that the diversity, flexibility, and multilevel character of this movement were particularly adept at responding to the political opportunity structure presented by the mad cow crisis and European integration. Both the mad cow crisis and the introduction of GMOs had simultaneously local, national, European, and international dimensions. The anti-GMO movement could capitalize on the issue salience of the mad cow crisis because it was able to effectively mobilize at each of these levels and to some extent mobilize one against the other. In the context of intense public scrutiny, the combination of grassroots mobilization, media-savvy politics, and government lobbying of the anti-GMO movement outmatched the resources and influence of the pro-GMO countermobilization.

European Mobilization against GMOs

A number of authors have noted that European consumer and environmental NGOs have been critical in mobilizing opposition to GMOs, and their success explains the relative stringency of European regulation in these terms (Schurman and Munro 2003, Bernauer 2003, Bernauer and Meins 2003). Bernauer and Meins (2003) argue that the European anti-GMO movement mounted a successful campaign against GMOs for at least three reasons: (1) because it has piggybacked on negative public opinion toward GMOs and public outrage toward regulatory authorities in order to mobilize protest against GMOs; (2) because European consumer groups have created effective alliances with producer groups, though the producer groups have not principally been motivated by protectionist rent seeking; and (3) because it has successfully leveraged multiple access points associated with multilevel governance in Europe. They argue, by contrast, that American NGOs have not mobilized as effectively because U.S. consumers are in general more favorable toward GMOs and more trusting of public authorities, and because they confront a more unified pro-GMO producer coalition.

In this section, we treat the Bernauer and Meins argument as a starting point from which to examine European anti-GMO mobilization. First, we examine the overall composition of the movement, based on an analysis of the frequency with which a particular NGO was mentioned in a specialized mailing list archive devoted to information exchange among a European network of anti-GMO groups.[3] The analysis demonstrates that the movement straddles many different specialized niches, including environmental, consumer, development, and agricultural sectors. We believe that the broad scope of participation must be related at some level to the mobilizing power of this issue. However, we also note that Reisner (2001) finds essentially the same social movement landscape in the United States as we find in Europe. So the mere scope and diversity of NGOs is by no means a sufficient explanation for successful European protest.

A second conclusion we derive from this analysis is the importance of two international environmental organizations—Friends of the Earth and Greenpeace—in the European anti-GMO mobilization. Their activity overshadows that of any other group. Since these two groups are also well represented in the United States, this finding further accentuates the argument that the difference between the United States and Europe cannot fundamentally be attributed to the more developed organizational infrastructure of the European movement.

Our analysis also suggests that the activity of environmental groups is more impressive than that of consumer groups. The activities of Greenpeace and Friends of the Earth far overshadow the activities of the most active consumers group, Consumers International. This is an interesting finding if you consider the claim that European protest is piggybacking on consumer outrage over the mad cow crisis. However, we might also note the existence of many groups specializing in genetic engineering (e.g., Gene Watch). These groups tend to focus on both consumer and environmental framing of the anti-GMO protest.

Farmers are also active in the movement, though we concur with Bernauer and Meins that there is little evidence that European GMO protest is a triumph for protectionist producers' groups. The farmers' groups involved tend to represent small farmers or organic farmers, and many of the organizations that represent larger farmers are conspicuously absent. Organic farmer associations appear fairly active in the movement, and the UK Soil Association, in particular, is quite impressive (see note 3, however, on the English language bias of our analysis). Finally, development organizations must be recognized. Concerns about poverty, sustainability, and autonomy of Third World farming were an important mobilizing issue that we were not fully sensitive to before conducting this analysis. Among groups focusing on sustainability, A SEED Europe, stands out. Based in the Netherlands, it has sought to provide coordination to the anti-GMO movement as a whole. Among groups focusing on Third World poverty, ActionAid and ChristianAid have been quite active.

We can also describe this anti-GMO movement in terms of local, national, European, or international protest. Here, we focus only on the organizational character, not the specific target of activity. For example, Friends of the Earth is clearly an international organization, but through its local chapter, it often targets local issues and authorities. However, in strictly organizational terms, we can identify the most important groups at each level. At the international level, Greenpeace, Friends of the Earth, and Consumers International are the most important actors overall. Among European groups, A SEED Europe, Ecoropa, Association of European Consumers, and European Farmers' Coordination might be mentioned. However, given that A Seed Europe is focused on areas outside Europe, we must conclude that strictly European organization is not strong. Most of the groups identified, in fact, were national rather than European or international in organizational identity. We found few mentions of strictly subnational groups. Keep in mind, however, that we are strictly describing organizational structure rather than activity. Many of the national groups may be much more locally rooted.

Based on our analysis of the GENET mailing list archives from January 1999 to May 2003, we can partially assess the level at which NGO activity took place. Note that this evidence must be evaluated with caution, because GENET is a European network. As reported in table 5.1, national activity is the predominant level of NGO action, followed by European, international, and subnational. The data are consistent with the claim by Bernauer and Meins that NGO activity operates at multiple political levels. We shall return to this discussion of the multilevel nature of NGO activity in our discussion of Greenpeace and European protest.

Turning to the claim about anti-GMO public opinion and public distrust of authorities, we now briefly summarize the evidence from public opinion polls. In the most direct comparative polls based on 1996–1997 data, Gaskell et al. (1999) find that Europeans were less supportive of GM crops and foods than Americans.[4] In the 2001 Eurobarometer poll, nearly 71 percent of Europeans surveyed reported that "I do not want this kind of food" and more than 56 percent believed that "GMO-based food is dangerous" (Bonny 2003, 4).[5]

What accounts for the difference? Gaskell et al. investigate the amount of press coverage in the United States and Europe and find that it was

Table 5.1
Level of activity of NGOs (based on evaluation of GENET mailing archive, January 1999–June 2003)

Level of activity	Number of memos
International	41
European	47
National	80
Subnational	13
Uncoded	23

similar until 1991. Thereafter, biotechnology received considerably more coverage in Europe. Through 1996, however, the increased European coverage was not distinctly more negative than American coverage. A more significant difference, they suggest, is the issue of institutional trust. Europeans appear to have much less trust in public authorities than do Americans. Although Europeans are more knowledgeable about biotechnology than Americans, they also hold far more negative images of food biotechnology. We suggest that this may be related to recent European food scares.

An obvious source of public outrage was the public handling of mad cow disease. We have already noted the coincidence of timing in 1996 between the identification of a probable link between BSE and Creutzfeldt-Jakob disease and the first imports of GM soya and maize. It is clear from Eurobarometer surveys that European attitudes toward GM crops and food became significantly more negative between 1996 and 1999 (Gaskell, Allum, and Stares 2003; see their table 5). It is also clear that in many European countries (Germany is a prominent exception), public debate about GM foods began only in 1996 (PABE 2001). More specifically, a UK Parliamentary Office of Science and Technology study found that a significant number of news articles about genetic modification also mentioned BSE, particularly in the early phases of the debate (Parliamentary Office of Science and Technology 2000). BSE created great citizen distrust of government expertise (Jasanoff 1997).[6]

A Critical Transnational NGO: Greenpeace

In our country-level analyses of Italy and France and our European-level analysis of the GENET archive, Greenpeace emerges as a critical actor in the anti-GMO movement (see also Purdue 2000). Greenpeace's organizational resources dwarf others in the anti-GMO network, with the partial exception of Friends of the Earth (FoE). Greenpeace has chapters in forty countries and over 1,000 full-time staff members, and 2002 total revenue for Greenpeace International was 37.2 euros, of which 26.1 euros were spent on campaigns.[7] FoE has chapters in sixty-eight countries and approximately 1,200 full-time staff members, but International FoE's 2002 total revenue was only 1.5 euros, of which 433,542 euros were spent on campaigns.[8] These financial numbers do not include national offices, but are significant because international offices coordinate transnational movements, such as the European anti-GMO struggle. FoE prides itself on decentralization, which gives it great strength in individual countries (e.g., Great Britain) but in turn makes it less of a player internationally. It is important to note that while Greenpeace is a large organization, the bulk of its revenue comes from small, individual donations, proving the depth and commitment of its grassroots support, which in turn provides critical resources for mobilizing public events.[9] Greenpeace also conducts surveys across Europe to determine public opinion and develop campaign strategies, resources used by smaller organizations in the anti-GMO movement.[10]

Greenpeace was founded in 1971 and has been campaigning against GMOs since the early 1990s, while many other organizations became involved with GMOs only in the mid-late 1990s.[11] Its long-term experience at mobilizing campaigns and its relatively early engagement against GMOs allowed it to build knowledge and capacities that other organizations did not have when GMOs finally became a major public issue in 1996. However, flexibility is what allowed Greenpeace (and the anti-GMO movement in general) to exploit contested governance and win early successes against pro-GMO actors.

We have defined contested governance as a phenomenon outside routine politics. We argue that flexible mobilization is an important asset under conditions of contested governance. Flexibility requires the ability to (1) balance long-term and short-term goals, (2) conduct symbolic and institutional politics, (3) operate at multiple spatial or political levels, and (4) use diverse frames and networks. Greenpeace and the European anti-GMO network were more flexible on each of these dimensions than the pro-GMO network.

Much like the anti-GMO network, the pro-GMO network comprises diverse actors and interests. A detailed study of the pro-GMO network would include biotech companies, research universities, seed companies, and industrial producer organizations. However, biotech giant Monsanto was central to the pro-GMO network, much as Greenpeace was central to the anti-GMO network, and this comparison will frame our analysis.

Both Greenpeace and Monsanto have strong long-term capacities, but Greenpeace has the advantage in short-term planning. Greenpeace devotes considerable resources to research and network building for campaigns that will not produce results for several years ("Greenpeace Means Business" 1995). Monsanto also devotes considerable resources to expensive scientific research in the hopes of developing products that will yield future financial gain (Charles 2001). However, Greenpeace balances long-term capacities with a tradition of rapid-reaction activism, and Greenpeace International retains approximately half of its budget and 25 percent of staff time available for contingency planning ("Greenpeace Means Business" 1995). Greenpeace was able to intensify its activities in 1997 as public distrust of GMOs grew, and specific activities ranged from handing out magnifying glasses to shoppers in Germany to help them find GMO labels, erecting large banners highlighting farms that grow GMO crops, suing the French government for allowing the growth of GM crops, organizing a worldwide campaign to pressure states not to accept Monsanto's attempt to patent seeds, directly pressuring food companies and supermarkets not to accept GM-tainted foods, to suing the U.S. Environmental Protection Agency for threatening the future of organic culture.[12] Monsanto tried to develop an advertising campaign in the fall of 1997, but did not release anything until June 1998, when public opinion had already been consolidated against GMOs. At that point, Monsanto's actions were seen as manipulative and counterproductive (Charles 2001).

Greenpeace has a broad repertoire of protest tactics, from symbolic grassroots demonstrations to institutional lobbying of governments. As a large, multinational company, Monsanto had been lobbying governments to influence regulation since the 1980s but had never focused on public information campaigns (Charles 2001).[13] Furthermore, Monsanto's corporate structure relied on research and sales to farmers and was less concerned with consumers (Boyd 2003). Monsanto's enormous financial resources may benefit the long-term struggle over GMOs once food safety politics become routinized. But in the context of public distrust of governments and producers, Greenpeace was much more effective at influencing public opinion than Monsanto was.

Greenpeace's success with rapid-response initiatives that captured public attention can also be attributed to strong, flexible links between the international organization and its national chapters. Greenpeace International sets the general policy direction but tries to respect the needs of different regions (Spencer 1991). Each campaign is run by an international coordinator, who promotes Greenpeace's global vision while delegating regional and national specifics to regional and national campaigners.[14] This international coordination allowed Greenpeace to quickly roll out anti-GMO activities across Europe, while the strength of the local chapters allowed Greenpeace to adapt national campaigns to national specificities. Monsanto is a large multinational company that conducts business in numerous countries but lacks the local flexibility that helped Greenpeace in Europe. Upper-level Monsanto executives in Europe suggested a preemptive public information campaign in the mid-1990s that might have better countered Greenpeace's campaign before it completely swayed the public, but it never materialized because the St. Louis home office underestimated European resistance to GMOs and overrode European executives' wishes (Charles 2001).

Finally, Greenpeace used diverse frames and networks more effectively than Monsanto. Greenpeace initially opposed GMOs as genetic pollution. Later, Greenpeace's demonstrations portrayed GMOs as a threat to public health and a danger to individual liberty, while its government and business lobbying framed GMOs as an issue of accountability to public concerns. These diverse frames fostered diverse partnerships that allowed Greenpeace to reach broader constituents and achieve more rapid success. Monsanto's frames and networks were more constrained because the public and its competitors saw it as a mercenary capitalist company. This lack of trust led to failed attempts at information sharing and strategic marketing cooperation with Novartis and Dupont between fall 1997 and spring 1998, the period in which the anti-GMO movement was rapidly building (Charles 2001).

The Anti-GMO Movement in France

The story of GMOs in France is that of a country strongly in favor of GMO testing throughout the 1990s that suddenly changed directions in

1998 due to the emergence of contested governance and the rapid mobilization of a flexible anti-GMO movement.

The two most important NGOs for mobilizing anti-GMO public opinion in France were Greenpeace France and Confédération paysanne (CP).[15] Greenpeace International and Greenpeace France had been anti-GMO since the early 1990s, but were largely unsuccessful in their early campaigns.[16] When agricultural and food safety reform became a public issue in the mid-1990s, Greenpeace France responded rapidly with demonstrations on farms and in research laboratories and stores that used and sold GMO products. Greenpeace France also conducted an intense public information campaign, publishing a blacklist of companies that used GMOs and urging boycotts and public pressure on food giants Danone, Nestlé, and Unilever (Joly et al. 2000). Finally, Greenpeace France lobbied the Conseil d'État and testified against the authorization of BT176 corn, which eventually led to the October 1998 decision to reverse precedent and ban GMOs in France.[17]

While CP is much smaller than Greenpeace, its dramatic demonstrations and charismatic leader, José Bové, were crucial for pushing public opinion against GMOs. Immediately after Novartis's GM crops were authorized in France in 1997, CP staged well-publicized attacks on GM crops and sabotaged supplies of GMO seeds, while also participating in public hearings on GMOs.[18] While Bové and the CP had been active for decades, their fame skyrocketed in the late 1990s, largely due to the August 12, 1999, destruction of a McDonalds franchise in Milau. The event brought Bové's mustachioed caricature to global attention and made him a constant news story in France (Abitbol and Couteaux 1999). It became easier and easier to get media attention for GMO crop destructions in 2000 and 2001, and the CP was very savvy about using the highly publicized trials as a (free) platform to spread its anti-GMO, pro–sustainable development message, to French and international audiences.

Greenpeace France, CP, and the larger French anti-GMO movement exhibited the same kinds of flexibility we attributed to Greenpeace Europe and Greenpeace International: the abilities to (1) balance long-term and short-term goals, (2) conduct symbolic and institutional politics, (3) operate locally and internationally, and (4) use diverse frames and networks.

In France, Greenpeace, CP, and several smaller organizations, including Ecologica EUROPA (Ecoropa), Les Amis de la Terre, OGM Dangers, and the Green Party, conducted public information campaigns throughout the 1990s and worked together to reach diverse constituents quickly in 1997 as the public crisis of contested governance emerged. By contrast, the first pro-GMO public action was a 1997 *Livre blanc* published by professional syndicates to educate consumers about GMO benefits, an approach that was seen as manipulative, in part because the anti-GMO movement had already convinced the public that GMOs were harmful (Joly et al. 2000). By the time pro-GMO forces moved to pitch their products, the battle for public opinion had already been lost.

The French anti-GMO movement showed considerable range between institutional and symbolic politics. Greenpeace and Ecoropa were successful with institutional politics, and CP and Bové dominated the symbolic public arena.[19] The pro-GMO movement had been successful in institutional politics throughout the 1990s as France was active in GMO testing and ready to receive GMO products in fall 1996 and spring 1997 despite a smattering of early protests. However, in the face of growing consumer distrust, biotech companies were unable to market themselves to the public. The series of food safety scandals in the 1990s shook public confidence in the safety of their food, as well as in the large companies and governments trying to sell GMO products. In addition, the French public considered multinational companies like Monsanto and Novartis the largest (and most evil) beneficiaries of the economic liberalization that threatened traditional French values, culture, and local farming economies (Bonny 2003). Biotech companies were impotent in response to this stigma, and after releasing the ill-received *Livre blanc*, industry reverted to institutional lobbying. As a result, while many European nations have seen slight increases in support for GMOs since 1999 (largely due to increased public confidence in food safety institutions that were reformed in response to the crises of mid- to late 1990s), French public opinion has become increasingly hostile to GMOs, up to 75 percent against in 2002 as opposed to 65 percent in 1999 and 46 percent in 1996 (Gaskell, Allum, and Stares 2003).

The French anti-GMO movement showed considerable flexibility between international and local organization, with international resources, nationally salient ideologies, and grassroots local protest. Greenpeace was essential for compiling knowledge from across the world and sharing that information with local and French organizations. Monsanto was less attuned to regional differences and underestimated European resistance to GMOs. Biotech's inattention to local specificities was especially damning in France, where a vibrant antiglobalization movement laments the loss of French government control over the local economy and national and local identities (Berger 1995, Meunier 2000). Economic autonomy from international influences is extremely salient in French politics, and agriculture is believed to be a central part of the economy. In a recent SOFRES poll, 71 percent of respondents thought agriculture was an important part of the French economy that needed to become even more important, while 81 percent of respondents thought French farmers deserved aid even if it meant that French products were more expensive than imports.[20] CP was active in its symbolic and literal defense of small French farmers and local French traditions, and was very successful in outmaneuvering its biotech opponents. As such, the French public remains supportive of small farmers and against multinationals that push products like GMOs. In 2000, 64 percent of the respondents thought the quality of food products had declined in the past ten years, the number one goal for twenty-first-century French agriculture was "to contribute quality products to Europeans,"[21] and in 2001, 62 percent of respondents thought there were not enough food safety regulations.[22]

The final aspect of flexibility—the ability to use different frames and networks—was crucial because the poor performance of pro-GMO actors in this area prevented them from aligning with local traditions that might have punctured the anti-GMO movement's dominance. Anti-GMO actors shared information and resources and accessed increasingly diverse constituents as the public crisis emerged in 1997. By contrast, biotech companies found it difficult to enter the symbolic struggle because they were stigmatized as capitalist invaders. In addition, biotech was slow to establish cooperation with the potential allies of consumer and agricultural organizations, neither of which were opposed to GMOs on principle but had various concerns about labeling and regulation that Monsanto's aggressive stance would not accommodate (Joly et al. 2000).

The Anti-GMO Movement in Italy

The Italian anti-GMO movement also played an important role in shaping the Italian government's position with respect to that policy issue and, in so doing, also had an indirect European-wide impact. The major strength of the movement can be found in its coalitional and framing strategies, its ability to use different channels of communication to civil society, and its capacity to act on multiple territorial levels.

Two events in 1996 contributed to push the GMO issue onto the agenda of Italian social movements. The BSE crisis, which exploded in 1996 in the United Kingdom, soon came to influence public opinion in Italy. Several cases of BSE have been found in Italy since 2001, but the alarm was sounded earlier. In 1996, Italy banned meat imports from the UK (Ansa 1996). The other event that mobilized public opinion was the importation of GM soy from the United States in November 1996. Greenpeace, the first Italian NGO to campaign against GMOs, began its campaign in 1996.[23] According to Greenpeace, the BSE crisis and the GMO issue are directly linked because the banning of animal feeds that resulted from mad cow disease has increased the importance of soy as an alternative protein source. Most of the soy imported in Italy is GM soy (Greenpeace Italia 2002). In 1997, public concern about GMOs exploded (Sassatelli and Scott 2001).

The anti-GMO movement in Italy has taken the shape of two advocacy coalitions. The first coalition is composed of the environmental groups Verdi Ambiente Società (VAS), Greenpeace, and Legambiente, a major farmers' association (Coldiretti), the consumers group Federconsumatori and Codacons (Coordination of Associations in the Advocacy of the Environment and Protection of Consumer Rights), as well as the National Confederation of Artisans and Small and Medium-Sized Industry (CNA) and the Association of the Italian Cooperatives (COOP). These groups created a coalition to lobby the Italian government through joint position documents and joint campaigns. The second, more broadly based advocacy coalition, Mobiltebio, is composed of 500 Italian NGOs (including the environmental NGOs WWF Italia, Legambiente, and Lav, the organic farmers AIAB and AMAB, the social promotion organizations Arci and the social centers Carta di Milano). Activated for the first time against the international biotech fair, Tebio, which took place in Genoa in 2000, this coalition pushed the government to maintain the moratorium against GMOs.

The environmental NGO VAS was particularly influential in shaping the government's position toward GMOs in 1999 and 2000. In 1999, VAS criticized the commercialization of products without complying with European Community norms. The Italian minister of health endowed the Istituto Superiore di Sanità with decision-making competence over GMO commercialization. In December 1999, the Istituto declared seven GM raw materials incompatible with the requirement of "substantial equivalence," as required by EC Community regulation 258/97 (Il Sole 24 Ore 2000). In response, the Italian prime minister, Giuliano Amato, issued a decree in 2000 (*Decreto Amato*) that banned the commercialization of four types of GM corn as incompatible with the authorization procedure. These products were among those targeted by VAS in 1999 (CNN Italia 2000). In October 1999 the EU Standing Committee on Food accepted the Amato decree. Since the decree legitimizes the ban on the commercialization of GM products, it placed Italy among the countries supporting the international moratorium against GMOs. Italy's stature reinforced the decision of these states to continue the ban.[24] Although VAS did not have a major impact on public opinion, it contributed to making decision makers and the other NGOs in its coalition aware of the problem.[25]

Greenpeace Italia also played a major role in the Italian anti-GMO movement. It adopted both an education and a direct action strategy. Its educational campaign was directed at consumers and took place in both supermarkets and in the squares of cities and towns, where GM-free organic products were advertised. Coldiretti and Aiab cooperated with Greenpeace in the organization of these organic food fairs. This educational campaign was accompanied by direct action, like labeling supermarket products with GM ingredients or raised with GM feeds. In December 2002, Greenpeace organized a blitz against AIA, a firm that sells animal products such as poultry and eggs. After several mass demonstrations in front of the firm, Greenpeace activists met with an AIA quality engineer to express concern about the presence of GMOs in the feed products used by the firm.

The association of small farmers, Coldiretti, engages in both conventional lobbying and less conventional action and directs its lobbying activity at both the national and the EU levels. Coldiretti has a Brussels office that closely follows EU lawmaking. At the national level, it operates jointly with the other Italian consumer and environmental groups. Less conventional activities are carried out on a local basis. Through the *semina sicura* (safe sowing) project, Coldiretti tried to make agriculture entrepreneurs aware of the need for retail certification and the conservation of information necessary for product traceability. Furthermore, it drafted legislative bills for several councillors and political groups in the Italian regions to encourage regional laws in favor of GMO-free areas.

The framing of the biotechnology debate also varies across different NGOs in the Italian anti-GMO movement. Broadly, an antiliberalization framing coexists alongside a framing that values the preservation of national and regional traditional production. NGOs adopting the antiliberalization framing, including many groups associated with Mobiltebio, regard themselves as linked to the antiglobalization movement. Promoted by the Lilliput network and inspired by the Seattle, Davos, and Washington demonstrations, their goal is to fight the "hyper-liberalist and neo-colonial trends of the multinationals" (*Greensite News* n.d.). They oppose "robberies, made by the biotech multi-nationals, of the huge variety of the genetic patrimony that is located in the South of the world." They seek to link the fight against "wild globalization" with the contribution of environmentalism, animal welfare, feminism, and the movement committed to fair trade and social aid to the developing world. Actors adopting the preservation of national and regional products framing are primarily represented by agriculture and consumer groups and regard themselves as distinct from the antiglobalization movement.[26] Coldiretti is the major group promoting the Italian products and defending them from territorial homogenization and delocalization. According to Coldiretti, Italian farm enterpreneurs should be free to choose to grow GMO-free crops. The fight against GMOs is considered a necessary condition to confer value on regimes to protect Italian products (Coldiretti 2003). Using a language consistent with the one used by the EU institutions, these regimes advocate the implementation of the principle of precaution (Ansa 2003). These regimes are supported by conservative groups, such as the right-wing political party Alleanza Nazionale (AN). The representative of the youth movement of AN states, "We do not have ideological opposition against biotechnology research, but we believe that the uncontrolled inclusion of GMOs in our agro-food system would bring a change in its nature. Italy competes in the global market thanks to its many quality labels. The indiscriminant use of GMOs would kill our system of excellence" (Alleanza Nazionale 2002). This group is not opposed to economic globalization, but rather advocates the economic interest of Italian producers in the global market through the principles of labeling and traceability of GMOs and the development of GM-free crops in Italy. They are concerned about the "national interest" and believe that "the agro-food patrimony of a Nation is part of its broader cultural patrimony and therefore it should not be changed in its nature, but enhanced and affirmed in the global competition." They argue that "the national interest is for us more important than the interest of the big multinationals."

The anti-GMO campaign has found broad support among political parties in Italy. The degree of activism of the government against the GMO issue has been high during the whole EU legislative process on the topic. The ministers who gave major attention to the problem, besides Giuliano Amato, include Edo Ronchi and Alfonso Pecoraro Scanio. In 1999 Ronchi, the environment minister, supported the moratorium established that year by the environment ministers of France and Greece against the import authorization of new transgenic food. According to Ronchi, the moratorium should last until legislation on labeling is approved (Ansa 1999a). The Italian government orientation toward GMOs appears in the institution-building process started in 2000 for the scientific assessment of the potential risks of the products containing GM ingredients. It created a committee in the Ministry of the Environment to investigate the effects of GMOs, a commission of experts in the Ministry of Health aimed at evaluating the pros and the cons of biotechnology in health care, and a committee within the Ministry of Agriculture to control GMO experiments. Nevertheless, in the second Amato government, the minister of health, Umberto Veronesi, showed a more open attitude toward GMOs and, in the second Berlusconi government, the minister of production activity, Antonio Marzano, has argued against the maintenance of the moratorium.[27] This change in the position of some of the Italian political elites is paralleled by the development of European biotechnology policy, which has shifted from the debate on the regulation of the process of GMO production to the issue of labeling of biotechnology products.

The pro-GMO movement in Italy has not been strong. Interest groups that are not part of the anti-GMO social movement and are involved in agriculture and food production did not spend sufficient resources to lobby the Italian government or the EU; above all, they lacked cohesion. The organization of agriculture entrepreneurs, direct workers, tenant farmers, and sharecroppers, Conferazione Italiana degli Agricoltori (CIA), does not consider biotechnology a priority issue (*Federalimentare* n.d., CIA n.d.). The association of biotech groups, Assobiotec, did not start to publish press releases addressing the GMO legislative process before 2000. Confagricoltura, an association representing broader farm interests, chose not to present any amendment to the EU draft regulation on labeling and traceability and to delegate its lobbying activity to its umbrella organization, COPA.[28] The pro-GMO movement has also lacked the cohesion of the anti-GMO movement. The pro-GMO groups have not formed a coalition and do not speak with one voice to the government.[29]

The Anti-GMO Movement as a European Movement

The European anti-GMO movement involves activists from all the EU member states, targets EU-level institutions and organizations, activates transnational NGOs, and is linked to the international antiglobalization movement. Nevertheless, anti-GMO campaigns are tailored to local and national contexts and member state governments, and local firms remain important targets for the activists. The anti-GMO movement in Europe is therefore better understood as a multilevel movement rather than as a strictly transnational movement. In this section, we investigate the European dimensions of this movement, while trying not to lose sight of how European mobilization relates to other levels.

The multilevel organization of the anti-GMO movement is composed of four types of groups:

- Groups with national constituencies located within the nation-states (e.g., Legambiente, Confédération paysanne)
- Groups with national constituencies that have both national and European branches (e.g., Coldiretti)
- Groups with an international constituency and based in Brussels (e.g., Friends of the Earth Europe, CPE, and the Greens)
- Groups with a transnational constituency that have both national and European branches (e.g., Greenpeace)

As a result of this articulation of the social movement, the anti-GMO protest has been able to mobilize different levels of public opinion and create a multifaceted advocacy coalition encompassing activists and supporters with a broad spectrum of interests and priorities that can take advantage of the opportunities provided by the EU. The major anti-GMO groups represented in Brussels are the environmental NGOs Greenpeace and Friends of the Earth and the consumer group BEUC. They channel the views of their member groups into policy demands at the EU level. They are European in their organization (their personnel are recruited on a European basis) and in their target (the European institutions). They lobby the European Parliament and European Commission and closely follow the legislative process. By acting as insider pressure groups, these NGOs aim to play the role of agenda shapers. Furthermore, the European environmental and consumer NGOs have sympathizers within EU institutions. The Green groups in the European Parliament (EP), in particular, are important allies, but other political parties are also committed to finding solutions to environmental and consumer problems. The European Commission is staffed by officials who may also exercise their discretion in favor of environmental and consumer NGOs. Ruzza (2000) calls these social movement sympathizers "institutional activists."

Linkages between the anti-GMO movement and the antiglobalization movement, and the transnational character of the key NGOs, have also contributed to the Europeanization of the mass protest. Several

European-wide protest events have taken place with respect to the GMO-policy. These events can be grouped in three major types:

· Protest targeted directly at EU institutions (e.g., the rally of Green parties in front of the EP, July 17, 2000)

· Protest against European-level firms (e.g., against the European branch of Monsanto, May 22, 2003)

· Solidarity between social movement organizations in different states (e.g., the mobilization of Italian Greenpeace activists in support of the French activist José Bové)

The anti-GMO movement has been successful in activating issue-specific mobilization at the EU level. Nevertheless, such protests have been less frequent at the European level than they have at the national level (see table 5.1). With reference to the GMO protest that took place between 1995 and 1997, Kettnaker (2001) argues that actions targeting the EU were more institutional and polite than the actions directed against national governments. National states are still the level of governance most likely to attract mass protest.

At the initial stage of the political process, the NGOs target the European Commission in order to affect the way the problem is framed. Later, they target the EP and the Council of Ministers to affect decision making. Since biotechnology law is subject to the co-decision procedure, both the EP and the Council of Ministers play a crucial role in the political process. With respect to implementation, the national government and the local authorities are the targets of the social movement protest. Environmental, agriculture, and consumer NGOs have also brought their case to the European Court of Justice (ECJ): since 1998, eighteen cases related to GMOs have been brought in front of the ECJ.

Although national groups focus on national lobbying and protest and European groups specialize in European lobbying and protest, national and European groups also create cross-level alliances. Consider the different levels of mobilization represented by the following events:

EU level

· April 24, 2003. Coordination Paysanne Europaenne (CPE), International Federation of Organic Agricultural Movements (IFOAM), Greenpeace European Unit, Friends of the Earth Europe (FOEE), and European Environmental Bureau (EEB) issue a joint press release on the roundtable on GMOs organized by the European Commission.

· March 3, 2003. FOEE, Greenpeace European Unit, and EEB issue a joint press release on the coexistence of GM and non-GM agriculture.

· March 27, 2003. FOEE, Greenpeace European Unit, and EEB issue a joint press release on GM crop contamination.

EU and national levels

· September 29, 2003. Greenpeace European Unit, Greenpeace Germany, and Greenpeace Belgium jointly issue a press release about the Greenpeace action that took place in Brussels and Vienna. Greenpeace activists handed out bags of certified GM-free seeds from Austria to agriculture ministers from Austria, Belgium, Germany, and Italy arriving at the Council of Ministers building.

· August 26, 2003. FOEE, Greenpeace, Amigos de la Tierra, and Greenpeace Spain jointly published a study about the effects of GM crops in Spain.

EU, national, and international levels

· July 17, 2003. The CPE, Confédération paysanne, and the international NGO Via Campesina asked for the immediate release of José Bové.

The social movement against biotechnology in Europe encompasses a broad range of interests, including representation of farmer groups. As the French and the Italian cases have shown, farmer organizations within the member states build alliances with the anti-GMO movement. Also at the EU level, the major farmers' organization, COPA-COGECA, supports the movement promoting a labeling policy and recognition that GMOs pose a potential threat to biodiversity and human health (COPA-COGECA 2002). In this sense, the European anti-GMO movement does appear somewhat more inclusive than the American movement, which lacks significant support from organizations representing agriculture interests. The American Farm Bureau considers the use of biotechnology in agriculture as an advantage for the environment and does not support labeling as a policy option (Kelly 1999).

A second finding of an analysis of press releases and position papers of European NGOs involved in anti-GMO protest is that there is a significant degree of homogeneity in the concerns they express. Each of the Euro groups takes into account the implications of GMOs for agriculture, the environment, and the consumer.[30] The most recurrent concepts in their press releases refer to consumer and farmer freedom of choice, environmental contamination, and seed purity.[31] Nevertheless, the positions of anti-GMO NGOs vary on four points:

· *The stress each puts on these issues*   Greenpeace, FoE and EEB focus on the environmental impact of GMOs; BEUC, Eurocoop, and Eurocommerce focus on consumer concerns; COPA-COGECA, IFOAM, and CPE focus on farmers' interests.

· *Their attitude toward a tolerance threshold for GMOs*   The environmental NGOs and CPE are the most radically opposed to GMOs; the other groups adopt a more pragmatic position. The environmental groups CPE and IFOAM do not accept any tolerance threshold for GMOs and underline the goal of seed purity, whereas BEUC, COPA and COGECA, Eurocommerce, and Eurocoop consider the presence of traces of GMOs in food unavoidable and therefore propose a limited acceptance of biotech products in food.

· *Their attitude toward science*   The environmental NGOs present scientific evidence of the negative effect of contamination for the environment in their position papers. By contrast, other NGOs view EU institutions as responsible for scientific risk assessment.

· *Their interpretation of the "polluter pays" principle*   They differ according to whether manufacturers (BEUC), growers (Greenpeace), or producers and users (IFOAM) should be held liable for costs resulting from the presence of GMOs. COPA-COGECA and EUROCOOP argue that farmers must not be held liable for costs.

In sum, NGOs have been able to mobilize anti-GMO protest by adjusting their strategies to the political authorities and constituencies that they target. The movement has been able to Europeanize its protest by adjusting to the political opportunity structure of the EU while preserving the national specificities of social mobilization. Finally, their ability to involve multiple interests has allowed them to activate a broad constituency and create an advocacy coalition that makes their voices relevant among the decision makers.

Conclusion

We have argued that the anti-GMO movement successfully became the interlocutor between public opinion and government authority due to their diversity, flexibility, and multilevel organization. In the context of preexisting issue salience of the mad cow crisis and the emerging antiglobalization movement, the anti-GMO movement in Europe moved quickly and effectively to seize the initiative to frame GMOs as a threat to biodiversity and farmer autonomy and an insufficiently regulated food safety issue. The movement mobilized diverse constituencies in the environmental, consumer, and development sectors and proved adept at utilizing both institutional and direct protest tactics. By contrast, the pro-GMO movement was slower and less adaptable to the context of contested governance.

Two findings from this chapter stand out in relation to the theme of contested governance. The first is that contested governance is not simply the outcome of conflict but also a precondition of deeper contestation. We found that contestation over mad cow disease created a window of opportunity for NGOs to mobilize attention to the GMO issue. We do not mean to imply that the anti-GMO movement simply exploited, in crass populist style, public anxiety about the safety of their food. For many in the anti-GMO movement, both issues were in fact fundamentally connected to a debate about problems inherent in the industrialization of agriculture. The second finding is that contested governance will shift the conditions for successful political mobilization and influence. It will do this in part by priming the context for the public to hear and respond to certain kinds of political messages. It will also do this by privileging certain forms of protest and political mobilization (direct action) over others (insider lobbying). In the context of contested governance, the anti-GMO movement simply outmaneuvered its opponents.

Notes

We thank Jenny Khuu for her able research assistance on this chapter.

1. Regulation (EC) No 1830/2003 of the European Parliament and of the Council of Ministers of September 22, 2003, concerning the traceability and

labeling of genetically modified organisms and the traceability of food and feed products produced from genetically modified organisms and amending directive 2001/18/EC.

2. We do not mean to imply that the anti-GMO movement is somehow responsible for politicization and contestation. Our point is simply that there would be less opportunity for politicization of science and risk assessment if they did not have the capacity to challenge the claims of industry and government.

3. This analysis is derived from the GENET mailing list archive for the years 1999 to May 2003. GENET is a European network of NGOs critical of genetic engineering. It has thirty-eight member organizations in fifteen European countries. The mailing list is designed to facilitate information exchange among organizations engaged in campaigns against GMOs. We examined each mailing list entry in the archive between 1999 and 2003, recording the number of times an NGO was identified in the communications. We were inclusive in our coding, including a group even if the "action" involved was merely commenting on a particular issue or event. For large federated groups like Greenpeace and Friends of the Earth, we lumped the actions of all affiliates together. Finally, note that we analyzed only the English-language mailing list and did not analyze the separate mailing list devoted to German-language communications. Hence, this analysis is certainly biased toward UK and Irish NGOs and probably European and international NGOs. Obviously, some groups could be placed under multiple classifications. We classified them based on our understanding of their primary mission. We thank Jenny Khuu for her research assistance.

4. We found variation in support and opposition across different kinds of biotechnologies. For example, Americans were less supportive of genetic testing than Europeans.

5. Zechendorf (1998) analyzes intra-European differences in attitudes toward agricultural biotechnology.

6. The connection to BSE, however, is not the whole story. The PABE focus group studies found that participants did associate BSE with the GM debate, but as representing the typical behavior of public institutions (PABE 2001). The 1991 Eurobarometer survey already finds a pronounced bias toward consumer and environmental organizations as sources of reliable information on bioengineering over public authorities. It also finds a more negative attitude toward bioengineering applied to crops, animals, and foods than toward other applications of biotechnology (e.g., medicines, micro-organisms; Eurobarometer 1991).

7. *Greenpeace Annual Report* 2002: <www.greenpeace.org/multimedia/ download/1/304797/0/gpiar2003www2.pdf>.

8. Friends of the Earth International Annual Report 2002: <www.foei.org/ publications/pdfs/ar2002.pdf>.

9. *Greenpeace Annual Report* 2002.

10. <archive.greenpeace.org/geneng> and Motavalli (1995).

11. FoE International was also founded in 1971, but it had less institutional consolidation than Greenpeace, preventing it from being as central to the anti-GMO movement across Europe.

12. <http://archive.greenpeace.org/geneng/>.

13. The notable exception to this preference for institutional lobbying among biotech companies was the British firm Zeneca, which released genetically engineered tomatoes in the summer of 1996 with an upfront public information voluntary-labeling campaign. The tomatoes were in fact very successful that summer.

14. Information obtained from a June 2003 interview with Yannick Jadot, campaign director for Greenpeace France, and Wapner (1996).

15. The centrality of Greenpeace France and Confédération paysanne is a common assumption among members of the anti-GMO movement in France.

16. <http://archive.greenpeace.org/geneng/>.

17. Information obtained from a June 2003 interview with Yannick Jadot, campaign director for Greenpeace France, and www.greenpeace.fr.

18. Information obtained from a June 2003 interview with Olivier Clement, Confédération paysanne employee in charge of GMOs, seeds, and large crops, and Bové and Dufour (2001).

19. Ecoropa was influential for behind-the-scenes lobbying of scientists to produce more rigorous studies of GMOs and testified with Greenpeace against BT176.

20. "The French and Agriculture," SOFRES poll conducted December 2000–January 2001; results available at <http://www.tns-sofres.com/etudes/pol/120101_agri_r.htm>.

21. "The French and Agriculture," SOFRES.

22. "The French and Globalization," SOFRES. Admittedly this number is down from 71 percent in May 2000.

23. Interview with the representative of Greenpeace Italia in charge of the GMO campaign.

24. Interview with a representative of Coldiretti.

25. Interview with a representative of Coldiretti.

26. Interview with a representative of Coldiretti.

27. Interview with a representative of Confagricoltura.

28. Interview with a representative of Confagricoltura.

29. Interview with a representative of Confagricoltura.

30. We think there may be two possible explanations for the homogeneity in policy framing. First is the need for intergroup cohesion. In order to build policy coalitions, groups have to use the same language and agree on the main issues to advocate. The second is adjustment to a shared belief in the EU institutions

that agriculture, environment, and consumer interests must be preserved. The language these groups use mirrors the terms used by the EU institutions in their programmatic documents. Radical demands and extreme left arguments (the no-global protest) are left aside and remain limited to the national level, where political polarization is higher.

31. Only Eurocommerce does not make explicit reference to the environmental impact.

III
Reforming National Food Safety Regulation

6

Is It Just about Trust? The Partial Reform of French Food Safety Regulation

Olivier Borraz, Julien Besançon, and Christophe Clergeau

Food safety has been a state prerogative in France since the beginning of the twentieth century. Yet it became a major political issue only recently, gaining top priority on the political agenda in the wake of the BSE crisis of 1996. Two reasons account for this. First, the BSE crisis revealed important dysfunctions in both beef industry practices and their supervision by the state, echoing similar dysfunctions in the UK and later Germany, and undermining public trust toward food products. Second, the blood transfusion scandal of the mid-1980s, with its political and administrative repercussions, promoted health safety as a priority on the political agenda along with issues of political accountability. To most observers, BSE seemed to reproduce the same mechanisms as the blood transfusion scandal, albeit in a different sector, but typical of a snowballing of crises (see chapter 1, this volume). Food safety became a subcategory of the more general theme of health safety.

This implied that the regulation of food safety was in some ways to adopt the more general features of a modern and efficient system of health safety regulation. The key words were, alongside *accountability, transparency, independence,* and *excellence.* These principles suggested an explanation of the previous crises and subsequently a solution: the scandals were the result of a regulatory regime marked by policy capture by private interests, a lack of transparency in the decision-making process, the absence of any diversity or discussion among experts, and insufficient resources and willpower in controlling the implementation of rules. Hence, only by providing independent expertise, a clear separation between risk assessment and management, possibilities for discussion and debate, and a clear definition of responsibilities and control mechanisms could such crises be avoided in the future and food safety be regulated efficiently. The 1998 law on health safety clearly upheld these principles to create a set of agencies in charge of risk assessment. Concerning food safety, AFSSA (Agence française de sécurité sanitaire des aliments) was to act as an independent agency assessing risks on the basis of expert knowledge, while the InVS (Institut de veille sanitaire) was to trigger alerts in case of epidemics due to food contamination and identify the culprits.[1] These two agencies were added to an already extremely complex and fragmented "regulation regime" (Hood, Rothstein, and Baldwin 2000) comprising a set of central ministries (namely agriculture but also consumer affairs and health), their respective field services, public-funded research centers, public and private laboratories (at the national or local level), professional technical centers, local government, the whole range of private actors (in the agrofood business), and consumer associations. Beginning in 1999, a series of crises in the field of food safety (dioxins, Coca-Cola, *Listeria*) played a role in stabilizing the central features of the new regime. The ministry of agriculture, heretofore in charge of food production policies, succeeded in maintaining ownership of food safety as a public problem against the ministry of health and its adjoining agencies. But the latter succeeded in imposing a stronger scientific expertise in the decision-making process.

This chapter argues that food safety regulation in France is a clear case of contested governance. The food scandals and crises all had to do with who should make decisions, and when and how they should be made. A break was called for from the previous corporatist model of comanagement characteristic of the agricultural policy sector, based on close relationships between public officials and representatives of the agrofood business. But the introduction of a new system of regulation implied strong shifts within this model, which caused tensions and conflicts. A break was also necessary with the way expertise was heretofore conducted within the public decision-making process. Once again, such a shift fostered contestation.

Hence, the answer to the question, "On what basis is food safety to be regulated?" seems to indicate that scientific risk assessment and a recourse to the precautionary principle when risk cannot be assessed have become predominant. But the question, "How is food safety regulated?" immediately points to the complexity of a regime in which agricultural issues still predominate and call for a more careful balance between health safety and economic interests. In its first part, this chapter shows that the transformations brought about in 1999 remain limited in scope and that tensions between public authorities have not altered a regulation regime dominated by the ministry of agriculture and its different partners.

The question, "Who should regulate food safety?" then calls for an assessment of the role of the agrofood business in managing and ensuring food safety. The second part of this chapter shows that public and private interventions are closely linked and progress jointly. Yet contestation is perceptible in the labeling of food products, where competition arises between public and private actors.

Finally, to answer the question, "Where is food safety to be regulated?" it is necessary to look at both the national and European levels. Although there seems to be an agreement around the issue of an open market for food products and the role of science in reducing trade barriers, conflicts arise within the procedures created precisely to base regulation on sound science and thus help lift potential obstacles to the free movement of goods. The third part of this chapter addresses contested governance between the different levels with regard to the guiding principles of risk assessment, along with the pressure exerted on the different regime components by private interests and public opinion.

Varying Trends in Public Regulation

The BSE crisis resulted in the creation of a new agency, which potentially challenged the previous regulation regime prevailing in food safety as well as in food production. AFSSA achieved important results in providing independent expertise on these matters but was not able to contest the ministry of agriculture's hold on the decision-making process

AFSSA: A New Actor in the Risk Regulation Regime
The French food safety agency AFSSA was created by the law of July 1, 1998, relative to public health surveillance and the monitoring of products intended for human consumption. It was a direct answer to the BSE

crisis and to the dysfunctions it revealed. But its origins are also grounded in the development of public health policies going back to the beginning of the 1990s in France. After the blood transfusion scandal, it appeared necessary to reinforce the expertise and management capacities of the ministry of health by creating independent agencies in charge of regulating health safety in drugs, blood, and transplants. These agencies were to provide scientific risk assessment to help set health regulation, improve the transparency of the decision-making process, and resort to the precautionary principle when confronted with scientific uncertainty; the administrations in charge of economic functions were to be separated from those with control and police missions (Tabuteau 2002). These developments were led by a team of civil servants in the ministry of health and by the Senate commission on social affairs. With the BSE crisis, several parliamentary reports suggested the creation of a new agency dedicated to food safety (Mattei and Guillem 1997, Huriet and Descours 1997).

The creation of AFSSA was destined to follow the same guiding principles mentioned above and untangle the close relationships between powerful agrobusiness lobbies and state officials. Economic stakes were no longer to prevail over health safety issues. After a heated debate between the administrations, ministries, and members of Parliament over the institutional structure and the powers of the agency, the law was passed, and AFSSA was created on April 1, 1999, as a governmental agency reporting to three ministries: health, agriculture, and consumer affairs.[2]

The agency's objective is "to ensure food safety, from the production of raw materials right through to distribution to the consumer." It has three main missions: (1) the assessment of nutritional and health risk for all categories of foodstuff; (2) a research and scientific support function, notably for animal health and diseases of animal origin; and (3) specific responsibilities in terms of veterinary medicines.[3] Regarding risk assessment, AFSSA can receive referrals from its three supervising ministries and from consumer associations. It can also have its own self-referrals. Three types of questions can be addressed to the agency. First, AFSSA must be consulted on all food safety draft legislation: laws, decrees, orders, and transpositions of European regulation. Second, it must be asked for recommendations on individual decisions relating to an industrial license (è.g., new additives or mineral water licenses). Third, it can be asked for advice in emergency situations or on general issues.

Despite the senatorial commission's wish, but due to pressures from the ministry of agriculture, the law separates risk assessment from risk management, the latter remaining in the hands of the central administrations. AFSSA is thus closer to the German Bundesinstitut für Risikobewertung (Federal Institute for Risk Assessment) (BfR) than to the British Food Standards Agency (FSA). But the law also provides for a close articulation between them: despite the fact that the agency does not have any police or control powers, it issues opinions, formulates proposals in terms of risk management, and assesses the inspection systems in terms of their efficiency or quality of their suitability to the objectives being pursued and of their independence. The agency has access to the information gathered by the authorities and can request measures to be implemented. But central government authorities make the final decision, free to follow or not the agency's recommendations.

Enhancing Scientific Advice: Positive Change
An evaluation of AFSSA's first four years of existence shows mixed results (Besançon 2003). Before the BSE crisis, the food risk assessment system was composed of different scientific committees under different ministries. The 1998 law gave the agency the task of rationalizing the system of expertise and defined three founding principles (already used to reform the European expertise system in 1997): excellence, independence, and transparency of risk assessment.

First, the creation of the agency allowed the dedication of more means to expertise than was the case when risk assessment was managed directly by the ministries: a special department with a staff of sixty was created, responsible for the assessment of nutritional and food safety risks. This department coordinates the work of 250 scientific experts belonging to ten external specialized committees on different types of food-related risks. These experts, drawn from a variety of disciplines and institutions, are appointed following public calls for application. When it receives a referral, the agency can ask a permanent scientific committee for advice or create an ad hoc working group. To accomplish its missions, AFSSA can also rely on the work of thirteen research laboratories employing 600 people. The new means allocated to food safety and the mix between internal and external expertise have improved the quality of risk assessment, which has become more collective and based on peer review.

Second, risk assessment has become more independent from political and economic interests. The agency has allowed a clearer separation between risk assessment and political decisions, so that there is formally less possibility for scientific opinions to be influenced by economic or political considerations. Representatives of the private sectors have been excluded from the new expert committees, and the research programs are exclusively publicly funded. Experts working for the agency have to declare their potential conflicts of interests, and these are made public.

Third, the expertise system has become more transparent. Due to the implementation of quality management procedures important progress has been made in tracing the assessment procedure from the question asked by the policymaker or the administration to the expert scientific opinion. Whereas the opinions of the former committees were not always made public, all the recommendations of the agency's figure on the agency's Web site.

AFSSA has proved to be efficient during several food crises that have occurred since 1999. In its first year of existence, French authorities were faced with crises caused by dioxins in chicken and eggs, intoxications due to Coca-Cola, and two *Listeria* epidemics. In each case, the agency gave a scientific opinion on the level of risk for public health that was immediately followed by risk managers. Policymakers could refer to scientific advice made independently and transparently. The agency succeeded in being recognized by the public authorities and public opinion as a full participant in regulating food safety (Besançon, Borraz, and Grandclément-Chaffy 2004). Moreover, the agency gained an international reputation when, at the end of 1999, the French government decided, on the basis of an agency recommendation, to maintain the embargo on British beef, thus opposing the expertise of the Scientific Steering Committee of the European Commission.

AFSSA allows not only better management of crises but also better management of food-related risks. Since 1999, it has published a number of recommendations on BSE risk control measures based on the precautionary principle. Following the development of the BSE epidemic,

AFSSA advised new protective measures, such as the withdrawal of risk material in cattle (e.g., central nervous tissue, vertebral column, intestines), the implementation of detection tests, and the ban on animal proteins used in animal feed. Such recommendations helped the ministry of agriculture manage the second BSE crisis in October 2000 and restore trust in public opinion toward beef and the policy process. The agency has also launched long-term assessment processes, such as the classification of foods in terms of *Listeria* risks, the risks of avian influenza for humans, and the risks and benefits of GMO. Since 2001, AFSSA has also helped the ministry of health to promote a policy on nutrition, the *Programme national nutrition santé*, by setting consumer and industrial guidelines. Some of these issues, such as the reduction of salt in prepacked food and the reduction of added sugar and fat to fight obesity, are examined in collaboration with professional representatives and consumer movements, which can provide data useful to the risk assessment.

In most cases, AFSSA's recommendations have been followed by the decision makers and translated into regulation. They have, in particular, received strong support from the ministry of health, which on these occasions has been able to uphold its role within the risk regulation regime against the ministries of agriculture and consumer affairs by gaining expertise and regulatory powers. Efficiency, transparency, and influence on the decision-making process are thus key factors in the general positive appraisal of AFSSA. The independence of the agency in producing expertise, along with the strong leadership exercised by its CEO, have proved decisive in reestablishing a strong link between scientific expertise and consumer trust. This result was upheld by the highly positive image gained by AFSSA in the media and the strong support expressed by the consumer movement.[4]

AFSSA between Risk Assessment and Risk Management

Despite the agency's successes, the new system of public regulation still presents a number of weaknesses due to ambiguities in the agency's institutional position.

AFSSA has to produce independent recommendations, but its scientific independence could be limited by the fact that it is not an independent regulatory agency but works under the supervision of three ministries. It is thus highly dependent on the budget the ministries decide to give it every year.[5] Between 1999 and 2003, the central administrations also took part in the provision of expertise, either as providers of referrals or as participants to most expert committees to which they furnished data. Furthermore, the research laboratories attached to AFSSA in 1999 still entertain strong links with the ministries, in particular the ministry of agriculture, thus reducing the agency's capacity to launch major research projects and health safety surveillance programs. All in all, AFSSA is much more dependent on the central government than can be expected from an independent agency, a situation that has encouraged its staff to promote procedures that guarantee independence in the expertise process.[6] Yet such procedures offer only partial protection.[7]

Moreover, the role of AFSSA in the decision-making process is still quite uncertain. AFSSA is like a candle in a (large) black box. The candle (production of expertise) sheds light on parts of the black box (the decision-making process), attracting attention on expert advice and giving the illusion of transparency. But what goes on before and especially after the intervention of AFSSA remains in the shadows.

Before calling on AFSSA to make a recommendation, there is often the question of the opportunity to ask for the agency's advice, since decision makers could feel bound by it; the problem also concerns the question addressed to the agency. Even if the agency has to be consulted on all food safety regulations, in some cases AFSSA has had to force its way in the decision-making process and demand that the authorities officially ask for its advice. Such was the case, for example, on the decision to lift the embargo on British beef (Setbon 2004). In other cases, using its self-referral powers, AFSSA reformulated the question or even answered a question it was not asked, as in the case of *Listeria* in 2000, when it reduced the level of *Listeria* acceptable in delicatessens even though it had been asked its advice on the reduction of "use by" dates (Besançon, Borraz, and Grandclément-Chaffy 2004). In other words, AFSSA has attempted with some success to gain ground upstream.

It has had less success downstream, after the recommendation is published. There are several reasons for this difficulty in shedding any light on this part of the process. First, the different ministries, and notably the ministry of agriculture, wish to maintain AFSSA in a position of scientific risk assessment, even though the law provides for an articulation between risk assessment and risk management. This attitude is perceptible in three cases. In the first case, when the agency makes proposals concerning the measures that should be taken, as it is allowed by the law, it may be accused by ministries of trespassing on policy grounds. The paradox is that the ministries often turn to the agency for advice on measures. This confusion is all the more acute given the status of the recommendations published by AFSSA. These consist of a risk assessment report produced by an expert committee to which is added the general advice of the agency, sometimes with proposals in terms of action to be taken. In a limited number of cases, the staff of the agency was criticized by the experts for providing advice that did not reflect entirely the expertise or took some liberties with the experts' conclusions. In other cases, the distinction between external expertise (that produced by the expert committees) and internal expertise (produced by AFSSA staff) appeared unclear. Although these tensions are rare, they underpin the ambiguous nature of the recommendations between assessment and management and their tendency to impinge on the regulators' role by making clear propositions or suggestions.

In the second case, AFSSA has no hold on the production of scientific information necessary to produce expertise. Although it has its own laboratories and research centers, it remains dependent on many other research institutions for scientific data, without having a voice in these institutions' research policies and programs. It has also to count on its ministerial supervisors for many of the data on which rest its assessment. And the central administrations rarely show goodwill in giving up their data.

Finally, AFSSA lacks the capacity to control, monitor, and evaluate the decisions taken by the ministries on the basis of its recommendations. It has no capacities whatsoever to control the implementation of decisions by administrative services or private firms. The data collected by the inspection services of the ministries of agriculture and consumer affairs or through procedures of self-control in the agroindustrial firms are not made public. In other words, if some progress has been made in the production of information by the agrofood business, this is essentially to the benefit of control services that will often choose to work with the firms rather than adopt a more rigorous stance toward them.

The second reason AFSSA has had less downstream success is that the separation between risk assessment and risk management is not only controversial but also incomplete. To evaluate an estimated risk, it is necessary to compare the risks and the benefits, the costs and the benefits of a measure of risk reduction, the potential risk trade-offs or the relative risks. In so doing, values are articulated that refer to political, economic, social, professional, and even ethical criteria. Yet this phase is often discarded, and the possibility of consulting the different stakeholder groups (producers, industrials, retailers, consumers) is not clearly organized, contrary to the British FSA.

AFSSA also has little means or legitimacy to introduce economic, political, or social considerations in its risk assessment. It can turn to industrial actors for information on the cost or technical feasibility of a measure before issuing a recommendation, but this is neither systematic nor officially promoted, the agency being careful to maintain its reputation of independence. In fact, this is a major weakness of AFSSA on which political, administrative, and private actors often base their criticism: recommendations founded solely on scientific assessment are likely to be criticized for their high cost, low feasibility, or important social and economic consequences, thus weakening the agency. For example, in October 2001, AFSSA recommended a ban on the consumption of sheep bowels on the basis that BSE might be found in these parts in the future. The French president, opening the annual agriculture exhibition, criticized the agency's opinion, which he said was not based on scientific proof, and he accused the agency of aggravating public worries and doubts. The implementation of this recommendation could have had a significant economic impact on sausage producers. And despite other advice that was much the same, the government never implemented this recommendation. But if AFSSA attempts to integrate other data, such as technical or economic concerns, it may be accused of making recommendations based on more than strict scientific data (thus losing its legitimacy).

The Conseil national de l'alimentation (CNA), an advising committee that represents organized interests, would like to contribute its socioeconomic expertise to the scientific assessment (Kourilsky and Viney 2000). In some cases, the central government has turned to the CNA when AFSSA's recommendations were not clear. In June 2001, for example, AFSSA published a recommendation to progressively put an end to the systematic destruction of the entire herd when one case of BSE was found. It suggested a step-by-step process in which the cattle would not be killed but simply kept out of the food chain until conditions made it fit for them to enter that chain. The recommendation was technically complex, and the government asked the CNA for advice: two days later, the CNA recommended to continue slaughtering the entire herd. The argument was that any other measure could cause public concern and that the costs of having cattle kept out of the food chain but not killed was too high for stock breeders (a slaughtered herd is subsidized). The minister of agriculture followed the CNA's advice, declaring that AFSSA's was not clear enough. In this case, the CNA proved to be both rapid and efficient in delivering advice. Nonetheless, its legitimacy remains weak, in particular given the fact that it comes under the authority of the ministry of agriculture. Furthermore, consulting it is not compulsory, it has no clear procedural rules, there is little actual deliberation among its members, its advice is often asked on very general issues, and its recommendations are published after a long delay. Since 2002, the government has abandoned the idea of promoting the CNA as a forum for socioeconomic interests. In 2005, the latter proposed different scenarios in terms of organizing socioeconomic expertise (CNA 2005), which have still to be enacted by the ministries in charge of food safety.

In most other cases, the consultation of organized interests falls to the ministries, which often rely on preexisting networks, lobbies, and policy communities to make decisions rather than consult with a large panel of representatives. As a consequence, some actors are excluded from the decision-making process (other than the directly concerned economic interests), and the criteria on which decisions are based are rarely made explicit.[8]

AFSSA thus attracts attention to a specific but very limited moment in the decision-making process. Its recommendations help legitimate the decisions taken, but these can also turn their back on scientific assessment if it is considered too costly or distant from economic realities.

Food Safety in the Field of Food Production

Decisions regarding food safety in France thus remain for the most part with the ministry of agriculture, working closely with representatives of the producers, agrofood industry, and retailers. AFSSA exercises influence on the decisions taken (with some exceptions) but little on their implementation. In other words, food safety, far from becoming a sphere of public intervention in itself, remains under control of the food production regulation regime. This regime has itself undergone recent transformations. The department in charge of food production at the ministry of agriculture (Direction générale de l'alimentation, DGAl) was reformed in 1997 in order to reinforce its legitimacy in the field of health safety. It no longer plays a role in agricultural economic policies but is solely in charge of food product safety. The 1999 law on agriculture enlarged its prerogatives to the control and surveillance of risks. As of 2001, the veterinarian field services gained independence from the other field services of the ministry of agriculture. The ministry has thus been able to use these reforms to enhance its leadership on food safety regulation. It is correspondent to the WTO, and the former director of the DGAl was elected in 2002 as vice president of the European Food Safety Authority (EFSA). The weakness of the ministry of health and the lack of interest on the part of the ministry of consumer affairs for food-related issues facilitated this evolution.

Thus, it is with an even stronger ministry of agriculture that AFSSA must negotiate its role in food safety regulation. The ministry has kept its powers on sensitive issues, using its own scientific committee to assess and authorize chemical substances. It has also fought to keep its leadership in the management of food crises. This became explicit during two *Listeria* crises in 2000, when AFSSA argued that the presence of *Listeria* and the risks for human health were the result of a complex system of interdependent relations, from the producers to the consumers, rather than the responsibility of an isolated actor. This implied adopting a general, systemic position, opposed to the sectoral logic of the different ministries defending their respective constituencies. But the latter, and in particular the ministry of agriculture, succeeded in restraining AFSSA to scientific risk assessment and thus preserved its capacity to act within their sector (Besançon, Borraz, and Grandclément-Chaffy 2004).

By creating AFSSA, government and legislators intended to strengthen scientific risk assessment in food safety regulation. And indeed, decisions taken by the public authorities seem more firmly based on scientific opinion. The role of science has been enhanced, giving greater legitimacy to political decisions. As the management of food safety addresses issues of perceived as well as objective risk, AFSSA's success results mainly from its capacity to enhance public confidence in the policy process. But the institutional configuration still holds many ambiguities, allowing AFSSA and its supervisors to play on the boundaries of risk assessment and risk management (Jasanoff 1990). And policymaking, implementation, and evaluation remain in the realm of the ministry of agriculture.

The Public-Private Regulation of Food Safety

If private actors participate in the decision-making process, mostly through professional lobbies, they also play an active role in managing and ensuring the safety of food products. This role has been growing since the 1980s, prior to the major food scandals; but these have offered producers, the agrofood industry, and retailers the opportunity to rein-force their role in food safety. In part, this process is strongly correlated with growing public intervention, in particular in those aspects related to traceability and self-regulation. But this process can also be a source of tension between public and private actors through the issue of label-ing. Altogether, the push toward stronger public regulation in the field of food safety has not altered a long-term trend of regulatory delegation to the private sector. In contrast with the situation in the United States described by Grace Skogstad (chapter 9, this volume), public and private regulation go together, either on a complementary basis or in a more contested fashion.

Managing Food Safety
In 1983, the French law on consumer safety asserted the principles of product safety for public health: it reinforced the control powers of state services and required that firms voluntarily implement systems of control. Given the lack of resources to enforce its rules along with a clear

preference for industrial self-control, public intervention defines objectives or thresholds and then expects the private sector to adopt the necessary measures to respect these objectives and ensure they are achieved. This makes it easier for the state to check that the procedures are followed, all the while delegating to private actors the responsibility for exercising controls. This public-private partnership aims to guarantee the safety of food products through a flexible system adapted to the development of innovations and the free movement of goods.

The same strategy was later adopted within the EU with the achievement of the common market. France played an important role in the adoption of European Council Directive 93/43/CEE of June 14, 1993, which fixes general rules of hygiene for food products and requires that firms adopt procedures of self-control based on the hazard analysis and critical control point (HACCP) method. Following this method, private actors assume the safety of their processes, while state field services control procedures at the secondary level. But apart from HACCP, other norms, standards, and quality insurance schemes have also been enacted. Concerned with the procedures adopted by producers rather than by the results, they point to a number of steps and measures that must be followed precisely. They often result in the production of written data based on measurements.

As policy instruments, they serve three purposes. The first has to do with the general regulation frame described above of delegating to private actors the implementation of regulatory measures. The second purpose is also related to regulation. In some cases, regulation exists but fails to achieve any result in ensuring risk reduction. An example is a 1997 decree on the use of sewage sludge in agriculture. Although producers of sludge respected the regulation, farmers, buyers of food products, firms, and retailers refused to use any sludge on the lands they worked on or depended on for their products. Professionals of sewage sludge in agriculture decided to standardize the processes of production, storage, and spreading through an insurance quality procedure, a solution that helped firms and retailers lift their bans. But at a closer look, the procedures consisted mainly of producers of sludge making a commitment to follow regulation, and it gave to insurance quality firms the task of controlling the procedure's application (instead of state field services) (Borraz and d'Arcimoles 2003). This is quite close to the German Quality and Safety standard (chapter 8, this volume). The third purpose has to do with familiar procedures in the agrofood business. Agrofood firms and retailers alike refuse to control their suppliers' compliance with regulations, considering this to be a state prerogative. Furthermore, they have little trust in the fact that their suppliers actually comply with regulation and that this regulation is effective in reducing risk. The picture is somewhat different once they are confronted with norms, standards, and insurance quality procedures. Not only do they themselves use such instruments, but they believe that through the methods used to elaborate these instruments (a large consultation of the different interested parties rather than a top-down approach), their voluntary nature, and the threat represented by the withdrawal of a certification in case of noncompliance (notified by an independent third party), these instruments are more efficient.

Alongside these evolutions, crises underpinned the need to trace products. Once again, France was at the forefront when it affirmed a general principle of traceability for all food products in the 1999 law on agriculture, a principle picked up by the EU in 2002. Hence, standardization made its way in the food industry before the food safety crises, but public authorities found in these further justifications for delegating more controls to firms, along with greater accountability in case of noncompliance. Standardization is thus part of a general trend in which public authorities are convinced they can achieve better results in implementing regulation through private actors and thus prevent the emergence of new scandals. The crises have encouraged its extension to farm products, submitted before to very specific and often ineffective regulatory measures. Issues of safety, initially foreign to this trend, actually served the purpose of standardization. These elements thus have a common evolution: the management of food safety today is largely run by private actors, under the state's approval and scrutiny. The emergence of a food safety regulation regime has had little impact on this general trend.

Competing Labels

The emphasis on quality in food products initially had nothing to do with issues of safety. But with the food safety crises and the importance of perceived risks, quality was considered a path to bring back consumer trust in the safety of food products. Once again, a trend prior to the crises, marked by strong public-private interactions, resulted in stronger forms of delegation to private actors on the part of public authorities. But this process proved to be more contested.

The policy of quality food reaches far back (Stanziani 2005). Before the 1980s, the labeling of French food products was controlled by the state. The labels referred to the origin of the product (place and methods of production) as a sign of quality. The best-known example are the *appellations d'origine*, created in 1919, which became the AOC (*appellations d'origine contrôlée*) controlled by the INAO (Institut national des appellations d'origine) in 1935.[9] Other examples are the *Label rouge* founded in 1960,[10] dietetic products in 1966, biological food in 1981 and 1988, and the "mountain label" in 1985. In 1988, the Commission nationale des labels et certifications de produits took responsibility for delivering certifications of conformity with national specifications. Public authorities and farmers' lobbies alike had come to the conclusion that these labels could offer a solution to the crisis farmers were going through in terms of outlets for their products and revenues (Sylvander 1995). These "specific quality products" represented in 1995 10 percent of the agrofood market. They were seen as an important source of growth, whereas twenty years before, they were conceived only in terms of compensation for smaller producers.

Hence, quality became an important component of an agricultural policy based on standardization on the one hand and certification on the other. "Through standardization and certification, the politics of quality aims to adapt the structures of agro-food production to fragmented markets. It is also targeted towards a globalisation of quality products inside the European market through harmonisation" (Nicolas and Valceschini 1995, 31). These procedures were important in anticipation of the 1992 common market, and France fought hard to gain recognition by the European Commission of these labels and specifications: labeled products were threatened by the principles of free movement and mutual recognition. By achieving European recognition, French authorities were able to protect smaller producers in certain specific areas.

Meanwhile, these labels came to be challenged by other quality signs, including major retailer brands. Through these, retailers exerted pressure on prices but also imposed on the producers their own quality standards and control procedures. In some cases, these brands were produced solely by the retailers and imposed on their suppliers. In others, they were negotiated between retailers and professional groups in a specific field. Food production saw a proliferation of norms, labels, and signs of quality by which producers, agrofood industry, and retailers guarantee the quality of their products (through its origin, ingredients, or methods used) and its compliance with public regulation. The content of these norms, labels, and signs can be approved by the state, but in some cases they are simply commercial brands or logos, on which public authorities exercise little control.

With the 1996 BSE and subsequent crises, these signs evolved. Quality referred not only to the origin of the product but also to its safety. Retailers, quickly followed by agrofood industry, issued labels for GMO-free products, vegetables that had not been grown on land on which sewage sludge had been spread, food that respected strict methods of production in order to eliminate all risks and other criteria. Often these measures were not based on any legal specifications or scientific data but simply considered that suspicion of a given product or its methods of production, likely to frighten consumers, called for strong measures. Here, the risk is not so much for human health as for the financial stability of firms and retailers that suffered important losses following the BSE crisis.

The BSE crisis also gave major retailers the opportunity to enter into negotiations with producers of fresh farm products (vegetables, fruits, meat, fish) in order to promote *marques de filières* (brands tied to a specific product). Whereas the previous brands concerned solely industrially transformed food products and were designed to put pressure on the giant multinational food corporations with which retailers were at war, the new brands were worked out with the producers of fresh products and then approved by the ministry of agriculture as certified products. Compliance with the specifications was controlled by third-party certification companies. Thus, Carrefour developed the *Filière qualité*

Carrefour, which covers more than sixty fresh products, and Auchan has its own policy of "reasoned agriculture," which certifies 100 products (de Fontguyon et al. 2003).

Organizations such as INAO that placed major emphasis on origins and methods of production were destabilized by the importance given to issues of food safety, on which they had little to say. Quality labels controlled by the ministry of agriculture came under strong pressure: either they included health safety measures but were accused of making decisions based on scarce scientific data and capable of dashing the policies led by other ministries (as in the case of sewage sludge, whose use in agriculture is encouraged by the ministry of environment); or they excluded such measures and were then accused of being too lax, with the risk of losing their legitimacy (Borraz, d'Arcimoles, and Salomon 2001). In a limited number of cases, producers were able to devise a label that combined origin, method of production, and safety; such was the case with mussels (Dubuisson-Quellier 2003).

This shift toward quality labels mixing origin and safety is part of a more general strategy by retailers to enhance their control of the production chain, from farmers to agrofood firms, in order to impose price reductions and a more stringent control on food products. The food safety crises came at a time when retailers were getting the upper hand in their battle with the agrofood industry, and it gave them the opportunity to reinforce its conditions imposed on farmers. In this competition for more stringent safety rules, industry had to adapt quickly, and the larger firms were faster to do so than the smaller ones. Meanwhile, the labels promoted by the ministry of agriculture in close association with the farmers' lobbies were often outdated and had to adapt to this new situation. In this competition, the smaller firms and farmers were the first to suffer: between the stringent regulation imposed by the state, on the one hand, and the conditions imposed by the buyers, on the other, the costs were often too high. Some small and medium firms were either closed or bought by larger firms in a movement toward concentration.

While in matters of managing food safety, public and private interventions are closely linked and publicly driven, the implementation of food safety through quality procedures is more competitive and partly led by private interests. Contested governance on these matters results for the most part from the lack of control exercised by public authorities on the labels produced by agrofood businesses, which tend to entertain the confusion between quality and safety issues in the name of consumer information. This has often prompted public authorities to endorse similar confusion in publicly approved labels.

In sum, the regulation of food safety in France is characterized by a strong mix of public and private interventions. Market incentives are closely linked to public initiatives, making it difficult to draw a clear line between the public and private spheres. But the growing role of private interests does not entail weaker public intervention: on the contrary, they tend to reinforce each other, resulting in a tight set of rules and norms.

Regulating Food Safety within a European Regime

If food safety is contested among public authorities and between public and private actors, it is also a subject of discord between the national and European levels of government, even though the reforms engaged at both levels followed similar principles. Hence, it is necessary to frame these reforms within their political context.

Common Trends in Regulating French and European Food Safety

European food safety regulation was initially motivated by the desire to lift all obstacles capable of impeding the free movement of goods. Since the early 1980s, the only derogation possible to free movement was to prove that health safety or consumer rights were threatened.[11] By legally harmonizing these fields, European regulators aimed at lifting these potential obstacles. Yet the definition of common health safety norms did not pursue a high degree of protection in terms of public health but rather resulted from the identification of the lowest common denominator acceptable, based on the available scientific data. Thus, in order to achieve free market rules and procedures, scientific expertise was given a specific role in the regulatory process.

The idea that procedures that rest on expertise are needed in the regulatory process goes back to the early 1990s, with the common market nearing completion and the WTO coming into existence. European member states were prompted to organize their own processes of expertise under the pressure of a directive on scientific cooperation (Clergeau 2004).

In France, the Centre national d'études et de recommendations sur la nutrition et l'alimentation was founded in 1992 to coordinate existing scientific research institutions. It is on this occasion that the idea of a French food safety agency first emerged, based on two key ideas: to rationalize and legitimate national expertise and to preserve the political authorities' capacity to define rules (Clergeau 2000). The BSE crisis did not alter this trend. AFSSA, when it was later created, was confined to the production of scientific expertise, while the management of risks remained in the hands of central government ministries. The same story was repeated at the European level. France, along with a few other countries, fought hard to prevent the European Food Safety Authority (EFSA) from having any competence in the field of risk management. Like AFSSA, EFSA is confined to the production of scientific expertise; and the definition of rules and norms still belongs to public authorities.

The transformation of the food safety regulation regime in France and in the EU rests on two similar principles, followed by a third principle after negotiations within the WTO.

First, public intervention is destined to reduce measures or actions capable of impeding market procedures by fighting technical and sanitary rules that distort competition and by regaining and stabilizing consumer confidence after the food scandals. The role of science, in this perspective, is to provide objective arguments against these market risks. Expertise offers information capable of reducing transaction costs and ensuring optimal market procedures. Public and private interventions in France converge on this matter: risk assessment and standardization rest on two different types of expertise, but both contribute to a reduction in transaction costs, as is also the case in Germany (see chapter 8, this volume). Government interventions at the national and European levels aim at preserving the role of the market rather than introducing social or ethical criteria to regulate food safety.

Second, reforms are limited to what is judged necessary to bring back public trust in food safety policies and keep the market in good working order instead of setting out to radically transform agricultural policy or widen the decision-making process. Reforms in food safety are based on a strategy of "blame reengineering" (Hood, Rothstein, and Baldwin 2001). After a series of scandals that threatened political authority in France and the EU, governments turned to creating systems capable of protecting them from future crises by turning the public opinion's attention toward independent institutions; but they did not abandon their prerogatives in order to assume responsibility for their action outside periods of crisis. Thus, public authorities promoted simultaneously independent scientific expertise, on the one hand, and the precautionary principle, on the other. The latter offered the opportunity to postpone the former by integrating nonscientific factors in the decision-making process. The precautionary principle is recognized by European and French environmental law alike.[12] Furthermore, European treaties since Maastricht recognize the right of a member state to maintain more rigorous norms in order to uphold public health. The Amsterdam treaty goes further and authorizes a country, once harmonization has been achieved, to adopt stricter rules if it holds new scientific evidence. In both cases, the European Commission must examine these measures and their possible generalization in the face of the available scientific evidence. The French government has made full use of the safety clauses allowed by the different directives and the opportunities offered by community law.

Finally, within the WTO, the EU and its member states acted jointly to promote scientific expertise in the definition of international rules and to achieve official recognition of the precautionary principle. But the promotion of this principle was accompanied by efforts to legitimate factors other than science in international procedures: namely, cultural, social, or ethical factors that underpin the specific conception of food and agriculture in Europe, based on an original social model (Clergeau 2003). Although this dimension is rarely made explicit between the EU and its member states, it determines the values and attitudes of the different actors and in this sense is also a component of the food safety regime.

Contested Decisions

The French and European food safety regimes thus rest on a triple foundation: the setting of rules and norms on the basis of scientific expertise; the dialectical relationship between independent agencies and recourse to the precautionary principle; and the social, ethical, and cultural dimensions of food and agriculture. Grace Skogstad (chapter 9, this volume) reaches similar results when describing the divergences or convergences between European and North American food safety regimes.

This may help to explain why a high level of contestation can still be observed, even though the different reforms upheld similar objectives in terms of decisions based on sound science. The apparent convergence in policies should not hide the strong divergences between the different levels of government in terms of dominant values and norms, democratic institutions, or partisan politics. These variables, along with strategies of blame reengineering, result in the reforms producing unintended results and in the maintenance of a high level of contestation (chapter 7, this volume).

The conflict over the embargo on British beef in France offers a case where scientific expertise is at the root of the controversy. The European SSC published in 1998 its recommendation to lift the embargo decided in March 1996 on the basis of the technical scheme for exportation (DBES) elaborated by British authorities. The European Commission decided to lift the ban, and the French ministry of agriculture undertook to transpose this decision into national regulation. AFSSA, which the public authorities had not consulted, managed to have the ministry of agriculture ask it officially for advice; more important, the minister proclaimed that whatever the result, he would follow the agency's recommendation. In September 1999, the committee within AFSSA charged with BSE produced a text expressing views opposed to those of the SSC. In particular, AFSSA considered that if the British engagements seemed satisfactory on paper, the real issue was how the DBES would be implemented—and on this point, AFSSA felt there was not enough data to prove its effectiveness. The SSC had indeed given its advice under the postulate that the measures were effective but did not feel it was its role to assess this effectiveness. AFSSA considered that until proof was given as to the way the protocols were implemented and until the results could be measured, it was necessary to adopt the precautionary principle since the risk could not be clearly assessed (Setbon 2004). The French government followed the advice and maintained the embargo, thus starting a conflict with the European Commission. In the fall of 1999, the SSC and AFSSA tried to come to an agreement while French and British authorities negotiated further measures. But in December, AFSSA still considered that the risk of infected beef meat being introduced on the continent existed and that, on this basis, the ban should be maintained. Early 2000, the European Commission decided to challenge the decision before the European Court of Justice. The embargo was finally lifted by France in October 2002 on the basis of the data collected by British authorities showing that the risk was now the same in Great Britain and in France.

In this case, not only did French and European scientific experts diverge on their analysis of the existing data, in part because the questions addressed to them were not the same (Godard 2001), but the French authorities followed AFSSA in promoting the precautionary principle, thus setting a standard for decision making in the field of food safety. This posture was all the more acceptable given that the French beef industry was still weak due to the financial consequences of the 1996 crisis. By maintaining the ban, the French government was able to protect the sector against a drop in consumer trust—public opinion being in favor of the embargo. On other less politicized issues, public authorities did not follow AFSSA's advice to use the precautionary principle, as in the case of sheep bowels. Or, on the contrary, they called on this principle without awaiting the agency's advice, as with processed animal proteins used in animal feed.

Nonetheless, the case of the French embargo on British beef and the controversy between the UK and the European Commission over the ban on the use of sheep intestines in sausage casings (see chapter 7, this volume) highlight the fact that the resort to scientific risk assessment neither fosters consensual decisions nor automatically promotes a more liberalized internal market. In fact, both cases underpin different approaches to the use of risk assessment in food safety regulation. In France, AFSSA played a major role in promoting the use of the precautionary principle, thus putting forward human health as a priority; but this was acceptable only as long as such advice did not go against deeply entrenched political and economic interests. In the UK, the FSA clearly devoted much attention to public concerns about BSE in sheep along with the long-term interests of the sheep farming industry, but as Rothstein shows, the critical variables are the "varied configurations of pressures on different regime components." Thus, the role of scientific expertise cannot be separated from the wider risk regulation regime within which it takes place and the influence exerted by different interest groups, the market structure, and public opinion.

GMOs offer another example of contested governance. Initially France was at the forefront in the promotion of GM crops: the first country to file an authorization, it successfully opposed in 1996 the ban on GMOs asked for by a majority of the other member states. In 1997, it authorized the sale and use in culture of transgenic corn—but banned transgenic soy on the grounds that there existed a risk of contamination for wild plants. The issue was thus managed following scientific risk assessment and under the rules of the common market. But under the pressure of anti-GMO mobilizations in early 1998, led by Greenpeace and José Bové's Confédération paysanne, public opinion turned hostile to GMOs. Several reasons can account for this: the lack of any social justification for this new technology, uncertainties concerning health and environmental risks, the feeling that an innovation uncalled for was being imposed, criticism toward a food and agricultural model foreign to French cultural traditions. These reasons reflect a mix of ethical and cultural criteria that go beyond scientific risks. The citizens' conference in June 1998 expressed this general lack of support for GMOs. And in September 1998, the Conseil d'Etat, on the basis of the precautionary principle, annulled the decision to authorize transgenic corn, arguing that proper risk assessment had not been conducted.[13] This decision led to France's joining the opponents to GMOs on the European level since corn had been authorized by the European Commission on the basis of scientific risk assessment. The Conseil d'Etat's decision compelled the French government to contest European legislation and ask for a reform in the authorization procedures for GM crops. Coupled with new scientific evidence confirming the existence of health and environmental risks, this led to the moratorium decided at the EU level in 1999 (Kempf 2003).

Four years were necessary to reform the authorization, labeling, and traceability of GMOs. During this period, French authorities were able to find a consensus within EU institutions without reopening the debate on GMOs in general. But the reform, mainly concerned with expertise and market procedures, largely ignored the ethical and cultural arguments put forth by public opinion. Risk assessment was reinforced in the authorization procedure, and legislation was passed on the traceability and labeling of GMOs in food products. In the European Commission's opinion, this was enough to ensure compliance with mandatory requirements in terms of consumer information and health and safety measures.[14]

Given the absence of direct political pressure on the European Commission and the lack of any scientific evidence confirming the dangers of GMOs, the Commission, once the new legislation was passed, lifted the moratorium and undertook to authorize GM crops. The French government delayed as long as it could the approval of new GMOs and formed a minority on this issue within the Council of Ministers. In parallel, AFSSA opposed the scientific committees' and later EFSA's risk assessments of Bt11 corn, judging that the existing scientific data were insufficient to assess the risks for human health. Thus, it is highly probable that in years to come, new debates will emerge, given that public opinion still remains hostile, while neither scientific controversies nor the divergences between AFSSA and EFSA have declined. Due to the lack of a majority within the European Council of Ministers, the European Commission will go ahead and authorize new GM crops, thus fostering new conflict with some member states.

These issues concern EFSA. The situation of the new agency is not yet clear in regard to the network of national food safety agencies and, more precisely, the role the agency would like the network to play. Will EFSA depend on this network to promote a common approach to risk estimation and evaluation? And will this reduce the opportunities for controversy between the national and European levels of government? Or, on the contrary, will EFSA attempt to produce its own expertise without relying on the national agencies, thus potentially fostering new controversies?

AFSSA could rely on EFSA to affirm its role as a national correspondent, for instance, through the forum of national agency CEOs, thus gaining some autonomy from the French central government. For the moment, French authorities have managed to keep the AFSSA apart from their negotiations with the European Commission. This could change.

Through the network of national agencies, AFSSA could become a spokesman for French industry and consumers at the European level, a role these interest groups are awaiting the French agency to play actively. Hence, AFSSA looks toward the European level to find new leeway and in due time may be in a position to defend a European viewpoint against national interests.

Conclusion

Food safety emerged as a political theme when agriculture and food production were undergoing deep transformations, mainly under the impulse of European policies. In a sense, the BSE crisis and the debate around GMOs revealed, as much as they partook in, the calling into question of the common agricultural policy. They also revealed the growing number of individuals and organizations claiming a voice in agricultural practices (notably consumer and environmentalist movements). As the Introduction to this book suggests, they became "entangled in larger controversies about multilevel regulation and trade liberalization." But this did not lead to radical reform of agricultural and food production policies.

The BSE crisis, along with mounting criticism against agricultural practices degrading the quality of water and controversies over the use of sewage sludge, pig manure, or urban waste, contributed to the idea that farmers were becoming a threat to the health of the French population—an idea radically opposed to the previous image of farmers as benefactors, feeding the population in the postwar years, then gaining worldwide influence through their exports. But the controversy over GM foods offered the opportunity for a counterattack in which farmers changed status from culprits to victims. The opposition against GMOs was based on the refusal to see multinational corporations impose their seeds on farmers. It gave farmers the opportunity to claim their autonomy, against the joint efforts of seed producers and large retailers, to reduce their role to that of a simple worker on a chain. In so doing, they were able to link their cause to wider debates within the WTO.

For French farmers and their lobbies, change was nonetheless radical: all of a sudden, they found themselves vulnerable to outside competition, reduced aid, and public disapproval. They had to adapt to the growing importance of food safety on the national political agenda and structural reforms such as the common agricultural policy. Given the political, economic, and social importance of farmers in France (who represent less than 3 percent of the working population), public authorities chose to preserve the autonomy of the food production system. This meant keeping food safety in the realm of food production, maintaining the ministry of health at a distance, restricting the role of AFSSA to that of scientific expertise, and limiting the influence of consumer and environmentalist movements. This was achieved sometimes through conflicts: health officials contested the control exercised by the agricultural policy community, retailers gained influence in the organization of farm food production, and social movements criticized the power of the farmers and their lobbies. Nonetheless, the ministry of agriculture maintained its hold on food policy, including food safety.

Finally, were all these reforms just destined to bring back trust in the system and policy of food production? The answer seems to be yes if one looks at the absence of change within the agricultural policy community, along with the pursuit in the delegation of regulatory powers to industry and retailers in the food production system. But on the reverse side, regulation now rests more firmly on sound science and offers a higher level of protection for consumers. More important, the dynamics between the different independent agencies, on the one hand, and around the political status of the precautionary principle, on the other, could reinforce the status of scientific risk assessment in the decision-making process and thus lead in due time to wider policy shifts. But this will occur only if the decision-making process widens to include stakeholders and addresses issues of accountability.

Notes

1. InVS took the place of the Réseau national de santé publique (RNSP) created in 1992. It gained its legitimacy through the management of collective food intoxications.

2. The agency has an administrative board composed of representatives of the state, consumer organizations, trade organizations from agriculture and the food industry, retail and distribution sectors, veterinary pharmaceutical industries, and

representatives of the agency's staff. The board is responsible for its annual report, investment programs, budget, and the accounts. A scientific board "monitors the consistency of scientific policy." But power is essentially in the hands of the CEO, named by the government and responsible for the decisions, opinions, and recommendations issued by the agency.

3. AFSSA has the power to issue, suspend, or remove licenses for the sale of veterinary drugs.

4. A parliamentary report in 2005 acknowledged the global improvement in risk assessment due to AFSSA (Saunier 2005).

5. Its budget for 2002 was 85.2 million euros. Ninety percent of its income comes from the central government (mainly the ministry of agriculture), local authorities, and international bodies.

6. As of 2003, representatives from the three supervisory ministries are not allowed to participate on the committees, except to answer questions on request.

7. The current CEO likes to point out that the agency is "a dependent organisation giving independent advice" (Hirsch 2001).

8. Two counterexamples confirm this point: the citizens' conference on GMOs in the spring of 1998 and the *Etats généraux de l'alimentation* held in 2000 gave a number of stakeholders the opportunity to take part in a general debate. Yet in both cases, these consultations had little or no impact on the decisions taken (Joly and Marris 2003).

9. A definition of the specifications to be respected in order for a product to benefit from an AOC is first worked out by the producers and approved by the INAO, followed by the ministries of agriculture and finance. The aim of AOC was the promotion of place-based products (wines and later cheeses in 1955) in order to protect French products against imports and help identify these products at export and, after World War II, to protect small-scale productions against the impact of agricultural policy.

10. Originally concerning free-range poultry and later extended to other meat and dairy products, there are today 365 *labels rouges*, mostly destined to the domestic market.

11. Art. 30 of the EC Treaty.

12. This was added to the French Constitution in 2005 as part of an environmental protection charter.

13. The Conseil d'Etat is the highest jurisdiction in administrative law in France.

14. Regulation (EC) 1829/2003 and Regulation (EC) 1830/2003.

7

From Precautionary Bans to DIY Poison Tasting: Reform of the UK Food Safety Regulation Regime

Henry Rothstein

Food safety . . . is a high priority for the Government. . . . As the Chairman of this new organisation I recognise that gaining and retaining the trust and confidence of consumers are vital to our success. We will be judged by how we act, and we are clear that our behaviour must match our intentions. Our core values—putting the consumer first, openness and independence—underpin the delivery of our primary aim of protecting public health and the interests of consumers in relation to food.
—Sir John Krebs, chairman of the Food Standards Agency (FSA 2000)

Food safety has long been a subject of contested governance in the UK. In the nineteenth century, popular outrage at a series of food scandals, such as the adulteration of flour with white lead and sugar with ground glass, led to the introduction of basic legislation to control food safety. In more recent times, UK food safety scandals have echoed around the world and have similarly focused attention on improving food safety regulation. As Chris Ansell and David Vogel point out in chapter 1, food safety lends itself to conflict because of the exceptional complexity of the market and regulatory structures and the wide range of public, private, and state actors who have often conflicting stakes in regulatory processes and outcomes. Many food safety conflicts, however, concern a series of problems that lie at the heart of risk governance more generally; defining the nature and assessing the scale of risk; setting risk tolerances; and allocating, organizing, and implementing risk management responsibilities. This chapter considers the nature of some of those conflicts and assesses how successfully they have been handled in the context of recent reforms to the UK food safety regime, and, in particular, the creation of the UK's Food Standards Agency (FSA).

The creation of the FSA in 2000 heralded a new era for food safety regulation in the UK that was long overdue. The BSE crisis in the 1990s capped a litany of problems that the old Ministry of Agriculture, Fisheries and Food (MAFF) had struggled with and failed to manage. Indeed, rarely had a national government ministry in the developed world achieved such global infamy. Slack controls on BSE contributed to the downfall of the Conservative government in 1997, but it took three more years for the FSA to replace MAFF as a nonministerial government department to advise government on food safety policy.

The creation of the agency specifically addressed many of the problems that had afflicted the old regime and reflected similar reforms in other countries (see chapters 6 and 8, this volume). First, MAFF had been afflicted by inherent conflicts of interest because of its dual responsibilities to regulate food safety and promote the food and agriculture business. The creation of the FSA reduced those conflicts by removing responsibilities for business promotion and giving the agency the right to publish its advice to ministers to restrict possibilities for direct political interference. Moreover, the agency was created as a stakeholder-style board comprising up to twelve members to help prevent regulatory capture and provide a balance of skills and experience.

Second, the old regime had been poorly linked up. Horizontal relations between the Ministry of Agriculture and its weak policy partner, the Department of Health, were poor, and vertical relations between central government policymaking and local government enforcement were virtually nonexistent, a problem that became a crucial component of the BSE story. That institutional fragmentation was addressed by consolidating food safety responsibility within the FSA and giving the agency extended monitoring powers over local government enforcement.

Third, decision making had been opaque, which gave little opportunity for external interests to expose regulatory capture and contributed to a public and scientific credibility crisis. That problem was addressed by enhancing the transparency and accountability of the regime.

The agency set out three guiding principles to help it improve the quality and effectiveness of food safety regulation. Those principles of "putting consumers first," "openness," and "independence" have been echoed in other newly created agencies across the EU. France's Agence

Française de Sécurité Sanitaire des Aliments (AFFSA), for example, stresses the importance of excellence, transparency, and independence, while the European Commission's (EC's) European Food Safety Authority (EFSA) emphasizes the principles of excellence, integrity, and openness (Byrne 2002). These principles have been readily internalized by FSA staff and are, at least nominally, reflected in many FSA policy processes. The FSA, for example, carries out extensive consultations with consumer groups and has set up a dedicated consumer consultative committee. Its board holds its meetings in public, as do many of its scientific advisory committees, and it publishes a considerable amount of material on which it bases its decisions.

Much hope has been held out for the style of reform adopted within the UK food safety regime. Prime Minister Tony Blair has said that "bodies like the Food Standards Agency . . . have shown that more open processes, based on evidence, are more effective at handling risks and winning public confidence than secrecy" (Cabinet Office 2002). Consumer groups have given the agency qualified support (National Consumer Council 2002), food retailers have supported the FSA's focus on the food chain rather than just farmers, and opinion polls suggest that consumer confidence in the agency rose from 50 percent in 2000 to 60 percent in 2003 (FSA 2003c). One example of rising consumer confidence was in 2004 when the FSA successfully managed to allay consumer fears about levels of dioxins and PCBs in Scottish farmed salmon to the extent that salmon sales increased.

There are, however, at least three important reasons why such reform may not be able to deliver hoped-for results. First, risk regulation regimes are complex systems that comprise policymaking and implementation components that can span multiple levels of government and encompass both statutory and nonstatutory systems of control (Hood, Rothstein, and Baldwin 2001). Food safety regulation is no exception, bringing together supranational, national, and local government activity; business self-regulation; organized private actors; and even individual lay consumers. That means that there are limits to what the FSA might be expected to achieve. For example, the UK is just one guest at the EU dining table where most food safety policy is decided. At the national level, the FSA only advises government on food safety policy, and it also sits between other major government departments such as the Health and Environment ministries, which have overlapping responsibilities on nutrition policy, pesticide approvals, and veterinary residues. Moreover, the FSA has limited powers over food safety surveillance and enforcement, because those activities fall under the responsibility of local government in the UK.

Second, and relatedly, individual components of the food safety regime are likely to be shaped by different factors, thus limiting the extent to which the FSA guiding principles can be put into practice throughout the regime (Hood, Rothstein, and Baldwin 2001). General public opinion, media salience, organized public and private interest pressures, and professional worldviews are likely to have different configurations, profiles, and leverage at different points in a regime. For example, national policymakers may be more sensitive to national media headlines than local government food safety inspectors or supranational policymakers, while the activities of local government inspectors are more likely to be shaped by the compliance culture of shop floor regulatees than supranational or national policymakers. In that context, there may be marked variation across the regime as to how far the public interest can be served, or indeed, how the public interest is itself conceived.

Third, reforms can have unanticipated side effects. For example, critics of U.S. health and environmental policy in the 1980s showed how greater transparency led to dysfunctional adversarialism in the policy process and increased reliance on rule-driven decision making (Jasanoff 1990). More recent work on risk regulation regimes has also shown how institutional responses to greater transparency can be heavily conditioned by blame-avoidance considerations and can have undesirable side effects that mitigate the gains that openness may bring (Hood, Rothstein, and Baldwin 2001).

This chapter therefore examines recent policymaking by the FSA in order to examine three questions. First, it considers to what extent FSA decision making has been aligned with its own guiding principles and to what extent those principles are reflected in practice throughout the regime. Second, it considers what factors can best explain divergences between principles and practice. And third, it considers what impacts such factors have on regulatory outcomes. By studying deviations between intention and practice, it may be possible to identify critical factors that shape the implementation of reforms to food safety regulation.

In order to assess the reforms to the UK food safety regime and their impact on policy processes and outcomes, this chapter considers how the regime has dealt with two recent cases: BSE in sheep and food allergens. BSE in sheep was the subject of a policy conflict between the FSA and EC in 2002, and food allergens were the subject of a policy initiative by the FSA in 2003. The predominant regulatory problem in both cases concerned information asymmetries, but the policy responses appeared inconsistent, ranging from awareness raising to precautionary bans. The cases highlight how interpretations of scientific evidence, precaution, and the public interest can vary between different levels of government and the difficulties of putting guiding principles into practice.

Empirically, the chapter draws on a range of documentary sources, attendance at FSA public meetings, and in-depth face-to-face and telephone interviews with relevant state officials and scientific advisers at both the UK and EU level, and business and consumer representatives who have had to remain anonymous for confidentiality reasons.

BSE in Sheep

The first case study concerns how the FSA dealt with the sensitive subject of BSE in sheep in 2001.[1] In the 1990s, BSE in cattle had been the straw that broke MAFF's proverbial back, and since then, there had been residual concern that BSE had infected sheep and goats. Although no cases had been found by 2001, it was known that sheep and goats had consumed the same feed that infected cattle during the 1980s and that they were experimentally susceptible to the disease. Moreover, unlike cattle, if they were infected, the disease was likely to be distributed throughout the carcass and could be passed through subsequent generations. The problem was that BSE was difficult to distinguish from scrapie, an endemic disease in British sheep and goats. A government-funded study had to be abandoned in 2001 after samples had become contaminated by cattle brains, and it was therefore not known at that time whether sheep and goats were free of BSE or if scrapie was masking BSE infection.[2]

When the FSA turned to the issue in 2001, it was confronted with a classic policy dilemma of how to trade off the risk of mistakenly assuming harm and the risk of mistakenly assuming safety in the absence of evidence. The FSA had three broad policy options. First, as sheep and goat meat was relatively substitutable with other meat, the agency could have opted for a labeling and a public information campaign about the potential risks. Such a campaign would have been consistent with a core philosophy of the agency to promote informed choice among consumers (FSA 2001).[3] Second, the agency could have adopted a more paternalistic option of introducing some form of ban on sheep and goat meat and products. Or third, the agency could have chosen to do nothing on the grounds that there was no evidence that BSE was in sheep and goats.

There had been an EU ban on the sale of certain sheep and goat organs since the mid-1990s, but in 2001, the FSA established a participative process to consider whether more should be done. The FSA first held an open stakeholder meeting that was attended by over a hundred stakeholders, and then a smaller stakeholder group was established that met three times. The group focused on sheep and was presented with conflicting risk assessments. One study suggested that sheep intestines that were used as casings for the "luxury end" of the sausage market could contribute up to a third of the total human exposure to potential BSE risks from sheep (Ferguson et al. 2002). Another study conversely suggested that processing practices reduced the risks from casings, so that they accounted for just 9 percent of total potential exposure, while more than 80 percent came from lymph nodes found throughout the sheep carcass (DNV 2001). Confronted by these conflicting risk assessments, the group assumed the worst-case scenario for natural casings and recommended a precautionary ban on the use of sheep intestines and that the FSA should communicate to the public the theoretical risks from mutton and goat meat (FSA 2002b). That recommendation went out to consultation and was then considered by the FSA board during a public meeting in June 2002.

The board's response reflected all three policy options available to it. First, the board issued general advice that consumers could reduce their theoretical risk by avoiding sausages with natural casings, mutton, and meat from older goats (FSA 2002c, 2003a).[4] Second, the board paternalistically followed the stakeholder group's proposal to ban the use of sheep intestines for natural sausage casings within the European regulatory framework (FSA 2002c). Third, the board explicitly stated that it did not advise against the consumption of sheep and goat meat, despite the likely widespread distribution of infectivity throughout carcasses if animals were infected (FSA 2002c).

The recommended ban on sheep intestines was forwarded to the European Commission's Scientific Steering Committee (SSC) (now replaced by the European Food Safety Authority), which was holding a key meeting on BSE in sheep that month. The SSC reviewed the studies considered by the FSA in camera, as well as additional work sponsored by the natural sausage casings manufacturers that suggested processing practices could reduce the risk from casings even further (DNV Consulting 2002; Koolmees, Berends, and Tersteeg 2002). In contrast to the FSA, the SSC concluded that sausage casings did not present a potentially higher risk than carcass meat and, in an accompanying press release, made the risk management recommendation that no more action should be taken unless a theoretically possible risk became a probable risk (SSC 2002b).

The EC was therefore reluctant to introduce the FSA's proposed ban, but it did eventually introduce a compromise ban on the use of sheep ileum, a particularly potentially infective part of the small intestine. That ban, however, broadly put contemporary practice on a statutory footing. Under a voluntary UK Code of Practice, the ileum was already routinely removed by processing machines and disposed of as unfit for human consumption. At the time, practices around Europe were unknown, but subsequent research suggested that other techniques to remove the ileum were roughly equivalent in terms of risk reduction. This case therefore raises the question of why the FSA went further than expected in recommending a precautionary ban on sheep intestines while simultaneously not advising against the consumption of sheep and goat meat, but the EC rejected the ban in favor of a policy compromise that simply put current practice on a statutory footing.

Food Allergy

The second case concerns the FSA's work on food allergy (this section draws on Rothstein 2005). Until the early 1990s, fatal food allergy was a rare disorder, but the prevalence of food allergies has been steadily increasing in the West. Most allergies are caused by a relatively small number of foodstuffs, such as nuts, peanuts, milk, eggs, wheat, soya, and seafood (Committee on Toxicity of Chemicals 2000). Almost 2 percent of adults and between 5 and 8 percent of children are thought to have a food allergy (James 2001; Macdougall, Cant, and Colver 2002; Royal College of Physicians 2003). There are still considerable uncertainties, however, about the range of foods that elicit allergic responses, their thresholds of activity, and the number of people affected. Most reactions are not fatal, but there are approximately ten confirmed deaths from food-induced anaphylaxis each year in the UK, and possibly more deaths from food-related asthma that go uncounted. Commercial catering, where ingredient control is often relaxed and cross-contamination happens easily, is responsible for over two-thirds of those deaths (Pumphrey 2000).

Anaphylaxis can be treated by prompt injections of epinephrine, but the rapid onset of the symptoms means that timely and competent intervention is not always possible. The main regulatory challenge posed by food allergens therefore is how to ensure the provision of reliable information to help consumers make rational consumption decisions and employ effective risk mitigation strategies. When the FSA turned its attention to food allergy, however, it was confronted by a complex web of statutory and private regimes that only partially helped consumers.

Prepacked food was covered by European labeling rules, but those rules did not require labeling of contaminants and exempted labeling constituents of compound ingredients that comprised less than 25 percent of foodstuffs. In contrast, catered foods and foods sold loose did not have to be labeled but were covered by general product description law and the caveat emptor provisions of food safety law that prohibited the sale of food that was not of the "nature or substance or quality" demanded by the purchaser (Food Safety Act 1990). Putting the onus on customers to engage in dialogue with food business staff to assess allergen content was consistent with addressing information asymmetries, but the criteria for legal compliance were unclear. Conventional food safety issues, such as food poisoning or chemical contamination, were covered by the food hygiene regulations, which set out the requirements for hazard analysis and control—the so-called hazard analysis and critical control point (HACCP) requirements. It was unclear, however, whether those regulations applied to food allergens. As a consequence, a significant number of food businesses failed to provide consumers with robust information in the absence of explicit requirements on how to deal with allergenic foods or even a specified list of foods that were allergenic. One study found, for example, that one-fifth of take-away meals requested to be peanut free contained peanut protein (Leitch, Walker, and Davey 2005).

There was also poor monitoring and enforcement of the statutory regime. MAFF had established a research program on food allergy in 1994 to improve basic scientific knowledge, undertook limited awareness-raising campaigns, and encouraged business self-regulation.[5] It did not, however, conduct any surveillance on allergen contamination of food and was reluctant to issue food hazard warnings about contamination. Local government food safety inspectors rarely conducted monitoring or enforcement activities unless inspectors had specialist expertise or deaths had occurred in the area, and they rarely published the results of monitoring activity because of concerns for commercial confidentiality and preventing public alarm (British Nutrition Foundation 2000; Leitch, Blair, and McDowell 2000).

Enforcement was particularly difficult. Inspectors had only low levels of allergy awareness and training. Recourse to law was difficult because it was expensive and the caveat emptor framework meant that cases often hinged on unwitnessed dialogue between businesses and, sometimes deceased, customers prior to consumption. Moreover, the lack of clear legal compliance criteria meant there was inconsistent and severe underenforcement. For example, enforcement officers felt that the provision of incorrect information by waiting staff, or mistakes in taking an order or preparing food, did not merit the same level of punishment as supplying food that was microbiologically contaminated, even if it resulted in serious incidents or fatalities. Those problems meant that food allergens stayed low on the list of local government priorities. As one senior inspector put it, "Most allergy work was done by businesses with Environmental Health Officers (EHOs) as interested and embarrassed onlookers hoping that they would not be asked to advise businesses on allergen control."[6]

There was some secondary business self-regulation. During the 1990s, at MAFF's encouragement, many major businesses started to ignore the 25 percent rule, voluntarily label prepacked foods with "may contain" warnings, and integrate allergen management into their routine risk control procedures. They were also able to use their market power as commercial intermediaries to monitor and enforce adherence throughout their supply chains. Business best practice guides were not comprehensive, however, and there were considerable inconsistencies in business practice.[7] Outside the major supply chains, moreover, there were few mechanisms to change business behavior in the absence of effective state oversight.

Business and consumer activity was also shaped by collective consumer action. The Anaphylaxis Campaign, a group that represented consumers with food allergies, helped train and raise awareness among businesses, local government inspectors, and consumers. The group also sent out product warning alerts when notified by business and lay consumers. Indeed, to a major extent, identification of false composition claims or contamination often relied on "do-it-yourself (DIY) poison tasting" detection, whereby consumers would raise an alert after suffering a reaction.

Consumers therefore had to play Russian roulette with their food purchases. Food labels left consumers wondering whether the absence of information about allergens on a label indicated the absence of allergens from food or the absence of information about the presence of allergens in food. Moreover, when customers engaged in dialogue with businesses, it was hard for them to assess the robustness of the reply. Furthermore, the problems of poor information provision were often compounded by the varied behavior of consumers, which ranged from hypercautious to highly risk prone, the latter a common characteristic of children and students.

The FSA was faced with a range of policy options. The least consumer protective option would have been for the FSA to refrain from intervention. Business opportunities and tort law might have driven the slow development of business self-regulation, but only large businesses were likely to be sensitive to the potential financial and reputational consequences of legal suits. Until the establishment of sufficient supplies of allergen-free food, consumers would be faced with the problems of managing their risks in a mixed compliance environment. A second option would have been for the FSA to pursue an enhanced version of MAFF's soft regulatory strategy by raising awareness among businesses, inspectors, and consumers and encouraging the further development of business self-regulation in tandem with greater regulatory oversight. A third, tougher option to help ensure full consumer sovereignty would have been to require full information provision on ingredients and contaminants on labels and ensure some form of robust information disclosure for catered and loose foods with full regulatory oversight.

In 2003, following a stakeholder consultation, the FSA developed a package of proposals that broadly fell in the middle of this range of policy options (FSA 2003e). First, the agency continued to support a major £1 million a year program of scientific research that had been established by MAFF in 1994. Second, it had already successfully lobbied the EC to close the 25 percent loophole but further aimed to strengthen food labeling. Third, it aimed to improve information, guidance, and training for caterers and ensure that other agency initiatives on HACCP in catering establishments and traceability in the food chain "took due account of food allergy concerns" (FSA 2003e). Fourth, it aimed to improve information, guidance, and training for local government inspectors. And fifth, it aimed to provide advice to consumers to help them make informed choices about their food purchases and minimize unnecessary restrictions.

While that strategy was likely to bear some fruit, it left a number of important issues unresolved. In particular, the strategy did not address the legal inconsistencies between the stricter information provision requirements for ingredients of prepacked food and for foods sold loose and in catering and the absence of legal requirements to provide information on contaminants. Moreover, the strategy did not address the key legal ambiguities and institutional factors that additionally hindered compliance and enforcement activities. The food allergens case therefore raises the question of why the FSA preferred a soft regulatory strategy of encouraging behavior change rather than pursuing a vigorous and enforceable regulatory strategy aimed at ensuring consumer sovereignty by reducing information asymmetries.

Explaining Decision Making

At first inspection, decision making on food allergens and BSE in sheep and goats seemed inconsistent. Both risks were potential killers, and indeed, similar numbers of people were dying each year in the UK from food allergy and vCJD. Moreover, in principle, both risks could have been managed by market mechanisms if consumer sovereignty had been ensured by the provision of sufficient information. Of course, there were differences between the two risks. It was not known whether sheep and goats were infected with BSE, but if they had been infected, then all those who consumed infected meat could have been afflicted.[8] In contrast, food allergy was known to have fatal consequences, but only for a minority of the population. But these differences provide inadequate explanations of why risk management strategies varied widely from precautionary bans to do-it-yourself "poison" tasting. In order to understand these apparent inconsistencies, we need to examine the factors that shaped decision making in each case.

BSE in Sheep

The conflict between the FSA and EC on natural sausage casings could be argued to show that open processes produce more precautionary outcomes than opaque processes and that the multilevel governance structure moderates the scope for action of national authorities. Closer analysis of the decision-making process, however, suggests that divergences between the FSA and the EC cannot be explained by simple adherence of the FSA to its guiding principles, but are instead better explained by the different configuration and representation of interests in the two policymaking processes.

The first difference between the FSA and EC decision-making process was the role of scientific evidence and advice. In the UK, scientific advice was equivocal. Curiously, the Spongiform Encephalopathy Advisory

Committee (SEAC), the UK expert committee on BSE, was not asked to give a formal opinion on the conflicting risk assessments. Instead, scientific advice was provided by SEAC's chairman, who sat on the stakeholder group, while members of SEAC were consulted afterward as part of the public consultation on the stakeholder report. While the FSA recommendation was publicly supported by at least one SEAC member, other SEAC members interviewed for this research gave more equivocal views, including one who would not have supported the FSA's interpretation of evidence (FSA 2002b). In the absence of clear scientific evidence, there was no strong scientific lobby pushing either way.

In contrast, scientists played a greater role in the EC decision-making process through the SSC, and the evidence base on processing practices was greater than that considered by the FSA's stakeholder group. While the SSC acknowledged the scientific uncertainties, it considered that there was insufficient evidence to suggest that casings presented greater risks than carcass meat. In other words, if BSE was in sheep, then a ban on sausage casings would do little to protect the public when compared against the greater consumption of carcass meat. As a senior BSE scientist and ex-member of SEAC put it, "If you want to reduce the risks by 50 percent, it would be more consistent to cut every sheep in half and throw half away."

The second difference concerned the configuration of pressures in the direction of tough regulatory action. In the UK, 70 percent of the UK population claimed that BSE concerns affected their eating habits and BSE was still a campaign issue for consumer groups (FSA 2002a). Moreover, the FSA had reputational risk concerns, which were expressed by the deputy chair of the FSA board when she argued during the public board meeting that the board members should remember the failing BSE years by which the FSA would be judged. Indeed, it could be speculated that the agency needed an early win to help establish itself as the consumers' champion. According to some regulatory actors, BSE had such a political sensitivity that "doing nothing was not an option" (FSA 2002b).

In Europe, BSE also had a considerable public salience; according to a Eurobarometer survey in 2001, just less than 80 percent of Europeans expressed some form of concern. For example, beef consumption in

France fell by nearly 40 percent in 2000 after a cow was diagnosed with BSE just as it was about to be slaughtered for consumption. Moreover, the BSE crisis had had serious consequences for the EC and indeed was leading at the time to the establishment of a new European Food Safety Authority. BSE in sheep and goats was not, however, a sink-or-swim issue for the EC. It did not have to establish its reputation on the issue and therefore could perhaps afford to be more relaxed than the FSA.

The third difference concerned the configuration of pressures against tough regulation. In the UK, the public backlash that occurred over the ban on beef-on-the-bone in 1997 suggested that the public would not weather overly paternalistic regulation. More important, however, the sheep industry would have resisted any tough regulation in the absence of evidence that there was BSE in the sheep flock. Removing lymph nodes and other infective material from sheep meat required high surgical precision and was therefore technically unfeasible. A ban on meat from mature sheep would have cost £115 million in lost sales and could have decimated the UK sheep industry, already crippled by low livestock prices and the previous year's foot-and-mouth epidemic (FSA 2002b). A ban on goat meat would have similarly decimated the goat meat and related products industries. The natural sausage casings industry, however, was a smaller and less well-organized industry. Natural sausage casings accounted for only 15 percent of the UK sausage market, and a ban on such casings would have cost only £6.5 million in lost casings sales. Moreover, while the sheep farming industry was uneasy about a ban on casings, it did not reject the proposal outright, having learned the lesson from BSE in cattle that such measures are sometimes necessary to maintain long-term consumer confidence (FSA 2002b). From the FSA's viewpoint, therefore, not only was the recommendation precautionary but it was also easy to implement and proportionate.

From a European perspective, however, natural sausage casings had a greater market presence. The European market was worth £200 million in casings sales and much more for sausages: Germans alone eat 11 million sausages with natural casings each day. Moreover, if natural casings had been banned, it was doubtful that substitute casings manufacturers could have met the demand. The market size meant that the

EC would have had great difficulty proposing a ban without good evidence that BSE was in sheep.

The fourth difference concerned the representation of different interests within the UK and EU policy processes. In the UK, the FSA claimed that the casings industry had opportunities to feed into the participative process through the initial open meeting and through the farming and meat industry representatives on the stakeholder group, and the public consultation prior to the board meeting. The natural sausage casings industry, however, claimed that it was not given the impression at the open meeting that casings would be singled out for a specific ban and that the twelve-member stakeholder panel was unrepresentative. The panel included five FSA representatives, including the chief executive, the board chairman and deputy chair; two senior scientists; two consumer representatives; a farmer; a meat and livestock representative; and a member of the Welsh Assembly Government. It did not include natural sausage casings industry representatives and other key stakeholders, such as retailers and abattoirs. Moreover, the FSA shortened the time for public consultation on the stakeholder report from the recommended twelve weeks to two to ensure that the board could take a decision before the SSC met in Brussels. That meant that the casings industry had only limited time to prepare a response, and board members had only a limited time to prepare for the board meeting. In addition, there was only limited time for discussion of the substantive issue—under thirty minutes. Some board members expressed unease, but there was a strong steer toward a consensus view that this was an important public health measure, and the recommendation was passed.

In the EU process, there was a different balance of interest representation. Professional scientists played a greater role in assessing the scientific evidence, and natural casings manufacturers were also better represented because they were able to submit additional evidence to the SSC, which the FSA stakeholder group had not seen. In addition, the EC invited the natural casings manufacturers to a specially convened meeting in November 2002 with officials from FSA and AFFSA. Moreover, the SSC meetings were held in camera, and there was no consumer representation at the EC meeting in November.

Finally, there were also internal institutional factors that shaped decision making. The FSA was committed to making independent decisions, but that guiding principle was mitigated in two ways. First, senior board members had conflicts of interest; the FSA board chairman chaired the stakeholder group, and the deputy chairman was also a stakeholder group member. Rejection of the stakeholder group recommendation by the FSA board therefore presented a potential embarrassment. Second, the FSA was able to lessen its burden of accountability by forwarding the board recommendation direct to Brussels, so that casings manufacturers had to take their case to Europe to argue for its rejection.

In the case of the EU process, the EC had been given a strong steer by the SSC. The SSC was strictly a risk assessment body, but in a press release accompanying its opinion, it made the risk management recommendation that no more action should be taken until what is a theoretically possible risk becomes a probable risk (SSC 2002b). That meant that the EC would have been in conflict with its own scientific advisory committee had it pursued the proposed ban.

This analysis suggests that the conflict between the FSA and the EC is not easily explained by the FSA being more consumer focused, open, or independent than the EC. On the one hand, the FSA appeared to be more consumer focused than the EC insofar as it proposed a precautionary ban on a sheep product. On the other hand, the FSA's proposed ban appeared to be neither precautionary nor proportionate when judged against the weaker actions proposed for other cuts of potentially riskier goat and sheep meat, the latter being considerably more widely consumed. Similarly, from the point of view of openness, while the FSA process involved consumer representatives in decision making, it gave less opportunity for the involvement of scientists and the casings industry than the EC process. The FSA decision therefore aligned with a particular pattern of interest representation within the decision-making process and reflected the dominant concern that the FSA needed to be seen to be doing something. Casings were easy to deal with and had only limited impact on the UK sheep and goat farming industry. From that point of view, the FSA recommendation was not so much a precautionary ban but rather more a sacrificial lamb. Indeed, the final agreement to ban the use of the ileum, which put current practice onto a statutory footing, was consistent with a face-saving policy compromise.

Food Allergens

In order to explain the FSA's soft regulatory strategy on improving food allergen control rather than ensuring the provision of robust information on allergenic ingredients and contaminants, it is necessary to examine a range of factors that shaped FSA activity.

First, there were basic scientific uncertainties that made it difficult to create an enforceable regime. Although more was increasingly known about food allergens, there were still considerable uncertainties about what foods should be classed as allergens and at what thresholds. Those uncertainties made it difficult to set legal standards for trace contaminants, though less so for allergenic ingredients, which are the cause of most deaths.

Second, the policymaking architecture of the regime constrained the FSA. Labeling of prepacked food was an EU trade issue, and that had historically posed a problem for MAFF when it tried to close the 25 percent labeling loophole. Despite widespread support for change, the EC had been hindered by a lack of resources and conflicts over the labeling of nonallergenic ingredients. Eventually the FSA assisted in amending the Labelling Directive to close the 25 percent loophole and establish a list of common food allergens, although it still did not deal with contaminants (2003). The EU constraint, however, might be overestimated, as arguably member states could unilaterally introduce tougher controls because food allergens presented established risks to health (European Court 1979). The FSA, however, has shown no willingness to go down that route.

The FSA did have clearer policy discretion to act on loose foods and catering because they were not intracommunity trade issues. Some form of declaration of ingredients for loose foods and catering would have been consistent with prepacked food, and such unilateral action by member states was permitted under a provision of the European Labelling Directive. Indeed, a precedent for such action had been set in 2000, when rules were introduced that required all food businesses to declare GM ingredients (Statutory Instrument 2000). The FSA was reluctant to go it alone on allergens, however, and preferred to wait for the final implementation of the amendment to the Labelling Directive before considering whether to make equivalent changes for loose and catered food.

Third, there were conflicting public interest pressures. There was some general public support for improving information provision along similar lines to that on GM food. According to one survey, just under a third of the public wanted allergy information on catered and loose foods, and just under two-thirds of those wanted information to be provided on a menu (MORI 2000). Food allergy had a relatively low media salience compared to other food safety issues, but it had put government under some pressure in the past; a widely reported cluster of deaths in 1993, for example, had been responsible for starting MAFF's work on food allergy. In addition, the FSA was under pressure from the Anaphylaxis Campaign to improve the enforceability of the regime in relation to ingredients and contaminants.

There were also public concerns, however, that pushed in the opposite direction. Regulation would impose an unequal distribution of costs and benefits on allergic and nonallergic consumers. Indeed, according to one poll, one-fifth of consumers were not interested in allergen information at all (MORI 2000). In addition, there was concern that overuse of "may contain" warnings could be resented by people with food allergies because of restrictions on their purchasing habits and lead to a backlash among the general public. There was also concern that overuse of "may contain" warnings could mitigate their risk management value if they fell into disrepute; fatal incidents had occurred following consumption of products with "may contain" warnings that had proved safe in the past.

Fourth, there were business drivers of change. Many businesses wanted to abolish the 25 percent labeling loophole for allergens and increasingly wanted greater legal clarification and guidance on managing food allergen risks (British Nutrition Foundation 2000). Those factors were consistent with the FSA's aim to improve labeling, raise business awareness of food allergen issues, and enhance guidance and training. Business attitudes were conflicting, however, on the extent to which the regime should be voluntary or enforceable. Caterers were especially concerned that the introduction of an enforceable regime would be costly, inflexible, and impractical. There were 400,000 caterers in the UK, and most of them were independent and had fewer than four, usually poorly trained, transient, and sometimes non–English speaking staff. Kitchen culture often worked against accurate recipe following and recording of ingredients and contaminants. Moreover, catering suppliers had varied compliance cultures. Allergy management had been introduced into the training qualification in 1995, but that had had limited impact. Creating an enforceable regime in that context would be very difficult, especially given that there were only about 1,500 local government food inspectors and they found it hard enough to get small catering businesses to comply with hazard analysis requirements for basic food hygiene issues. As one FSA official put it, "There was not a hope in hell that half the catering industry would be able to guarantee the information given to consumers."

Fifth, the FSA was constrained by personnel and institutional resource issues. Allergy policy was the responsibility of a handful of officials who had only limited time and resources at their disposal, limited allergy expertise, and relatively few policy analysis and advocacy skills. Officials, for example, were unwilling to quantify the costs and benefits of different regulatory options or contemplate the UK taking unilateral action beyond EU requirements. There was also little overall policy ownership to ensure that the system for managing allergens, from policymaking to enforcement, was functioning. A number of actors interviewed for this research were also skeptical about the role of the FSA Communications division in driving the policy agenda, fearing that it led to short-term populism at the expense of longer-term strategic thinking. One example was the policy focus on the wording of "may contain" labels rather than what and when to label.

Finally, there was a cultural and legal perception among many businesses and state officials that food allergies were a human health problem rather than a food safety problem. On that view, it was inappropriate to apply the same kind of legally binding rules that applied to conventional food safety issues such as the food hygiene regulations. Jurisprudence went some way to supporting that view. The preexisting susceptibility doctrine in tort law (or the eggshell skull rule, as it is colorfully known) suggests that there is no liability if the wrongdoing would have caused no damage to someone of reasonable robustness and the injury suffered by the victim was not foreseeable by the defendant.[9] Food allergies were relatively rare and so, from that point of view, it was unreasonable for sufferers to expect foods to be free from undeclared allergen contamination or require businesses to conduct a hazard analysis for allergen risks.

Cultural and legal perceptions of the problem were changing, however, as food allergies were becoming more common and widely recognized. In particular, European requirements on labeling allergenic ingredients of prepacked foods and the routine incorporation of food allergy into hazard analysis systems by some businesses made it harder to argue for the applicability of the "eggshell skull" rule. Most significant, the European Commission in a personal communication interpreted the food hygiene regulations to apply to both the intentional and unintentional incorporation of food allergens into foodstuffs, whether prepacked or not.[10] That view was consistent with according consumers with food allergies greater rights under food safety law and introducing a considerably tougher enforcement regime than existed.

The FSA was moving in the general direction of viewing food allergy as a food safety risk. After some internal debate, the agency issued advice to caterers that businesses could be prosecuted if they supplied food containing allergens that customers had specifically asked to avoid. The agency was also committed to ensure that work on introducing HACCP principles into catering establishments should include food allergy issues. Unlike the European Commission, however, the FSA did not state that food allergens were covered by the food hygiene regulations. Instead, the FSA considered that the European Commission's opinion was "a reasonable one" but that "ultimately only the courts can interpret the law".[11] While that was strictly the case, the courts were likely to rely on the FSA to clarify and flesh out the practical application of the law. The ambiguous position of the FSA on that point therefore could dispose the courts, and indeed enforcement authorities, to take a lenient view of business behavior at the expense of robust information provision.

The FSA therefore was confronted by a number of conflicts that it resolved by pursuing an enhanced version of MAFF's strategy to seek changes through soft rather than hard regulatory strategies, such as increasing knowledge, raising awareness, and encouraging the development of business best practice guidelines. The approach adopted was to work with the grain of current practice in order to balance the public interest aspects of introducing an enforceable regime against the concerns of the catering industry and potential public backlash over "may contain" warnings. Indeed, the FSA explicitly stated that it would be "difficult to effect practical changes in the way food allergens are handled in all catering establishments and there will always remain a degree of responsibility with the individual consumer" (FSA 2003e). That approach recognized the limits of what could be achieved, but the consequence was a regime that failed to fully redress the information asymmetries for consumers with food allergies.

Conclusions

The UK's FSA is one of a new breed of food safety agencies that have swept the EU in recent years. It is evident from the companion chapters on France and Germany that like the UK, those countries have used crises as policy windows to confront structural problems of institutional fragmentation and gaps in expertise, policymaking, and implementation; regulatory capture; and transparency and accountability deficits. Moreover, regulatory competition between member states and the EC in food safety governance has put member states under additional pressure to beef up their food safety activities if they are to play a senior role in EU decision making.

The variation among the reformed regimes, however, shows that food safety agencies come in different flavors. In the UK, for example, risk assessment, management, and communication functions were combined within the FSA and kept at arm's length from ministers, while in France, AFSSA was given responsibilities for risk assessment and communication but risk management was firmly left in the hands of central government. The way in which different institutional architectures affect how issues play out in different countries deserves further sustained research, but this chapter highlights some of the problems that are arising.

This chapter examined the impact of reforms in the UK through the lens of two contemporary food safety issues. At the heart of each issue was the division of responsibility for managing risk between the state, business, and individual consumers. In principle, both risks could have been managed by ensuring the effective operation of market mechanisms, yet the profile of regulatory decision making and activity across the whole regime showed that sometimes the state intervened more heavily than expected and sometimes less. Further case study work is required to assess the generalizability of the findings, but these cases do permit some conclusions to be drawn.

First, the chapter shows how UK reforms have only partially reduced institutional fragmentation in the food safety regime and have left opportunities for conflicts to arise between regime components that can constrain the pursuit of overall regulatory goals. For example, conflicts have arisen between national and supranational levels of policymaking, such as the EC's rejection of the FSA's proposed ban on sheep intestines or the EC's more aggressive stance on the relevance of food hygiene regulations to food allergens. The reluctance of local government inspectors to enforce food safety law in relation to food allergens is another good example of regulatory incoherence.

Such conflicts are endemic to risk regulation regimes. The companion chapters on the French and German regimes, for example, highlight poor linkages between policymaking and enforcement. Moreover, in France, the institutional separation of risk assessment and management functions provides further opportunities for horizontal conflicts within national government. One example was the conflict over sheep intestines, which AFSSA, like the FSA, proposed to ban, but in the French case was overruled by the president. Indeed, chapter 6 vividly describes the boundary-setting politics of organizations trying to extend their own, or constrain each other's, remits within the fragmented national policymaking structure.

The case studies in this chapter also highlight the difficulty of aligning practice with guiding principles by both the agencies that espouse them and other actors in the regime beyond the control of those agencies. The FSA's first principle of putting consumers first is clearly flexible. Evidence of that flexibility is provided by the inconsistent approaches taken by the agency toward sheep intestines and sheep meat, allergens in prepacked food and catered food, and BSE in sheep and food allergens in general. That should not be surprising because assessment of the public interest entails complex trade-offs between different interests such as consumer choice and consumer health and conflicting business interests.

Indeed, the case studies in this chapter show how the balance of pressures from public opinion, concentrated private interests, public interest groups, and regulatory professionals plays a key role in shaping how the public interest is conceived and reflected at different points in the regime. For example, the FSA's recommended ban on sheep intestines was consistent with the agency's reputational concerns as the consumer's champion, the representation of consumer groups within the policy process, and the strategic long-term interests of the sheep and goat farming industry at the expense of the commercially smaller natural sausage casings industry. In contrast, the EC's rejection of the FSA recommendation was shaped less by the reputational concerns of the EC and consumer groups but more by scientists and the natural casings industry, which had a greater market presence in Europe than in the UK.

For food allergens, the FSA strategy of winning hearts and minds on catering, rather than intervening to ensure full consumer sovereignty, broadly balanced the interests of consumers with food allergies against the commercial interests of the catering industry, the difficulties of achieving behavior change, and the risk of public backlashes at the growth of "back protection" labeling. That balance of interests on food allergens appears to have been differently tipped at the EU level, while enforcement activities by local government inspectors appear to have been dominantly shaped by institutional resource constraints, legal uncertainties, and knowledge deficits.

Indeed, the food allergy case highlights the fact that sometimes consumer and business rights and responsibilities are simply not well worked out within regulation. For some regulatory actors, food allergens are consumer health risks and therefore not covered by the panoply of food safety law. For others, food allergens are food safety risks, and therefore consumers have a right to robust information at the very least. There has been some research on how the lay public and regulators conceive of risk, but contested conceptions of risk and the allocation of rights and responsibilities by regulatory actors is much less well investigated and deserves further research (see Rothstein 2003).

Moreover, the interpretive flexibility in putting consumers first presents an important challenge to the adoption of the precautionary principle within risk regulation (European Commission 2000b). While precautionary action is often advocated in situations of scientific uncertainty, it is often difficult to judge the precautionary nature of proposed action precisely because of the presence of scientific uncertainty. The BSE in sheep case clearly shows how in situations of scientific uncertainty, different regulatory actors within the regime can equally construe conflicting policy options as precautionary and proportionate depending on the framing of risk management questions and the choice of evidence. Equally, food allergens shows that the FSA had a marked reluctance to even encourage precautionary warnings because of fears that such warnings could generate other kinds of problems.

The FSA's second principle of openness is a common theme of risk regulation reform, and the FSA has undoubtedly gone to some lengths to fulfill it. Overall regime openness, however, has been limited by a number of factors, such as the choice of consultation mechanisms, the construction of legitimate stakeholder representation within policy processes, and the contingent demands and practices of regulatory actors that are beyond the control of the FSA such as the EC and local government enforcement. The varied inclusion and exclusion of different regulatory actors by the EC and FSA when consulting on the issue of BSE in sheep was, for example, a factor in shaping the conflicting conclusions that were reached. Similarly, the nondisclosure of surveillance data on food allergen contamination by local government because of concerns for commercial confidentiality and the maintenance of consumer confidence conflicted with the FSA's policy commitment to publish all such data. Chapter 6 points to similar problems in operationalizing openness and consultation in France. Indeed, the swings and roundabouts profile of openness and key stakeholder representation across regulatory regimes suggest that the operationalization of openness is highly dependent on local institutional practices and pressures.

The case studies in addition suggest that the principle of independence is also a flexible concept and can be mitigated in a number of ways. Independence for the FSA has been popularly conceived as independence from political interference and dominant agribusiness pressures. Nevertheless, the cases suggest that the structure of policy processes can create path dependencies that work against independence. For example, the involvement of senior FSA board members in the BSE stakeholder group made it more likely that the FSA board would accept the stakeholder group recommendations. Similarly, the EC was given less room for maneuver when the SSC extended its remit beyond risk assessment to send out a strong risk management signal on BSE in sheep. Chapter 6 points to similar problems in France, where budgetary dependencies and reliance on experts from supervisory ministries mitigated AFSSA's independence.

Moreover, the independence of national regimes that sit within supranational settings needs to be considered. For example, when the FSA forwarded its recommended ban on sheep intestines directly to the EC, the natural casings manufacturers were forced to argue their position at the European level rather than through UK processes. That finding provides further evidence that complex regimes present considerable opportunities for blame-shifting responses that reduce the accountability of any one institutional actor for decision making (see Hood, Rothstein, and Baldwin 2001).

In general, the case studies in this chapter show that reform of the food safety regime has not resolved conflicts in this domain of highly contested governance. Conflicts between different groups of regulatory actors over the nature and scale of food safety risks, risk tolerabilities, and institutional responsibilities, processes, and capacities for managing risks seem to be an inevitable part of the regulatory landscape of food safety regulation. Indeed, given the often competing preferences of different groups such as private interest groups, regulatory professionals, or civil society organizations, regulatory reform should not be about eliminating conflicts but managing them in a way that best serves the public interest.

The UK experience, however, seems to suggest that simple adherence to a predefined list of principles is insufficient guarantee that policy outcomes will be socially optimal. Indeed, the chapter shows the importance of considering the conceptual flexibility inherent in the meaning of apparently worthy guiding principles and the institutional constraints on their operationalization. The FSA has undoubtedly been successful so far in working toward its key priority of improving public confidence in the food safety regime. However, as this chapter shows, and as chapter 6 observes in relation to France, improving food safety and confidence in the food supply do not necessarily always coincide. That finding presents an important challenge to improving food safety and indeed risk regulation in general.

Notes

I thank Michael Huber, Hazel Gowland, and Ian Leitch for their helpful comments on this chapter, as well as the practitioners interviewed for this research who will have to remain anonymous. The views expressed in this chapter are mine. The support of the Economic and Social Research Council (ESRC) is gratefully acknowledged. The work was part of the program of the ESRC Centre for Analysis of Risk and Regulation.

1. This section draws on Rothstein (2004).

2. That situation changed marginally in early 2005, when it was discovered that a French goat had died three years previously from BSE and a Scottish goat that died in 1990 may have been infected. The confirmation that BSE could spread on the farm prompted further testing in member states, but as none of the 140,000 other goats tested across Europe up to that point had tested positive, the incidence of BSE in goat herds was still unknown.

3. Market failure analysis considers the need for the state to correct for potential failures in market or tort law processes (Hood, Rothstein, and Baldwin 2001). From that perspective, regulatory intervention would be expected only where the costs of individuals' informing themselves about risks and/or opting out of risks through market or civil law processes are high.

4. The FSA also issued particular advice to Muslim and African Caribbean groups where older (and hence riskier) goat and sheep play a particular dietary role and recommended voluntary country-of-origin labeling of baby food containing sheep meat.

5. MAFF had conducted some limited awareness-raising campaigns among caterers and retailers and issued advice on the consumption of peanuts by children and pregnant and breast-feeding mothers (COT 1998).

6. Personal correspondence with I. Leitch, senior environmental health officer, Omagh District Council, April 17, 2003.

7. For example, by 2003, guidelines had been produced by British Retail Consortium, the Food and Drink Federation, the Institute for Food Science and Technology, and the Institute of Grocery Distribution. The sectoral guides to good hygiene practice that were used as guides to both business and enforcement, however, remained virtually silent on food allergens. Only the guide relating to retail food sales referred to allergens, but it simply referred readers to the Anaphylaxis Campaign for further information (personal correspondence with Leitch, 2003).

8. Recent research suggests that certain people have a particular genetic susceptibility to BSE risks.

9. Thanks to Colin Scott for making this point.

10. Personal communication with J. Husu-Kallio, Health and Consumer Protection Directorate-General, European Commission, Sept. 17, 2003.

11. Personal communication with S. Hattersley, head of Branch 2, Chemical-Safety and Toxicology Division, Food Standards Agency, February 9, 2004.

8

Governance Reform of German Food Safety Regulation: Cosmetic or Real?

Bodo Steiner

With the emergence of the first BSE case in Germany in November 2000, the fast erosion of consumer confidence into the safety of meat products led to a rapid restructuring of government agencies and policy instruments related to food safety.[1] Similar to the release of information about British BSE cases in Germany in 1996, the arrival of the first German BSE cases in 2000 led to a highly intense and emotional reaction among German consumers (Loy and Steiner 2004). This intense, though periodic, mass-level attention to BSE is an important attribute of contested governance (see chapter 1, this volume) that has proven to be more dramatic in Germany than in France or Britain (see chapters 6 and 7, this volume). In November 2000, the mass-level attention to BSE not only led to a reduction of beef eating by more than half, but had repercussions for the entire food marketing chain, the animal breeding industry, the catering business, and EU farm policy as a whole ("A New Type of Farming" 2001, Fox and Peterson 2004).

Under political pressure, the federal minister of agriculture announced the establishment of a new ministry branch solely devoted to food safety only one week after the first BSE case was reported.[2] Up to then, the Health Ministry was fully responsible for handling food safety issues. One month after the first BSE case, Chancellor Schröder announced that BSE had become one of his-priority issues (*Chefsache*). When the federal ministers of agriculture and health refused to consider further swift changes, Schröder forced them to resign in January 2001 and named a lawyer from the Green Party, Renate Künast, as the new minister of agriculture. For the first time in German history, the minister of agriculture came from outside the sector. In addition to the changes in personnel, the Ministry of Food, Agriculture and Forestry was renamed the Ministry of Consumer Protection, Food and Agriculture.

In the light of these changes, an important question to ask is: to what extent do the observed institutional governance modifications reflect continued contested governance in terms of public distrust, when it challenges the legitimacy of institutional arrangements related to food safety (chapter 1, this volume)?[3] This chapter attempts to address this issue by exploring the scope and effectiveness of visual changes in governance in Germany, including the policy instruments that were implemented to address food safety issues and particularly the eroding trust in public authority. The key role of regaining trust in public authority in this process is echoed by policymakers themselves. Künast identified this as her top priority, emphasizing that "trust through change must be our motto" (Künast 2002). David Byrne, European commissioner for health and consumer protection, announced, "Clearly there is a need to develop trust. The food safety agencies, which have been established in many European countries, serve as good examples. These agencies create a credible and visible distance between different government structures with the broad aim of increasing transparency which, in turn, bolsters public acceptance and confidence" (Byrne 2004). However, before exploring to what extent these calls for public trust and reduced contestation were more than cosmetic rhetoric, this chapter first considers some specifics of Germany as they relate to food safety and food markets in general.

German consumers could be characterized as highly price sensitive. Discounters, for example, have gained a market share of close to 40 percent, which is higher than in any other European country (M+ MPlanetRetail 2002).[4] At the same time, only a small fraction of consumers purchase organic meat, which consumers perceive as being safer than conventional meat products.[5]

Given Germany's traditional reliance on state intervention since the Bismarck era, a shift toward more industry-led initiatives in the food sector seems, at first sight, to be more challenging and more appropriate than in other European countries. Industry-led initiatives, such as the 2001 voluntary national quality assurance scheme Quality and Safety (QS), can be highly desirable in a world of increasingly differentiated food produce. With increasing complexity in the food system, a greater reliance on market mechanisms that exploit the informational advantages of decentralized market participants has advantages over state intervention. This is because competitive forces can deliver efficient price discovery by exploiting local and idiosyncratic information (Hayek 1945) and by giving important incentives, for example through reputation, that are necessary for the functioning of quality assurance schemes.[6] At the same time, increasing complexity calls for a stricter separation of tasks between markets and government and a stronger government focus on auditing mechanisms and liability law.

Indeed, we observe an increasing degree of government intervention along those dimensions when considering the food safety–related regulations initiated by Künast, or EU directives related to food safety. To emphasize, such intervention can generally be justified, since it is well known that without intervention, the market fails to deliver the optimal level of safety at the margin. The underlying problem of inadequate or asymmetric information can be addressed not only through the regulation of liability but also by public information provision and through the mandatory implementation of minimum quality standards or guarantees.[7]

The case for government intervention with regard to setting minimum product quality standards is a critical one in the context of this chapter.[8] In a world of increasing proliferation of brands and private quality assurance systems, the problem of transparency and heterogeneity of product quality standards can often be addressed more efficiently through mandated quality standards, since certified quality standards reduce information cost to consumers about the safety level of quality attributes. Significantly, product quality standards rather than process quality standards enable the industry to choose the most efficient way of achieving a given level of food safety.[9] In sum, since markets can help to resolve failures related to food safety through competition and reputation, and since governments can take an important role with regard to liability and information provision, a balanced, accountable, and transparent division of responsibilities poses the greatest challenge to a government trying to regain consumer confidence and assure an optimal degree of food safety at the margin.[10]

This chapter explores the newly emerging mix of market and government initiatives in Germany with regard to food safety, as exemplified by QS and the reform of governance structures at the federal level. Following a discussion of the changing scope of governance with regard to food safety, the chapter discusses the effectiveness and efficiency of the emerging reform elements of the new governance structures. In doing so, this chapter tries to answer to what extent food-safety-related governance in Germany remains contested. Finally, this chapter aims to provide an outlook on emerging tensions between governance modes, since these tensions are likely to determine the accountability, competence, and efficiency of forthcoming food safety regulations.

The Changing Scope of Governance

Given the federal structure and the institutions that are associated with a "social market economy" such as in Germany, we expect that the underlying system of governance as related to food safety is distinctly different from other economies (Chandler 1990).[11] However, before exploring several changes in Germany's governance structure related to food safety, it is essential to identify what is meant by scope of governance, governance structure, and their role in shaping an incentive structure that underlies economic activity and political distress.

Following North (1990), Nelson and Sampat (2001), and vonTunzelmann (2003), the *scope of governance* can be captured by three key elements: process, structure, and control. In the context of this chapter, we consider governance *processes* as the changing roles and relationships of agents and agencies in the course of the BSE events in Germany.[12] Governance *structure* relates to the different forms through which decisions are made. Structures can thus induce and govern collective decision making. Finally, the capability of governance (competence) needs to be captured: *control* refers to the power to make economic and policy decisions through different structures.

In identifying the key parameters of regulatory organizations in OECD countries, Scott (2003) suggests that there are at least three main combinations of form and power: organizations established and given power by statute; organizations established without direct state involvement, through contracts or incorporation, but empowered by state legislative instruments; and nonstate organizations exercising private regulatory power (p. 309).[13] For example, consider the contrast between conventional modes of governance that rely on lengthy legislative processes, and more flexible governance modes such as those that rely more heavily on regulatory agencies or voluntary standards (e.g., QS). Lengthy legislative processes are more vulnerable to political and lobbying influences due to their structure as compared to the more robust and flexible structure of regulatory agencies in a social market economy, which are likely to undergo appropriate checks and balances. They are, therefore, more likely to be accountable and democratically legitimate (Persson, Roland, and Tabellini 1997). This is perhaps where the economic view of scope of governance is echoed most closely in the political view of contested governance, in terms of its challenge to the legitimacy of existing institutional arrangements, and in terms of its sectoral or multisectoral scope (chapter 1, this volume). Consider that the new institutional economics literature refers to a governance structure as the institutional framework within which the integrity of a transaction is decided (Williamson 1979, 235). The elements of such an institutional framework, the institutions themselves, are the humanely devised constraints that structure political, economic, and social interaction (North 1991, 97). According to North (1991), these institutions consist of the informal constraints (sanctions, customs) and formal rules (laws, property rights) that define part of the choice set of economic agents and thus determine the profitability and feasibility of engaging in economic activity (p. 97). These informal constraints and formal rules lie at the heart of those conditions that either challenge or support the legitimacy of existing institutional arrangements, and can therefore be directly associated with contested governance in the sense of Ansell and Vogel (chapter 1, this volume).

Given a mix of formal and informal constraints, the power of making economic and policy decisions through the above structures often fails to deliver equity and efficiency. We can identify several forms of failures that are responsible here: market failure, government failure, corporate failure, and network failure. There are two reasons why these different modes of failures should not be considered in isolation in the context of our analysis. First, we are interested in exploring changes in the scope of governance following the BSE outbreak in Germany as they relate to the changing scope of contestation. Consider that the interrelationship between different modes of failure can be directly linked to the BSE outbreak. Government failure exacerbated market failure by relying on intransparent decision making and thus hampering economic incentives. Due to inappropriate liability rules at the farm and processing level, as well as inadequate and asymmetric information in the provision of ruminant feedstuff, a market failure emerged. But inadequate liability rulings at the level of public authorities, and thus the failure to align incentives between principals and agents in the political hierarchies, were also most likely important reasons for the BSE outbreak.

As a further example, consider the UK, where the specified bovine offal ban failed for at least two reasons. First, it failed because of noncompliance of industry participants. Second, it failed because government officials who were in charge of designing and enforcing the ruminant feed ban did not act in the interest of society. Government officials decided to lower the temperature for treating animal protein in feedstuff processing while their decision-making process took place in the absence of public scrutiny.[14] Therefore, the conditions that led to the outbreak of BSE may be regarded as a prime example for contested governance. Ansell and Vogel (chapter 1, this volume) argue that contested governance is particularly likely where intense public scrutiny confronts an extensively institutionalized policy sector in which day-to-day routine decisions are delegated to experts or administrators with little ongoing attention or interest from the public.

The second and related reason that supports an analysis of the interrelationship between the above modes of failure relates to the three ideal types of governance modes: markets, networks, and hierarchies (Thompson et al. 1991).[15] Importantly, two types of hierarchies can be distinguished here, the corporate hierarchy (large firms) and a country's political hierarchies.[16] This division between governance modes is particularly relevant here, since this chapter argues that a transparent and sharp distinction between the roles of markets and political hierarchies is desirable in resolving contested governance with regards to food safety. The following sections explore these issues more explicitly, by analyzing the key dimensions of changes in the political hierarchies in Germany, and by examining changes in a market-led initiative, both of which aim to address contestation in food safety matters.

A Voluntary National Quality Assurance Scheme: Quality and Safety (QS)

The shift in incentives for the German food demand chain to implement a large-scale QS scheme after the BSE events is a further reflection of the shifting balance of regulation away from publicly mandated food safety regulations and more toward industry-led initiatives.[17] Several authors have explored general incentive and adoption issues of such quality assurance schemes at the industry level (Henson and Caswell 1999; Caswell, Bredahl, and Hooker 1998).[18] However, given the scope of this chapter, the following sections attempt to describe the functioning of the QS scheme, highlight its actual and potential weaknesses, and explore its broader relevance in the context of German food safety regulation and contested governance.

The following discussion focuses on the new QS scheme for three main reasons. First, in contrast to the limited coverage of other retailer-led schemes, the QS scheme reaches across the entire demand chain for meat and meat produce as well as fruit and vegetables.[19] Second, it takes an interesting intermediate position in terms of incentive provision to the food demand chain, as it combines elements of a voluntary industry-led quality assurance scheme and a publicly mandated set of food safety regulations. Third, largely due to the composition of its members, the cautious criticism of Minister Künast (Die Zeit 2003, Agrar.de 2003), and a recent BSE test scandal (Putz 2004), QS has become a focus of public debate that longs to be viewed through the lense of contested governance.

In October 2001, representatives from the German farmers' federation, the federations of feed processors, meat processors, and retailers joined together with the Central Marketing Association of German Agriculture (CMA), to form a limited liability corporation with the objective of establishing a national label and quality assurance scheme for conventionally produced meat and meat produce.[20] Each of the federations has a veto right and sends two representatives to an advising committee, whose task is twofold. First, it sets the control criteria according to which independent auditors are asked to classify and accredit system participants.[21] Second, it defines and interprets the criteria according to which the assigned label is set up and communicated to the outside world.

Two further institutions were established: the sanctioning committee and the board of trustees. The sanctioning committee consists of three members: a lawyer, a judge, and an expert sworn to impartiality. This committee rules over system participants that have not adhered to the control criteria established by the advising committee. It then imposes penalties according to guidelines that are established by the advising committee. The other institution is the board of trustees, whose functions lie in public relations and advising the sanctioning committee.[22] In order to reduce a centralized administrative burden, key demand chain members, such as cooperatives, packers, and slaughterhouses, have become the local administrative centers for producers, who then become associated producers.

The structure of controls has three dimensions: the firm-level self-control, an independent auditing, and a control of the auditing. Currently this control of the auditing is performed by the QS corporation itself or by independent auditors chosen by QS. Independent auditing occurs randomly, but auditors have to announce their visit at least one week in advance. The auditors check on physical criteria such as hygiene and administrative criteria such as documentation. Some criteria are exclusion criteria, but after passing those, each farm obtains an index number. Depending on the percentage of criteria fulfilled, farms get classified as QS standard 1, 2, or 3. For example, a pork producer who has been classified into QS standard 1 has three years before he can expect the next auditor on his farm (two years for QS standard 2, and one year for QS standard 3). There are several incentive problems with this system. First, it is not made public into which QS standard a system participant (and thus his product) has been classified. Second, the auditing frequency differs according to species (higher for beef than for pork) and level of system participant (key distinction between farmers and local administrative centers). Third, the auditing frequency and stringency is particularly low at the retail level. As soon as more than 10 percent of retail outlets in a given chain have achieved a given QS standard, this

QS standard will automatically be granted to all the remaining outlets. Once a retail chain has been granted QS standard 1, only 10 percent of its outlets will be randomly selected for auditing (15 percent annually for QS standard 2 and 20 percent annually for QS standard 3).

Given the inexperience with this type of quality assurance scheme, it is of interest to examine the practical implications for the alliance members further. Beyond the mandatory federal requirements in terms of documentation of origin and medication, the use of antibiotics is more strictly regulated under QS. Growth antibiotics were permitted for the production of piglets and in the early fattening stages of pork production until January 2004. A total ban on growth antibiotics has now been implemented throughout the life cycle of all animals. However, the use of GM feedstuff as well as the use of fully slatted floors in pork production is still permitted (Putz 2004). Another important implication for farmers is the compulsory monitoring of Salmonella status, which exceeds the general mandatory federal regulations. The data about the Salmonella status of an individual animal as well as a classification of the entire farm are fed into a central Salmonella database. From there, farmers and slaughterhouses can access the data. Initially sow herds were exempt so the coverage of the Salmonella monitoring was incomplete until January 2004. Further, there are no implications and specifications on the farm or any other level regarding GMOs or animal welfare criteria. As slaughterhouses, processors, and retailers have to comply with federal regulation regarding traceability in any case, there is no additional impact from QS.

Since the initiation of the QS system, the first certified produce appeared on the markets in September 2002, while the first QS meat was sold through Wal-Mart. Clearly, that was a message to all those who believed that QS would automatically guarantee higher retail and producer prices.

However, for the first time in German history, a voluntary national quality assurance scheme was established. As regulators are interested in the efficient provision of a desired level of food safety, this should be seen in a positive light since we need to consider economies of scale associated with safety-specific capital.[23] With QS, as with other schemes of vertical integration, firms can obtain the necessary minimum efficient scale of production. Nevertheless, after one year, QS had achieved only a limited coverage of the entire sector with about 50 percent of pork and 32 percent of beef produced under the QS label (October 2003). This is surprisingly low, given that QS originated as a result of safety problems in the beef sector. Beginning in early 2004, QS auditing also started in the fruit and vegetable sector. Furthermore, system participants hope that QS would improve international competitiveness of QS-certified fruits and vegetables, since QS audits will be embedded in the global system of EUREPGAP audits.[24]

With the key objective of establishing a quality assurance scheme that covers the entire food demand chain based on hazard analysis and critical control points principles, the QS scheme has achieved standards only slightly greater than Germany's mandatory standards: its criteria rest generally on existing mandatory standards and are distinct only in terms of a more extensive data management system (which is meant to improve traceability) and increased Salmonella monitoring. According to those criteria, QS fulfills EU Food Safety Law 178/2002 in terms of traceability and self-control.

In sum, what are the most critical points of the QS system? Given its limited coverage in terms of total production, it appears that the system's credibility remains limited as long as there is leeway for members of the demand chain to circumvent the system. More striking is that the very reason for establishing the QS label does not appear to be taken seriously. According to Foodwatch, an independently funded German organization for consumer rights in the field of agricultural and food policy, nine German farms were identified where QS-certified beef was not tested for BSE (Putz 2004). Furthermore, considering the institutional structure of the QS system, the role of the sanctioning committee appears questionable in two ways. First, a potential conflict of interest emerges because the sanctioning committee imposes sanctions according to guidelines that were established by the advising committee. Second, and most important in the view of the declared objective of improving transparency, the names of the system members who violated the QS criteria and were punished with sanctions are not made public. Further, the lack of transparency with regard to participants' QS classification and the low auditing frequency deserve to be emphasized again. Also, the Salmonella monitoring scheme is insufficiently rigorous, as there are no bacteriological examinations of the animals required.[25] Problems with establishing a more rigorous Salmonella monitoring scheme can only be anticipated from the fact that the German government had previously led a voluntary national eradication and disease control program, which was abandoned by the end of 1999 due to lack of participation.

Some critical issues extend further to the butchers and the retailers. The butchers' association has refused to join the label, based on two points. First, butchers argue that the additional compliance costs will not be counterbalanced by a higher consumers willingness to pay. Second, the butchers believe that their quality standards are already above QS standards. Results from a recent study (Loy and Steiner 2004) suggest that butchers have indeed been able to charge higher prices compared to supermarkets.[26] As several studies have confirmed, German consumers appear to value the personal relationship with a butcher more than placing their trust in an "anonymous label" (Nielsen 1998, Wirz 1996). The fact that butchers have not joined the QS system, although they currently account for about 40 percent of meat sales in Germany, is a further indication of the inability of the QS corporation to communicate the label's benefits to consumers, beyond those that are conveyed through the current mandatory standards.

Further, consider the retail level. The QS scheme started as a retailer-led quality assurance scheme, with its first meat being sold through Walmart. Many producers and food processors were thus implicitly forced to adopt QS standards or lose their outlets. Clearly, with an increasing concentration at the retail level, it is important to keep antitrust issues in mind.

In total, and accounting for the tightened standards as compared to the initialization stage, QS appears to have only slightly lifted the overall level of food safety beyond the current mandatory state regulations. However, it appears striking that a quality assurance scheme was put into place with little rigor first, before more stringent measures were adopted. This may be rational with regard to minimizing system participants' initial compliance costs. But it is unlikely to be a successful long-term strategy with regard to regaining consumer confidence and market share. Consider that at present, the QS label appears to carry a low informational value, since it is difficult to communicate to consumers the differences between the QS label and the required standards objectively. Beyond the complexity of the underlying standards, a low consumer valuation is also anticipated due to a continuing lack of consumer trust. This is due not only to the fact that most of the information about QS originates from its system members, but also because German consumers continue to be surprised by undesirable substances in the food demand chain (May 2002: nitrofen in organic wheat; July 2003: dioxin in feedstuff).

Nevertheless, due to its broader scope and larger scale than previous industry-led quality assurance schemes, the implicitly improved standard harmonization could in principle be seen in a positive light with regard to consumer information. Consumer choice could be improved due to the reduction in the complexity of labeling and standards information. Due to the greater comparability of standards, transparency leads to greater competitive pressure on other sector participants to differentiate themselves. A continuing proliferation of domestic and international retailer- or producer-led quality assurance schemes could be expected to appear on the German market. Consumer gains could thus be in terms of price, but whether consumers gain in terms of information provision is likely to be determined by how industry players and the government find a balance between standards regulation and label proliferation.[27]

Further, since QS system participants have developed the Salmonella monitoring system based on the European Parliament's regulation on the control of salmonella, QS is likely to serve as the basis for a faster and more efficient introduction of the expected mandatory regulation.[28] In the future, it should also guarantee a smoother compliance with the European Centre for Disease Prevention and Control (ECDC) (COM 2004) which started to operate in May 2005. But beyond the Salmonella criteria in QS, it is also the establishment of a central database that has anticipated recent EU regulation with regards to traceability.[29] Given these potential harmonization benefits, it will be interesting to continue to observe the forthcoming governance interplay between political and corporate hierarchies, especially after the recent reform of federal ministries and regulations in Germany.

The Reform of Food Safety Regulation in Germany

The most visible change in the scope of governance that can be associated with food safety issues relates to the renaming of the Federal Ministry of Food, Agriculture and Forestry the Federal Ministry of Consumer Protection, Food and Agriculture (BMVEL) in January 2001. This occurred only one day after the federal minister for health and the federal minister for agriculture were forced to resign.

The following section outlines the changes in governance structure before attempting an assessment of these reforms. Throughout, this section will relate to a study of the German court of auditors, which was initiated by Chancellor Schröder at the end of 2000 ("von Wedel Report"; von Wedel 2001). This 127-page report, which was published in July 2001, is particularly insightful for two reasons. First, its editor was the president of the German federal court of auditors and, at the same time, the federal commissioner for operating efficiency in public administration.[30] Second, the report came about with the cooperation of experts of the court of auditors, the BMVEL, as well as an advising committee that consisted of representatives from farmers, consumers groups, and science.

The renaming of the ministry had an immediate structural consequence. The Federal Ministry for Consumer Protection (BgVV) was placed under the jurisdiction of the BMVEL and finally dissolved in November 2002. The BgVV's responsibilities were then taken over by three federal institutions: the BMVEL, the newly created federal institute of risk assessment (BfR), and the newly created federal office for consumer protection and food safety (BVL), with the latter two both created in November 2002. The BfR is responsible for risk analysis, risk communication to policymakers and the public, and cooperation with the European Food Safety Authority (EFSA) (Agrarbericht 2003). Risk management responsibilities (including the admission of pesticides) and the coordination of joint control functions between the federation and the federal states were taken over by the BVL. The reform of these institutions has very much followed the blueprint of the von Wedel report.[31]

The report's criticism focuses on three traits of the previous scope of governance: the fragmentation of food safety–related responsibilities across federal ministries, the lack of an independent scientific center advising the BMVEL, and the lack of coordination between the federation, the federal states, and the EU in matters of food safety.

Fragmentation of Responsibilities
After the immediate reorganization of the BMVEL in January 2000, there were still food safety–related tasks for which the BMU (federal ministry for the environment, nature conservation, and nuclear safety), the BMWI (federal ministry for the economy and technology), and the BMG (Federal Ministry of Health) were responsible. The von Wedel report found that there were eighteen subordinate federal institutes engaged in food safety matters. In order to address this fragmentation, lack of coordination, and in response to the chancellor's intention that food safety matters should be concentrated within the BMVEL, the report contained two main suggestions. First, food safety tasks should be bundled within the BMVEL after a reorganized working structure of its departments. Second, a complete reform of the central policy department within the BMVEL was proposed to account for future strategic issues such as policy planning, coordination in research, and coordination in EU matters. While the bundling of food safety responsibilities has taken shape in the current BMVEL, the second proposal of the von Wedel report has not been implemented.

Establishment of an Independent Scientific Center for Risk Analysis
Within the structure of the previously established federal ministries, there was no scope for interdisciplinary risk analysis related to food safety. Therefore, the von Wedel report proposed the establishment of such a center with the following tasks: (1) collect, analyze, and evaluate information on food risk (risk analysis and risk communication) in order to provide objective and preventative policy advice; (2) serve as an intermediary between the BMVEL and national and international research institutes; and (3) serve as representative to the EFSA. The report rec-

ommended that this center be part of the BMVEL (in budgetary terms, with an independent governing status), that it have the power to contract research projects out, and that it be guaranteed independence through similar principles and measures that rule for the Deutsche Bundesbank. Given the unresolved budgetary issue and faced with the difficult task of overcoming principal-agent (incentive) problems that would underlie such an associated center, it is not surprising that this part of the proposal has not been put into practice in its original form.

The BfR in its current form considers itself to be the scientific body of the Federal Republic of Germany in matters of food safety. Legally it is a self-governing public institution, which is meant to provide the necessary scientific independence. It aims to prepare expert reports and opinions on questions of food safety and consumer health protection on the basis of internationally recognized scientific assessment criteria (BfR 2003). With the help of risk analyses, it aims to formulate action options for risk reduction. Its tasks include the provision of scientific advice to the federal ministries concerned with food safety matters and the publication of original research and risk assessments to the public in a transparent and comprehensible manner.[32] Further, the BfR is engaged in scientific cooperation with other international institutions and organizations that are involved in consumer health protection and food safety. The BfR takes a role that more closely resembles that of AFSSA in France (see chapter 6, this volume), since its role as a public body for risk assessment is strictly separated from risk management. This contrasts with the UK reforms, where risk assessment, management, and communication functions are combined within the FSA (see chapter 7, this volume).

Addressing the Lack of Coordination at the National and EU Levels

In anticipation of the foundation of the EFSA, the von Wedel report focused on organizational weaknesses at the level of the federation, as well as on the division of responsibilities between federal states and the federation. In the past, the federation was only partly responsible on food safety matters. The responsibility was limited to the creation of laws at the level of the federation, as well as to cooperating responsibilities with EU institutions. Given Germany's constitution, the central role of the federal states was and still is in the sphere of execution (monitoring food quality, feedstuff, and the private veterinary sector). In order to fulfill the joint tasks of the federation and the federal states in terms of risk management, risk evaluation, and risk communication, the von Wedel report suggested the creation of a more output-oriented "coordinating agency of the Federation" (KSB). Created in its governance structure as a mirror image to EU governance structures, this KSB has been established through the BVL (federal office for consumer protection and food safety). Its associated responsibilities lie in the establishment of a central internal data network for food safety issues and the harmonization of control standards and crisis management, such that the KSB functions as intercept for the European Rapid Alert System. However, two recommendations of the von Wedel report have not been followed so far: that the data collected through the KSB be made public and that the KSB be used as a mechanism for exploring the legal appropriateness of existing liability laws.

Beyond the reform of the BMVEL and its related institutions, the government enacted several other initiatives. On August 6, 2002, a law for the "new organization of consumer health protection and food safety" was passed in the upper house of the federal government. This legislation established not only the BfR and the BVL, but also relabeled the pesticide regulation, the epidemic regulation, and the feedstuff regulation to provide conformity with the newly labeled BMVEL. The government also invested about $13 million to support the national research initiative on TSEs (transmissible spongiform encephalopathies). In addition, the government has reformed the liability laws by integrating consumer rights into the BGB (the German civil code), making it easier for consumers to sue individual firms and for consumer groups to sue associations.

Continued Contestation or Improved Competence, Accountability, and Legitimacy?

The 2001 Agriculture Report of the BMVEL, published on February 14, states that "the BSE scandal marks the end of agricultural policy of the old type. In the future, consumer protection in these sensitive areas of

agricultural and food policy will be given priority over economic interests (Agrarbericht 2001)."[33]

In an attempt to explore the issue of remaining contestation in the
above context and in the sense of Ansell and Vogel (chapter 1, this
volume), it appears necessary to ask which traits of the reformed scope
of governance can be linked to continuing public distrust in authority
that challenges the legitimacy of existing institutional arrangements. This
chapter suggests that the lack of the following governance traits as
related to food safety can be used to reflect upon this issue:

Competence[34]
· The capacity to select and replace ill-founded food safety policy
instruments
· The capacity to design and implement well-founded food safety policy
instruments (e.g., the capacity to judge whether risk is acceptable or not)

Accountability
· The aptness of institutions to respond to changing demands and
insights from citizens (democratic accountability from within)
· The readiness of governing institutions to respond to evolving scientific knowledge and feedback from other democratic institutions (external democratic accountability)
· External and internal accountability require transparency: only when
the operation of governance structures is transparent can a critical flow
of information be returned from citizens and science to the institutions
themselves.

A further issue that is not covered in the above view of competence
and accountability, yet which emerges in the context of Germany's
federal system, is the characterization of governance in terms of centralization versus decentralization and its effect on the competence of
governance. It appears that the reduction in fragmentation of food
safety–related responsibilities through the establishment of the BMVEL
in its current form has led to a more competent scope of governance.

Further, with the established separation of risk management from risk
analysis and risk communication through the BfR and BVL (which
mirrors European governance structures as implemented in the EU Food

Safety Law 178/2002), accountability has also been, in principle, improved.

Regarding transparency, this chapter has stressed the lack of it on several occasions above, including in the context of the BfR. This may prove to be the greatest weakness in terms of improving the food industry's and government's accountability.

In sum, it appears that contestation in food safety matters has been reduced when judged in terms of competence and accountability. Initially, and following the decree of Chancellor Schröder for organizational reform in January 2001, a mere rebundling of responsibilities has been observed, without effective reform efforts related to food safety issues.[35] Largely due to the von Wedel report, this temporary peak in politicization has subdued. However, only the emergence of critical safety situations will prove how accountable and competent the governance structure will remain.

Effectiveness and Efficiency in a Changing Scope of Governance

The following section presents a brief assessment of effectiveness and allocative efficiency as it relates to the current scope of governance in food safety matters.

Effectiveness   In order to consider the effectiveness of the reformed institutions more explicitly, the following criteria are employed:

(i) Achievement of goals inherent in the implemented regulations and policies

(ii) Appropriateness of regulatory burden in its context

(iii) Facilitation of verification and traceability

(iv) Strengthening of liability law

(i) The von Wedel report has established the fragmentation of the old Ministry of Agriculture as one of the main deficiencies to be resolved. Since the goals of the report were, in this respect, put largely into practice, it appears that the current governance structure represents a major—and yet overdue—improvement. However, without knowledge of the time allocation of individual ministries and branches on food safety–related aspects and the corresponding achievement of specific goals, it is difficult to provide further judgment.

(ii) Given the bundling of responsibilities and the reduction in fragmentation, the regulatory burden through multiple and overlapping governance structures is likely to be reduced. The establishment of the BfR is important for improving the effectiveness of food safety regulations through conducting and promoting research in general, and through the use of cost-benefit analysis in particular. Since it is currently unknown to what extent the BfR uses cost-benefit analysis in the regulatory process (no such information was made public until June 2005), only the observed promotion of research and the associated establishment of a data network hint of an improvement in terms of regulatory effectiveness. Further, the above caveat in terms of lacking data transparency looms large.

(iii) The government's attempt to establish a voluntary Salmonella monitoring scheme that ensures traceability and facilitates verification has failed. Instead traceability has been achieved through the QS's Salmonella monitoring scheme and the central Salmonella database.

(iv) Finally, with regard to producers, consumers, and consumer groups, liability rules have been improved.

Efficiency   Efficient governance mechanisms are those that align incentive problems between agents that frequently occur due to the separation of ownership and control (Williamson 1998). Good governance thus aims to align incentive problems in order to permit the realization of (mutual) gains between agents. There are several ways by which the achievement of such gains may be hampered. In the face of the previously discussed changes in scope of governance, this section will briefly focus on issues of authority, liability, and risk.

Authority, Decentralization, and Efficiency   As Aghion and Tirole (1997) have emphasized, a gain in terms of efficiency can be made by giving up some control, that is, giving away real authority, even though formal control remains a top priority.[36] Considering the stricter bundling of food safety–related tasks at the federal level, the improved communication between federal ministries due to the reduction in overlap of responsibilities, together with a more transparent decentralized federal governance structure, it is likely that the current governance structure is more efficient than previous ones.

Liability and the Provision of Information   From an efficiency point of view, it is desirable to use food safety regulation and liability rules jointly in order to control for risk related to food safety hazards (Shavell 1984, Skogh 1989, Antle 1995).[37] Although an improved regulation of the provision of risk-related information helps to ensure and preserve consumers' freedom of choice, informational failures need to be addressed through standards and liability.[38] Since 2001 we have observed tighter liability rules that should strengthen deterrence. Together with an improvement of risk assessment, communication, and management that appears to have been made (through the establishment of the BfR and the BVL), it is likely that the balance between regulation and liability has been improved.[39] So far, considering information made public, it does not appear that much risk-related research has been performed in relation to food safety matters. It appears that in striving for more efficient risk regulation, the BfR should address important issues, such as: how do consumers respond to different communication efforts of the government, and how does consumers' capacity to use differently formatted information vary?[40]

In sum, the reformed food safety regulation appears suited to improve efficiency through the emphasis on information provision, standards, and transparency as these help to safeguard consumers' freedom of choice.[41] Since we observe some improvements in liability law and standards regulation and would expect that fewer resources are needed to achieve the acclaimed risk-related goals in the newly reformed governance structure, efficiency gains should be observed. Nevertheless, the lack of deterrence due to the reduction in potential liability that comes with the limited publication of risk data is likely to hamper efficiency (it is also in this sense that the QS scheme is inefficient by not publishing the identities of firms that defected).

Risk Standards, Cost-Benefit Analysis, and the Issue of Risk Perception
When risk standards (standards to protect health) are used for choosing among different food safety regulations, a major concern is that the costs

of different policy options may not enter into the design of risk standards, and standard setting is likely to reflect evidence of risk biases and responsiveness to political factors (Viscusi and Hamilton 1999). This calls for the use of cost-benefit analysis. Furthermore, since governance decisions at the federal level need to account for private efforts to ensure food safety such as the QS initiative, cost-benefit analysis should be used to facilitate the identification of effective intervention points in the food demand chain and the identification of efficient mixes of mandatory and voluntary quality management systems (Unnevehr and Roberts 1997, Caswell 1998).[42] The general importance and pitfalls of cost-benefit analysis for regulatory decision making are well established (Nichols 1991; Arrow et al. 1996). But importantly with regard to food safety, standard cost-benefit has also been refined to take account of scientific uncertainty, in ways that balance the precautionary principle against the benefits of waiting to learn before taking action (Gollier 2001).[43] This raises three issues related to the legitimacy of the BfR, the BVL, and the governance reforms as such. First, since it is unknown, at this stage, to what extent the BfR makes use of cost-benefit analyses, it is difficult to judge how efficient the operations of the BfR and BVL are along these lines (there are no publications that reveal its actual use, although the BfR's Web site proclaims that it is "developing concepts" for cost-benefit analysis (BfR 2005)). Second, from the published information it is not known to what extent the precautionary principle is actually integrated into cost-benefit research at the BfR. Third, even if this is done, it is not evident what role the precautionary principle takes as part of the reformed food safety regulations. However, in providing reformed institutional arrangements that reduce distrust in public authority and thus reduce challenges to legitimacy, the specification of a clear and transparent role of the precautionary principle in a newly emerging scope of governance should be given high priority.

Given consumers' different capacities and thus efficiency of using various forms of information, it is to be expected that consumer heterogeneity will pose further challenges to the work of the BfR and the BVL.[44] Since German consumers have proved to be more sensitive than other European consumers with regard to food safety scandals and the provision of food safety information, consumer heterogeneity and the resulting problem of efficient allocation of risks should be part of the BfR's research agenda. An interdisciplinary research effort appears particularly appropriate, just as the von Wedel report has suggested, since this is likely to help in analyses to adjust the subjective risk to the objective one.[45] Future research could control for these aspects by taking advantage of the strengths of choice experiments from surveys, combining it with market data (Louviere et al.1999; Louviere, Hensher, and Swait 2000).

In sum, risk research should not degenerate to a governance marketing effort that aims at reducing perceived risk associated with search, experience, and credence attributes. Rather, a multidisciplinary research effort on risk perception is important for an efficient design of governance structures and a regaining of institutional legitimacy, since knowledge of perceived risk helps to rationalize and depoliticize risk assessment and those governance options that both the BfR and BVL have on their agenda. In doing this, those interested in the effectiveness and efficiency of the evolving scope of governance in Germany may wish to consider Viscusi's findings as their paradigm: "As in the case of risk perception biases, the most disturbing aspect of these potential market failures is that the government policies intended to eliminate the shortcomings often appear to be driven by the same set of influences" (Viscusi 1990: 261).

Conclusion

Six weeks after the first BSE case emerged in Germany, the foundations were laid for a sweeping reform of governance structures related to food safety: within forty eight hours, both the minister of health and the minister of agriculture were forced to resign, and a lawyer and member of the Green Party became head of the former Federal Ministry of Food, Agriculture and Forestry. The ministry was simultaneously renamed the Federal Ministry of Consumer Protection, Food and Agriculture. This chapter has explored an emerging mix of market and government initiatives in Germany with regard to food safety, as exemplified by an industry-led, voluntary national quality assurance scheme and the reform of federal level governance structures involved in food safety issues. Since

both mandatory regulations and markets, through reputation and competition, can serve to provide appropriate incentives and constraints with
regard to food safety matters to actors in the food industry, the functioning and implications of QS were considered together with the
reforms of governance structures at the ministerial level.

Before the actual changes in the different aspects of governance were
discussed, an attempt was made to explore the key elements of scope of
governance—that is, structure, control, and process—together with the
evolving mix of types of governance modes in a more general context.
This permits a clearer assessment of governance elements that follows
with regard to aspects of competence, accountability, effectiveness and
efficiency. In turn, it enables us to explore the extent to which the changing scope of governance faces ongoing public distrust that challenges the
legitimacy of those newly reformed institutional arrangements (chapter
1, this volume).

This chapter suggests that the QS scheme has lifted the overall level
of food safety only slightly above the one supplied by the current mandatory state regulations. This is largely due to an attempt to implement a
more rigorous Salmonella monitoring system and the need to satisfy all
members of the demand chain that participate in the QS system. A low
informational value of the label is asserted, since it is difficult to communicate to consumers the differences between the QS label and the
generally required mandatory standards objectively. But beyond the
complexity of the underlying standards, a low consumer valuation is also
expected due to a continuing lack of consumer trust. Public distrust has
only recently received a boost due to allegations of failures in BSE testing
(Putz 2004). However, given the broader scope and larger scale of the
QS scheme compared to previous industry-led quality assurance schemes,
the implicitly improved standard harmonization should, in principle,
positively affect consumer information and consumer choice. Nevertheless it appears that in practice the standard harmonization has taken
place at such a low level that those informational gains to consumers are
outbalanced by the fact that the QS label masks shortcomings that are
not likely to be anticipated by consumers (neither GM feedstuff nor
animal welfare criteria are currently part of the QS certification; the
auditing procedures are not stringent enough to be effective). As a result,

diminishing consumer trust may spill over to other existing or forth-coming labeling schemes.

However, since QS system participants have developed a Salmonella monitoring system based on the European Parliament's regulation on the control of salmonella, QS could serve as the basis for a faster and more efficient introduction of the forthcoming mandatory regulation at the EU level. In the future, the QS scheme should also guarantee smoother compliance with the proposed European Centre for Disease Prevention and Control (ECDC). But beyond the Salmonella criteria in QS, it is also the establishment of a central database, and thus traceability, that is antici-pating forthcoming EU regulation. In sum, the introduction of QS appears to have brought little, if any, immediate consumer gains in terms of improving consumer choice and information, yet its pioneering char-acter and large scope across the food demand system appear to have brought some gains with regard to the implementation of future institu-tional and regulatory changes. Since the German government must ulti-mately defend itself in terms of traceability measures and Salmonella monitoring in relation to the EU, these regulatory gains from QS may help to reduce contested governance in the interplay between market-led and government-led food safety initiatives.

The chapter goes on to explore governance changes with regard to the restructuring of German federal ministries and the government's initia-tives with regard to liability issues and information provision. Along with the criticism and reform proposals of a report of the German court of auditors, the chapter considers three aspects of the scope of governance before 2000, which are all relevant to exploring the extent of distrust in public authority and the legitimacy of the underlying institutional arrangements. First, the fragmentation of food safety related responsi-bilities across federal ministries; second, the lack of scientific advice and research that links more directly with the Ministry of agriculture; and third, the lack of coordination between the Federation, the federal states, and the EU in matters of food safety. Accounting for the most recent governance changes, it appears that the governance in food safety matters is less contested in the sense of Ansell and Vogel (chapter 1, this volume), and as judged in terms of competence and accountability. Given the bundling of responsibilities and the reduction in fragmentation that has taken place, the regulatory burden is also likely to be reduced.

The establishment of the federal institute of risk assessment (BfR) and the federal office for consumer protection and food safety (BVL) in November 2002 was a credible attempt to separate risk analysis and risk communication from risk management. This approach is similar to the developments in France with the introduction of AFFSA (see chapter 6, this volume), but differs sharply from the UK approach, in which risk assessment, management, and communication are combined within the FSA (see chapter 7, this volume). The creation of the BfR is important for improving the effectiveness of food safety regulations through conducting original research and promoting research in general, and through the use of cost-benefit analysis in particular. Since it is currently unknown to what extent the BfR uses cost-benefit analyses in the regulatory process, only the promotion of research and the associated establishment of a data network suggests that regulatory effectiveness is likely to be improved. Also, liability rules have been improved for producers, consumers, and consumer groups. Nevertheless, lacking transparency with regard to data access to the outside world remains a problem.

Finally, this chapter attempts to make a brief efficiency assessment of the emerging governance structures. Considering a more focused and decentralized division of authority together with tighter liability rules that should strengthen deterrence, the governance reform promises efficiency gains. Together with an improvement of tasks related to risk analysis, communication, and management, it is likely that the balance between regulation and liability has been improved. Further, the reformed food safety regulations appear suited to improve efficiency through the emphasis on information provision, standards, and traceability, as these help to safeguard consumers' freedom of choice. Nevertheless, the lack in deterrence due to the reduction in potential liability that comes with the limited publication of risk data is likely to hamper efficiency.

Also, the recent and repeated defeat of the government's "information law" for consumers at the upper house of parliament must be seen as a setback for restoring trust in public authority. Further, extensive consumer consultation, as it is practiced in the UK through a dedicated consumer consultive committee (chapter 7, this volume), is also largely missing in practice, although the BfR proclaims risk communication as an interactive process and dialogue. These two conditions are all the more important with regard to continuing contested governance, since effective risk communication is essential for building credibility, trust in public authority, and thus enhancing the legitimacy of institutional arrangements.

In view of the danger that the costs of different policy options may not enter into the design of risk standards and that standard setting is likely to reflect evidence of risk biases and responsiveness to political factors, this chapter suggests that cost-benefit analysis should be implemented at various stages in the planning and decision-making process of German food safety regulations. It is not currently evident whether or to what extent the BfR is making use of these tools. Further, a multidisciplinary research effort on risk perception, which should be linked to the BfR, is important and should be initialized in order to account for critical issues related to consumers' risk perception. To initialize such an effort appears important for an efficient design of governance structures, since knowledge of perceived risk helps to rationalize and depoliticize risk assessment and those governance options that both the BfR and BVL have on their agenda.

A final comment is in order with regard to the internal accountability and thus legitimacy of German governance structures related to food safety. Following the BSE crisis in Germany, it was a report by the German court of auditors that came about with the cooperation of consumer groups, farmers, and ministry officials that proposed sweeping changes in the scope of governance. Many of these changes have been implemented, anticipating forthcoming developments at the EU and international levels (Codex Alimentarius). In this sense, it appears that Germany's federal system has, due to its reliance on consensus building, been successful in improving the legality, effectiveness, and contestation of German food safety regulations.

Notes

Funding was provided by the Volkswagen Foundation. The hospitality of the Department of Agricultural and Resource Economics, University of California, Berkeley, made this research possible. I gratefully acknowledge both.

1. See Loy and Steiner (2004) for a review of the history of the BSE crisis in Germany and an exploration of price-setting behavior in the beef supply chain

related to the 1996 BSE events. Fox and Peterson (2004) provide more detailed scientific background on BSE and a chronology across Europe.

2. The Health Ministry was, up to then, fully responsible for handling food safety issues.

3. "Throughout his book, North [1981] . . . argues that good institutions will simultaneously support private contracts and provide checks against expropriation by the government or other politically powerful groups. There is a growing consensus among economists and political scientists that the broad outlines of North's story are correct: the social, economic, legal and political organization of a society, i.e., its 'institutions,' are a primary determinant of economic activity." Acemoglu and Johnson (2003: 4).

4. In 2002, the sales of discounter Aldi alone grew by 16 percent (M+MEurodata 2003).

5. Organic share of total food production in 2000: 2.2 percent (Hamm, Gronefeld, and Halpin 2002).

6. As we know from information economics, there is a role for government intervention, since Hayek's (1945) fundamental insight into market efficiency only holds when markets operate in the absence of imperfect information. A more refined argument would also need to take account of trade and industrial organization issues, such as the observed increasing concentration in the German food industry. These issues raise new concerns related to multilevel governance. Issues related to credence attributes will be discussed below.

7. Evidence of this is found in Regulation (EC) No. 178/2002, which created the European Food Safety Authority and established traceability at all stages in the food marketing chain.

8. Both extrinsic quality attributes (e.g., "QS label") and intrinsic quality attributes (e.g., "organic") have an impact on the quality perception of consumers. Intrinsic quality dimensions include, therefore, process attributes that are not observable at the point of purchase and may thus lead to market failure (even from ex post observations, the buyer can never be certain of the quality of the services he or she purchased (Emons 1997)). The literature (Nelson 1970) has therefore differentiated credence attributes from experience attributes (whose utility is assessed after purchase by actual consumption) and search attributes (which can be determined by inspection without the need for consumption).

9. In this sense, the European Commission has opted for efficiency: the White Paper on Food safety promotes food safety standards and emphasizes that food safety is related to the attributes of the products, not to a specific method of production.

10. Persson et al. (1997) make this call for accountability and transparency very clear in their analysis of political accountability: "Another relevant problem is how to increase the accountability and transparency of decisions in the European Union: witness the handling of the mad-cow disease by the European Commission" (p 1199).

11. Scholars in other areas, for example finance, have argued that we can distinguish national systems of governance, as defined by their methods of decision making and the underlying balance of power (Albert 1993). Consider also that presidential and parliamentary democracies involve different incentive structures, informational asymmetries, and thus scope for abuse of power (Persson, Roland, and Tabellini 1997).

12. This is meant to include changes in information processes, such as changes in a newly regulated information exchange between local and federal ministries.

13. "Paradoxically the last of these is often the most independent and most powerful because of its capacity to combine each of the three regulatory functions of rule-making, monitoring and enforcement, without the involvement of any other organizations." (Scott 2003, 309).

14. Fox and Peterson (2004) also emphasize the importance of cross-contamination of feed, in mills, and on farms, which is difficult to detect because of a lack of reliable tests.

15. "The key feature of networks . . . is the way cooperation and trust are formed and sustained within networks. In contrast to either hierarchy or market, networks coordinate through less formal, more egalitarian and cooperative means." Thompson et al. (1991, 18).

16. See Libecap (1992) for early evidence of the interrelationship between these hierarchies, as they were shaping the first federal food quality guarantees in the United States (1887–1891).

17. See Fearne, Hornibrook, and Dedman (2001) for previous retailer-led beef quality assurance schemes in Germany.

18. Buzby, Frenzen, and Rasco (2001) consider the adverse consequences on firms that may result from market forces (reputation, market share, revenue), food safety regulations (penalties) and product liability law (legal and compensation expenses).

19. A quality management system is in place in the dairy industry. The objective of the dairy industry is to align it with the QS system.

20. Most of the following factual information originates from the official website of QS: <www.q-s.info/de.>

21. Auditors operate according to DIN 45011.

22. The board of trustees consists of twelve members. It is made up of academics, politicians, a union representative, a member from the German consumer association, and a representative from the sugar industry.

23. This point deserves further emphasis since German meat production, particularly of pork, is characterized by much smaller production units as compared to other European partners. The lack of large, homogeneous supplies is likely to lead to further competitive pressure, as German processors and retailers are likely to look beyond the German border as soon as others have adopted QS standards.

24. Key specifics of EUREPGAP are: transparency, recognition of existing schemes and programs via benchmarking, and an easy to adopt good agricultural practice protocol that is based on a master HACCP plan (no full HACCP exercise at the farm gate).

25. No judgment can be made regarding the actual status of infection; it is merely possible to judge whether an animal had contact with Salmonella in the past.

26. Also, in the wake of the 1996 BSE crisis in Germany, they appear to have been able to adopt a more consistent pricing strategy, as reflected in lower price variability (Loy and Steiner 2004).

27. Consider also that the German government does not intend to replace QS by any national set of regulations (BMVEL 2003).

28. See directive 2001/0176 (COD) and 2001/0177 (COD), as in COM(2003) 434, 16.7.2003.

29. EU Food Safety Law 178/2002 took effect on January 1, 2005.

30. Since January 2002, Dr. von Wedel has been a member of the European court of auditors.

31. Following the von Wedel report, a working group on the "reorganization of consumer health protection" was convened in the BMVEL and published its findings and proposals in December 2001 (BMVEL 2001).

32. "The assessment results will, in principle, be made publicly accessible whilst maintaining the confidentiality of protected data." (BfR 2003).

33. "Der BSE-Skandal markiert das Ende der Landwirtschaftspolitik alten Typs. In Zukunft hat der Verbraucherschutz in diesen sensiblen Bereichen der Agrar- und Ernährungspolitik Vorrang vor wirtschaftlichen Interessen." (Agrarbericht 2001).

34. Williamson (1998) differentiates governance structures in terms of their cost and competence.

35. "Es unterblieb eine umfassende interne Reorganisation, mit der Anliegen des gesundheitlichen Verbraucherschutzes entsprechend ihrer politischen Bedeutung gebündelt worden wären." (von Wedel, 2001; 27).

36. Aghion and Tirole (1997) focus on a moral hazard setting (agents can take actions that are unobserved to others) with costly monitoring, which appears most suited in the present context.

37. When it is inefficient to address market failures through tort liability, there is need for regulation.

38. Issues related to inadequate and asymmetric information (credence qualities) have been discussed above. Liability can be shared, in a hierarchy, or it can be shifted among agents, each of which has different efficiency implications. Sunding and Zilberman (1998) analyze the case of shifting liability among firms and consumers, when agents follow what are perceived to be reasonable actions that result in accidental injury.

39. With "tightened" liability it will be more feasible to sue with lower transaction costs. Further, the legal instruments will be more suited to provide deterrence, assuming that firms correctly anticipate the compensation that would be imposed by the legal rules (Viscusi 1989a). An improvement of liability rules along those lines will, through the reduction of transaction costs, help to ensure that a level of food safety is provided that is socially optimal. Consider that lower transaction costs may also be achieved through the court system itself, due to clearer liability rulings.

40. Viscusi and Magat (1992) discuss the conditions under which different types of information provision instruments are effective. Just et al. (2002) extend existing models of value of information by incorporating consideration of individuals' varying capacity to use differently formatted information and variation in their information needs.

41. The current refusal of the QS system to make the Salmonella status public could also be seen in this light: if the Salmonella status is disclosed, consumers could overestimate the uncertain outcome of contracting Salmonellosis with a certain probability. The level of meat demand would thus be suboptimal. However, a transparent system means also that scientists and the media have a role in transmitting the information to consumers such that these market failures can be averted.

42. See Unnevehr and Roberts (1997) for a discussion of cost-benefit analysis in the context of microbial food safety.

43. The precautionary principle asserts that uncertainty should never be used as a reason for postponing risk prevention efforts (Gollier 2001).

44. It is well known that it is important to account for the endogeneity of risk: consumers differ in their marginal productivity of self-protection (Ehrlich and Becker 1972, Shogren and Crocker 1999).

45. See Viscusi (1989b) for analyses that account explicitly for the relationship between consumers' perception of risk and actual risk.

IV

The European Dimension

9

Regulating Food Safety Risks in the European Union: A Comparative Perspective

Grace Skogstad

The desirability and safety of foods produced using the techniques of modern agriculture have provoked wide debate and controversy in the member states of the European Union (EU). Are milk and beef produced from animals injected with hormones safe? What about the genetically modified foods that are the products of plant biotechnology? And who should make the final decision on whether these products pose acceptable or unacceptable risks to human health? Over the past twenty years, the answers to these questions have divided European citizens from one another, pitted them against their governments, and forced European decision makers to reform food safety legislation and regulatory structures. EU regulations regarding beef hormones and GM crops and foods have also triggered trade disputes with Canada and the United States, where these same products have elicited far less controversy.

This chapter examines the contested governance of food safety regulation internal to the EU and across the North Atlantic as one rooted in conflict over the authoritative basis on which food safety should be regulated. This dimension of governance is arguably the most fundamental; other dimensions of governance—who should regulate food safety, where, and how—derive from conflict over the authoritative basis of regulation. Contestation over the authoritative basis of food safety regulation is conflict over the different priorities that should be assigned to scientific expertise, market incentives, and democratic norms in food safety rule making. It is therefore also conflict over who should regulate food safety: scientific experts, private firms, or politically responsive elected officials. And, further, it is controversy over where and how regulation should proceed: in regulatory agencies free of political interference, by self-regulating private actors, or in democratically accountable institutions. Insofar as these various dimensions of governance are interlinked, a widespread challenge to the legitimacy of the most fundamental dimension of rule making—its authoritative basis—is also a challenge, as the editors of this book observe, to "the legitimacy of existing institutional arrangements."

The discussion that follows documents the reality of contested governance in EU food safety regulation, seeks an explanation for it, and demonstrates why it has created transatlantic conflict. Consistent with theorizing in the Introduction to this book, it links contested governance in the EU to food safety scares, goals of market integration, the institutional framework of multilevel and dispersed decision making, and cultural beliefs about the role of science and technology in promoting public goods. Collectively this setting has led to a mediative food safety regulatory policy style to legitimize food safety regulation. This style combines strong democratic norms with a weaker belief in the authority of science and makes food safety regulation a process of consensus building across state and civil society actors. It differs from the Canadian and American food safety regulatory styles and constitutes a source of transatlantic tensions. Canada, and the United States on some issues, display a technocratic food safety regulatory policy style in which decisions are taken on the basis of technical expertise, largely free of the influence of civil society actors, and with their political implications denied. On other issues, the U.S. food safety regulatory style is one of adversarial legalism or private interest governance. The former describes a pattern of politicized regulatory policymaking with the courts playing a major role in its resolution; the latter, self-regulation by private firms with state oversight. As with the EU, the Canadian and American regulatory policy styles have their origins in each polity's institutional framework, historical experiences of food safety regulation, and cultural beliefs that equate science and technology with innovation, competitiveness, and public welfare.

The chapter begins with an elaboration of the concept of policy style and its distinguishing features. It then examines the three cases of the use of growth hormones in cattle, the injection of dairy cows with recombinant bovine somatotropin (rBST) to stimulate milk production, and the genetic modification of foods. These case studies reveal different degrees of policy contestation across issues and polities, and distinctive food safety regulatory policy styles. The conclusion assesses the implications of the findings for continuing contestation around food safety regulation.

Regulatory Policy Styles

The term *policy style* captures the central and distinguishing features of policymaking and implementation in various political systems (Richardson, Gustaffson, and Jordan 1982; Vogel 1986). In identifying the distinctive elements of a policy style, Richardson, Gustaffson, and Jordan (1982) uncover the "legitimising norms for political activity" as these are reflected in the pattern of relations among state actors and between state and nonstate actors. Insofar as legitimate rule making rests on the perception that the exercise of political authority is proper and appropriate, an important constitutive element of a policy style is its authoritative rule-making principles and institutions. Given that legitimation standards are a "socially constructed system of norms, values, and beliefs" (Suchman 1995, 574), authoritative principles and procedures recognized as legitimate in one society may not be similarly regarded elsewhere.

Principles of Authoritative Rule Making

Regulating food safety risks is foremost an exercise in protecting public health and safety. It entails assessing the hazards to human health posed, for example, by a food additive, a contaminant such as a veterinary drug residue, or a new production process—a process known as *risk assessment*—and deciding how to manage those hazards—a process known as *risk management*. In all modern societies, risk assessment relies on scientific knowledge and methods of inquiry. Science is the traditional and internationally recognized basis of authority in food safety regulation; international law requires food safety measures to be based on scientific principles and scientific evidence. Notwithstanding that risk assessment is an inexact science—scientists can and do interpret the same data differently—the authority of science derives from a belief that its methods yield disinterested and neutral knowledge. Providing it protects citizens from hazardous food products *and* citizens believe in the neutrality of scientists and the fact-finding quality of scientific methods, science-based regulation retains legitimacy.

When these assumptions are challenged, scientific knowledge and methods of inquiry cease to be an exclusive legitimation basis for risk assessment and risk management. Relying solely on scientific knowledge to regulate food safety risks is likely to be politically contentious in the instance of novel food products and technologies because, at least in their early stages of production, there will be scientific uncertainty regarding their human health and and other effects. To the extent that scientific knowledge is perceived to be uncertain, there will be pressure for adoption of a precautionary approach that obliges governments to act prudentially to avoid risks to human health and safety. Thus, for example, in 1960 the United States inserted the Delaney Clause into the Federal Food, Drug, and Cosmetic Act (FFDCA). It prohibited food additives that were found to cause cancer in experimental animals or humans, despite many scientists' belief that low doses of these additives were not harmful to humans. New food products and technologies raise other issues that include their socioeconomic impacts and sometimes, their ethical implications. How, if at all, should these extrascientific considerations be factored into food safety regulation? This question suggests two other bases of authority as potentially legitimate underpinnings for food safety risk management: democratic processes of representative and participatory government and market mechanisms and incentives.

When science is the basis of authoritative rule making, those who exercise influence on regulatory outcomes possess scientific expertise: normally government regulators and developers of the technology or product being regulated. Even so, strong democratic norms of transparency and accountability usually require that regulatory governance by technical experts include opportunities for public participation, that regulators give reasons for their decisions, and that measures exist to prevent abuse of technical or administrative discretion. Food safety risk regulation based on democratic norms and processes goes even further in vesting authority in citizens and their elected governments. Regulatory procedures and outcomes that rely on democratic processes derive their legitimacy from adhering to democratic procedural norms like transparency, public input, and government accountability. In addition, policy outcomes reflect majority preferences, and elected politicians take responsibility for regulatory decisions and are directly accountable to their electorate for risk management.

Vesting regulatory authority in market mechanisms and incentives is a third potential basis for food safety regulation. Having established (often minimalist) regulations or guidelines for the conduct of private firms, government regulators take a back-seat role to "the market," which then decides the effectiveness of regulations or guidelines to secure efficient and effective policy outcomes. Market-based regulation leaves private firms with responsibility for food safety, subject to the oversight, albeit often remote, of public authorities. State (elected and appointed) and civil society actors have much less influence over policy outcomes than they do in regulatory governance based on democratic norms and processes. To be perceived as legitimate, industry self-regulation must be seen to serve the public interest, for example, by maximizing material benefits and consumer choice.

These three principles of authoritative rule making—or more accurately, the combination of them—are an important constitutive feature of a food safety regulatory policy style.[1] Which principle dominates is contingent on a number of factors, including the institutional framework within which food safety regulatory policies are formulated and implemented, as well as a society's collective historical experiences and cultural beliefs.

The Institutional and Legal Context

Formal and informal organizations, rules, and practices define who can participate in rule making, the resources needed to be influential, and the rules (majoritarian or unanimity) employed to make decisions. Institutional frameworks that offer few access points to nonstate actors and concentrate decision-making authority in bureaucratic officials in a single ministry, and who are armed with policy expertise, lend themselves to a technocratic regulatory policy style. Decision makers have little need to accommodate a broad range of interests or to rely on nonstate actors for their expertise.

Food safety regulation in Canada comes closest to meeting the requirements for a technocratic regulatory policy style even though the
Canadian institutional framework does not concentrate decision-making
authority with respect to food safety in a single ministry. Health Canada
sets food safety standards and administers regulations pursuant to the
Food and Drugs Act that are aimed at preventing the production or sale
of dangerous products. However, it is not responsible for the enforcement of food safety standards and guidelines; that task, through inspection, for example, is dispersed across ministries and agencies of the two
orders of government. The framework facilitates a technocratic regulatory policy style because officials within Health Canada do their work
generally free of parliamentary pressure.

Providing they have sufficient in-house expertise, Health Canada officials also have considerable potential to be independent of civil society
actors, even if they normally have a cooperative relationship with regulated actors (Harrison and Hoberg 1994, Turner 2001). Food safety regulation is based on scientific data, which Health Canada has possessed
in-house, at least until government-imposed financial constraints, since
the mid-1990s (Moore 2000; chapter 2).

Institutional frameworks that disperse rule-making authority across a
plurality of weakly coordinated and poorly resourced state actors do not
lend themselves to technocratic rule making. They are more open to nonstate actors who become allies for state actors hungry for their policy
expertise, financial backing, and political support. This institutional
framework is said to characterize U.S. legislative and policy implementation processes and result in a regulatory policy style of adversarial
legalism (Harrison and Hoberg 1994). Adversarial legalism as applied to
policy implementation (none of the three issues under discussion entailed
new legislation) captures the possible politicization that results from congressional oversight and judicial review of the Food and Drug Administration's (FDA) implementation of the major food safety statute, the
FFDCA. Although the concentration of rule-making authority in the
FDA can give rise to technocratic rule making on noncontroversial regulatory matters, Congress is likely to use its authority to call public hearings and request investigations when regulations become politically
salient. Further, statutory provisions require formal notice and comment

procedures on proposed regulations and allow administrative appeals and citizen petitions. These institutional features give American citizens ample opportunities "to intervene in administrative proceedings, to question the expert judgements of government agencies, and ultimately to force changes in policy through litigation" (Jasanoff 1986, 56).

Not captured by this formal institutional framework is the American reliance on strong private liability laws to regulate market transactions. American food developers are legally responsible for ensuring that foods are safe and comply with safety standards. They are expected to undertake premarketing testing, as prescribed by FDA regulations and in accordance with scientific protocols and procedures, and present these data to FDA to confirm the safety of a new food additive. However, foods that are "generally recognized as safe" are exempt from FDA's regulatory premarket approval. This legal framework lends itself to a regulatory style of private interest governance.

The institutional framework of food safety regulation in the EU—dispersed policymaking authority across member states and EU institutions as well as unanimity or supermajority decision-making rules—necessitates a consensual, mediative regulatory policy style. Democratic decision-making procedures are imperative in this "polity under construction," which is constantly required to justify the growing authority of EU-level institutions. The European Commission has the sole right to initiate and draft legislation. Much foodstuff legislation is designed to harmonize differences in member state legislation that threaten a single internal market in which products circulate freely. Its passage requires agreement between the Council of Ministers and the European Parliament. Until 1987 (throughout the debate on the safety of beef hormones), Parliament could only delay legislation; the Council of Ministers could pass legislation without its consent. The implementation of the Single European Act in 1987 gave the EU legal authority to protect the health of member state citizens and their rights as consumers. It also increased Parliament's legislative powers (on the 1990 legislation to regulate GM products and the early policy responses to rBST milk). The Council of Ministers could ignore parliamentary amendments only by unanimity among its member states. If it incorporated parliamentary amendments into a revised legislative proposal, then only a qualified majority of the council was needed to pass the legislation. The passage of the Treaty on the European Union in 1992 gave Parliament codecision powers in public health, consumer protection, and environment legislation. As refined in the Treaty of Amsterdam (implemented in May 1999), the codecision procedure means that if an absolute majority of the Parliament and a qualified majority of the Council of Ministers (sixty-two of eight-seven votes) fail to agree on legislation, including on amendments proposed by either body, the legislation dies. A Council of Ministers committed to new legislation (on regulating GM products) thus has strong incentives to take Parliament's views into account.

This framework of multiple state actors provides multiple access channels for nonstate actors and is sensitive to consumer interests. The Treaty of Amsterdam states that a high level of consumer protection should be integrated into all EU policies, an obligation that the European Parliament has championed (Pollack 1997).

The consensus building necessary for the passage of legislation carries over to the administration of legislation. It requires agreement among member state representatives in regulatory committees of the European Commission. The high thresholds of agreement for new legislation and its implementation lead to food safety policy outcomes that are not dictated by scientific considerations. Although historically the European Commission sought the advice of scientific committees in regulatory decision making, it reserved the right to take into consideration nonscientific factors, including consumers' expectations (Hankin 1997).

History and Culture

Historical experiences of food safety regulation and cultural attitudes toward science and risk also affect food safety regulatory policy styles. Science-based, technocratic regulation presupposes faith and trust in science to solve regulatory problems, including those posed by the risks of new technologies. So does private interest governance when the rationale for self-regulation is based on private firms' possession of requisite technical expertise. North Americans appear to possess such a faith in science and regard it as yielding universal and objective facts that provide the basis for impartial regulatory decisions (Isaac 2002, Jasanoff 1995). They also place "strong faith in the ability to manage risk, either by technical means or through compensation" (Gaskell et al. 2001, 101).

Compared to North Americans, Europeans in general appear to have less faith in science and to be less willing to rely on it to provide policy solutions. Survey data show a deterioration over time in Europeans' faith in the ability of science to produce benefits, with the preponderant view being that science and technology are not "a panacea" and should be subject to "social control" (Eurobarometer 2001, 30, 37). The EU's constitutional endorsement of the precautionary principle (in the 1997 Treaty of Amsterdam) at a time when the United States appears to be moving away from it is evidence of different understandings of science in North America and Europe (Jasanoff 2003, Vogel 2003). A precautionary approach assumes that expert knowledge provides "only a partial characterisation of possible hazards" and gives credence to the views of lay citizens (Jasanoff 2003, 229). It leads to a European regulatory approach in which science is not "an absolute truth" but provides political officials only with "knowledge with a confidence interval" on which to make risk management decisions (Haniotis 2000; see also Commission of the European Communities 2000a, 2000b).

Different transatlantic experiences of regulatory policy success and failure at risk management have undoubtedly contributed to the greater European skepticism of science-based regulation. Ulrich Beck (1992, 1999) argues that Europeans' experiences with regulatory failures that have created environmental disasters have caused public attitudes toward science and technology to change dramatically. He argues that a risk society has developed characterized by a loss of faith in scientists and scientific evidence to provide answers on how to deal with the hazards that are the by-products of modern industrial society. Others point to food safety and health scares—the BSE crisis, dioxin-contaminated poultry feed, tainted blood in France—that have discredited government regulators and the scientific experts on whom they relied to protect public health. The BSE crisis in particular undermined the idea of scientists as "objective" and "independent" (Joerges and Neyer 1997, 612). Scientific experts who had advised the European Commission on BSE were blamed for jeopardizing human health by underplaying the nature and severity of the crisis, and governments were seen as a party to this duplicity (Chambers 1999, Eurobarometer 2001).

The significance of these regulatory failures is their effect of undermining the legitimacy of technocratic styles of regulatory policymaking at both the national and EU levels (Majone 2000). Restoring regulatory credibility requires not simply better and more independent science. It requires that decision makers embrace forms of regulatory governing that encompass democratic criteria of accountability, transparency, and public participation.

Regulating the Risks of Hormone-Fed Beef

The safety concerns raised by injecting bovine animals with hormones to stimulate their growth are that residues of these hormones will remain in the meat of these animals and pose a hazard to human health. At issue were three hormones that occur naturally in animals and two that are synthetically produced.

In the United States and Canada, approval of the growth-promoting hormones was a routine decision, taken by the responsible administrative officials in Health Canada and the FDA. The application by the developer of the hormone products was confidential until the approval process was completed. The North American institutional framework of delegated agency responsibility, confidentiality of information pertinent to the approval of veterinary drugs, and exclusive reliance on scientific data as a basis of regulatory approval depoliticized the regulatory decision. The result was a technocratic regulatory policy style.

Such depoliticization of the approval of hormones was impossible in the EU regulatory system. The issue unfolded in the early 1980s against a decade-old backdrop of considerable consumer concern about the illegal use of a growth hormone in veal production in France and Italy and in an institutional setting that was porous to mobilized interests. This context required mediation of state and societal interests and resulted in lower priority being assigned to scientific knowledge than to consumer interests and broader political and economic objectives of market integration through harmonized food safety standards across member states.

In 1980, the European Commission prohibited the administration to farm animals of several hormones, except for therapeutic purposes, and the subsequent marketing of meat from animals treated with these hormones. Directive 81/602/EEC excluded the five growth-promoting hormones from the ban, pending examination of their effects on human health and the adoption of an EC rule. The Council of (Agriculture) Ministers, where the decision would ultimately be taken to ban the growth hormones, was divided. Some of its member countries had banned all or some of the hormones, while others had approved some of them. The scientific advice that the European Commission solicited determined that the three naturally occurring hormones posed no harm to human health, but that further data were needed to determine the effects of the two synthetic hormones. In the light of this scientific advice, the commission proposed the controlled use of the three natural hormones for growth promotion purposes and reexamining the ban on the two synthetic hormones on completion of their scientific evaluation.

The proposal was immediately opposed by the European Parliament and the Council of Ministers. The European Parliament, which had the power to delay but not block the proposed legislation, took up the cause of consumer groups who opposed legalizing the use of beef hormones. Faced with this concerted opposition, the European Commission reversed its position and, contrary to scientific advice, proposed a ban on the use of the growth-promotion hormones. The Council of Ministers accepted the commission's proposal on December 31, 1985, offering multiple reasons for doing so. As defined in Directive 88/146/EEC, a ban would protect public health and safety; harmonize member states' regulations regarding the hormones; through harmonization, end the distortions in intracommunity competition and trade in animals and meat from hormone-injected animals; and bring about an increase in beef production by assuaging consumer anxieties. In justifying the ban to their irate North American counterparts, whose hormone-fed beef was blocked from entering the EU, European officials and politicians elaborated the balance of democracy and science in food safety regulation. The agriculture commissioner, Franz Andriessen, stated that "scientific advice is important, but it is not decisive. In public opinion, this is a very delicate issue that has to be dealt with in political terms" (quoted in Vogel 1995, 158).

Regulating the Risks of rBST Milk

Approval of a drug to stimulate milk production in lactating cows, recombinant bovine somatrotropin (rBST), was controversial in Canada, the United States, and the EU. Concerns centered on the drug's potential harm to the cows into which it was injected and to human beings who drank their milk. The adverse effects on dairy cows included the possibility of an increased incidence of infected udders and various reproductive problems. The human health concerns were rBST's possible link to breast cancer and premature growth in infants. Scientific reviewers in Canada and the United States found no ill human health effects, while reviewers in the EU did not rule out their possibility. Reviewers in all three countries agreed that animal health data showed statistically and biologically significant animal ill health effects. American regulators judged that these potential risks were manageable by individual dairy farmers; Canadian and EU regulators came to the opposite conclusion and banned the hormone. An important additional dimension to the debate was whether socioeconomic considerations should play a role in the regulatory decision.

United States

The 1993 decision by the FDA to approve an application from Monsanto to license Prosilac (rBST) was preceded and followed by political controversy. Farm, consumer, rural advocacy, and food policy groups opposed rBST, as did legislators from major dairy-producing states who worried its use would drive small farmers out of the dairy sector by resulting in the overproduction of milk and undermining government price supports. Consumer groups threatened to boycott milk from cows given the hormone if the drug were approved. Prior to its approval, Congress held hearings on the potential impact of the drug. Even after the drug was approved, senators from dairy states persuaded Congress to impose a ninety-day moratorium on the first sales of the product. Congressional representatives pursued conflict-of-interest allegations against FDA employees with an association with Monsanto, and they requested the General Accounting Office to investigate the mandatory drug trials and report on human health effects. The U.S. Center for Food Safety and two dozen other consumer groups petitioned the FDA to reverse its authorization decision (Mills 2002).

In approving the product, the FDA adhered to its narrow statutory remit. It resisted pressures to consider the economic consequences of the drug. Instead, it sought to assuage consumer and congressional concern by actively promoting the human safety of rbst (Gibbons 1990). It also rejected a request that rBST milk be labeled. Because there were no significant differences between rBST and non-rBST milk, the FDA argued that labeling would be misleading and in violation of laws that preclude labeling other than for health reasons. Its 1994 guidelines recommended that dairies not be obliged to inform consumers whether cows are treated with rBST.

The courts also played a role in rBST regulation. When Vermont introduced mandatory labeling of rBST milk, it was challenged by a coalition of food producers. In *International Dairy Foods Association v. Amestoy* (1996), the court ruled illegal the mandatory labeling, stating that the U.S. Constitution protects the right to silence as well as to speech. From the perspective of the court, the violation of this right was not justified by the intent to ensure consumers' right to know.

Canada

The debate touched off by Monsanto's 1990 application to license rBST in Canada was similar in many respects to that which unfolded in the United States. Dairy farmers, dairy processors, environmentalists, and consumers mobilized against rBST, similarly concerned about its health effects and socioeconomic consequences for Canadian farmers. An additional dimension to the Canadian debate was the schism among regulatory authorities within Health Canada over the drug's safety and the integrity of the regulatory process itself. Some officials publicly alleged that Health Canada was under pressure from drug sponsors to approve the drug. In addition, scientists who had not been involved in the human health review spoke out publicly that there was insufficient evidence on which to base the 1990 decision that the drug posed no human health risks (Mills 2002, Turner 2001).

Public mobilization around the extrascientific (including socioeconomic) concerns raised by rBST led two parliamentary committees to hold hearings on the impacts of the drug on dairy farming in Canada. Over sixty organizations and individuals, representing dairy farmers, dairy processors, consumers, government departments, and the companies producing rBST, appeared before the committees. In keeping with the request of dairy farmers who were concerned about consumer reaction to milk from rBST cows, the House of Commons committee recommended a moratorium on its use. The Canadian government then negotiated with rBST manufacturers a one-year moratorium on its sale. However, the government rejected another committee recommendation to investigate the socioeconomic effects of rBST. Possible socioeconomic effects, it stated, were not a regulatory criterion "because these factors could pre-empt decisions based on safety, and effectiveness" (quoted in Mills 2002, 89).

In 1995, Health Canada declined Monsanto's application for licensing rBST, citing flaws in its experimental design. Controversy continued, most of it from within Health Canada, regarding the regulatory approval procedures and the earlier finding that rBST produced no adverse human health problems. The Canadian Senate called hearings to investigate the rBST evaluation process, and the government commissioned two external expert panels to review the bureau's decisions on human and animal safety. The two external panels produced findings consistent with the eventual 1999 decision of Health Canada regulators not to approve rBST.

European Union

In 1990, the Council of Ministers imposed a one-year ban on the use of rBST, pending completion of scientific studies on the hormone's quality, safety, and efficacy. Socioeconomic considerations were a factor in the decision, as were worries about the cohesion of the single market (Brinckman 2000). The possibility that some member states might authorize rBST while others did not created the prospect of both a rise in milk production when there was already a surplus and a disruption of the common milk market. Further, because the drug was expensive, there was worry that it would be used disproportionately by agribusiness, thereby undermining the competitive position of small-volume dairy farmers and hastening the long-term consolidation of the dairy farm sector (Vogel 1995, Cherfas 1990).

The initial one-year ban was extended in 1991 and 1992. In early 1993, the European Commission's scientific committee, the Committee of Veterinary Medicinal Products (CVMP), advised that rBST posed no health risks to either humans or animals. Nonetheless, the Commission proposed continuing the moratorium on the marketing of rBST, arguing its right (in exceptional cases) to take into account criteria other than those of quality, safety, and efficiency when deciding on a possible authorization of veterinary medicinal products. It referred to possible consumer reactions to rBST and possible negative impacts on the milk quotas used to maintain farm incomes within the dairy sector. It also stressed that the prohibition of rBST would be a purely internal EU matter since imports of rBST dairy products to the European Union were unaffected. In line with the European Commission's proposal, in December 1993 the Council of Ministers extended the moratorium on the grounds that it needed further time to examine all the implications of rBST for the EU (Brinckman 2000).

Before the expiration of the moratorium in 1999, two scientific committees concluded that the product had an adverse impact on animal welfare and was associated with a higher-than-normal incidence of adverse effects on dairy cows' health. Another scientific committee raised concerns about gaps in the knowledge of its effects on human health. When the European Commission referred these reports about the adverse animal health and welfare effects of rBST to the CVMP and asked it to review its 1993 opinion, the CVMP confirmed its previous opinion that the substance was safe. Even so, citing scientific findings of adverse animal welfare and health effects, the commission proposed, and the Council of Ministers agreed to, a permanent ban on rBST effective January 1, 2000.

Comparing rBST Regulatory Policy Styles

The public controversy and legislative scrutiny that surrounded rBST did not affect American and Canadian regulators' decisions. They were based only on the evaluation of scientific evidence relating to rBST's safety. Pressures by legislators (in Canada) and organized interests (in both Canada and the United States) to consider the social and economic impact of rBST were not addressed and not a factor in the regulatory decision. However, they were in the EU and appear to have been an important ingredient in the regulatory decision.

As with the Canadian beef hormone issue, the Canadian regulatory policy style is one of technocratic regulation. Throughout the nine-year regulatory approval process, top-level officials in the bureau tried to keep their review immune from external influence. They consulted primarily with the manufacturer and provided only minimal cooperation with the parliamentary committees and government-appointed task force (Turner 2001). Their final decision was based solely on their interpretation of scientific evidence regarding the drug's effects on cows and was oblivious to the extrascientific concerns the product raised. The U.S. regulatory policy style conforms to "adversarial legalism": state and nonstate actors squared off with one another, and the courts ultimately had a role to play in the labeling of rBST products. In the EU, a mediative policy style was evident, as divisions across state and nonstate actors were resolved in the optimal solution of a regulatory ban.

Regulating Genetically Modified Foods

Genetically modified (GM) foods are the products of plant biotechnology and are produced from organisms in which the genetic material has been altered in a way that does not occur naturally by mating or natural recombination. Most GM crops have been modified for insect resistance or herbicide tolerance. They raise environmental and human health issues, the latter including increased allergenicity, toxicity, and antibiotic resistance.

United States
In the mid-1980s the Office of the U.S. President made the decision to regulate biotechnology products and processes under existing statutes (the FFDCA) and institutional arrangements (United States 1984). This decision was based on the FDA's belief that GM food is "substantially equivalent" to a conventionally produced food that is "generally recognized as safe." It did not therefore require special legislation to regulate it (Jasanoff 1995). Because Congress took little interest in GM food and

no new legislation was introduced specific to the regulation of plant biotechnology, the opportunities that the legislative process allows for public debate were foreclosed. The decision not to introduce legislation specific to GM crops and foods was also governed by the belief that plant biotechnology was an innovative technology that would give U.S. agriculture a competitive edge internationally. The regulatory task therefore was and is to "balance protecting and informing the public with encouraging innovation" and to "find solutions that will ensure the safety of the food supply, but will not stifle innovation of new technologies" (Ronk et al. 1990).

The resulting regulatory process left biotechnology developers with major responsibility to ensure the safety of GM foods, subject to weak oversight of government regulators. A 1992 FDA guidance encouraged, but did not require, industry to engage in "voluntary consultations" with the FDA regarding potential safety concerns of new plant varieties intended for food use prior to releasing them on to the market.[2] It stated that U.S. manufacturers of GM products have the legal duty to ensure the foods they market are safe and comply with legal requirements, thereby requiring them to internalize food safety risks "because a safety risk quickly becomes a commercial crisis" (Isaac 2002, 190). The guidance document further clarified that GM foods would not be labeled to indicate their method of production.

Controversy around GM products' regulation has surfaced recently. Public interest organizations representing consumers and environmentalists criticize the adequacy of the scientific underpinnings of regulatory decisions. Since disclosure of safety data is voluntary, critics charge that the FDA has had difficulty obtaining scientific data from developers to evaluate GM foods and that biotechnology firms supply additional requested data to FDA only about half of the time (Fabi 2003). The non-labeling of GM products, a policy intended to avoid their discrimination, is also increasingly a source of consumer criticism. Public opinion data show that large numbers of Americans want GM food to be labeled as such (National Science Board 2002). Notably, however, those who question the benefits of plant biotechnology or turn away from its products are a decided minority.

Canada

Canada also relied on existing statutes and procedures to regulate plant biotechnology products. Health Canada's 1994 *Guidelines for the Safety Assessment of Novel Foods* stipulated that the safety of biotechnology products would be appraised using the same procedures that applied to all products with "novel traits": products without a history of safe use in Canada or that have been altered to cause some significant change in the food's properties. As in the United States, premarket approval for each GM product was seen to be overly onerous and unnecessary. Nor are GM foods labeled as such. However, unlike in the United States, developers of novel foods must notify Health Canada regulators in advance of their marketing. This regulatory framework was guided by the desire to promote innovation and, through it, international competitiveness. An additional concern was to harmonize Canadian GM regulatory policies with internationally accepted standards (Moore 2000).

The Canadian government's decision to rely on existing legislation to regulate GM foods and plants meant that no wide public or parliamentary debate surrounded their introduction in Canada. The government did take efforts to solicit organized interests' views. The 1994 guidelines were preceded by a 1993 "multistakeholder" workshop that included consumer and industry representatives, and a second 1994 workshop was devoted to the issue of labeling GM foods. However, critics charged that neither workshop considered issues beyond the safety of GM foods, ignoring their social, economic, and ethical dimensions (Abergel and Barrett 2002).

Until the late 1990s, there was little public controversy around GM foods and certainly nothing on the European scale (see below). Criticism focuses on the lack of labeling of GM foods, the scientific integrity of the regulatory process, and the failure to take into account nonscientific considerations in approving GM products. With regard to labeling, public opinion polls consistently show that Canadians would prefer mandatory labeling of GM foods. A parliamentary committee held hearings on the issue, and a government backbench member of Parliament introduced a mandatory labeling motion. Although the latter initiative failed, a government-appointed advisory body has produced voluntary labeling guidelines with respect to GM foods. With regard to its scientific foundation, an Expert Panel of the Royal Society of Canada, commissioned by the government of Canada, found significant deficiencies in existing risk regulation procedures and argued they did not warrant Canadians' confidence (Royal Society of Canada 2001). A second government advisory body also concluded that more scientific rigor and transparency were needed (Canadian Biotechnology Advisory Committee 2002). However, both advisory bodies stressed there is no evidence that GM foods approved to date are unsafe.

European Union
Unlike Canada and the United States, the EU passed legislation specific to the regulation of GM crops and food. The 1990 Directive 90/220/EEC established procedures for the approval of GM crops and foods for release into the environment and onto the EU market. The Novel Foods Regulation (258/97/EC) was adopted in 1997 and specified approval and labeling requirements for foods containing or derived from genetically modified organisms. This regulatory framework has recently been updated with a new directive (Directive 2001/18/EC; see Commission of the European Communities 2001b) and new regulations regarding the approval, labeling, and traceability of GM products, including foods (Regulation 1829/2003/EC and 1830/2003/EC; see Commission of the European Communities 2003a, 2003b).

The new regulatory framework, fully effective April 2004, differs in several significant respects from that in North America. Provisions in earlier EU legislation that require GM foods and crops to undergo mandatory case-by-case risk assessments prior to their licensing are retained. Scientific risk assessments must be released to the public, which also has the right to be consulted prior to commercial release of GM products. The simplified authorization procedure in the 1997 Novel Food Regulation for GM foods considered to be "substantially equivalent" to existing foods—and which continues to prevail in the United States and Canada—is abandoned. Traceability provisions will allow GM food to be tracked through all stages of production, processing, and marketing. Comprehensive mandatory labeling provisions will clearly identify products containing and derived from genetically modified organisms (GMOs), even when the GMO cannot be detected

(Commission of the European Communities, 2003a, 2003b). And, as before, risk management—the final decision as to whether to authorize a GMO or GM product—is left to political authorities, not independent regulators or the developer.[3]

This admittedly onerous regulatory framework reflects a more than decade-long effort to resolve the high degree of political contestation that has surrounded GM products since the mid-1980s. The controversy over the terms under which GM products should be regulated has put member states at odds with one another, driven a line of cleavage through the European Commission, and cast biotechnology companies against consumers and environmentalists. The various plant biotechnology legislative initiatives are efforts to resolve this conflict, even while promoting treaty goals of establishing an internal common market free of interstate trade barriers.

The initial piece of GM legislation, Directive 90/220/EEC, attempted to forestall initiatives by member states to regulate biotechnology by establishing harmonized, EU-wide procedures for the release of GM products into the environment and onto the market (Cantley 1995, Commission of the European Communities 1990). Its rigorous and cumbersome features owed themselves to the context of the mid- to late 1980s: pervasive public unease over biotechnology, an environmental movement leery of the technology and sufficiently organized to wield considerable political influence (Gottweis 1999), and a European Commission sharply divided between those who wanted to promote plant biotechnology and those who wanted strict GM-specific legislation. The latter won out when the directorate-general responsible for the environment gained control over the initiation of GM legislation in 1986. The European Parliament also played a decisive role, despite its limited legislative powers. It championed a narrowly defeated motion to ban the commercial release of GM crops until binding Community-wide safety directives were drawn up (Cantley 1995).

The controversy inside the European Commission and across member states that had plagued Directive 90/220/EEC did not die away. In 1996, the commission used its legal authority to approve a GM maize and GM soya, despite strong public mobilization against the products. The commission's action was condemned by the European Parliament. Three member states prohibited the import and use of the GM maize in their countries, invoking the Treaty of Rome's "safeguard clause," which allows market restrictions on a product believed to constitute a danger to the health and safety of citizens (Barling 1997). Legislation specific to GM foods and food products was equally contested. The European Commission first proposed a regulation for the voluntary labeling of novel foods and novel food ingredients—including genetically modified—in 1992. Five years later the Novel Foods Regulation (258/97/EEC) was adopted. It had been delayed by consumer and environmental sympathizers in the European Parliament and the Council of Ministers who sought compulsory labeling (Barling 1996). The political compromise struck in the 1997 regulation failed to cover the labeling of all GM food products and prompted a series of additional regulations.

The most recent legislation represents the latest attempt to reconcile the internal tensions over GM foods and crops. Public opposition to GM products reached a new peak following the arrival of the first imports of GM products (soybeans) in Europe in 1996. The public turned overwhelmingly against genetically modified products and demanded that they be distinguished from non-GMO products for regulatory purposes (Eurobarometer 2001). Reacting to consumer concerns, over the period 1996 to 1999 European food processors and distributors removed GM soybeans from their products, and grocery retailers, processors, and caterers began providing GM-free products. Some member states reacted to the environmental and consumer opposition to GM crops and food by invoking the safeguard clause and not licensing GM products in their country. Others refused to approve applications for GMO release until the regulations were revised to take into account skeptics' concerns. In June 1999, the Council of Environmental Ministers halted any new GMO approvals pending reform of Directive 90/220/EC. Agreeing on legislation to end this de facto moratorium and reestablish the internal market in GM crops and foods has been difficult and has required considerable consensus building and compromise (Skogstad 2003).

Comparing GM Food Regulatory Policy Styles

Like the substance of the regulations themselves, GM food regulatory policy styles diverge sharply across the North Atlantic. The United States displays a situation of private interest governance: delegation of regulatory authority to private firms and reliance on strong liability laws to achieve public goals of safe food. It is rendered more legitimate by reliance on experts, whether federal regulators or the risk assessment personnel of GM developers, to perform the "hypothetical risk assessments" (Isaac 2002, 187). The U.S. regulatory style gives the public little opportunity to participate in decisions relevant to commercial marketing of GM foods and requires little public accountability from government regulators (Zweifel 2002). In Canada, a technocratic regulatory style prevails: "Participation in the regulatory decision-making process is narrow and judicious, in that it is limited to traditional actors and experts" (Isaac 2002, 199). Citizens, consumers, and environmental groups have historically had little access to the opaque decision-making process.

The regulatory style that characterizes EU-level regulation of GM foods has evolved from the early to mid-1990s when deliberations over whether to authorize the marketing of GMOs and GMO-derived products were confidential, officials gave only perfunctory explanations for their decisions, and interest groups were denied the possibility of judicial review of officials' in camera decisions (Hunter 1999). This technocratic regulatory style lost legitimacy and precipitated a legislative process and a GM regulatory framework consistent with a mediative regulatory policy style of consensus building across state and societal actors (Skogstad 2003).

Conclusion

The contested governance that characterizes regulation of the products of modern agriculture in the EU, and which knows no North American parallel, is best understood as political contestation over a core dimension of governance: the basis or authoritative principles of rule making. In a context of multilevel governance, construction of an internal common market, and supranational (EU) institutions with fragile legitimacy, resolving this fundamental conflict has required that democratic norms be given a high priority and scientific expertise a lower priority than in North American food safety regulation. The resulting policy outcomes—on hormone-fed beef and genetically modified products—have.

This response of the EU to contested food safety governance has clearly created transatlantic tensions, which bilateral diplomacy has failed to resolve. Multilateral trade dispute bodies have come up short as well. And yet, as observed in the Introduction to this book, the problem will not go away. Food safety regulation and trade liberalization are linked, and science-based risk assessment has become the authoritative basis for mitigating the trade impacts of distinctive food safety regulatory regimes. What, then, are the prospects that the EU will converge on science-based risk assessment or that North America will move away from it to embrace the more comprehensive framework of the EU?

Legislative and institutional reforms in the EU have fortified the role of scientific expertise in food safety regulation. These reforms include a permanent European Food Safety Authority, staffed with independent scientists whose advice must be solicited in food safety regulation. (See chapter 11, this volume.) EFSA's mandate enhances the possibility that scientific expertise as a basis for food safety regulation will become more legitimate and, further, that EU regulatory policy decisions will be analogous to those in Canada or the United States.

In North America, although mobilized segments of the public have not been as concerned about the safety of GM products as their European counterparts, they have been and continue to be unhappy with regulatory principles that approve products solely on the basis of scientific evidence as to their safety. Critics have argued that "nonscientific" criteria, like the social, economic, and ethical consequences of novel foods and food additives, should have a legitimate role in food safety regulation. To date, they have not become politically salient, but were they to do so, they would be a catalyst to a regulatory framework like that in the EU, which is not solely science based.

The possibility of transatlantic convergence around the authoritative principles and institutions of food safety regulation should not be minimized. However, as revealed in this chapter and observed in this book's opening chapter, food safety regulation in the EU is embedded in broader goals and controversies about European integration. This context necessitates that primacy be given to democratic norms of decision making and ensures, at least for the short term, that risk management will remain formally with accountable politicians, not with arm's-length administrators or private companies as in North America. EU food safety regulation is also embedded in EU law and treaty provisions, which include consumers' right to know and the application of the precautionary principle when there is scientific uncertainty about the risks of a food. Although WTO litigation may yet restrict the scope of the precautionary principle (see chapter 13, this volume), its potential as a continuing source of transatlantic policy divergence—and conflict—in the near future cannot be dismissed.

Notes

1. This conceptualization draws on Renn's (1995) distinction among different styles of using scientific expertise.

2. The FDA reports that no GM products have been approved for commercial use without FDA consultation. Firms consult the FDA in order to minimize their liability risk. In 2001, the FDA issued a proposed rule that would convert the current voluntary premarket notification system for GM foods into a mandatory requirement for the submission of safety data and related information 120 days prior to marketing. The proposed rule would mean that GM foods could not be marketed without a favorable response from the FDA. As of August 2005, the FDA had not taken action to issue a final rule.

3. A qualified majority in the Council of Ministers can adopt or reject a European Commission proposal to authorize a GM product.

10

Food Safety and the Single European Market

Alberto Alemanno

The recent food safety crises that have outraged Europe probably constituted the most serious challenge to the European integration process during its first fifty years of existence. These food scandals dramatically showed the inadequacy of the way in which food laws are created and implemented by the European Community (EC) institutions and the member states, highlighting the complexity of the European system of governance and the limits of its functionalist approach to integration. Relying for too long on "improvisational compromises" (Lister 1995, 285), the European governance of food safety became contested. Unlike the legislation existing in most of the member states, the EC food policy has developed in a piecemeal fashion, being based on a variety of different legal bases provided in the European Community Treaty in order to serve different policy objectives.

The European Community began regulating the food sector, like many other sectors, in conjunction with its effort to eliminate trade barriers arising from different domestic legislation in order to establish an internal market. However, various peculiarities of foodstuffs, such as their long-rooted tradition at national levels and their risk component, have increasingly involved the community by requiring more and more supranational legislative intervention. In particular, EC institutions have assumed new tasks that are largely related to what is generally referred to as risk regulation (Breyer 1993, Vogel 2001). Thus, under the public opinion pressure induced by the food scandals, the community became aware that regulating the food sector only through the economic lens of the internal market could be inadequate in addressing the new challenges brought by the generally new perception of risk. In other words, its traditional functionalist approach to integration was proving unsuccessful in handling reality.

While undermining the credibility of the EC's food safety regulatory system and balkanizing the functioning of the internal market, the food crises of the 1990s brought their own impetus for reforming the EC food regime, leading to calls for an agency solution. Under the pressure of mounting political and public opinion, the European Community had to rapidly design a new approach to consumer health and food safety, moving away from its economic-oriented system toward an approach enlightened by consumer protection and food safety concerns. Through the publication of several policy documents, such as the Green Paper on the general principles of food law and the White Paper on food safety, the community launched an effective and exemplary policymaking process leading to the creation of the European Food Safety Authority (EFSA), originally promoted as a "European FDA" (European Commission 2000a, 1997a).

This chapter provides a narrative account of the historical evolution that has occurred in European food policy in the wake of the food scandals. Since the FDA analogy has been largely invoked during the debate leading to the establishment of EFSA, the chapter also explores the extent to which the U.S. Food and Drug Administration actually represented a model for it. A comparison between the EFSA and the FDA that focuses on their respective powers and institutional organizations shows that this is not, if it ever was, the case.

Historical Background of European Food Law

There were four main periods in the evolution of the EC food policy. The first phase is the *genesis*, stretching from 1962 to the mid-1980s. During this foundational period, the community, animated by the goal of establishing an internal market for foodstuffs, pursued a detailed harmonization program consisting of adopting directives that set up compositional standards for individual foods. The second period, the *new approach*, developed between the Single European Act of 1986 and the BSE row in 1997. This phase is characterized by the introduction of an innovative approach to harmonization based on the mutual recognition principle combined with the use of the minimum harmonization method. The BSE and other food scandals triggered the development of a third phase, the *Europeanization of food risk*, lasting from 1997 to 2001. During these years, the European Commission transformed its policy efforts expressed in its communications into a concrete legislative proposal laying down a new food safety regime for Europe in order to avoid the balkanization of the internal market. The entry into force of Regulation 178/2002 and the establishment of EFSA symbolize the current phase: the *global approach* to food safety.

The Genesis: the European Standards of Identity (1962–1985)

The EC's food legislation has come into being as a result of the gradual harmonization of national rules, which was necessary in order to guarantee the free movement of foodstuffs and prevent distortions of competition in the establishment of the single market. Thus, the EC food law has traditionally been conceived of as a set of rules prompted mainly by the desire to eliminate trade obstacles within the European internal market and having the force of law in all member states. Like several other European policies, the legislative framework of food law has been primarily designed to answer economic rather than safety or societal concerns. In fact, no explicit reference to public heath or consumer protection was made in the Treaty of Rome until the adoption of the Single European Act (1986) and the Maastricht Treaty (1992).

The primary influences on the development of the EC's food law have resulted from the Common Agricultural Policy and the program for the realization of the internal market, whose implementation and surveillance remain to a great extent the responsibility of member states (Lugt 1999).

For almost three decades, the EC maintained this economic approach to food law by using Article 100 (current Article 94) of the EC Treaty to harmonize a few specific areas of national food legislation. Because the different national provisions on food appeared to be the main obstacles in achieving a single marketplace for foodstuffs, it was necessary to proceed to the harmonization of this legislation. The task was not self-evident because national regulations of foodstuffs were not only profoundly diverse but also embodied different administrative traditions.

Similarly, in the United States, before Congress enacted the 1906 Federal Food and Drugs Act (which became the Federal Food, Drug, and Cosmetic Act in 1938), the governmental involvement in food regulation was based on the commerce clause. At that time, the regulator's main purpose was "to protect against fraud in the marketplace" rather than to pursue a free trade objective in contrast to the situation within the European Community (Barton Hutt 1984, 1). However, the economic purpose has also found its way in the United States. As has been stated (Echols 1998, 530), "Regulators in both jurisdictions ultimately derive their legal authority to define and control food safety risks from their constitutional power over the free or interstate movement of goods and both share some aspects of that authority with their constituent states." In accordance with the traditional approach to harmonization, the EC prepared nearly fifty vertical directives aimed at establishing compositional standards for individual food—the so-called recipe laws. The first "Euro-product" conceived by EC legislators was chocolate.

These standards dictating permissible ingredients and prohibiting products that do not satisfy these requirements from using a designated trade description were highly detailed and inclusive. The common goal pursued by these directives was to ensure the free movement of foodstuffs within the European Common Market rather than promoting health and consumer protection goals. The latter were tackled only to the extent that it was necessary to ensure regular intracommunity trade and were mainly left to the choice of the member states (Vos 2002).

This total harmonization approach to food law was not limited to Europe at that time. These EC food recipe laws recall to some degree the food standards of identity promulgated by the U.S. FDA until the 1970s. However, unlike the EC standards, the U.S. recipe laws were primarily aimed at preventing "economic adulteration, by which less expensive ingredients were substituted so as to make the product inferior to that which the consumer expected to receive when purchasing a product with the name under which it was sold" (Barton Hutt and Merrill 1991, 99). In short, the U.S. standards were conceived not as promoting trade but rather as a tool of consumer protection. However, while the FDA abandoned this strategy in the 1970s, the EC realized the failure of its traditional approach to harmonization only in the 1980s. Two factors paved the way to the failure of recipe laws. First, Article 94 of the Treaty of

Rome (1957), requiring unanimity for the adoption of the directives, turned out to be inadequate in promoting the creation of the internal market because it enabled member states to block any European Commission action with which they did not agree. Second, sensitive questions of culinary cultures and traditions contributed to render the decision-making procedure extremely cumbersome and time-consuming by making it sometimes impossible for states to attain unanimous agreement. These difficulties for harmonizing food quality requirements for all foodstuffs led the commission to rethink its traditional approach, leading to a new strategy of harmonization.

The New Approach: Mutual Recognition Principle and Minimum Harmonization Standards (1985–1997)

In 1985, the European Commission decided to abandon its titanic effort to introduce universally applicable recipe laws for all European-made foodstuffs and launched the New Approach to Harmonization of national legislations (European Commission 1985a), in particular to those related to foodstuffs (European Commission 1985b). In doing so, the commission relied on the mutual recognition principle formulated by the European Court of Justice (ECJ) in the 1979 *Cassis de Dijon* judgment. According to this principle, a member state should allow the free circulation in its territory of goods produced or marketed in conformity with the rules, tests, or standards found in another member state that offer an equivalent level of protection to its own rules, tests, or standards. Suddenly it appears there was no longer a need to harmonize all the food legislation of member states by agreeing on common food quality requirements for "Euro-bread," "Euro-chocolate," "Euro-beer," and so on.

The ECJ endorsed this interpretation of the *Cassis* judgment by holding that the protection of consumers cannot be a legitimate ground on which a member state may prohibit the marketing in its territory of foodstuffs that are compositionally different from those generally sold there. According to the court, the consumer protection objective could be achieved by the inclusion of additional information on the labeling of products indicating differences in compositional and production methods existing in the exporting member. This measure allowed individuals to make informed choices.

The principle of mutual recognition, while preserving all traditions, richness, and diversity existing among the different national culinary traditions, allowed the community to realize an internal market without having to adopt hundreds of vertical directives (European Commission 1985a). In accordance with the new strategy, EC food legislation would henceforth be limited to the harmonization of national rules justified by the need to protect public health and other consumer interests, notably consumers' need for information and the necessity to ensure fair trading and provide appropriate official controls (European Commission 1985b). The idea was that the EC could lay down harmonized rules only on a horizontal basis to set forth the "essential requirements" necessary for the free circulation of foodstuffs. The mutual recognition principle combined with a reinforced labeling regime guaranteeing consumer information would have realized an internal market for foodstuffs.

However, the *Cassis de Dijon* doctrine did not immediately lead to an acceleration of the harmonization process, as Article 94 ECT still required unanimity. Only in 1987 did the Single European Act incorporate, in line with the EC's "New Approach on Technical Harmonization and Standards," Article 95 (former 100A), requiring a qualified majority in the legislative process instead of unanimity, thus speeding up the harmonization process.

As a part of this approach, the EC adopted some framework directives, the so-called new approach directives, dealing with essential requirements in the fields of additives, labeling foods for particular nutritional needs, hygiene, and official controls in order to establish basic standards and guiding member states in the development of more detailed rules. National food legislation, constrained by the respect of the framework directives, would have been accepted within the European Community by virtue of the mutual recognition principle. The existing vertical directives would have remained in place, and the EC would still have been in charge of periodically updating and replacing their texts. However, in principle, the EC was not to issue new vertical harmonization legislation—not only to preserve the culinary richness of member states, but also to avoid introducing legislative rigidity that would prevent innovation and commercial flexibility.

Although the EC tried in these years to reorient its food policy toward the achievement of new goals, such as the protection of public health or consumer protection, these aspects of EC food law were still neglected at the time and implemented in a way functional to the economic requirements of the internal market. The only priority was the completion of the internal market, widely publicized by the 1992 single-market program. Although much national food legislation had already been harmonized at the EC level, European food law continued to develop in a fragmented fashion. There was no unifying text that clearly defined the responsibilities of the parties concerned. There is no doubt that before 1992, following more than thirty years of legislative activity, EC food law was still mainly focused on issues of trade and the free movement of goods rather than on safety issues. Although a significant number of EC legislative texts were adopted, one could not properly speak of a pan-European common food policy.

The Emergency: Toward the Europeanization of Food Risk (1997–2002)

In the mid-1990s, in the wake of several food outbreaks and food scares, it became clear that the free movement of foodstuffs could no longer be the overriding principle of EC food law. Food safety was not only a consumer's concern, but also a condition for proper functioning of the internal market. It was necessary to figure out how to reshape this European policy.

The BSE crisis heavily contributed to spreading this awareness among citizens and institutions by showing the inadequacy of the existing regulatory regime in ensuring a high level of protection of public health and consumer protection. As Chalmers (2003, 532) notes, "The BSE crisis marked a Year Zero for the European Union food regime by forcing both member states and the Community to acknowledge the shortcomings of the existing European approach to food safety issues."

Facing a motion of censure from the European Parliament for alleged mismanagement of the BSE crisis, the Santer Commission promised to revise its internal organization and establish a new food regulatory regime. It also made reference, for the first time, to the idea of establishing an independent European food agency.

The first highly symbolic step was the adoption, in May 1997, of a long-awaited Green Paper on the General Principles of Food Law in the EU (European Commission 1997a) aimed at launching a public debate on how the EC should best regulate the area of food law. The EC seriously envisaged the possibility of adopting a general directive on food law, containing definitions of the fundamental terms of food law, particularly the term food itself. Such an EC-wide definition was considered essential to determining the scope of the EC food laws. In this text, although not putting into questions the fundamental goals of EC food law, the EC stressed that "the *BSE* crisis has highlighted the need for a European food policy centered on the requirement that *only foodstuffs which are safe*, wholesome and fit for consumption be placed on the market. Health protection in relation with consumption of foodstuffs is to be an absolute priority at any time and not only something to be looked at in emergency situations." The protection of public health was gradually entering EC food law policy as a goal deserving as much coverage as the economic goals related to the CAP and free movement.

Along these lines, the Amsterdam Treaty, agreed by the EU's political leaders on June 17 and signed on October 2, 1997, fully acknowledged public health protection and consumer protection as objectives of the European integration process and conferred on the commission new responsibilities to their attainment.

The next step in reshaping food law was the EC's publication of the "Communication on Consumer Health and Safety" (1997b). This text set out the action the EC was taking to reinforce the manner in which it obtains and makes use of scientific advice and operates its control and inspection services in the interest of consumer health and food safety. The new approach, which was also a new political direction, was based on three general principles:

• Separation of legislative responsibilities (risk management) and those relating to scientific advice (risk assessment)
• Separation of legislative responsibilities and those relating to controls and inspections
• Enhanced transparency and dissemination of information throughout the decision-making process and monitoring activities

In order to better satisfy these objectives and enhance consumer health protection, the Directorate-General (DG) XXIV of the European Commission was reorganized.

The division between responsibility for legislation and scientific consultation was realized by entrusting the latter to DG XXIV, renamed DG for Consumer Protection and Health (DG SANCO), which became responsible for the scientific assessment system. The European Commission had in particular placed the management of all the scientific committees working in the field of foodstuffs and responsibility for inspection and control under the authority of this DG and had reorganized the relevant DG as having responsibility for consumer health. Thus, the scientific committees were distanced from the legislative wing of the commission services, being subjected to the exclusive control of a DG totally oriented to consumers. At the same time, they were removed from direct industrial pressures. In particular, the committees were regrouped and coordinated by the Scientific Steering Committee (SSC) in order to achieve greater synergy and effective coordination.

The proper functioning of these committees was to be based on three main principles: excellence, independence, and transparency. To satisfy the principle of excellence, scientific evaluation had to be undertaken by eminent scientists. The principle of independence required scientists serving in the scientific committees to be free from interests that might be in conflict with the requirement of providing independent advice. As for control and inspections, the new approach aimed at providing a harmonized system of control for all parts of the food production chain, following three main orientations. First, in view of the broad range of areas covered by the legislation, control and inspection were to follow a scheme of priorities established by risk assessment procedures, and, second, they were to ensure that the entire food production chain is covered (from "plow to plate"). Third, the control activities were to be exercised through the introduction of formal audit procedures enabling the EC to assess the control systems operated by the national authorities. This new regime had to be implemented through the Food and Veterinary Office (FVO). The 150 FVO inspectors, situated in Dublin, Ireland, are in charge of monitoring the observance of food hygiene, veterinary, and plant health legislation within the EU (Lugt 1999).

The EC response to the new regulatory challenge was based on the assumption that good management would have helped in solving the difficulties that had arisen from the possible ways of dealing with scientific advice.

In particular, the "Communication on Consumer Health and Safety" introduced a new way to deal with risk analysis by breaking it down into two distinct components: risk assessment and risk management. This crucial conceptual distinction would subsequently be reiterated in all EC documents and legislative texts relating to scientific expertise. This distinction aimed at enabling decision makers to act with the best knowledge of scientific data relating to a certain phenomenon. Once the risk assessment is carried out by an independent body of experts, it is possible to act at the risk management stage by deciding whether to authorize a certain activity or substance on the market. Although that communication represented only a first rough reaction to the new challenges of food safety, these efforts to protect consumer health by focusing on scientific advice, risk analysis, and control and inspection heralded the future European food authority and the newly established regulatory food safety regime.

Two years after the changes undertaken in 1997, the director general of DGXXIV, H. Reichenbach, charged three scientists—Philip James, Fritz Kemper, and Gerard Pascal—with assessing the existing system of scientific advice and eventually coming up with a better system in terms of independence, transparency and excellence (James et al. 1999).

Their report, submitted to the newly appointed European Commission in December 1999, sketched out the blueprint for a European food authority and was immediately endorsed by the new Commission President Prodi in his first speech before the European Parliament as one of the priorities of his mandate.

Meanwhile, several events contributed to speeding up the food safety policy reform by decidedly counteracting the member states' resistance to the establishment of an independent European food authority: the ongoing BSE crisis, growing consumer concerns about the safety of GM foods, and the dioxin contamination outbreak in Belgium. In the wake of these food emergencies and consumer scares, the European Commission proposed to combine the envisaged radical reform of the food regulatory framework with an innovative institutional reform by publishing the White Paper on Food Safety on January 12, 2000 (European Commission 2000a).

By launching a debate and involving the governments and all other parties affected by the new regime, this paper expressed the need for a major structural change in the food safety regime to ensure the twin objectives of ensuring the highest standard of food safety and restoring consumer confidence. In order to achieve these goals, it proposed the establishment of a European Food Authority (EFA) within the framework of a broader EC food safety legal reform mainly driven by the need to guarantee a high level of food safety.

The guiding and somewhat revolutionary principle of the White Paper was that food safety policy must be based on a "comprehensive, integrated approach" throughout the food chain; across all food sectors; between the member states; at the EC external frontier and within the EC; and in international and EC decision making for and at all stages of the policymaking process. The assumption was that a comprehensive, integrated approach would lead to a more coherent, effective, and dynamic food policy.

Following the two 1997 communications, the Green Paper and the Consumer Health, the European Commission confirmed the central role of risk analysis as "the foundation on which food safety policy is based" and described its three components: risk assessment (scientific advice and information analysis), risk management (regulation and control), and risk communication.

Relying on this conceptual framework, the White Paper proposed to entrust the EFA with particular responsibilities for both risk assessment and communication on food safety issues, while denying it any role in risk management. Thus, the scope of the mandate to be given to the EFA reflected the "generally accepted need to functionally separate risk assessment and risk management" already sketched out by the European Commission in its Communication on Consumer Health.

Moreover, the White Paper advocated the adoption of eighty-four distinct measures (involving around thirty directives and regulations) forming a complete and coherent body of legislation covering all aspects of food products from farm to table. The new legal framework should have virtually covered the entire food chain, including animal feedstuffs, animal health and welfare, hygiene, contaminants and residues, new types of food, food additives and flavors, packaging materials, and ionizing radiation.

The Global Approach: The New Food Safety Regime and the EFSA (2003–Present)

It took more than two years for the European Commission to transform the White Paper into a proposal for a regulation "laying down the general principles of food law, establishing the European Food Authority, and providing for urgency measures in matters of food safety." This proposal, published in March 2001, contained all the main features originally sketched out by the White Paper and was subsequently adopted, with few amendments, as Regulation (EC) No. 178/2002 on January 28, 2002, with a title only slightly modified. Its legal basis can be found in Articles 37, 95, 133 and 152 (4) b of the *ECT.*

This regulation represents the first attempt to address all aspects of food safety at the EU level by laying down a comprehensive EU food policy horizontally covering all stages of production, processing, and distribution of food and feed (from farm to fork), thus encompassing raw materials, intermediate products, and finished food products as well as feedstuffs (Art. 3.3). Being addressed to not only EC institutions but also the member states, the scope *ratione personae* of this policy is unusually broad (Gonzalez Vaqué 2003).

The overriding principles of the new EC food regime are that food law enacted by either the community or its member states should seek to achieve a high level of protection of human health and consumers' interest while ensuring the effective functioning of the internal market. The regulation seeks to achieve these twin principles in two main ways:

• It establishes a comprehensive EC-wide food policy, addressed to both the community and its member states, by setting forth general principles (Arts. 5–10), obligations and requirements of food law (Arts. 10–21), and some procedures in matters of food safety (Arts. 50–57).

• It creates a new independent agency: the European Food Safety Authority (Arts. 21–49) (see chapter 11, this volume).

Operation of the EFSA

Referral to the EFSA

Unlike the previous system, where only the European Commission could request advice from the scientific committees, the EFSA may respond to requests for scientific advice from a variety of entities, such as the member states, national food authorities, and the European Parliament. However, where consultation is mandatory under European Community law, the Commission continues to have exclusive authority to obtain scientific advice from EFSA. Furthermore, the EFSA, acting ex officio, may carry out scientific assessment on any matter that may have a direct or indirect effect on the safety of the food supply, including matters relating to animal health, animal welfare, and plant health.

Legal Status of EFSA Scientific Opinions

Although the EC institutions are expressly required to take the EFSA's opinions into account when drafting a community measure (Art. 22 (6)), the EFSA lacks formal authority to reach binding resolutions on potentially contentious scientific issues. In other words, it does not have the final word in the event of diverging scientific opinions between its own decisions and those issued by other bodies. This may be inferred from Article 30 of the regulation that while establishing a procedure aimed at solving problems arising out from "diverging scientific opinions," it attributes neither an authoritative nor a mediating role to EFSA, but simply "vigilance" and "cooperation" duties. This outcome is even more surprising if analyzed in the light of the EFSA's ambition to become "the point of reference in risk assessment" for the whole community.

More precisely, under the regulation, the EFSA has to exercise vigilance in order to identify at an early stage any potential source of divergence between its scientific opinions and the opinions issued by national food agencies or other bodies carrying out similar tasks (Art. 30 (1)). Where there is a conflict between its opinion and those of bodies carrying out similar tasks, the EFSA must contact the body in question to ensure that all relevant scientific information is shared and identify potentially contentious scientific issues. Where accommodation is not possible despite EFSA's effort and the body is either a community agency, a commission scientific body, or a member state body, the EFSA is "obliged to cooperate" either to resolve the differences or to present a joint document, which will be made public identifying the uncertainties and the "contentious scientific issues."

A prima facie reading of these provisions clearly shows that EFSA has not been entrusted with the power to act as the ultimate body of scientific advice in the EU. To understand the practical consequences stemming from this decision, it is sufficient to remember the crisis involving France and the United Kingdom and regarding the European Commission's decision to lift the embargo on beef exports in July 1999, two years after the BSE outbreak. The French food safety authority (AFFSA) and the Scientific Steering Committee strongly differed on the scientific interpretations of the risks associated with beef. France, relying on its scientific opinion, refused to lift the embargo on British beef in contravention of the EU scientific data, and the European Commission brought France before the European Court of Justice claiming a violation of EC law. This case clearly exemplifies the likelihood that in spite of the high degree of integration within the EU, conflicts may arise in the future between national authorities and the EFSA on contentious scientific issues.

The introduction of a mere duty of cooperation does seem to fall short in providing an effective answer to the fundamental question of the relationships between the EFSA and the national authorities responsible for food safety issues. The institution of an advisory body, as a mechanism of exchange of information between the national authorities and the EFSA, is unlikely to prove decisive in overcoming the difficulties arising from diverging scientific opinions. Thus, the current regulatory framework and the institution of the EFSA does not seem to be likely to put an end to the competition in scientific matters pertaining to food among national authorities in the member states. These provisions certainly cast some doubt on the possibility that EFSA will become "the scientific point of reference for the whole Union" as announced by the regulation.

Nevertheless, outside the case of diverging scientific opinions between the EFSA and other bodies carrying out similar tasks, the EFSA's opinions are likely to produce some significant indirect normative effects. In particular, its opinions have the potential to become a source of constraint not only for the EC institutions but also for the member states and private parties.

As for the EC institutions, the recent *Pfizer Animal Health* judgment (2002) has clearly established a general duty to consult the available scientific reports prepared by experts on behalf of the EC. The EC institutions would be allowed to depart from this duty only in those exceptional circumstances where equivalent scientific evidence can be found and a justification for relying on it is provided. There are therefore good reasons to believe that these constraints in the use of scientific expertise will be maintained by the EC courts with regard to the EFSA's opinions by transforming them in de facto authoritative measures.

The EFSA's opinions are likely to acquire some authoritative value over national decision makers as well. Although the regulation introduces the presumption that in the absence of specific EC provisions, all food is deemed to be safe where it complies with the specific national provisions of the country where it is marketed (Art. 14 (9)), the same regulation imposes on member states the duty to take account of the results of risk assessment, in particular, the opinions of the EFSA when regulating the food sector. In sum, although domestic authorities are not procedurally required to consult the EFSA, they are required to abide by its scientific opinions in passing new legislation (Art. 6(3)). It would therefore seem impossible for the national authorities to depart from the EFSA's opinions without giving some reasons justifying their rejection.

Finally, the EFSA's position also has the potential to acquire some legal significance for private parties. The regulation also imposes a general obligation on private business operators engaged in production, processing, and distribution to ensure that food placed on the market is safe (Art. 14(1)). Any breach of this duty gives rise to two separate violations of EC law: breach of the general obligation to ensure that food is safe, established by Article 14 of the regulation, on one side, and violation of the product liability directive on the other. Although national courts are not required to consult the EFSA while investigating these violations, they are likely to rely on its scientific opinions. In other words, if the EFSA has issued an opinion suggesting that a product is unsafe, it would be extremely difficult for a private individual to prove the opposite.

In conclusion, while the EFSA's opinions have not been expressly granted a direct regulatory authority, they are likely to acquire a de facto legally binding value for both the EC and the member state authorities when passing legislation and a strong probative authority for private business operators placing unsafe food on the market. More generally, it can be reasonably expected that the EFSA's opinions will structure the terms of debate on several issues by influencing enforcement within the member states and public opinion. Finally, it remains unclear and difficult to predict whether the EFSA will play a role in trade relations with third countries.

EFSA and the FDA: Some Elements for a Comparison

Missions

If compared with the imposing institutional and substantive framework of the U.S. FDA, the newly established EFSA comes across as a weak authority. Its resources and its powers are far from being like those that make the FDA one of the most authoritative administrative agencies in the world. However, these agencies pursue different missions: while the FDA protects the public health of Americans citizens by monitoring the safety and effectiveness of products entering the market (or already in use) and by enforcing the Food and Drug Act against those in breach of its provisions, the EFSA is a scientific advisory body charged with providing independent and objective advice on food safety issues associated with the food chain.

Regulatory Universes

By assuming a linear relationship between science and political decision making, the EC or has shaped its food institutional framework in accordance with a functional distinction between risk assessment and risk management. Accordingly, while the EFSA has been conceived as the risk assessor, the body in charge of doing risk assessment on behalf of the EC institutions, the European Commission, has remained the risk manager, in charge of adopting the decisions. Both entities exercise their functions in conformity with the risk analysis framework (the *Grundnorm*) sketched out by the regulation, which allows the European Commission to take into account, apart from the scientific opinions, "other factors legitimate to the matter under consideration" and the precautionary principle.

The FDA's universe differs greatly from the EFSA's in the following respects:

• Its substantive powers overcome the rigid distinction between risk assessment and risk management functions since the FDA is in charge of both.

• Its decisions are more science based than those adopted within the EU. FDA risk managers are supposed to rely exclusively on scientific factors and not on social factors.

• Its institutional organization comprises approximately 9,000 employees in charge of monitoring the manufacture, import, transport, storage, and sale of a broad range of products throughout the United States and relies on about 2,100 scientists working in forty laboratories throughout the country.

• Unlike the EFSA, the FDA does not derive its powers from a regulation merely laying down general principles and requirements of food law. Rather, its power derives from powerful text such as the Food, Drug, and Cosmetic Act.

Moreover, the EFSA has been not only denied both regulatory and enforcement powers, but it seems to play a limited role even within its own area of competence: risk assessment. Although providing a common standard for conducting risk analysis throughout the EU to be followed by both the EC and the member states, the current regime does not empower the EFSA to impose its own scientific vision on the member states' competent authorities in case of diverging opinions.

Notwithstanding their relevant indirect effect not only on EC institutions but also on the member states and individuals, the EFSA's scientific opinions do not prevail in case of conflict with those elaborated by the national competent agencies. It follows that the lack of authoritative power is likely to produce conflicts analogous to those already seen in the past between the EC scientific authorities and the national competent bodies.

Does this outcome weaken or strengthen the EFSA's functioning and the overall EC food policy? Unlike the United States where arguably all local food differences have been obliterated (Schlosser 2002), Europe still shows long-rooted culinary traditions symbolizing strong identity values. Thus, a claim by a domestic food authority that a certain good is safe or unsafe is likely to involve not only an assertion about science, but also the willingness of this country to bear or not bear the level of risk considered acceptable in order to continue or reject a certain local tradition. In contrast, the assertion made at the EC level about the safety of a product to be marketed throughout the EU is both a claim about its risk component and a political claim aimed at favoring economic integration and free trade within Europe. Along these lines, conflicts about food safety within the European context inevitably involve a tension between a European (universal) and a national (local) vision of both safety and the sociocultural perception of a particular food (Chalmers 2003).

Against this backdrop, giving the EFSA the last word on all scientific contentious matters would have amounted to forcing the establishment of a pan-European food safety standard, inevitably leading to the obliteration of local traditions. Thus, although the lack of authoritative power in scientific matters may be seen as weakening the EFSA, it expresses the EC dislike for the mounting trend toward a standardization of the food supply by revealing at the same time the strong member states' willingness to defend their national perception of risk (Testori Coggi 2003).

Therefore, under the current regulatory framework, it is up to the European courts, and not to the EFSA, to solve conflicts arising between national and EC EU's scientific opinions. More precisely, the EC courts are called to conduct a delicate balancing exercise between the local and the universal visions of risk (Alemanno 2001, 2005).

The case involving the French refusal to lift the embargo against British beef two years after the BSE outbreak symbolizes the logic followed by this approach. Although the ECJ condemned France for not having lifted the embargo as requested by EC law, it also recognized that traceability of UK beef, essential up to the point of sale in order to enable a consignment that did not meet the conditions of the EC law to be recalled, was not guaranteed at the time of the European Commission decision of

July 23, 1999, lifting the ban, in particular regarding meat and products that had been cut, processed, or rewrapped.

It follows that in case of divergent scientific opinions between the EC and the local risk assessors, the EC courts are called on to carry out the difficult task of reconciling conflicting visions by looking at the value of domestic measures to the local population in relation to the damage to the community (free trade) interest.

This approach condenses local differences without providing a single, objective standard for "safety enabling economies of scale and trade liberalization across the Union" (Chalmers 2003). This seems to be confirmed by Article 1.1 of the regulation, which states that in ensuring a high-level protection of human health and consumers' interest in relation to food, it must take into account "the diversity of the supply of food including traditional products, while ensuring the effective functioning of the internal market."

In sum, the new EU food regime constitutes an attempt to extend the mutual recognition model, originally developed to avoid standardization of food identity throughout Europe, in the field of analysis of risk between the EU and the member states. Although the regulation provides for the first common model of analysis of risk applicable to both the EC and the member states, it does not give the last word in scientific matters to the EFSA, but rather introduces a presumption of safety for all products found in compliance with EC law or, lacking EC provisions, for foods conforming to the national food laws of the member states. Should the community or a member doubt the presumed safety of a particular food, the question is decided by the EC courts, and the burden of proof lies on the party claiming the product is unsafe. Similar to what happens when the mutual recognition principle does not work because of a lack of trust among member states, it is up to the courts, not to the EFSA, to weigh the conflicting interests, thus striking a balance between the local and the universal interests involved.

Different Cultures

This chapter suggests that the main institutional and substantive differences between the EFSA and the FDA may ultimately be understood not only as a result of different systems of governance and regulatory environments but also as a reflection of entirely different societal contexts. In recent years, Europeans and Americans have developed conflicting perceptions of risks and, inevitably, different cultural norms regarding food safety (see chapter 9, this volume). This seems to be due to the complex interplay of cultural models that we, as humans, use to interpret the environment and the world around us. In other words, the public perceives the risk within its own cultural model.

Conflicting perception of risks may significantly influence how these authorities respond to given risks by elaborating divergent risk analysis methods. It is becoming increasingly clear that risk perception plays a crucial role in the mechanics of risk management. Thus, scientists and nonscientists look at risks from different perspectives. While the scientific approach is rational, dealing with probabilities and science-based studies, other people, being more value driven, behave according to perceptions rather than relying on facts (Coleman 2001).

By taking the social factor into account within its risk analysis, the EC seems to be more willing than the FDA to address the dichotomy existing between the perceptions of scientists and nonscientists. This may be seen by many as an irrational position, potentially hiding protectionist intent. But for many others, experience has shown that one day's scientific "truth" may turn out to be based on a partial understanding (as the unquestionable benign nature of nuclear power was put into question by successive studies).

A comparison of the perceptions of the riskiness of some foods and their production processes shows the impact on food regulation of tradition in Europe and of science in the United States. While Europeans tend to favor traditional foods and are skeptical about new technologies, Americans have always been more in favor of new technologies than traditional food processing. This is best reflected in the European reluctance to consume GMOs and the U.S. resistance to the consumption of unpasteurized raw milk cheeses (Echols 1998, see also chapter 9, this volume).

In sum, a comparison between the EFSA and the FDA clearly shows that culture and tradition play a silent though crucial role in regulatory processes and the resulting rules. It remains to be seen whether the European Commission/EFSA approach will prove more satisfactory in protecting citizens' public health than the long-standing and more scientific-based attitude symbolized by the FDA. The ambition nurtured by the Europeans is that EFSA, though following a different path, could one day be described, much like the FDA, as "one of the most venerable institutions, whose employees have long memories and a tradition of dedicated, sometimes single-minded public service—in sum a strong commitment to the job of regulation" (Barton Hutt 1984, 4).

Conclusion

The creation of the EFSA and the enactment of the new food policy regime stem directly from the wave of contested governance that slapped Europe at the end of the 1990s. It would have certainly taken longer for the EC to conceive this reform if several food scandals had not rendered its system of governance contested by showing the absence of a centralized European scientific assessment and a unifying text setting out the fundamental principles of EC food law. By producing a collapse of public trust in the European institutions, the contested governance of European food safety has not only accelerated this reform but has considerably helped the EC food law to get rid of its original sin, its pro-market bias, by illustrating the importance of ensuring the safety of the products throughout the community. Under the new policy, only foodstuffs that are safe, wholesome, and fit for consumption can be sold to consumers.

By ceasing to be a fragmented area of community law, European food law rests for the first time on comprehensive legislation covering the entire "farm to fork" distribution chain and directly enforceable in all EU member states. The role of EFSA in the implementation of the new food regime is far from that of the FDA within the U.S. context. This is due not only to the authorities' different missions and diverging regulatory universes, but also to the conflicting perceptions of risk developed by their respective citizen-consumers. With risk analysis the *Grundnorm* of the new regime, one could have expected the EFSA to become the authoritative scientific body for the whole EU and having the final word in scientificly contentious matters. But member states did not want to make the EFSA an oracle spelling out the "truth" in all scientific matters (Podger 2003). Rather, they wanted to preserve the right of their national food agencies to carry out scientific studies, thus expressing their specific perception of a certain risk.

While this approach is likely to bring about conflicts among member states, it expresses the European attempt to defend its cultural patrimony and culinary richness against the mounting trend toward the obliteration of local traditions led by the multinationals of processed food. Accordingly, in case of diverging opinions between the EFSA and national food authorities, it is up to the EC courts, and not to the EFSA, to solve these conflicts by striking a balance between the universal and the local values. However, this judicial involvement could be reduced if EFSA is able to establish an effective network with the national food agencies aimed at solving scientific conflicts before they reach the EC courts. Therefore, the EFSA's success will mainly depend on the creation of a network between it and the national agencies so as to give to all European consumers good reason for a high level of confidence in the food that they eat.

The EFSA is still in its infancy. It remains to be seen to what extent it will become entrusted by the 450 million European consumers by acquiring a reputation, as achieved by the FDA, although in a completely different constitutional, regulatory, and societal environment.

11

The Creation of the European Food Safety Authority

Laurie Buonanno

The European Food Safety Authority (EFSA) joined the pantheon of European information agencies in 2002 after several years of member state disagreement over food bans, consumer uncertainty as to the safety of European food supplies, and institutional failures to achieve satisfactory reforms to Europe's food safety regime. The EU has increasingly established independent agencies to oversee specialized policies, but the circumstances surrounding EFSA's formation (the EU's thirteenth agency) differ from that of most of its predecessors (including the European Environmental Agency) in three important ways.

First, the food policy regime became a highly charged area of public contestation fueled by sensational media coverage, circumscribing the maneuverability of European institutions and member state governments. Second, EFSA was the first agency established by a regulation of both the Council of Ministers and Parliament after David Byrne, commissioner for DG Health and Consumer Protection during the period under discussion, determined that food safety policy fell under Articles 95 (internal market) and 153 (public health), both of which are subject to Article 251 (codecision and qualified majority voting). This brought the European Parliament into a process in which it had never had more than a consultative role. Third, this policy reform was accompanied by subtle power shifts among European institutions and between these and member states.

Actors

From Harmonization to Comitology

Although many of the European statesmen who agreed to the EEC Treaty (1957) sought a federal Europe, their aspirations were constrained considerably by the institutional mechanisms available to international organizations: the harmonization of national laws through EU regulations and directives.[1] Article 95, the Consolidated Treaty establishing the European Community (TEC) establishes the conditions of the Single European Market (SEM), subject to Article 30 (the safeguard clause). Thus, the European Economic Community's (EEC) earliest policy instrument for achieving the SEM relied heavily on the adjudication of cases in the European Court of Justice (ECJ) and member state courts, with all the attendant problems of governing by case law. Predictably, member states felt free to ban the importation of products on grounds of protecting consumer health, exercising their right to do so under Article 30. Despite Article 95, clause 3, which speaks to the necessity of derogations based on scientific evidence (rather than, for instance, cultural predilections), the EU experience mirrored that of international trade in the same time period.

While the Kennedy Rounds resulted in a dramatic lowering of worldwide tariffs, this effect was greatly diminished by the proliferation of opaque Non-Tariff Barriers (NTBs). The ECJ confirmed the necessity of proving a scientific basis for derogations under Article 30 when it promulgated the principle of proportionality in the *Cassis de Dijon* case (February 1979), overruling Germany's ban on the importation of the French black currant liqueur. *Cassis* established the principle of mutual recognition (see chapter 10, this volume, for a more detailed discussion): a product lawfully produced and marketed in one member state could not be prohibited in another. All actors—member states, the European Commission, and business interests—became disenchanted with harmonization's slow pace as a tool for market integration; consequently, the commission's White Paper (1985) proposed regulatory committees (as did the Milan Council Summit of that year), culminating in the 1987 Council of Ministers' decision clarifying the use of comitology beyond agriculture (Nugent 2003).

Agreement to the SEM affected the food regime in two ways: quali-fied majority voting replaced unanimity in the Council of Ministers, and the extension of comitology across the DGs working to implement the SEM strengthened the council's ability to exercise institutionalized over-sight of the European Commission's regulatory activities. With respect to this second point, much of the implementing legislation for food policy is issued as commission regulations and directives taken in the relevant DGs. While comitology refers to all three types of committees—advisory, management, and regulatory—it is on the latter two that national offi-cials sit and can block (management procedure) or must approve (regu-latory procedure) commission decisions.

The comitology system enhances administrative efficiency without greatly strengthening the commission in its dealings with the council. Nugent (2003, 139–140) suggests four reasons that this might be so: first, controversial policies are regularly referred to a council meeting; second, the commission is uniquely positioned to know when a particular regu-latory measure will face serious opposition in the committee and must act accordingly to broker compromises; third, when the member states cannot agree on the establishment of a committee, the council will reserve implementing powers for itself; and, fourth, the "Council tends to be jealous of its powers and would move quickly against the Com-mission if it thought comitology committees were being used to under-mine Council power."

Joerges (1999a, 312) applauds comitology because it eliminates the "need to construct non-majoritarian institutions." As a middle way between mutual trust (harmonization) and independent (regulatory) agencies, the comitology system, or deliberative supranationalism (Joerges and Neyer 1997), is "a conceptual alternative of the well-known dichotomies between functionalism or supranationalism, on the one hand, and intergovernmentalism, on the other" (Joerges 1999a, 312). Comitology opens and monitors the SEM "without replacing these States with a Europeanized equivalent" (Joerges and Neyer 1997, 321–322).

But comitology's critics question its legitimacy, characterizing it as nontransparent, undemocratic, unaccountable, and prone to unstable policymaking. Weiler (quoted in St. Clair Bradley 1999, 76), for example, describes comitology as "a phenomenon which requires its very own science which no single person has mastered," while Chambers (1999, 100) refers to comitology as "the Council in the Commission," part of the "constitutional fudge which glues the Union together by filling the fundamental gulf between federalism and intergovernmental co-operation. Like fudge," he tells us, "it doesn't make a very stable glue when the temperature rises." The European Parliament and consumer groups have never been comfortable with comitology, for similar, but not identical, reasons. Members of the European Parliament (MEPs) resent their exclusion from policymaking and chafe at the closed-door meetings of the comitology committees. Consumer groups think that without oversight of comitology committees, business interests are being advanced at the expense of consumers. These perceptions made for a natural alliance between the Parliament and consumers.

BSE Crisis: The European Parliament's Investigations

In its 1996–1997 Committee of Inquiry into BSE, the European Parliament identified four factors underlying the BSE crisis: the comitology committee, member state inaction in the Council of Ministers, overlapping competencies in the European Commission DGs, and regulatory capture. With respect to comitology committees, the Parliament found (European Parliament, 1997):

The complexity of the commitology [sic] system and the lack of transparency of the procedures inherent therein make it even more difficult to apportion responsibilities be it with respect to the institutions or to the committees, and enables one institution to shift political and administrative responsibilities on to another. . . . By virtue of the opaqueness, complexity and anti-democratic nature of its workings, the existing system of commitology [sic] seems to be totally exempt from any supervision, thereby enabling national and/or industrial interests to infiltrate the Community decision-making process. Although the powers of the Standing Veterinary Committee were delegated by the Council, it is the Commission that exerts control over it. However, the committee's work is based on the opinions of the Scientific Veterinary Committee, and it is clear that the UK was able to control this latter committee through the convening of the meetings, the agendas and attendance, and the drafting of minutes.

In the course of its investigations, the Parliament also discovered that the Agriculture Council had rejected a commission proposal (June 1990) to prohibit the exports of meat from the UK, and two other councils had been made aware of the potential danger of BSE to humans: the Council of Health Ministers discussed it on several occasions, and the Council of Research Ministers had, without committing funds to the endeavor, recommended further research.

The Medina Report (European Parliament 1997, 14) also concluded that overlapping competencies in the DGs contributed to inadequate monitoring of food-borne diseases:

Public health protection competencies are compartmentalized between a number of different Commission departments (as regards possible food risks). The BSE affair has been handled variously by: DG VI (Agriculture), DG III (ex-Internal Market, now Industry), the Consumer Protection Service (currently DGXXIV), and the Directorate for Health and Safety (DG V). This compartmentalization has hampered the coordination and efficiency of the services concerned, has facilitated the shifting of responsibility for maladministration between the various services of the Commission, and points up the lack of an integrated approach, a phenomenon exacerbated by DG VI's arrogating primary management of the BSE issue to itself.

Regulatory capture also appeared to play a role in the escalation of the BSE crisis. For instance, the commission revealed that it had been subject to intense political pressure from UK government officials not to include BSE checks in the general slaughterhouse inspections.

Reforming the System

The European Commission reacted swiftly to the Medina findings—and working under the threat of EP censure—disbanded the principal advisory scientific committees and transferred staff from a variety of DGs to an expanded DG XXIV (Health and Consumer Protection). The commission also complied with the Parliament's call for a joint (EP/Commission) body, with a fixed term of office to monitor and review the implementation of its recommendations (European Parliament 1997).

As food crises continued to rock the EU, Eurobarometers and other opinion polls (see Kjærnes, Dulsrud, and Poppe chapter 3, this volume) reported low levels of trust for EU policymakers among European consumers. The European Commission engaged three leading European scientists (who also served on commission scientific advisory committees), to evaluate "whether an independent agency type structure could lead to further improvements in scientific advice at the EC level" (James, Kemper, and Pascal 1999). But EU independent agencies can take two forms: a regulatory body exercising legislative, executive, and judicial authority or an information agency designed to serve as a point of contact for an issue network of public and private actors operating on many levels and in various spheres in the policy space. So while support for the agency approach seemed to be congealing among Parliament (Medina Report), the commission (e.g., in speeches by Jacques Santer and in his testimony to the EP's BSE Committee of Inquiry), and the December 1999 Helsinki European Council, which mentions the "possible establishment of an independent food safety agency," disagreement focused on the extent of its remit. Specifically, would an independent agency assess and communicate risk (information agency), or would it also be expected to manage risks (regulatory agency)?

The James, Kemper, and Pascal report (1999) is rich reading on many levels, not least because in their work as national and European scientific experts, they were in the center of the maelstrom of European food scares. Pascal, for example, has held positions in EU food policy since 1986 as a member of the DG III (then DG XXIV in reorganization) Scientific Committee for Food (1986–1997) and its chair from 1992 to 1997; member of the Multidisciplinary Scientific Committee on BSE, 1996–1997; member of the Scientific Steering Committee (DG Consumer Health and Food Safety) since July 1997; and chair of the Scientific Steering Committee since November 1997 (Pascal 2004). Pascal, a French national, found himself in the crossfire between French and British agricultural regulators when, in October 1999, in his position chairing the commission's SSC, he was accused first by the British tabloids of favoritism toward France (before a decision was made), and when the SSC unanimously recommended to lift the global ban on British beef exports, the French media stepped in where the British left off, and he was branded a traitor to France.

Concurring with the Medina Report, the European scientists concluded that the existing regulatory structure had advantaged industrial interests at the expense of consumer safety and that the comitology system endangered the public health of Europeans. In short, the internal market had outpaced the capacity of European institutions to regulate the common market in foodstuffs. Believing that the 1999 commission reorganization could not ensure safe food, they advocated for a European response to a "European crisis." Accordingly, they developed a blueprint (see Figure 11.1) for a European Food and Public Health Authority (EFPHA), a regulatory agency with the combined scope of the U.S. Centers for Disease Control (CDC) and the Food and Drug Administration (FDA). In defending the designation of "authority" (rather than "agency"), they wrote that "it is distinctive and immediately specifies a different entity from the Agency concept which is so familiar to Commission officials and Member State policy-makers. It has also, in English, the ring of excellence and the ability to respond which may be helpful given the recent crises" (James, Kemper, and Pascal 1999, 40). In brief, they proposed to usurp much of the power then currently reserved for the commission, council, and member states. Europe needed to make a bold break from its past: "Systems need to be in place to show the links

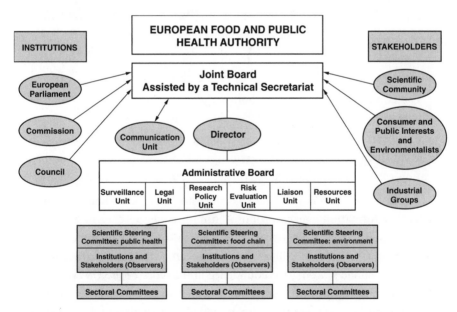

Figure 11.1
Scientists' proposed structure for the European Food and Public Health Authority.
Source: James, Kemper, and Pascal (1999)

with policy-making, risk management, control and audit processes which are capable of rapid and effective action" (14).

The new authority must be independent of governments, they argued, because the public had lost faith in the neutrality of scientific analysis and governmental regulations, especially in relation to agricultural and corporate interests. EFPHA would not only restore consumer confidence in food but would reduce industry frustration, "exasperated by the complex and protracted system for clearing their products." Finally, EFPHA would bring accountability to an anarchic system in which "national ministers, the Commission and European Parliament all seem to be involved, but where responsibility for specific issues or crisis management is hard to discern."

Events outpaced the proposed reforms. Between the time of the commissioning of this report (May 1999) and its publication (December), the Santer Commission resigned in disgrace and Romano Prodi was appointed commission president. The commission's (2000a) response to the James, Kemper, and Pascal report, the White Paper on Food Safety rejected the regulatory solution, citing three reasons:

· Transfer of regulatory powers to an independent authority could lead to an unwarranted dilution of democratic accountability.

· The commission must retain both regulation and control in order to discharge the responsibilities placed on it under the treaties.

· An authority with regulatory power could not be created under the current institutional arrangements of the EU and would require modification of the existing provisions of the EC Treaty.[2]

David Byrne soon launched a vigorous campaign defending the White Paper's information agency proposal in numerous speeches in which he drew a stark contrast between U.S. and European regulatory power (European Commission 2000e): "Looking across the Atlantic, I saw the American public placed great confidence in the work of the US Food and Drug Administration. An institution that was science-based. But also an institution that was involved in management and legislation. I concluded that such a model, while attractive in itself and clearly working for the US, would not be appropriate for the European scene. I wanted to ensure that risk assessment and risk management would be separated. Such an approach would be in line with the provisions of the Treaty, which entrusted management, and legislation, to the Commission, Parliament and Council." The EP Committee on Legal Affairs and the Internal Market (2000a) supported Commissioner Byrne's interpretation in a draft opinion: "A transfer of power does, however, entail a shift of competencies, which are thus removed from the sphere of influence of the bodies legitimised by the Treaties. . . . Legal provisions on food safety exist at both national and European level. It is, however, extremely doubtful whether a Food Authority could carry out local checks or impose sanctions, even in order to enforce the rules, or whether this would be desirable."

The White Paper: Interests and Food Law

After a four-month period of public comment on its White Paper on Food Safety (European Commission 2000a, 7), the EU submitted its proposal to the Council of Ministers and Parliament. The commission received opinions from interest groups, business enterprises, and EU institutions.

Analysis of Opinions on White Paper

Table 11.1 summarizes the opinions of the decision makers with respect to a number of critical issues. On the key issue of risk management, consumer organizations and retailers favored including management in the authority's competence. The regulated interests—food/drink and agriculture—preferred the current system (management in the European Commission and member states) but were more open to the possibility of risk management being centralized in the authority. While some respondents expressed an interest in relocating managerial responsibilities to the authority, this was not especially salient. The sectoral opinions reveal a recurring theme: the necessity of streamlining the review process (in the licensing of GMOs, evaluation of hormones and antibiotics) and the expectation that the agency approach would increase the turnaround time on the issuing of scientific opinions, and therefore commission rulings. Unequivocally, all European institutions agreed that risk management should remain a commission responsibility, although the Economic and Social Committee agreed with the commission that in the

Table 11.1
Attitudes toward a European food authority

	Risk management	Risk assessment	Risk communication	Urgency in creating an EFA	Subsidiarity	Democratic accountability and transparency
Interests						
Food and Drink (*n* = 25)	Medium	High	High	High	Medium	Medium
Agriculture (*n* = 10)	Medium	High	High	High	Medium	Medium
Consumers (*n* = 8)	High	High	High	High	Low	High
Retail and distribution (*n* = 3)	High	High	High	High	Low	High
Others (*n* = 13)	Varied	Varied	Varied	Varied	Varied	Varied
Parliament						
Environment, Public Health, Consumer Policy	Low	High	Low	High	Medium	High
Economic and Social Committee Councils	Low	High	Low	High	Low	High
Agriculture	NA	NA	NA	NA	NA	NA
Consumers	Low	High	Not addressed	Not addressed	Not addressed	High
Internal market	Low	High	Not addressed	Medium	High	High
European Council	Low	High	Not addressed	Medium	High	Not addressed

Note: High = favorable toward competency; low = unfavorable toward competency.

undetermined future, the issue of competency for risk management might be revisited.

The opinions of European institutions and interests were virtually identical in in supporting a shift of risk assessment from the commission to an independent agency. But with respect to risk communication (the commission's rapid alert system, RAS), the Economic and Social Committee, and the Parliament disagreed that competency should be shifted to the authority, questioning whether the new authority could be held accountable for failures in the RAS. In the EP's Committee on the Environment, Public Health and Consumer Policy (European Parliament 2000b), "The Rapid Alert System which allows the rapid identification and notification of urgent food safety problems, should continue to be the responsibility of the Commission, working closely with the Member States and the EFSA, but that in due course it may be appropriate for the Rapid Alert System to be operated within the EFSA."

As might be expected, preserving member state subsidiarity (food inspections, transposition of EU legislation into national law) was of greater concern to the Council of Ministers than to Parliament or the Economic and Social Committee, while the food/drink and agricultural sectors considered subsidiarity primarily in the context of promoting transparency and fairness in the SEM. With respect to transparency and democratic accountability, there was substantial support for making scientific assessments and methodology widely available, with Parliament and the Consumer Affairs Council both emphasizing this point. The Consumer Affairs Council reported that all of the member states "expressed themselves in favour of public availability of the information related to scientific opinions according to the procedures guaranteeing transparency," and the Internal Market Council reported similar agreement among member state representatives.

Consumer group opinion differed markedly from the results of Eurobarometer 49—Food Safety (Eurobarometer 1998), which found that consumers were more likely to trust food regulated at the national (66 percent) compared to the European level (43 percent). (Just 29 percent of the respondents expressed trust in producer-only controls.) Naturally, consumer group opinion would hold less weight than institutional (council, Parliament, ECS) and sectoral opinion, not least because of the collective action problem (Olson 1971). So while consumer groups favored the transfer of regulatory competency to the authority, their ability to speak on behalf of European consumers was questionable. A 1999 Eurobarometer collected data on the relationship between EU citizens and consumer groups. European consumers tend to trust information provided by consumer associations (50 percent), compared to 25 percent for national and 20 percent for European authorities. While 67 percent of Europeans would like "consumer organizations to have more influence in their country" (p. 7), only 4 percent reported membership in a consumer association and 50 percent did not know any consumer organization in his or her country (p. 13). This is the case despite European Commission funding to promote pan-European consumer groups (Young 1997). And although Europeans hold positive attitudes about consumer organizations, 50 percent of Europeans thought public services should distribute information, while 10 percent thought this task should belong to private services (p. 83). When asked whether "protecting the interests of consumers," should be a public or private task, 40 percent responded in favor of the former, only 13 percent agreed with the latter.

EFSA and the New Food Law

The European Commission published its food law proposal on November 8 (European Commission 2000a), which mirrored its proposal for a new food safety regime set forth in the White Paper. After Parliament and the Council of Minister's first reading, the former removed the Rapid Reaction Force from the EFA and returned it to the commission (a predictable move, given the lead committee's opposition to its removal, as expressed in its opinion to the White Paper). The commission presented a revised law on August 7, 2001, returning the Rapid Alert System to the commission (European Commission 2001a) and making some adjustments to the original legislative proposal for purposes of clarification. Only one more important change was to occur: Parliament inserted "Safety" into the title of the new agency.

Thus, the European Food Safety Authority was created on January 28, 2002 (legislation came into force February 21, 2002). It set up its management board nine months later and began work in 2003 after appointing scientists to its eight advisory panels. (See Figure 11.2.) EFSA worked out of its temporary headquarters in Brussels, awaiting word from the European Council on its permanent home: Would it be Helsinki or Parma? Finland cited the Edinburgh Council (1992) decision, which had (irresolutely) promised member states lacking an EU agency preference in council site selection for newly authorized agencies. But not only did some member states challenge Finland's claim to the EFSA—most indefatigably Prime Minister Silvio Berlusconi in his campaign on behalf of the city of Parma—but EU commissioners (Romano Prodi, David Byrne) opposed a Helsinki headquarters, preferring Luxembourg or Brussels. The Berlusconi presidency may not have delivered an EU constitution, but it did succeed in securing EFSA's headquarters for Italy, bringing to a close a contentious chapter in EFSA's founding and first years of operation ("Finns Feel Hard Done by on EU Agency" 2003, Whitehead 2004).

EFSA describes its mission as to "share its findings and listen to the views of others through a *vast network* [emphasis added] that will be developed over time, as well as interacting with experts and

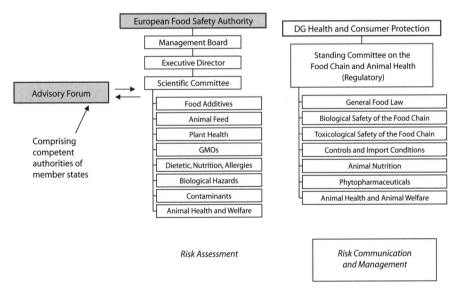

Figure 11.2
European Food Safety Policy Network.

decision-makers on many levels" (EFSA 2004). Figure 11.2 depicts the current European food regime. Representatives of member states' national food safety authorities sit on EFSA's Advisory Forum, while the scientists who staff its Scientific Committee and Panels serve in an advisory capacity. The regulatory function remains in the commission's Standing Committee on the Food Chain and Animal Health.

EFSA occupies the center of a network of member state regulatory bodies that exchanges and disseminates scientific opinions, while at the same time is itself a member of the commission's risk and communication network (European Commission 2002). This arrangement is typical of the independent agency's relationship with the commission and the former's relations with national authorities. Although the functions of Europe's independent agencies differ (Kreher 1997), they share a mandate to establish and maintain policy networks among national authorities, interests, and experts. The EU makes extensive use of policy networks for three reasons. First, European administration is understaffed as compared to the public administration of member states (Dehousse 1997, Majone 1996, Nugent 2001). Second, Wessels (1997) attributes the proliferation of networks to the commission's failure to institute EU-wide corporatism. Third, according to Dehousse (1997, 259) networks help the EU "expand the scope of its influence in the administrative sphere . . . [while] greater centralization is politically inconceivable."

Conclusion

This chapter has explored the establishment of the European Food Safety Authority in the context of the politics of European integration, particularly with respect to institutional and member state objectives. It addresses three questions. First, how did the European Union deal with political saliency and extensive media coverage of European food shocks? Second, how has the insertion of a new institutional actor (European Parliament) into the food policy legislative process influenced the policy outcome? Third, can one detect a reconfiguration of member state and European institutional power in the new European food safety regime?

The EU as a whole probably gained credibility among Europeans for taking leadership to resolve the food crisis. This was a highly salient issue on which member states made highly publicized mistakes—Belgium and dioxin, UK and BSE, Germany and BSE, France and its lax regulations of feed practices. But consumers came to realize that this was not just *their* country's problem but a European problem that required, at least in part, a European solution. In short, Europe was presented with the opportunity to resolve a crisis. It did so with the EFSA and a little luck besides. (No food crises have arisen since EFSA's establishment.) In sum, what seemed a European public relations disaster was deftly turned into an opportunity to demonstrate European competency in governing the SEM.

This conclusion leads to the second point regarding the new, more visible role of Parliament in codecision with the council. Parliament benefited from the favorable media attention it received in its now famous BSE Committee of Inquiry. BSE gave Parliament the hot-button issue it had sought since becoming directly elected in 1979, and it ably performed the role of fearless watchdog of European consumers. But not only this, the Parliament proved itself a competent and significant legislative partner in a key reform issue facing the European Union. The Parliament, in establishing itself as the European institution best able to represent the wishes of the European polity, brought a degree of credibility to the process that the commission and council could not. This is an important contribution that significantly assisted the commission and council in achieving consensus on policy reform with the European Council and national governments.

The commission's power as external negotiator in relation to the Council will likely increase with EFSA. Armed with reports from scientific experts working through an independent agency (rather than the commission's own advisory and regulatory committees), the commission can better overcome objections of member states that habitually keep the commission on a tight leash in WTO and other multilateral trade negotiations. At the same time, shifting the advisory function out of the commission enables it to focus less on assessment and more on implementation, tasks sometimes blurred when the commission was responsible for chairing and servicing the advisory committees. The commission too gains at the expense of national authorities by establishing a "European" standard of scientific expertise. This is a well-recognized phenomenon in federal systems, where the best and the brightest are lured to the higher level of government. Finally, the commission, by establishing food law based on legislative mechanisms, achieves a measure of democratic legitimacy in the area of food law that is not possible through the comitology system.

Parliament too gains, in its relationship with the council, by establishing itself as not only a coequal in issues thought to go to the heart of sovereignty and subsidiarity (protecting the life and health of member state nationals) but as a professional body of equivalent ability as that of the council in a key policy area. The Parliament also gains in relation to the council in inserting itself in an area that overlaps substantially with agricultural policy, the latter being a policy area that the Parliament has long sought (especially with regard to the CAP) colegislative authority with the council. This point should not, however, be overstated: the EP failed to leverage the BSE crisis into inclusion of codecision in agricultural policy (European Parliament of 1997, 36–37), first in the Treaty of Nice and more recently in the European Constitution.

Significantly, the BSE hearings strengthened the European Parliament's quest to have access to information discussed in the commission comitology committees. Specifically, the Parliament's position in relation to comitology committees was strengthened when the 1987 council decision laying down the comitology committees was revised in 1999. Although the EP remains dissatisfied with its powers in relation to these committees because it cannot stop or amend a comitology decision, it is now provided with fuller information about the work of the committees, and if it thinks a committee has exceeded the powers given to it in the enabling legislation, it can ask that the matter be reconsidered (see Buonanno and Nugent 2002).

Paradoxically, member states also benefit, despite the soft power invested in the authority. This is because food safety disagreements pitted member state national authorities against each other. Most famously, this was the situation in the protracted debate between the British (FSA) and French (AFSAA) authorities. As chapter 6 (this volume) discusses, the commission issued a global ban on the export of British beef on March 27, 1996 (Commission Decision 96/239/EC). By 1998 the British government had made sufficient changes in its regulatory policies to prompt the commission's Scientific Steering Committee (SSC) to recommend on October 29, 1999, that the commission lift the ban. All but Germany and France did so.

Chapter 6 notes that while the French government planned to abide by the commission decision, the new AFSSA objected on the basis of the precautionary principle. So while Germany lifted its ban on March 29, 2000, the French government, following the advice of AFSAA, continued its ban. (Before the ban, the French market represented 30 percent of British beef exports, its largest export market.) The European Court of Justice ruled France's ban illegal on December 21, 2001, but with the French government still banning British beef, the commission sent an Article 228 TEC notice to France in April 2002 and on July 17 decided to refer the case back to ask the court to request the imposition of a daily fine of 158,250 euros (Defra 2002). Meanwhile, President Chirac asked (June 13, 2002) the AFSAA to issue an opinion on British beef. The AFSSA declared British beef safe on October 2, 2002, and the French government lifted its ban. It is expected that EFSA will be in a better position than the Commission's expert committees to not only provide scientific opinion less subject to member state influence (or the appearance thereof), but to be able to broker disputes between national authorities, themselves members of the EFSA's advisory structure.

EFSA's evolving role in the EU's most contentious food safety issue of GMO licensing is a good bellwether of the Europeanization of food safety assessment. With Regulation (EC) No. 1829/2003 of the European Parliament and Council (see also the commission's implementing Regulation (EC) No. 641/2004), which came into effect January 1, 2005, the EU shifted risk assessment for GMOs out of the national authorities to EFSA. While an application is still to be submitted to the national authority of the applicant's member state, it now must be forwarded to EFSA. This new process likely strengthens, albeit incrementally, the commission's hand in its dealings with those member states resisting the licensing of new applications for marketing GMOs in the EU. Although the commission experienced a setback in the June 2005 Council of Environment Ministers decision (under qualified majority voting) permitting Austria, France, Luxembourg, Germany, and Greece to continue their bans of GMOs authorized prior to the EU moratorium, the council deadlocked on the commission's directive to authorize importation of Monsanto's MON 863 (corn variety engineered to resist corn rootworms).[3] The commission, in authorizing its importation for use in animal feed, ended the EU's six-year moratorium. The commission's approval was based largely on EFSA's April 2004 assessment the MON 863 was as safe as conventional maize, a point reiterated in the many commission statements on this issue.

On closer examination, the council's voting pattern is more suggestive of mutual respect for national law in a highly contested policy area than an anti-GMO vote. Even heavily GMO-cultivated Spain voted to permit continuation of the bans in company with most of the member states. (The UK supported the commission's directive, Finland and Sweden abstained, while Portugal voted to lift one of the bans and the Czech Republic another.) As a wholly new application, authorization for MON 863 did not overturn national bans; Monsanto made the first application under new EU laws dealing with traceability, cultivation, and assessment of GMOs. The council was well aware that in the event it did not act on the commission's directive, the commission held the legal authority to approve MON 863. As the EU moved to end its embattled ban on GMOs, it did so by shifting responsibility from member states to supranational authorities. EFSA now joined the commission in this dubious honor as an institution for member states to blame for unpopular decisions, a familiar tactical maneuver in the increasingly federalized European political landscape.

Whether local tastes and practices differ substantially so as to affect food safety debates is questionable. Apart from those few cases regarding Italians, Greeks, or French who do not wish to pasteurize cheese and Belgians who seek a strict definition of chocolate, these are marginal rather than mainstream. They are also hardly unique to Europe. If there are any areas of substantive contestation in this realm, it is more likely to be in European taxation policy, where, for instance, the commission faces tough battles in harmonizing alcohol excise taxes between central and eastern European (Scandinavian booze cruises to the Baltic states) and the wide disparity among the EU-25 in national rates applied to wine and beer.

Jürgen Habermas (2001) and other cosmopolitans suggest that western Europe has created a new norms-based form of government that supersedes the nation-state. The concept of contested governance engages this notion by suggesting that in such a highly contested policy area as food safety characterized by multi–level regulation, uneven integration, politicization of science and risk assessment, and disparate norms among members in international organizations, actors are unlikely to agree to how policy will be implemented. Although some observers have bemoaned the loss of a historic opportunity to establish greater European authority in the food safety policy regime, this chapter has illustrated that incremental policy developments may be accompanied by potentially significant shifts in institutional power. The fifty-year history of European integration has been characterized by incremental progress in policy areas that are later confirmed by history-making treaties. So while EFSA may have been seen as a tepid response to a decade of food shocks, the act of its establishment has probably strengthened the European Parliament's role as a legislative actor, increased the EU's democratic legitimacy and accountability, and resolved a long-standing problem the EU has experienced in international forums by providing food safety assessments informed by European scientific expertise and the ability of Europe to speak with one voice.

Notes

1. Regulations and directives are defined in Article 249 of the TEC. A regulation is binding in its entirety and automatically enters into force on the day it is adopted. Directives leave room for member state discretion in their transposition into national law as well as an extended time frame (usually two to three years) for their adoption. (EU legislation—regulations, directives, decisions, and recommendations—can be promulgated by the commission, the council, or the council and Parliament.)

2. The third assumption is hotly contested by EU jurists. Weiler (1999, 343, 344) writes that "the only question is whether the Court knowingly or unknowingly turns a blind eye to the fictions of both the Council and Commission when they apply their *Meroni* circumventions." Everson et al. (1997, 12) argue that "neither

Article 4 nor the *Meroni* doctrine are writ in stone, and it should no longer be simply assumed that they act as a legal bar to the evolution of European agencies."

3. Under EU law, the commission submits GMO recommendation to the Regulatory Committee, which can approve or reject the proposal. In the Monsanto case, the Regulatory Commission did not give an opinion. The commission, therefore, needed to submit the proposal to the competent council (environment ministers), which must act on the directive within three months. If the council does not take action, the commission can adopt the directive.

V

The International Dimension

12

Protection or Protectionism? EU Food Safety and the WTO

Alasdair R. Young and Peter Holmes

The European Union's attempts to manage differences over food safety among its member states have provoked differences with its trading partners. The conclusion of the Uruguay Round of multilateral trade negotiations, which both tightened international disciplines on food regulation and established binding dispute settlement, increased the significance of such trade disputes, because they now have the potential to lead to domestic food safety rules being found incompatible with international obligations. Such decisions are highly politically sensitive as food safety has become extremely politically salient within the EU in the wake of several high-profile food safety failures.

This chapter assesses the extent of the challenge posed by World Trade Organization (WTO) obligations for EU policy autonomy with regard to food safety. It thus concentrates primarily on the "where should food safety be regulated?" aspect of contested governance. In particular, the location of food safety governance is contested within the EU—between the member state and emerging EU levels—at the same time as new multilateral rules impose disciplines on EU (and national) food safety regulation. These multilateral disciplines affect two other facets of contested governance: On what basis should food safety be regulated, and how should it be regulated?

This chapter argues that the dynamics of the market integration process within the EU tend to produce common rules that are fairly trade restrictive, even though the aim is protection, not protectionism. While this tendency helps to address concerns about the legitimacy of EU-level food safety regulation, some of the EU's rules have fallen afoul of the EU's multilateral obligations. Further, a number of features of the EU's policymaking process—particularly its highly legalistic character and high thresholds for policy change—arguably may make it more difficult for the EU than for other polities to comply with adverse WTO judgments. That said, the evolving interpretation of the WTO's obligations through the dispute settlement process and developments in the EU's food policymaking process are reducing the differences between EU and WTO approaches to food safety with regard to on what basis and how to regulate. As a consequence, the likelihood that future EU rules will fall afoul of its international obligations is also reduced, which should also help to mitigate the at-what-level-of-governance aspect of contested governance.

This chapter begins by mapping the EU's experience with WTO dispute settlement with respect to food regulations and contextualizing it with respect to the EU's experience in other policy areas and other countries' experiences with respect to food safety. This discussion is augmented by identifying EU food safety rules that irritate its main trading partners but have not (yet) been the subject of WTO complaints. The chapter then seeks to explain why the EU has particular problems with WTO rules in the area of food safety, compared to both other countries and other policy areas. Having established where the EU butts up against multilateral obligations, the chapter investigates the precise nature of those obligations. It then turns to the issue of compliance and investigates how the EU has responded to adverse WTO judgments. The chapter concludes by drawing out implications for the EU's future relationship with the WTO with regard to food safety.

The EU's Experience in Context

This section identifies EU food safety rules that have caused trade frictions and contextualizes the EU's experience with the WTO. As table 12.1 illustrates, the EU accounts for the vast majority, of an admittedly small number, of disputes concerning food safety. This share exaggerates the situation, as multiple complaints, by different trading partners, concern the same regulations: two concerning the ban on hormone-treated beef and three against the moratorium on approvals of genetically modified (GM) crops.

Table 12.1
The relative importance of food safety in complaints against the EU (through 31 December 2004)

	Total number	EU number	EU share
All complaints	324	50	15%
Regulatory	35	12	34
Food regulation	29	10	34
Food safety	7	5	71

Although very few food safety measures have been the subject of WTO disputes, there are a number of EU food safety rules that have caused trade frictions but have not (yet) led to formal trade disputes (see box 12.1). The measures raised by the EU's trading partners in the SPS (Sanitary and Phytosantitary) Committee do not represent all of the EU's food safety rules that affect trade. The United States, for example, has raised a number of EU food safety measures outside the committee, including the ban on hormone-treated beef (discussed below), the ban on rBST milk, the ban on some antimacrobial treatments in poultry production, the third-country meat directive, and wine-making standards (USTR, 2002).

Although not comprehensive, the measures raised in the SPS Committee provide the best source of comparable data among countries. This reveals that the EU's trading partners have raised the adverse trade effects of EU food safety measures in the WTO far more than those of any other country (see table 12.2). This strongly suggests that whatever the perceptions of European consumers, the EU's food safety rules are often more risk averse than those of its trading partners.

Why Are EU Rules Particularly Problematic?

An important reason why the EU's food safety rules have tended to pose problems for its trading partners is a side effect of the process of agreeing on common rules within the EU.[1] As explained below, the dynamics of trading up (Vogel 1995) mean that common rules tend to be set close to those of the most risk-averse member government.

Box 12.1
EU food safety rules affecting trade

Restrictions on shellfish
Pesticide and antibiotic limits in honey (Directive 96/23)
Regulations on genetically modified food and feed
Notification G/SPS/N/EEC/150 on traceability and labeling of genetically modified organisms and food and feed
Directive 2000/42 on pesticide residues
Legislation on the fungicide thiabendazole (TBZ)
Import restrictions on soy sauce
Information on dioxin
Measures on food treated with ionizing radiation
Emergency measures on citrus pulp
Measure on establishments operating in the animal feed sector
Maximum levels for certain contaminants (aflatoxins) in foodstuffs
Trade restrictions in response to cholera
Restrictions on the importation of fruits and fruit juices
Restrictions on honey imports
Maximum levels for aflatoxins in corn and sampling contaminants in food
Notification G/SPS/N/EEC/196 on maximum residue levels in plant and animal products
Notification G/SPS/N/EEC/191 and Add.1 on food and feed controls
Source: WTO (2004).

The EU's single-market program, launched in 1985, aims to liberalize trade among the EU's twenty-five member states. Where possible, it has sought to do so simply by having the member governments recognize each other's rules as being equivalent in effect, if not the same in detail: the mutual recognition principle. Such an approach is entirely beneficial for third-country products, as meeting one member's requirements permits access to the rest.

Even among the EU's relatively homogeneous member states, however, many national regulations cannot always be assumed to be equivalent in effect. This is because there are a number of legitimate reasons that national regulations diverge (Hancher and Moran 1989, Previdi 1997). These differences stem from cultural differences (see chapter 2, this volume), different mixes of public and private regulation (see chapters 2 and 9, this volume), and/or different political institutions (see chapter 9

Table 12.2
Food-safety-related trade concerns notified to the WTO's SPS Committee,
January 1, 1995–December 31, 2003

| Country | Concerns related to . . . | | | | |
	Food safety	Animal health	Plant health	Other	Total
EU	15	10	3	1	29
China	3	2	2	0	7
South Korea	3	2	0	2	7
Australia	2	6	5	0	13
Japan	2	2	7	1	12
Czech Republic	2	1	1	0	4
United States	1	6	7	0	14
Brazil	1	2	4	1	8
Canada	1	5	0	0	6
Indonesia	1	2	2	0	5
Chile	1	3	1	0	5
Panama	1	1	1	1	4
Slovak Republic	1	1	2	0	4
Honduras	1	1	1	0	3
New Zealand	1	1	1	0	3
Poland	1	1	1	0	3
El Salvador	1	1	0	0	2
Philippines	1	0	1	0	2
Romania	1	1	0	0	2
Singapore	1	1	0	0	2
Switzerland	1	0	1	0	2
Egypt	1	0	0	0	1
Iceland	1	0	0	0	1
Malaysia	1	0	0	0	1
Rest of world (29 countries)	0	31	6	2	39
Total	45	80	46	8	179

Notes: SPS Committee's totals based on total number of measures, a number of
which are imposed by multiple countries. Excludes notifications made by the government in question and measures adopted by EU member states. BSE-related
restrictions are classified under "animal health"; the EU's rules on genetically
modified crop approvals are classified under "other."
Source: WTO (2004).

and, contrast chapters 6, 7, and 8, this volume). One increasingly important reason for differences in the stringency of national regulations is different attitudes toward the management of risk (Isaac, Banerji, and Woolcock 2000; Vogel 2001b; chapter 11, this volume). As a consequence of the resulting significant differences in regulation among its member states, the EU has frequently engaged in positive integration—agreeing on common rules—in order to achieve market integration. When common rules are agreed, there is the potential that they will impede imports from outside the EU.

This is not to say that regulatory approximation within the EU does not bring benefits to third-country firms by eliminating the need to comply with multiple national requirements and by increasing transparency. However, although it is possible that the common rules may be less restrictive than the national ones they replace, the tendency has been for them to be more stringent.

Within the category of harmonized product regulations, rules that govern how products are produced present particular problems for third-country firms. So-called process regulations do not generally present barriers to trade; however, they can present a problem when the production process is considered to have altered the product. This seems to be a particularly common problem with respect to food safety. The WTO disputes concerning the EU's rules on hormone-treated beef, GM food, and wine making all fit into this category, as do the residual dispute concerning antimicrobial treatments in poultry production, the shelved dispute about rBST milk, and the resolved dispute over the third-country meat directive.

The Dynamics of Market Integration

When the EU adopts common rules, the dynamics of market integration press for regulatory approximation at a strict level—"trading up." The energy for approximation comes from the negative impact that divergent national rules have on trade within the EU. Stringent product standards, in addition to protecting consumers, provide benefits to domestic firms by protecting them from other European competitors whose products do not meet those standards. Those competitors may decide that it is simply worth complying with the rule in order to gain access to the market. Alternatively, they might try to have the rule overturned under EU law.

Under EU law, however, member governments have the right, albeit within limits, to enforce strict national rules despite the mutual recognition principle. As noted above, the mutual recognition principle applies only when the assumption of equivalence holds. Further, Article 30 of the Treaty of the European Community permits restrictions on trade for a number of public policy reasons, including the protection of human health and safety. It is possible, therefore, that a government's more stringent regulation will be upheld by the European Court of Justice (ECJ). As a consequence, there are incentives for a stringent-standard country's trading partners to negotiate a common rule in order to eliminate the disruptive impact on trade of different rules (Vogel 1995, Young and Wallace 2000). The more important the market of the stringent-standard country, the greater the incentive. Thus, governments with more stringent regulations play an agenda-setting role within the EU.

When common rules are negotiated, the government with legitimately (under EU law) more stringent standards is in a strong bargaining position. So long as there is no agreement, its industry is protected from foreign competition while those of its trading partners are hurt by being denied access to its market. Consequently, the costs of no agreement fall more heavily on its trading partners. In addition, particularly given the importance of food safety, the government with stricter standards might pay a political cost for compromising and might expose its citizens to danger. The government with little to gain and potentially much to lose from an agreement has a strong incentive to hold out for an agreement close to its preference, while those that have most to gain have stronger incentives to compromise (Garrett and Tsebelis 1996, Moravcsik 1993, Putnam 1988).

Because regulatory decisions within the EU are adopted by a qualified majority vote, no individual government can block a rule.[2] Consequently, a stringent-standard government needs assistance to resist a common rule that would require it to relax its standards. Such assistance is usually forthcoming either from other member governments (to form a blocking minority) or from the European Commission or European Parliament. The Danish, Dutch, German, Finnish, and Swedish governments regularly supported stricter measures. Although just shy of a blocking minority under the pre-2004 decision rules, they were often supported by additional member governments on specific measures.

Crucially, the European Commission, because of its agenda-setting role in advancing proposals, often has the ability to choose the winning coalition. For a number of reasons, not least its concern to bolster its legitimacy with the EU's citizens, the commission tends to advance proposals that will command the qualified majority of member governments favoring more stringent rules rather than the one favoring less stringent rules (Peters 1994, Young and Wallace 2000). This tendency has been reinforced by the increasing application of the precautionary principle, which is anchored in Article 174 of the treaty, in consumer and environmental policy (Woolcock 2002; and see chapters 11 and 13, this volume).

Another reason for the commission to favor stricter proposals is that it reduces the risk of disruption to the internal market. Article 95 of the treaty permits, albeit subject to strict disciplines, member governments to adopt or retain rules stricter than agreed common rules. Consequently, a stringent-standard government that was deeply unhappy with a less strict common rule might take its chances with the EU's legal system and retain or adopt stricter rules. Although it might ultimately have to comply with the common rule, it would at least delay the impact of the measure and earn itself political points at home. In the meantime, trade within the single market would be disrupted. Thus, the commission has an incentive to prevent defection upward by pushing for stricter rather than looser common standards.

The emergence of the European Parliament as a colegislator on single-market measures has also reinforced the tendency toward stricter standards. This is because the Parliament has repeatedly sought to promote consumer and environmental interests (European Commission 1991; Judge, Earnshaw, and Cowan 1994). This advocacy is related to the Parliament's receptiveness to civic interest organizations, which have also become increasingly active and effective at the European level since the mid-1990s (Webster 1998, Young 1997).[3]

As a consequence, consumer and environmental measures within the EU are often supported by an influential advocacy alliance of member governments, supranational institutions, and civic interest groups (Young and Wallace 2000). Such advocacy alliances, coupled with the catalyst of trading up, have created a political dynamic within the single market that favors the adoption of stricter common standards (Peterson 1997, Sbragia 1993, Scharpf 1996, Vogel 1995; Young and Wallace 2000).

Nonetheless, governments with the most stringent standards do not always get all that they want. As a sweetener to get the government with the most stringent regulation to accept a common rule that is not quite as strict as its own, EU rules may incorporate escape clauses that permit member governments to adopt more stringent national rules under specified circumstances. Such provisions provide scope for the dynamics of trading up to continue to press for stricter standards even after a common rule has been adopted. In addition, measures adopted over the intense objection of a stringent-standard government often include provisions requiring that the issue be revisited within a specified, relatively short time (Young and Wallace 2000). This creates a process through which standards are ratcheted up over time.

These dynamics are illustrated by two high-profile examples: the ban on hormone-treated beef and the rules for approving genetically modified crops. As both examples are covered extensively elsewhere in this book, the discussion here is restricted to brief summaries that concentrate on the dynamics discussed above. The EU's ban on hormone-treated beef clearly illustrates the process of trading up and the influential role of an advocacy alliance (see box 12.2). The informal moratorium on GM crop approvals and the subsequent revision of the directive on the intentional release of genetically modified organisms illustrate how escape clauses can provide opportunities for trading up even after common rules have been agreed (see box 12.3).

The Implications of Enlargement

Enlargement, by increasing the diversity of membership, will complicate the already delicate regulatory balance within the EU (Holmes and Young 2001). Given the limitations of mutual recognition among the existing membership of the EU, enlargement will create pressure either to agree to even more common rules or to rely more heavily on national treatment, which would not eliminate impediments to trade within the EU. The former course is more likely than the latter. Whether

Box 12.2
The ban on hormone-treated beef

In the 1980s, the member governments had markedly different assessments of the safety of five hormones used in raising beef (Council 1988). As a result, some banned all five, while others permitted all five, and others banned only some (Vogel 1997). These different practices impeded the free circulation of beef within the EU and raised concerns about the distortion of competition.

The European Commission's initial proposal to ban the two synthetic hormones but permit the controlled use of the three natural hormones received a hostile response from consumer groups, the European Parliament, the Economic and Social Committee, and most of the member governments (Princen 2002, WTO 1997). In the face of this formidable advocacy alliance, the commission (1985c) revised its proposal to ban the three natural hormones as well. Although some governments opposed such a ban, the ability of other member governments to exclude hormone-treated meat from their markets placed them at a disadvantage. The deck was further stacked against the opponents of a ban by the commission's questionable decision to advance the proposal under just Article 43, which enabled the new directive to be adopted by a qualified majority vote. This meant that the opposition of the UK and Denmark and the abstention of Ireland could not prevent the adoption of the directive.

Box 12.3
GM crop approvals

The procedures for approving genetically modified crops under the 1990 directive provide significant scope for any member government to impede the approval of any GM product. There is also a safeguard clause that permits governments under certain circumstances to exclude from their territories GM products that have been approved for sale in the EU. In 1998 the member governments stopped taking decisions, and several governments invoked the safety clause of the directive to prohibit the sale or import of even EU-approved varieties of GM crops.

The European Commission (1998), frustrated at the resulting fragmentation of the single market and concerned about the implications of the stalled approval process for the competitiveness of the European biotechnology and agriculture industries, proposed making the rules more stringent. Several governments stepped up the pressure for reform by declaring that they would not approve any new GM crops until a revised directive was adopted (Council 1999b). With the European Parliament also supporting more stringent rules, it is no surprise that the new directive places greater emphasis on precaution and environmental risk assessment and requires traceability, monitoring, and labeling throughout the production process.

enlargement will dilute the tendency toward higher standards, thereby accentuating the contestation of governance within the EU while easing the tension between the EU and its trading partners, is unclear. Enlargement will almost certainly reduce the power of the pro-stringent-standard member governments, but it is less likely to affect the preferences or power of the other components of the pro-strict-standard advocacy alliance, notably the European Commission and Parliament.

Summary

The need to grapple with the contested governance of food safety within the EU has tended to produce fairly stringent common rules. These rules have sometimes caused tensions with the EU's trading partners. These rules, however, while impeding trade, are not necessarily incompatible with the EU's WTO obligations.

WTO Jurisprudence and the Contours of Multilateral Obligations

In order to assess the EU's multilateral obligations, this chapter briefly reviews the key aspects of Article III (national treatment) of the General Agreement on Tariffs and Trade (GATT) and the Sanitary and Phytosanitary (SPS) and the Technical Barriers to Trade (TBT) Agreements as they have been interpreted in WTO disputes involving food safety. It summarizes the implications of the relevant WTO rules and jurisprudence and specifies in what ways the EU's policies may be incompatible with WTO rules.

The WTO's Rules

The first point to stress is that historically, the GATT left countries free to set whatever food safety standards they wished. Article III:4 imposed the constraint that such measures had to be applied in a nondiscriminatory way on imported and domestic goods, but the implications of this emerged only after the WTO's binding dispute settlement began to clarify the rules.

On the face of it, the nondiscrimination obligation of Article III is quite weak. It implies that a country's rules may be whatever it likes but must apply equally to home and foreign goods. By contrast, within the EU, the European Court of Justice (ECJ) very early on argued that any national differences between rules were capable of acting as obstacles to trade and had to be justified if they did so, and hence created an impetus toward first harmonization and later mutual recognition.

Concern that governments might try to offset trade liberalization in agriculture by introducing idiosyncratic health and safety standards that were easy for their own firms to meet but hard for foreign firms led to the demand for the SPS Agreement as part of the Uruguay Round. Its essential features are:

1. All food safety measures have to be based on a risk assessment and scientific evidence (Arts. 5.1 and 5.2).

2. Governments are free to set their own levels of food safety, but there is a general presumption that food produced to international standards is safe, and countries wishing to impose tighter or different standards have to show that there is scientific evidence to justify them (Arts. 3 and 4).

3. Governments may adopt provisional measures if there is inadequate scientific evidence on product safety (Art. 5.7).

4. Measures to achieve a given end must restrict trade as little as possible (Art. 2).

The TBT Agreement also qualifies governments' right to regulate. It requires that technical regulations be based on international standards "except when such international standards or relevant parts would be an ineffective or inappropriate means for the fulfilment of the legitimate objectives pursued" (Art. 2.4). Although the TBT Agreement applies to food, it is more relevant to labeling requirements than to safety.

The foregoing is a brief summary of the principle and intentions, but the devil in these matters is always in the detail, which requires an examination of how these disciplines have been interpreted by the Dispute Settlement Body (DSB). Notable among the issues that were left ill defined are where the burden of proof lies in the case of challenges and just what constitutes scientific evidence.

Before getting into the case law, it is worth looking at how the SPS Agreement fits with the rest of the structure of the WTO Agreement. The basic structure of the WTO is that the core regulatory discipline of the

WTO is expressed in GATT Article III:4, and the rules governing standards in general and food safety standards in particular are expressed in the TBT and SPS Agreements, which were adopted during the Uruguay Round. These key aspects of the multilateral framework are summarized in table 12.3.

WTO Jurisprudence
These rules leave significant scope for interpretation (see also chapter 13, this volume). Despite the Uruguay Round establishing a more robust process of adjudicating disputes, there have been relatively few WTO complaints involving food safety measures (see table 12.1). In fact, as table 12.4 indicates, the only complaint concerning an EU food safety measure to have produced a ruling by the time of writing (February 2005) has been the beef hormone case.

The appellate body in the beef hormone case (and in the sardine case, which was about labeling, not safety) declared that under both the SPS and TBT Agreements, governments have the right to choose the level of protection they want and do not have to justify their choice to the DSB. It also held that the burden of proof was on the complainant to show that there was no justification for the measures. This appears to mean that complainants have to show both that a measure was not based on international standards and that the risk assessment on which it was based was inadequate. In the beef hormone case, the Canadian and U.S. governments were able to convince the appellate body on both counts. The appellate body in the beef hormone case, however, insisted that it did not require proof of the necessity of a measure, but would have been prepared to accept any kind of scientific evidence that indicated there might be a risk, even if majority opinion was against it. Thus, the appellate body did not challenge the EU's wish to set a zero risk of cancer from hormones, but merely whether there was a rational link between this aim and the measures adopted. The EU's case in beef hormones was further weakened by not invoking Article 5.7 (which refers to provisional measures, which the EU's ban was not) as a defense, even though it made repeated references to the precautionary principle.

Neumann and Türk (2003) stress that the appellate body has repeatedly insisted, as in the asbestos case, that even under the more stringent

Table 12.3
Summary of key WTO obligations affecting food safety regulation

Obligation	Rule	Escape clause	Burden of proof
Art. III	National treatment—de facto but no formal obligation to harmonize	Art. XX, "General exceptions"	On complainant to prove violation of national treatment On respondent to prove necessity (*Asbestos*)
TBT	National treatment required, and regulations to be based on international standards unless ineffective to achieve national aims (Art. 2.4) Deviations must be least trade restricting	May use different rules if it has an aim that cannot be met by international standards. Aim unlikely to be questioned (*Korean Beef*)	Complainant must prove rule is not based on international standard AND if so, there is no good reason to justify (*Sardines*)
SPS	Base rules on scientific evidence Base rules on international standards Deviations must be least trade restricting No arbitrary inconsistencies between different regulations	Art. 3.3, 5.7 May use higher standard if there is some evidence it can reduce risk, or if evidence not complete	Complainant must prove rule is not based on international standard AND that if so, there is no scientific evidence to justify (*Hormones*)

Note: Parenthetical text refers to cases.

Table 12.4
WTO complaints involving EU food regulations (through December 31, 2004)

Case	Description	Type of issue	Complainant	Status	Panel favored	Appellate body favored
7	Description of scallops (French measure)	Labeling	Canada	Negotiated solution		
14	Description of scallops (French measure)	Labeling	Chile	Negotiated solution		
12	Description of scallops (French measure)	Labeling	Peru	Negotiated solution		
231	Trade description of sardines	Labeling	Peru	Appellate body ruling	Peru	Peru
263	Measures affecting imports of wine	Quality	Argentina	Negotiated solution		
26	Measures affecting meat and meat products (hormones)	Safety	United States	Appellate body ruling	United States	United States
48	Measures affecting meat and meat products (hormones)	Safety	Canada	Appellate body ruling	Canada	Canada
291	Approval and marketing of biotech products	Safety	United States	Panel established (Aug. 29, 2003)		
292	Approval and marketing of biotech products	Safety	Canada	Panel established (Aug. 29, 2003)		
293	Approval and marketing of biotech products	Safety	Argentina	Panel established (Aug. 29, 2003)		

Notes: Shaded groups' complaints concern the same regulatory measure. The complaints concerning the description of scallops actually targeted a French rule.

burden of proof requirements of Article III, "it is undisputed that WTO Members have the right to determine the level of protection . . . that they consider appropriate in a given situation" (WTO 2001, paragraph 168).

What the appellate body has often disputed, however, is whether there is sufficient evidence, including scientific evidence where appropriate, to show that a given measure really is necessary to achieve a declared aim. In the Korean beef case, which involved labeling rather than food safety, and hence fell under the TBT Agreement, the appellate body, for the first time, tried to clarify the meaning of *necessary* in this context and the obligation to use the least trade-restricting measure. The appellate body make it very clear, however, that a complainant cannot win by simply showing that there is in principle some logically available alternative measure that would restrict trade less. But it implied that it will allow a government more leeway when the objective of the measure in question is something as vital as the protection of human life, but may be more demanding in applying the least-trade-restrictive test to a TBT measure aimed at a lesser goal, such as administrative convenience (Marceau and Trachtman 2002).

This might give the impression that the appellate body is seeking to impose its own values and apply some sort of trade-off: when the value seems important, you can be very trade restrictive, but when it is a lesser value, you must pay more attention to the trade impact. This sounds like the ECJ's proportionality test, but Neumann and Türk (2003) argue ingeniously and convincingly that this is not what the appellate body has said and that it has no authority to weigh up food safety against trade effects. They argue that the appellate body adheres firmly to respect for the "right to determine the level of protection," and therefore when considering whether a measure is "least trade restrictive," it will examine only alternatives that are equally effective. Thus, there is no trade-off between effectiveness and trade impact. That there is an alternative measure that is almost as effective, but very much less trade restricting, would not be grounds for a measure to be found incompatible with SPS rules (Marceau and Trachtman 200, Neumann and Türk 2003).

On the other hand, once the appellate body has identified other measures that are equally effective, it will then set about the task of assessing the degree of trade restrictiveness. It is at this point that the importance of the objective comes in. Neumann and Türk (2003: 211) observe, "If the value to be protected is important, the measure is effective and the trade restriction is moderate, the measure is likely to be considered 'necessary' while an equally effective and GATT-consistent or less inconsistent alternative will be seen as being not 'reasonably available'." The appellate body will, on this view, never challenge the aim itself.[4] Such rulings have come in the context of Article III/XX cases, but as Neumann and Türk point out, Article 5.6, footnote 3 of the SPS Agreement is even more explicit that any alternative measure is not to be considered less trade restrictive unless it both "achieves the appropriate level of sanitary or phytosanitary protection and is significantly less restrictive to trade."

There is perhaps one qualification to the view that the DSB will never question the objective of an SPS measure, and that is the criteria of consistency. Article 5.5 of the SPS text says, "Each Member shall avoid arbitrary or unjustifiable distinctions in the levels it considers to be appropriate in different situations, if such distinctions result in discrimination or a disguised restriction on international trade." In the beef hormones case, the United States argued that tougher rules on beef than on pork might be seen as evidence of inconsistency and hence suggested that the beef hormone ban was really a disguised restriction on trade. The appellate body rejected this argument in this case, although it accepted a similar argument in the Australian salmon case.[5] The implications of this are that the EU should not have to worry about this provision so long as its food safety rules are consistent in reducing risk.

Before leaving the issue of WTO jurisprudence, it is worth commenting on the current complaints against the EU's procedures for approving GM crops by Argentina, Canada, and the Untied States. Although these complaints are very high profile, it seems unlikely that they, should they ever get as far as a ruling, will further clarify these key issues in the SPS Agreement. This is because the complaints are quite narrowly drawn and do not challenge the basis on which the EU takes its decisions.[6] Rather, they focus on the EU's "moratorium" on approvals and the refusal of some member governments to accept GM crops that have been approved by the EU (USTR 2004). Thus, the challenges are against the EU's failure to apply its own procedures and enforce its own rule rather than against the substance of those procedures and decisions. The complainants seem to have taken this tack because the EU's procedures, were they applied, are compatible with the SPS Agreement as it has been interpreted.[7]

Summary

The approach of the appellate body in clarifying the SPS Agreement and other related texts essentially affirms the right of the EU to choose whatever food safety objectives it wishes. Where there is any evidence at all of a risk from a food product, this is likely to leave the EU fairly free to choose its own policies—although the EU may find that measures to achieve these aims that also restrict trade will be vigorously scrutinized. Where scientific evidence is inconclusive, provisional measures may be applied, although what constitutes relevant scientific evidence is always (literally) disputable. It should be noted, however, that given the limited case law to date, the full implications of these rulings remain to be seen.[8]

The real potential problem lies with measures adopted in response to public fear of a health risk while all the scientific evidence appears to show a product is safe. In cases where tough labeling rules are enough to allow the public to avoid a perceived risk, there is little to worry about. But where a trade ban is imposed for the sake of reassuring the public, the appellate body of the WTO may find itself obliged to be more restrictive of regulatory autonomy than the ECJ has been in some comparable circumstances (Slotboom 2003). As this chapter shall argue, however, the evolution of the EU's procedures should mean that future EU rules will be less likely to be incompatible with its multilateral obligations.

Balancing Competing Governance Demands

The WTO's rules clearly have implications for EU food safety rules, even if these are greater with respect to means than ends. Consequently, the EU confronts two aspects of compliance with multilateral obligations: one concerning bringing existing rules into line with multilateral obligations, the other with ensuring that future rules are compatible. The first is narrower and concerns the EU's changing its rules in response to an adverse WTO judgment—the hormone-treated beef case is the only food safety example to date. The second is broader and involves reform of how the EU makes its food safety policy. An extreme variant of this second aspect, of concern to a number of anti-WTO activists, would be a regulatory freeze, with the EU ceasing to adopt food safety rules for fear of incurring the wrath of its trading partners and the WTO.

Bringing Existing Rules into Line

Although there are very few cases to go on, there is some indication that the EU has particular problems resolving food regulation disputes amicably. As table 12.5 indicates, food regulation complaints against the EU tend to result in panels more often than similar complaints against other countries. Further, when the DSB has ruled against the EU in food safety and other cases, it has had difficulty bringing its rules into compliance.

None of this should come as a surprise. There are strong indications that political systems in which there is a separation of powers have more trouble changing their rules than do more unified polities; witness the problems the United States had with changing its law on foreign sales corporations. Not only do any changes to EU food safety rules have to be agreed by both the European Parliament and the Council of

Table 12.5
Status of food regulation disputes (by respondent as of December 31, 2004)

	EU	Australia	Korea	United States	Japan	Rest of the world
Pending consultations for more than a year	1	1	2	2		4
Withdrawn						1
Negotiated solution	3 (1)	1	2			
Panel requested		2				
Active panel	3 (1)					
WTO judgment	3 (2)	1		1	2	
Sanctions imposed	2 (1)					
Total number	10 (4)	5	4 (3)	3 (2)	2	5

Note: Numbers are based on the number of complaints. Numbers in parentheses report the number of measures challenged (if different).

Ministers, but there is also a high threshold for change, with the Council having to adopt proposals by a qualified majority.

These difficulties apply to any rule change within the EU, but there is reason to expect them to be particularly pronounced with regard to food safety, as it is now such a hot-button issue. European publics are sufficiently sensitized to food safety that any politician perceived as not taking the issue seriously is risking his or her political future.[9]

Examination of the EU's response to the adverse judgments in the beef hormone case provides at least preliminary support for the view that institutional features of the EU are likely to make compliance with WTO judgments particularly challenging. As discussed above, the DSB found the EU's ban incompatible with its multilateral obligations in January 1998. After the WTO-adjudicated "reasonable" period for the EU to bring its rule into conformity expired, the United States and Canada imposed trade sanctions. The EU's response has been to confirm its ban on the basis of a new risk assessment. The new directive (2003/17/EC), which came into force on October 14, 2003, establishes a definitive ban on one hormone as a growth promoter and further restricts its therapeutic use and imposes provisional bans on the other five hormones while greater scientific understanding is sought. The WTO's judgment and the imposition of sanctions therefore did nothing to change minds about the safety issues or to galvanize significant support for substantive policy change.[10] Instead, the new measure is designed to address the procedural shortcomings of the initial ban—hence the emphasis on risk assessment and the use of provisional bans for those hormones where scientific uncertainty persists.

In the absence of substantive policy change, Canada and the United States have refused to lift their sanctions. Having failed to persuade them to accept the sufficiency of the rule change, the EU initiated WTO complaints against the Canadian and U.S. sanctions (DS321 and 320, respectively) in November 2004 in order to get a WTO ruling on the compatibility of its new measures with WTO obligations. Should the WTO rule in the EU's favor, it would clearly establish the regulatory discretion discussed above. A ruling against the EU would imply that multilateral disciplines are more constraining than the jurisprudence to date suggests.

Agreeing to New Rules That Fit

The institutional factors that make it difficult for the EU to change its existing rules to bring them into compliance with multilateral obligations arguably pose much less of a problem when it comes to adopting new rules that are compatible with multilateral obligations (Princen 2002). Rather than having to take positive action and overcome veto points, policymakers need only avoid adopting measures that contravene existing obligations.

The most extreme variant of this approach, and one that deeply concerns some anti-WTO activists (see, for example, Shrybman 1999), is that governments will simply refrain from adopting new rules that might provoke the wrath of trading partners and fall foul of WTO obligations. There is no evidence that this has occurred. For example, 23 of the 121 measures that the European Commission (2003) has brought to the attention of third-country authorities as affecting the importing of live animals and animal products into the EU were adopted after the DSB's judgment in the beef hormone case in February 1998.

Nonetheless, multilateral obligations do shape EU food policy. In line with the emphasis of WTO jurisprudence discussed above, the relevance of multilateral rules has been much more in terms of process than substance. This is evident in both the adoption of individual measures and, more significant, the development of the EU's new food safety policy, although here the impact has been reinforcing of internal trends rather than contradictory. The recent development of the EU's food safety regime is discussed in detail elsewhere in this volume (see chapter 11), so the discussion here concentrates on the relevance of international rules.

Grace Skogstad (2001) has identified three facets of EU food safety policy that interact with the SPS Agreement: policy objectives, programmatic idea, and policy style. We broadly agree with her analysis that EU and SPS share common policy objectives—ensuring that food safety rules are not discriminatory or arbitrary—but that there have been differences with regard to programmatic ideas, with SPS placing a heavier emphasis on science, and policy style, in which the EU is more willing to consider nonscientific factors. We also concur with her assessment that the recent reforms of EU food policy have reduced, although not eliminated, the scope for EU policy outcomes to be inconsistent with SPS disciplines.

The impetus for EU policy change, however, has been internal. The two driving forces have been the disruption to the single market caused by the particularly pronounced failure of mutual recognition with respect to food safety (European Commission, 1997a; Council 1999a) and the contribution of the BSE crisis to enhancing the legitimacy of European regulation (Skogstad 2001; chapter 11, this volume). These internal pressures precipitated changes in EU food safety rules while the hormone-treated beef case was unfolding (the panel reported in August 1997 and the appellate body in February 1998).

In early 1997 the European Parliament passed a conditional censure of the European Commission over its handling of the BSE crisis and threatened an outright censure vote if the commission did not respond to its demands concerning EU food safety (Peterson and Bomberg 1999, Peterson 2002). The Santer Commission responded by issuing a Green Paper on the general principles of food law in the European Union (Commission 1997a) and adopted a series of measures to rebuild confidence in the process through which it gathered scientific advice (OECD 2000). The Green Paper noted the need for EU food law to comply with the community's WTO obligations (Commission 1997), while the greater emphasis on scientific evidence echoed the programmatic idea of the SPS.

The EU's food safety reforms received renewed emphasis as a result of the perception that lingering dissatisfaction over the handling of BSE contributed to the European Parliament's confrontation with the Santer Commission over corruption in 1998–1999 (Skogstad 2001).[11] The Prodi Commission entered office with improving EU food safety policy as one of its top priorities (Skogstad 2001).

As a consequence, the commission separated bureaucratic responsibility for food safety from that for food production and consolidated it in one place: the Directorate General for Health and Consumer Protection (DG SANCO). It also sought to enhance its scientific capacity by creating the European Food Safety Authority. Further, the tasks of risk assessment, risk management, and risk communication were rendered distinct in the policy process (Skogstad 2001).[12] In addition, the commission and the ECJ have clarified the application of the precautionary principle in such a way that it requires, rather than eschews, risk assessment (chapter 13, this volume). These reforms and clarifications have moved the EU's approach to food safety regulation closer to that incorporated into the SPS Agreement. Arguably, however, rather than being driven by the requirements of the WTO, the reforms reflected acceptance of the same mainstream thinking that had informed the SPS Agreement.[13]

Within this policy framework, the European Commission tries to ensure that all food safety proposals are compatible with the SPS.[14] Once the proposal leaves the commission and enters the more political realm of the Council of Ministers and the Parliament, however, there is the potential for the proposal to be modified in ways that might not be compatible with the SPS Agreement, although the commission tries to alert the council and Parliament if it thinks this is the case. It is here, in the rough and tumble of legislative politics, that the greatest potential for EU rules to fall afoul of international obligations persists. Political compromises, particularly among twenty-five member governments and between the council and the Parliament, do not necessarily lend themselves to full consideration of external obligations. As alluded to earlier, enlargement may exacerbate this potential by increasing the demand for common rules and complicating further the political interests that must be reconciled.

Conclusions

With the EU's attempt to justify rather than change its ban on hormone-treated beef, it seems clear that given contested governance from below and above, the EU will try to respond to the latter in a way that does not compromise the former. The combination of the clarification of the WTO's rules and the development of the EU's food safety policymaking, particularly greater reference to risk assessment, however, should mean that new EU rules are less likely than in the past to fall afoul of its WTO obligations. The beef hormone ban may illustrate this nicely. Arguably, the original ban would not have been adopted under the EU's new food safety procedures because the risk assessment was incomplete. Conversely, the revised ban, which represents one of the first applications of the EU's new approach to food safety regulation, arguably is compatible with the WTO's disciplines, although the jury, in the shape of the DSB, is still out. Likewise, the challenge to the EU's rules on GM crop approvals attacks their lack of application, not their substance, which also reflects the new approach to food safety. If, as this suggests, practice within the EU and multilaterally is converging with regard to the "on-what-basis" and "how-to-regulate" aspects of contested governance, the contested nature of the location of food safety governance will also be eased.

Given the very politicized dynamics of market integration, however, there will always be a risk of clashes between EU rules and multilateral disciplines. This is particularly likely when profound public fears are not allayed by apparently overwhelming scientific evidence of product safety or when provisional measures remain in place long after a contrary scientific consensus has been established. This potential for problems will likely be exacerbated as a side effect of enlargement, which will arguably accentuate pressures for common policies and complicate political compromises. Given the dynamics of market integration, this will likely produce more rules that restrict trade and give rise to more challenges.

Thus, changes in the EU's food safety procedures are reducing the likelihood of contested governance between the EU and WTO, while changes to the EU's membership have the potential to increase contested governance. Which of these tendencies will be dominant remains to be seen.

Notes

An earlier version of this chapter was presented to European Food Safety Regulation: The Challenge of Multi-Level Governance, Second General Workshop, University of California, Berkeley, November 7–8, 2003. We are grateful to the participants, particularly Christine Noiville and David Vogel, for their comments. We also thank Leonardo Iacovone and Gabrielle Marceau for their comments and the practitioners who took the time to discuss these matters with us. All remaining errors are our own.

1. This section draws on Young (2004).

2. From 1995 to 2004, 62 votes out of 87 were needed for a qualified majority. Since enlargement, 232 votes out of 321, as well as a majority of the member states representing 62 percent of the EU's population, are required.

3. For discussion of civic interest group activism and impact with respect to genetically modified food, see chapter 5.

4. Neumann and Türk note that the wording of Article 2.2 of the TBT Agreement leaves open the very slight possibility that the appellate body could demand a trade-off between the effectiveness of a trade measure and its trade impact in the case of a low importance but still legitimate TBT objective, but as they point out, this would be inconsistent with the appellate body's philosophy.

5. WTO Appellate Body Report, *Australia–Measures Affecting Importation of Salmon*, AB- 1998-5, WT/DS18/AB/R (98-0000).

6. Interview with a senior U.S. trade official, Washington, D.C., January 11, 2005.

7. Interview with a U.S. trade official, Washington, D.C., January 14, 2005; USTR (2004, p. 1).

8. For other interpretations see Pauwelyn (1998) and chapter 13, this volume.

9. Interview with a DG SANCO official, Brussels, September 16, 2003.

10. Interview with a commission trade official, Brussels, September 18, 2003.

11. Interview with a DG SANCO official, Brussels, September 16, 2003.

12. Interview with a DG SANCO official, Brussels, September 16, 2003.

13. Interview with a DG SANCO official, Brussels, September 16, 2003.

14. Interview with a DG SANCO official, Brussels, September 16, 2003.

13

Compatibility or Clash? EU Food Safety and the WTO

Christine Noiville

Recent European food safety crises have led the EU to promote a new regulatory instrument: the precautionary principle (Christoforou 2003). First applied during the BSE crisis and later used in the regulation of GMOs or the ban on antibiotics used in animal feed, this principle has spread throughout the whole of European food safety regulation and has become its cornerstone (de Sadeleer 2002, Fisher 2002). It is not only a new regulatory instrument but also illustrates a new type of governance. Indeed, it goes further than the traditional principle of prevention, which constrains government to prevent risks only when their existence has been proven or appears highly likely. According to the precautionary principle, the absence of scientific certainty no longer justifies delaying the introduction of measures that could prevent potential harm. Under this principle, it is advisable, and even necessary, not to wait for a risk to materialize before evaluating or withdrawing from the market a product whose safety is dubious.

But what is the value of this European precautionary model within the framework of international law and particularly in international trade law? This issue has come to be all the more decisive as the regulation of food safety has had important international consequences and has become a source of growing strain in trade relations. It raises two key questions in terms of contested governance. First, in a multilevel governance scheme, where should decisions be made: at the EU level or by international trade institutions? Second, on what grounds should decisions be made: prevention or precaution?

Such dilemmas in the relationships between different levels of regulation on the one hand, between science, politics and regulation, on the other, have come to the forefront during the negotiations on the Biosafety Protocol, finally adopted in Cartagena in January 2000. Whereas EU representatives argued that the insertion of the precautionary principle in the protocol was necessary in order to achieve a high level of health and environmental protection for GMOs in international trade, the United States feared that this would open the door to trade restrictions lacking scientific basis. Since then, the gap has continued to widen as EU officials regard food as a central symbol of consumer and cultural sovereignty. In the past five years, international trade law has witnessed a series of disputes originating from the desire of the EU to restrict the trade of various foodstuffs in order to prevent a perceived health risk. The dispute relating to the EU ban on imported North American hormone-fed beef was only the first in a long series. Recently European restrictions on genetically modified foodstuffs have been challenged by the United States before the World Trade Organization's (WTO) Dispute Settlement Body. Consequently, it is essentially before this body that the question as to which type of risk governance prevails will be played out.

Some argue that even if the precautionary principle is not explicitly mentioned, WTO agreements leave adequate room for a precautionary approach to risk management (Victor 2000). But others hold that WTO law is incompatible with the precautionary principle (Hardstaff 2000). They recall that, confronted with the lack of any authoritative definition, the WTO's appellate body refused, in the hormone beef case, to consider it to be a principle of common international law (Noiville 2000, Scott and Vos 2002). According to this perspective, with the WTO loath to give the precautionary principle any legal deference, European consumers could find themselves exposed to food safety risks that their own governments have judged unacceptable.

This chapter aims to clarify this issue. Founded on recent EU case law, it begins by arguing that there is no philosophical opposition between the EU precautionary governance and free trade. With the passage of time, the meaning of both the precautionary principle and WTO legal corpus, especially the Agreement on Sanitary and Phytosanitary (SPS) measures, becomes clearer and leads to an adjustment of the EU's policy style with WTO obligations. But then the chapter takes a more cautious approach, discussing Holmes and Young's contribution as many technical details still need to be worked out. In particular, what will be the precise use and value of scientific data by the WTO? When will a precautionary measure be deemed founded by sufficient scientific data? How long may this measure last? At what conditions will it meet the new consistency obligation required by the SPS agreement?

All these technical details are not mere anecdotes. In working them out, conflicting rationales on the governance of risk issues—the use of science, the role of politics, the adequate level of regulation, and others—will inevitably surface. They will most probably be a source of significant tensions in the future. And in time they may, limit the scope of the precautionary principle within the EU food safety regime.

An Apparently Insuperable Conflict of Logic

It is worth beginning by looking at the SPS Agreement, since how it is interpreted will be critical. The European model is based on the precautionary principle, which authorizes protective measures to be taken in the event of scientific uncertainty. However, the SPS Agreement allows the use of such measures only if they are supported by scientific evidence, which would appear to represent a clear contradiction. Although the exact contours have been the subject of much debate, at least the overall aim of the precautionary principle is clear: in the event of a potential health risk, action must be taken without waiting for the risk to be confirmed by scientific evidence. Thus, doubt and uncertainty concerning the safety of a product can justify recourse to protective measures.

SPS Agreement and Scientific Evidence
The purpose of the SPS Agreement is to promote the use of harmonized sanitary and phytosanitary measures among member states (Preamble no. 6th and Art. 3.1). Since several international organizations have already made substantial contributions to this goal, states are invited to base their sanitary or phytosanitary measures on these organizations' international standards, guidelines, or recommendations. Thus, in the area of foodstuffs, all sanitary measures compliant with the Codex Alimentarius guidelines are presumed to be compatible with free trade obligations. If they deem it necessary, member states may introduce or

maintain sanitary or phytosanitary measures that result in a higher level of sanitary or phytosanitary protection (Art. 3.3). Thus, the European communities, which aim to make food safety a top priority, may choose to apply stricter regulations in this matter than the standards laid down by the Codex. But if these regulations give rise to a complaint, the EU would need to furnish scientific proof to justify their more stringent standards: sanitary measures must be "based on scientific principles" and must not be "maintained without sufficient scientific evidence" (Art. 2.2 and 3.3).

The concept of scientific principle incorporates two related requirements. First, before having recourse to a sanitary measure, the state is duty-bound to have analyzed the risk at stake. For example, does the existence of a given chemical substance in a foodstuff present any particular danger? What level of consumption is harmful to consumers' health? Second, this assessment must confirm that there is in fact a risk. In sum, only the existence of sufficient scientific evidence can legitimate the use of sanitary measures.

The authors of the SPS Agreement were quite aware that it may be too difficult to follow such a stringent standard. For example, when an epidemic breaks out or a disease spreads and is apparently linked to the consumption of a certain foodstuff or to the import of a particular animal, the state must act quickly. Before it has even made the necessary assessments and obtained scientific proof that the sanitary incident is indeed linked to the foodstuff, it must be able to provisionally withdraw it from the market or bar it from entering the country. This is why Article 5.7 of the SPS Agreement states: "In cases where relevant scientific evidence is insufficient, a Member may 'provisionally' adopt sanitary or phytosanitary measures on the basis of 'available pertinent information.'" But the text specifies immediately afterward that "in such circumstances, Members shall seek to obtain the additional information necessary for a more objective assessment of risk and review the sanitary or phytosanitary measure accordingly within a reasonable period of time."

Article 5.7 therefore grants states the authority to restrict trade of a foodstuff when they have misgivings about its safety, even in the absence of sufficient evidence. But this authority, which allows French law to use quarantine measures or product withdrawals, is only provisional. In the longer term, the requirement for scientific evidence prevails. Adopting a measure when there is uncertainty is possible, but maintaining it beyond a "reasonable period of time" is permitted only when there is sufficient evidence that such a risk exists.

Of all the areas that were regulated in 1994 by new GATT/WTO agreements, it was only in the sanitary and phytosanitary field that this requirement of scientific rationality was adopted. This is because in this area, experience shows that sanitary measures adopted by states diverge so widely that they are likely to frequently serve as trade barriers. Hence the architecture of the SPS Agreement was constructed around the concept of scientific evidence, a criterion judged to be more universal and more reliable for distinguishing between necessary and illegitimate sanitary measures.

Terms of the Opposition

The SPS requirement for scientific rigor that obliges states to make systematic evaluations is not inconsistent with the logic of precaution. Certainly, emerging as it did in the wake of various ecological and sanitary crises and doubt about the ability of science to provide definite answers, the precautionary principle calls for scientific data to be treated with some humility and for modest expectations to be entertained concerning absolute scientific certainties. Nevertheless, the precautionary principle does not rule out a scientific approach. On the contrary, it requires empiricism and hasty scientific analysis to be rejected in favor of inspections, evaluations, and maximum information gathering before a product about which there are safety concerns is marketed.

In addition, in an emergency, the SPS Agreement authorizes countries to withdraw a product from the market or to close their frontiers provisionally. Such measures clearly incorporate elements of the precautionary principle. When signs of contamination appear in poultry, beef, or Coca-Cola, the fact that Article 5.7 of the SPS Agreement allows a state to adopt such measures without having to wait for proof confirms the legitimacy of a precautionary approach.

But it is also important to realize that precaution cannot just be limited to provisional emergency measures adopted in times of crisis. Whether it is poultry or Coca-Cola, isolating a product, withdrawing it from the market, and carrying out evaluations in order to identify the causes of contamination constitute traditional forms of government regulation. But some persistent uncertainties regarding the effects of certain products cannot be resolved by a few months of research and thus require that measures be maintained beyond the provisional time frame. Take, for example, the BSE crisis: more than six years after the adoption of the initial emergency measures, the link between this pathology and Creutzfeldt-Jakob disease has not been proven, and consequently there was prolonged controversy about whether to lift the ban on British beef and under what conditions. Once the sanitary crisis has passed, managing sanitary uncertainty becomes a challenge.

More important, the precautionary principle requires that governments not wait for crises to occur but prevent them from occurring in the first place. The EU's rules for the approval of genetically modified food provide an emblematic example of this approach. Before they have caused the slightest damage, but for the sole reason that they derive from new techniques and that this innovation has spawned scientific uncertainty, the European Commission decided to wait before allowing mass introduction of these products into the environment and foodstuffs. Precaution here is not limited to managing a crisis or an emergency; rather, it represents a tool for regulating a new technological development, a process that is likely to be time-consuming as policymakers gradually become more familiar with the effects of a new mode of production. Nearly fifteen years after the first genetically modified plants were developed, some members of the scientific community still claim they are learning to formulate the relevant questions concerning their safety.

These uncertainties are not linked to a crisis but to a product's novelty, and are thus durable uncertainties. Taking the SPS Agreement literally, this type of uncertainty that persists and requires long-term risk management cannot exist, for by definition there are only temporary situations of uncertainty that can be rapidly allayed by further research.

This is where the heart of the conflict between the SPS Agreement and the precautionary principle may lie. In the SPS Agreement, precaution seems to be limited to the provisional measures adopted in an emergency. Once the provisional period has passed, the alternatives are simple: either objective scientific data clearly confirm the need to sustain the restrictions, or the latter are not backed up by sufficient scientific evidence and must be withdrawn.

Some observers have noted another point of conflict—one that derives from the obligation for proportionality in precautionary measures. The SPS Agreement carries a customary proviso in terms of international trade law: "any sanitary or phytosanitary measure is applied only to the extent necessary to protect human, animal or plant life or health," and "measures are not more trade-restrictive than required to achieve their appropriate level of sanitary or phytosanitary protection" (Art. 2.2 and 5.6). Is the precautionary principle compatible with these conditions? How can you prove that a precautionary measure is necessary when it is directed at an uncertain risk that is intrinsically hard to quantify?

Articulation

How might the precautionary principle and the SPS Agreement be reconciled? On the one hand, the EU has constantly sought to clarify the meaning of the precautionary principle and to submit its implementation to a series of prerequisites that are partially inspired by the SPS Agreement.[1] On the other hand, WTO jurisprudence clearly intended a genuine notion of precaution to filter down through interpretation of this agreement.[2] Hence, both the EU and the WTO have wrestled with striking the correct balance between permitting protection and prosecuting protectionism.

Prerequisites of the Precautionary Principle

The precautionary principle requires "a structured decision-making process" as well as "reliable scientific data and logical reasoning," according to the communication from the European Commission on the precautionary principle. Advocate General J. Mischo adds: "The precautionary principle has a future only to the extent that, far from opening the door wide to irrationality, it establishes itself as an aspect of the rational management of risks, designed not to achieve a zero risk, which everything suggests does not exist, but to limit the risks to which citizens are exposed to the lowest level reasonably imaginable."[3]

This sums up well a fundamental concept of EU law: that while it is necessary for scientific uncertainty to translate into legal consequences, it is important to discipline the precautionary principle so that it is not applied in ways that could prove useless or even dangerous, hindering innovation and paralyzing economic activity and international trade (Noiville 2000). Some of these conditions are likely to pose real problems in the event of a WTO trade dispute.

First is the prerequisite relative to the risk itself. What type of risk exactly justifies the implementation of a precautionary measure? Is a simple doubt enough, or must the risk be sufficiently probable? According to the EU, only a plausible risk, revealed by serious scientific evaluation, justifies recourse to a precautionary measure. Recourse to a precautionary measure presupposes that the potentially dangerous effects of a phenomenon, product, or process have been identified by scientific evaluation. Next, and more important, the measure cannot be based on a merely hypothetical approach to the risk, founded on mere conjecture that has not been scientifically verified. It may be taken only if the risk appears to be adequately backed up by the scientific data available. This is of major significance: scientific uncertainty can only be the basis of regulation provided it does not stem solely from an imaginary risk, in a purely intellectual hypothesis. It does not mean "throwing science in the dustbin," as has sometimes been claimed, nor does it diminish the need to undertake a serious evaluation of threatened risks. Quite the contrary: it obliges the EU and member states to renounce their often informal, sometimes empirical, mode of dealing with risks (Heyvaert 1999, Noiville and de Sadeleer 2001). If, as in the hormone beef case, the EU lost, as did Japan over agricultural produce and Australia in the salmon conflict, it is partly for their wait-and-see attitude: measures were adopted without any serious scientific evaluation[4] and without seeking to "document the risk on the basis of scientific data."

Another fundamental prerequisite concerns the conception of precautionary measures. Any measure adopted by the public authorities must be proportional to what is known about the risk. However the precautionary principle is expressed, there can be no doubt that its application does not have the effect of avoiding the application of other principles that are just as fundamental. This is particularly true of the principle of proportionality, which can be seen as inseparable from the precautionary principle. This is the viewpoint of the European Court of Justice (ECJ). The precautionary principle is not intended to be applied in the same way if public authorities are confronted by a rigorous but still largely theoretical hypothesis of a risk or with the threat of a risk backed up by reliable scientific data. There is a sizable difference between the two. Hence, the necessity of proportionality: the less a hypothetical risk is plausible, the less stringent must be the precautionary measures. From the wide array of tools available—ranging from legally binding measures on research projects or just recommendations—the regulator must not choose a measure that is more stringent than necessary. Thus, if the evidence of risk appears to be very slight, the regulator must choose a measure that is the least trade restrictive. In any case, the measure adopted should be subject to periodic review and amended as necessary in the light of new information. It is not a matter of, at the first hint of doubt, withdrawing a product from the market definitively, but rather of either submitting it to evaluation or withdrawing it temporarily and accompanying its withdrawal by research that will progressively attenuate the uncertainties, resulting in the measure's being either reinforced or slackened.

The stakes are high with regard to international trade law, The overall configuration of the appellate body's ruling in the hormone beef affair suggests that it is the disproportion between, on the one hand, the general and definitive ban on hormone meat in Europe, and on the other, the weakness of scientific argument developed by the communities, that constituted a crucial element in the condemnation of the latter.

These criteria—the verifiable nature of the risk and proportionality of precautionary measures, as set out in the communication from the commission on the precautionary principle—represents a codification of EU law, which the ECJ is responsible for enforcing. Thus, the precautionary principle may be less antithetical to the SPS Agreement than at first appeared.

An Interpretation of the Sanitary Agreement in Favor of Precaution

This assertion may seem surprising, because none of these three rulings—on Hormones, Salmon, and Agricultural Products—concluded that the risk invoked justifies trade restrictions. So how was this possible? In all three cases, a restrictive measure was adopted against products that were suspected of causing intoxication or disease. Hormone-fed beef was banned by the European Communities due to the cancer risk attributed to it; Canadian salmon was subjected to strict processing requirements by Australia in order to prevent any risk of pathogenicity for Australian salmon; American fruit was turned away on entry to Japan unless the American exporters could prove, for each variety, the absence of potentially devastating insects. Only the EU in the *Hormone* case expressly invoked the precautionary principle to support its ban, but all three disputes nonetheless raised the same question: Were the litigious sanitary measures based on scientific principles, as the SPS Agreement stipulates? Although the appellate body each time responded in the negative, it interpreted "scientific principle" in ways that were considerably different from the literal reading of the agreement. If these three measures taken by the EU, Australia, and Japan were ruled to be incompatible with international trade legislation, it is more for reasons of form than for reasons of content deriving from an absence of scientific evidence of the feared risk. On this key concept of the SPS agreement, WTO jurisprudence has distanced itself from literal interpretation of the text.

In reality, everything stems from the appellate body's conception of science, which is quite different from the almost idyllic concept expressed in the SPS agreement itself: if science constitutes the principal tool for settling trade disputes, it is because it is a bearer of truth, capable of providing objective evidence. However, in the *Hormone* affair, and then in the *Salmon* and *Agricultural Products* rulings, the appellate body based its approach on quite different reasoning. It understood that science rarely eliminates uncertainties. When a country is faced with an epidemic or fears a foodstuff may be allergenic, it must undertake scientific research, as this constitutes the necessary complement to its sanitary policy. But this research does not always come to a certain result or a monolithic conclusion. It may still leave uncertainties or pinpoint both a prevailing view representing the mainstream of scientific opinion and divergent views. Since scientific evaluation constitutes neither an absolutely reliable tool nor a means to obtain universal answers, its results alone cannot predetermine a state's sanitary policy. A sanitary measure does not have to conform to any of the scientific conclusions reached in the scientific studies. While "responsible and representative governments tend to base their legislative and administrative measures on "mainstream" scientific opinion, . . . equally responsible and representative governments may act in good faith on the basis of what, at a given time, may be a divergent opinion coming from qualified and respected sources" (*Hormones*, Appellate Body Report, no. 172, 194 note 12 and 213). Consequently, this only reinforces the Codex Alimentarius standards' absence of legally binding authority and the states' recognized freedom not just to contravene them, but more generally to autonomously fix the level of protection they consider most appropriate.

More concretely, all these understandings on the limits of scientific analysis end up by modifying the scope of certain key provisions in the SPS Agreement, particularly the obligation of scientific evidence required by Articles 2.2 and 3.3 and the Article 5.7 provision for provisional measures. If science does not always provide reliable and universal answers, the notion of scientific evidence becomes eminently conditional. WTO jurisprudence further weakens this notion. The concept of scientific evidence has been replaced by one of "reasonable relationship between the sanitary measure and the risk assessment." According to the appellate body, there need not be proof of a certain causal link or a scientifically proven correlation between the regulated product and the harm feared, but only a reasonable, logical relationship between the results of the assessment and the measure that is finally adopted. There is no need, in order to adopt a sanitary measure, to scientifically demonstrate that a product presents a sanitary risk, that is, that there is without any doubt a risk in consuming it. Rather, the results of the risk assessment must sufficiently warrant—that is, reasonably support—the SPS measure in question. While it is necessary to have verified the possibility of risk by scientific methods—otherwise a state could always maintain that a risk is always possible since zero risk does not exist—no consensus, not even of a "minimal degree" of risk, is required, provided there is a serious scientific claim of a possible risk. This is essentially what in community law constitutes one of the essential conditions for the adoption of precautionary measures.

In cases of scientific uncertainty, the SPS Agreement authorizes states to provisionally adopt stringent measures, while requiring that they review them "within a reasonable period of time" in the light of objective scientific assessment. The decision relative to agricultural produce provides clarification as to the meaning of a "reasonable period of time." Japan had provisionally adopted a measure destined to limit the potentially disastrous effects of an insect often found in imported fruit. But in reality, this measure remained in force for more than twenty years. It was therefore declared contrary to the SPS Agreement for two reasons. First, Japan, because of the wait-and-see attitude it adopted, made no effort to find out about what the actual risks were and instead waited for the fruit exporters to prove that their products were harmless. Second, this sanitary measure was applied for more than twenty years. Although the obligation to examine it in a reasonable period of time dates back only to January 1, 1995, when the SPS Agreement came into force, the appellate body considered that in this case, a reasonable period of time had been exceeded. But at the same time, the appellate body stated that "what constitutes a *reasonable period of time* should be based on the specific circumstances of each case, including the difficulty of obtaining the additional information necessary for the review *and* the characteristics of the provisional SPS measure." In Japan's case, it was easy to obtain this information, for as all the experts summoned to the WTO remarked, many studies already existed on the subject. But presumably if the pertinent information can be obtained only following long-term assessment or with gradual experience of the product, the reasonable period of time could extend beyond a brief interval. It is therefore conceivable that in these conditions, the innovation of a foodstuff or the techniques used to produce it could justify maintaining a sanitary measure for as long as is required to obtain reliable epidemiological data.

A Vast Issue: Terms of Technical Adjustment

Once the binary conditions of trade dispensations—evidence or lack of evidence, certain or uncertain—are replaced by more subtle but also more variable criteria—plausible, logical, reasonable—the actual application of the SPS Agreement depends on how it is exactly interpreted by the WTO.

The prerequisite appears to be quite simple: the sanitary measure must, as we have seen, be "reasonably supported" by a risk assessment. But as we have also seen, this criterion is more a point of reference than a specific threshold. Although one can surely notice, as do Holmes and Young in chapter 12, increasing similarities between EU and WTO case law, this will not prevent endless disputes.

What exactly is the "minimal degree of risk" short of which a sanitary measure would in principle be ruled illegitimate? While it has held in the hormone and salmon cases that the existence of a purely theoretical risk cannot justify adopting a precautionary measure, the appellate body has also been careful to specify that there is no quantitative requirement, that is, no requirement of a minimum magnitude of risk and that the panel must instead ensure, via an objective assessment of the facts, that the measure is sufficiently supported or reasonably warranted by the risk assessment. It is therefore up to the panel to evaluate, on a case-by-case basis, the significance, value, and credibility of the scientific elements submitted to it, some of which, one can hypothesize, may appear more important and convincing than others.

Consequently, the question of content or level of evidence—what must be demonstrated in each case to convince the panel—is all the more important. Many things remain ambiguous, however. For the measure to be "sufficiently backed up" by available scientific data raises the question of the range of scientific knowledge. Certain risks will have a bare minimum of experience to back them up, whereas in other cases, the hypothesis of risk will have been the subject of a theoretical model, but there will be no empirical confirmation whatsoever. Is this acceptable to the WTO? A similar vagueness characterizes the meaning of the term *temporary*. A temporary measure may last, but for how long? Maintaining a precautionary measure may depend on the evolution of scientific knowledge, but under what conditions will these be considered conclusive? This question is particularly pertinent in the case of GMOs since in this area, a decade of risk assessments has not sufficed to settle scientific controversy.

Organization of Scientific Expertise and International Trade Disputes

The stakes are twofold. First, there is the matter of how the panels employ scientific expertise. Second, how are risk assessments to be performed by international standards organizations, whose technical standards now have international legal standing?

Current practices require the panels themselves (after consultation with—and not agreement of—the parties) to decide on the number and quality of experts they choose to call in (Christoforou 2002). However, since any scientific opinion can be solicited by the panels, it will become necessary to define the notion of "scientific," as American courts have done. Finally, the panels' appreciation of scientific evidence must be closely checked: Did they perform their own assessment or dismiss certain data, while all they were meant to do was to undertake an objective assessment of the facts? All this should enter the appeal's field of scrutiny, which is not clearly the case today.

But the stakes involved in scientific assessment are not limited to dispute settlements. They also concern the execution of scientific assessment in the framework of international technical standardization bodies, for example, in the Codex Alimentarius (Sikes 1998). Whereas these standards once had legal value only if a state expressly stated its desire to conform to them, the SPS Agreement recognizes them as the reference standards regardless of whether they were adopted by a very wide or very small majority (McNeil 1998). Once the standard has been adopted by a "recognized body" of the international standardization community, according to the appellate body, there is no need to question how they were determined or to what extent they were disputed.[5] Hence, the necessity of providing a framework for scientific assessment at this stage in the elaboration of standards.

These stakes were only very recently perceived by scholars and states—for whom the precautionary principle was by nature a principle deriving from a political decision, and therefore of no concern to the work of the Codex, which involves conducting scientific assessments on given subjects (e.g., water, cheese, GMOs), then transcribing the results in the form of technical standards. But the scope of the precautionary principle in international trade cannot be reduced to scientific and technical expertise. It also directly depends on the degree of WTO control over a state's political choice.

Control of Political Choices

Any sanitary risk management measure inevitably entails political choices: once the scientific data are available, political choices become critical as member states judge which risks appear acceptable and which must be prevented at all costs. This is why the SPS Agreement leaves states free to set the level of sanitary protection they deem appropriate. On the surface, things seem clear. Once the risk has been identified, it is the state's responsibility to decide if it is acceptable, which may mean, for example, adopting an attitude of zero tolerance as the appellate body said in the salmon case. It is then up to the dispute settlement bodies to verify the state's scientific justification.

But although the appellate body's rulings to date have been respectful of state regulatory autonomy, as pointed out by Holmes and Young in chapter 12, there are still significant areas of ambiguity. It thus remains to be seen whether real autonomy can be maintained.

Risk Management as a Political Choice

It is almost a truism to say that any regulation of risk implies a political choice. For in themselves, scientific calculations, if removed from their political, economic, and social context, are not necessarily significant. Once the decision maker has the scientific data in hand, he is not free from the necessity of weighing up, arbitrating, and therefore choosing among more or less acceptable hypotheses (Noiville 2003). But the political choice is all the more inexorable when objective scientific data are either lacking or controversial. In instances of scientific uncertainty, the results of risk assessments cannot monopolize the political decision. They are but one aspect of a wider social choice, whose rationality does not depend solely on mere scientific data. Is the potential risk associated with the use of antibiotics in animal rearing or in the consumption of genetically modified foods acceptable, useful, or necessary? Is it worth taking? The precautionary principle raises questions not just about the risk itself but also on the wider issue of risk taking and product acceptability. Hence the particular form of trade disputes relative to food safety, where political considerations carry as much weight as scientific data. After all, states do not use their regulatory authority over food only for sanitary or "scientific" reasons; they also take into account the preference of their consumers, economic constraints, and defense of national cultural models. Take, for example, bovine somatotropine, whose potential sanitary risks are considered not worth taking in Europe, as the product does not bring any benefits to the farmer or the consumer. Another example is GMOs, whose acceptability is now subject to much public debate or to the prior evaluation of the products' socioeconomic impact.[6] In view of this interaction between scientific and political considerations, food regulation 178/2002/EC now says that "scientific risk assessment alone cannot, in some cases, provide all the information on which a risk management decision should be based, and that other factors relevant to the matter under consideration should legitimately be taken into account. The latter include societal, economic, traditional, ethical, and environmental factors." In other words, as the communication on the precautionary principle puts it, when science is unclear, "judging what is an 'acceptable' level of risk for society is an eminently political responsibility. Decision-makers faced with an unacceptable risk, scientific uncertainty and public concerns have a duty to find answers."

The key question is whether this political choice, which in theory is a matter for each member state to decide, will be second-guessed by WTO dispute panels. Let us examine two examples.

First, any import ban or regulation of a potentially dangerous product is subject to a "necessity test," according to both the SPS Agreement and the GATT Agreement (Marceau and Trachtman 2002). Traditionally, this requirement was twofold: the measure not only had to achieve the targeted aim of health protection but also had to be the least restrictive measure possible for international trade (SPS Agreement, Art. 2.1, 2.2, and 5.6). What scope is there here for the different values that led to this political choice? Not much, it would seem. A stringent measure is justifiable only if there are technical or economic constraints. For example, as Europeans are big eaters of pastries and cheese, the "admissible dose" of additives in these foods is lower in Europe than international standards allow.

Another example is that since a system for verifying a given hormone in animal rearing would not on its own enable fraud to be prevented, it is preferable to ban the hormone entirely rather than attempt to manage the risk. Beyond these kinds of considerations, cultural and social dimensions do not seem to matter to the WTO. Thus, even if GMOs are culturally unacceptable and give rise to consumer resistence, unless their danger has been verified, how can recourse to restricting them be justified? And can even a strict case-by-case assessment be warranted as required by EU law?

Above all, another challenge must be overcome, which also appears to be a powerful instrument for tampering with national political choices. This is the coherence test mentioned in Article 5.5 of the SPS Agreement. A simple example will illustrate the purpose of this provision. Suppose that the Belgian authorities imposed a heavy tax on wine for health protection purposes, without taxing beer at the same time. They would then be taxing differently two products presenting comparable risks. Is this difference not arbitrary or unjustifiable? Doubtless, since from a health point of view, it is common knowledge that wine is less harmful than beer. But by levying a heavy tax on wine, has not Belgium sought to favor national beer manufacturers to the detriment of foreign exporters of wine? Hence the coherence test. Acting as a complement to the principle of nondiscrimination, it aims to prevent members from setting a very high level of sanitary protection in one case and a very low one in another presenting comparable risks, with no other justification than the concern to protect their own trade interests.

The question is how this comparison will be carried out by the dispute settlement bodies. First, what exactly is meant by "comparable situations"? For example, by subjecting the marketing of transgenic soya to stricter regulations than conventional soya, has the European Communities made an arbitrary or unjustifiable distinction between "comparable situations"? Are the risk indexes of the former sufficient to prevent any comparison with the latter? More important, do the comparable situations require similar regulations? It is not necessarily unreasonable for two comparable risks in terms of mortality or morbidity to be subjected to different regulation. Whether in the case of cheese made of untreated milk, alcohol, mad cow disease, hormones, or whatever else, a whole series of technical, social, and cultural data can justify these risks being treated differently. For example, it is difficult to see how one could seriously compare the dangers of alcohol or the famous toxic Japanese fish fugu with those presented by the use of antibiotics in animal rearing. Would not the fact that the consumer willingly accepts the two former while he resists the latter make different regulations appropriate? Moreover, the evolution of public attitudes may explain why two comparable risks are treated differently. Thus, the risks of a hormone destined to be used in animal rearing today could appear unacceptable, while even ten years ago, another hormone presenting comparable risks may have been granted market approval.

Conclusion

As the meaning of both the precautionary principle and SPS Agreement becomes clearer, it appears that contrary to a still dominant belief in Europe, there is no insuperable philosophical opposition between precaution and free trade. But it remains to be seen how WTO dispute settlement bodies will manage all the complexities involved. Tensions in the public regulation of food, dilemmas in the relations between science and regulation, market promotion and consumer protection, public authority and public opinion that define contested governance may well reappear here, in what may seem at first glance to be mere technical details. It is here, then, that the real extent of EU policy autonomy in the area of food safety will be decided.

Notes

1. See the Communication from the Commission on the precautionary principle (COM(2001)final) and the European Court of Justice Case law, in particular, C-331/88 *Fedesa and Others* [1990] ECR I-4023, Case C-405/92 *Mondiet* [1993] ECR I-6133; Case C-435/92 *APAS* [1994] ECR I-67, Case C-180/96 *United Kingdom* v. *Commission* [1998] ECR I-2265, Case C-157/96 *National Farmers' Union and Others* [1998] ECR I-2211, Case C-179/95 *Spain* v. *Council* [1999] ECR I-6475, and Case C-6/99 *Greenpeace France and Others* [2000] ECR I-

1651), by the Court of First Instance (see, in particular, Case T-199/96 *Berga-derm and Goupil* v. *Commission* [1998] ECR II-2805, upheld on appeal by the Court of Justice in Case C-352/98 P *Bergaderm and Goupil* v. *Commission* [2000] ECR I-5291, Case T-70/99 *Alpharma* v. *Council* [1999] ECR II-2027, Case T-13/99 *Pfizer Animal Health* v. *Council* [2002], ECR II-3305, Case T-74/00 *Artegodan* v. *Commission* [2002] ECR II-4945, reversed by ECJ in Case C-39/03, *Commission* v. *Artedogan*, July 24, 2003).

2. *European Communities—Measures Concerning Meat and Meat Products*, Panel Report, August 18, 1997, Appellate Body Report, January 16, 1998; *Australia—Measures Affecting Importation of Salmon*, Panel Report, June 12, 1998, Appellate Body Report, October 20, 1998; *Japan—Measures Affecting agricultural Products*, Panel Report, October 27, 1998, Appellate Body Report, February 22, 1999; *European Communities—Measures Affecting Asbestos and Asbestos-Containing Products*, Panel Report, September 18, 2000, Appellate Body Report, March 12, 2001. These cases will be cited as *Hormones*, *Salmon*, *Agricultural Products*, and *Asbestos*.

3. *National Farmers' Union c. Secrétariat Général du Gouvernement*, C-241/01, conclusions of the Advocate-General J. Mischo, July 2, 2002, no. 76.

4. See, for example, *Salmon*, WTO, Appellate Body Report, par. 119.

5. *European Communities—Trade Description of Sardines*, Appellate Body Report, September 26, 2002, no. 227. Let us emphasize, however, that this conclusion would be relevant only for purposes of the TBT Agreement.

6. See the Cartagena Protocol on Biosafety.

VI

Conclusion

14

The Asymmetries of Governance

Christopher Ansell

People ask me: Why do you write about food, and eating, and drinking? Why don't you write about the struggle for power and security, and about love, the way others do?
—MFK Fisher, *The Gastronomical Me*

To write about food, we have argued in this book, is to write about the struggle for power and security. Whether we are talking about the emerging slow food movement, bioengineered foods, trade disputes about hormones in beef or milk, or the current debates about nutrition and obesity, food has emerged as a major topic of political debate at the beginning of the twenty-first century. This book has focused on the particularly intense conflicts around food safety regulation that emerged in Europe over the past decade. Our project sought to understand the sources of this conflict, the dynamics of contestation, and its implications for institutional reform, European integration, international trade, and the changing balance between public and private regulation.

In this concluding chapter, we review some of the common findings from the individual chapters. We also draw on these findings to revisit the main theme of the book, contested governance, as a way of suggesting some of its more generic features. Although conflict is a typical feature of most policymaking and governance, the conflict that characterizes contested governance is more pervasive and fundamental. It is characterized by challenges to the fundamental legitimacy of who should make decisions and where, how, and on what basis they should be made and implemented. The central claim of the book is that European food safety regulation over the past decade exemplifies contested governance.

Contested governance is characterized by challenges to taken-for-granted, routine, and institutionalized assumptions about public priorities and their relationship to one another. In European food safety, this is most dramatically illustrated by the deep challenge to the long-term, institutionalized relationship between food safety concerns and the promotion of agricultural markets. Specifically, food crises in Europe have galvanized attention to the potential conflicts of interest symbolized by the location of major food safety responsibilities in agricultural ministries. Regardless of whether these conflicts of interests were real or perceived, it is clear that they can no longer be treated as taken for granted, routine, or institutionalized.

Perhaps our most general point about contested governance is the need to analyze both the self-sustaining quality of contestation and the larger institutional and temporal contexts with which crisis events may interact. We stress this point because the saliency and dramatic quality of crisis events (notably, in this case, the mad cow crisis) leave many in little doubt as to the proximate cause of contestation. But this very saliency may lead analysts to neglect how crisis conditions interact with more subtle longer-term trends and with broader institutional tensions. It also neglects the snowballing of conflict characteristic of contested governance, in which conflict begets conflict. In the case of European food safety regulation, contestation has been clearly triggered by a series of food scandals, many of which are described in this book. Contestation has also been deepened and propelled forward by asymmetries in the perceptions and coping strategies of the various stakeholders affected by these food crises.[1]

The most notable asymmetry lies in perception and experience of risk trade-offs by consumers and producers, a tension that manifests itself not only in the conflict between the consumers and producers within a single nation but also between nations. Although liability regimes and public regulation partly redistribute these risks, consumers bear the ultimate risk of harming their health by eating unsafe food. There is little surprise that consumers (as individuals or nations) are more risk averse than producers. (See the discussion of information asymmetries between producers and consumers in chapter 2). For food safety, this risk asymmetry is partially offset by the strong interdependence of producers and consumers. Producers are obviously sensitive to demand, and scares can undercut demand.[2] Therefore, they are dependent on the trust that consumers have in the food regime and the food supply, as described in chapter 3. Reciprocally, consumers are obviously dependent on producers to produce healthy food. This interdependence means that both producers and consumers are likely to agree that some sort of regulatory system is necessary. However, they will disagree about the distribution of risk and the cost of regulation. And, of course, producers will be more inclined to favor self-regulation, as explored in chapters 2, 3, 4, 6, and 8.[3]

A second asymmetry at the heart of contestation over food safety stems from the first one. The asymmetries of risk perception and experience mean that the risk trade-off is partly a conflict of values that must ultimately be resolved by politics rather than science. Yet food safety concerns are also inextricably linked to science-based analysis. Indeed, the microbial and genetic nature of food safety risks guarantees that any serious analysis of risk must be founded on scientific analysis. Thus, science is absolutely necessary but ultimately insufficient. When risk perceptions and experiences are asymmetrical, science and politics will be inextricably linked and necessarily at odds. The international dispute over the precautionary principle has been at the epicenter of this tension. Noiville's analysis in chapter 13 of the relationship between the precautionary principle and scientific analysis argues that the meaning of precaution is not inherently antithetical to science. She argues, in effect, that the devil is in the details: the relationship must be worked out on a case-by-case, and often technocratic, basis. Nevertheless, the evolving relationship is fraught with conflict.

While the uneasy coexistence between politics and science is partly about the conflict between public risk perception and scientifically established judgments about risk, it cannot be reduced to this conflict. The characterization of the debate about GMOs as fundamentally a debate between the consumer fears of Frankenfoods and scientific evaluation of actual risks is misleading. As described in chapter 5, public and NGO concerns about GMOs are much broader than food safety. They also concern issues of corporate control, biodiversity, the ethics of bioengineering, and the industrialization of agriculture. However, these additional issues, which are both political and scientific, become intertwined with the food safety debate. The dispute about science versus politics becomes in part, then, a dispute about the issues that can be legitimately raised in scientific fora and whether claims to science-based decision making are really a political way of curtailing debate. In chapter 9 comparing European, American, and Canadian regulatory styles, Skogstad argues that the U.S. Food and Drug Administration (FDA), in approving rBST milk, "adhered to its narrow statutory remit" and "resisted pressures to consider the economic consequences of the drug." Of course, broader issue linkages are also symptoms of contested governance. The fact that FDA can adhere to its narrow remit is partially indicative of the fact that it has successfully resisted politicization of decision-making criteria.

The asymmetry between science and politics also shows up over time in an asymmetry between a heavy reliance on routine expert authority to make food safety decisions and the heightened political attention that such decisions receive during a crisis. This asymmetry between routine response and crisis response is one of the mechanisms that propels contested governance forward by creating an additional set of tensions. The conflict, symbolized by the infamous toxics crisis at Love Canal, is that experts respond to crisis by more strongly asserting scientific authority, while those at risk respond by insisting on political intervention reflecting their value trade-offs. Thus, public authorities come to be seen as "callous bureaucrats," while experts view the public as "irrational."

The dialogue of the deaf that commonly ensues from the asymmetries of science and politics goes to the heart of the issues of trust and legitimacy that are central to contested governance. The loss of trust and legitimacy in public and private institutions that characterizes contested governance is rooted in this dilemma. A first-order loss of trust and legitimacy arises from the food scandals themselves. As Skogstad writes, "The significance of these regulatory failures is their effect of undermining the legitimacy of technocratic styles of regulatory policy making at both the national and EU levels." And just as the legitimacy of technocratic styles suffers, so the importance of political factors is enhanced. Skogstad notes that public opinion has hence become a more important factor in European decision making than in North American. The genie is not easy to put back in the bottle once let out. Although Rothstein (chapter 7) and Kjærnes et al. (chapter 3) suggest that institutional trust in food safety has been restored to a significant extent in the UK, Kjærnes et al. suggest that trust has been more difficult to reestablish in Germany.

The asymmetry of science as routine expert decision making and politics as the jostling of democratic interests and values creates a dilemma. For example, what resources or strategies do food safety experts have to assuage public concerns about possibly unsafe food or to satisfy aggrieved stakeholders? As Bernauer and Caduff (chapter 4) put it, "In the food market perceived safety problems are at least as important as real risks because food is a credence good—consumers are rarely able to reliably assess on their own the safety of food products." One strategy (adopted in Britain) is to create public consultation mechanisms that incorporate public opinion and allow it to be considered. Another strategy is to sharply separate technocratic from political decision making—an approach adopted by France, Germany, and the EU. A third choice is a "marketizing" of decision making that relies on depoliticizing issues by making them subject to individual choice. This is a strategy that can be seen at work in the development of many labeling and quality schemes, as described in chapters 4, 6, and 8. A fourth strategy is to combine political and scientific criteria in a single decision-making framework. This is arguably the strategy embodied in the precautionary principle, which (in some versions) seeks to simultaneously incorporate both public opinion and science into decision making.

If the asymmetries of risk perception and science versus politics propel the process of contestation forward, it is also important to understand how the genesis and evolution of contested governance is shaped by broader institutional contexts and also long-term trends. In the context of food safety, the broader institutional context has been the creation of the European Union and a new international trade regime. For example, the unstable relationship between political and scientific modes of decision making in the European context cannot be simply attributed to the high salience of the issue following food scandals. It must also be partly attributed to the character of European institutions that give greater weight to political concerns in decision making. Skogstad (chapter 9) uses such an argument in part to describe the European response to

GMOs: "And, as before, risk management—the final decision as to whether to authorize a GMO or GM product—is left to political authorities, not independent regulators or the developer."

Food safety crises as a set of conjunctural events also interact with longer-term trends in food production and politics. As Borraz, Besançon, and Clergeau put it in chapter 6, "Food safety, as a political theme, emerged when agriculture and food production were undergoing deep transformations, mainly under the impulse of European policies." Alemanno (chapter 10) provides a broad historical overview of food regulation at the European level. His analysis indicates that while achieving common or mutually acceptable food safety standards has long been a basic concern at the European level, the concern about safety per se has been subordinated to the project of completing European market integration. He writes that "there is no doubt that before 1992, following more than thirty years of legislative activity, EC food law was still mainly focused on issues of trade and of the free movement of goods rather than on safety issues. Although a significant number of EC legislative texts were adopted, one could not properly speak of a 'common food policy.'"

Beyond European market integration, van Waarden (chapter 2) suggests that globalization of food markets has accentuated the tensions around food safety: "Internationalization makes it more difficult for consumers to have confidence in the food they are consuming: information asymmetries increase, the sense of risk and uncertainty becomes heightened, and trust in markets declines." We also see evidence of a shift in the relative power of different producers in the food chain from farmers to food manufacturers to food retailers (Bernauer and Caduff discuss the concentration of European food production and retailing in chapter 4; see also Connor 2003).[4] Although this book has not provided a systematic analysis of these issues, our analysis does point to the need to think in terms of long-term secular trends in food production, distribution, and safety in relationship to short-term crises. In the broadest sense, we may be witnessing a sea change in the relationship between agricultural (producer) interests and health (consumer) interests. Agriculture remains a politically powerful sector of society. However, there are many indications that its political sovereignty has eroded. In part, this conflict can

be linked to the industrialization of farming, which erodes the boundaries that defined agriculture as a distinct and autonomous sector. As this
autonomy erodes, new issues are increasingly injected into the debate.
For example, the GMO, rBST, and beef hormone cases all create linkages between environmentalism, the sustainability of family farming, and
consumerism.

The erosion of these boundaries creates opportunities as well as constraints for traditional producers. The image of farmers in recent years
has become less idyllic, and they are increasingly seen as sources of pollution. Borraz, Besançon, and Clergeau (chapter 6) observe, however,
that the GMO debate has allowed French farmers to partially reframe
this image: "But the controversy over GM foods offered the opportunity
for a counterattack, in which farmers changed status, from culprits to
victims. The opposition against GMOs was based on the refusal to see
multinational corporations impose their seeds on farmers. It gave farmers
the opportunity to claim their autonomy, against the joint efforts of seed
producers and larger retailers to reduce their role to that of a simple
worker on a chain." This example illustrates how contested governance
is not simply a symptom of crisis but also a process that creates
new opportunities for actors. Ansell, Maxwell, and Sicurelli (chapter 5),
for instance, describe how the mad cow crisis created an opportunity
structure particularly conducive for the mobilization of anti-GMO
demands.

Institutional Adaptation to Contested Governance

One of the major contributions of this book is to present a broad view
of how institutions will adapt in the context of contested governance. In
this section, we summarize some of the major findings from the book
related to institutional reform. We also try to suggest some of the generic
dynamics of institutional reform under such conditions and the types of
difficulties that institutional reform faces.

At the national and European levels, food safety institutions have been
significantly, even radically, reformed and reorganized in response to
food crises, mad cow disease in particular. Steiner (chapter 8) conveys
the dramatic institutional upheavals that occurred in Germany: "Six

weeks after the first BSE case emerged in Germany the foundations, were laid for a sweeping reform of governance structures related to food safety: within forty-eight hours, both the minister of health and the minister of agriculture were forced to resign, and a lawyer and member of the Green party became head of the former Federal Ministry of Food, Agriculture and Forestry, which was simultaneously renamed the Federal Ministry of Consumer Protection, Food and Agriculture."

One characteristic of contested governance is that it challenges institutionalized, taken-for-granted political relationships. And we have noted that in the food safety case, the challenge took aim at the perceived conflict of interest between agricultural production activities and food safety responsibilities. In the wake of mad cow disease, the major institutional reforms at both the national and European levels sought to address this conflict by strengthening the independence of food safety authority within agricultural ministries, relocating food safety authority to health ministries, or creating an independent food safety agency. Rothstein (chapter 7) describes the relationship between the old and the new food safety regimes in the UK as follows: "MAFF [Ministry of Agriculture, Fisheries, and Food] had been afflicted by inherent conflicts of interest because of its dual responsibilities to regulate food safety and to promote food and agricultural business. The creation of the FSA [Food Safety Authority] reduced those conflicts by removing responsibilities for business promotion and by giving the agency the right to publish its advice to Ministers to restrict possibilities for direct political interference." However, the challenge to existing relationships goes beyond institutional reform. Conflict-of-interest concerns also point the spotlight on cozy relations between agricultural agencies and the agricultural industry. At the EU level, as Buonanno (chapter 11) observes, the EU Parliament blamed "comitology" (the committees providing scientific and political advice to the commission) for allowing agricultural and national interests to be overrepresented in food safety decision making. Similarly, in France, Borraz, Besançon, and Clergeau (chapter 6) note that the traditional "comanagement" characteristic of the agricultural policy sector was fundamentally challenged. And in the UK, as Rothstein (chapter 7) notes, FSA created a "stakeholder-style board comprising up to twelve members to help prevent regulatory capture and provide a balance of skills and experience."

Conflict-of-interest problems are likely wherever public or private authorities must balance multiple objectives. The heightened issue salience we associate with contested governance typically leads to a fundamental refocusing of priorities, with the salient issue being given— temporarily at least—overriding priority. A common way of realizing this overriding priority institutionally is by creating a new agency that can make this new priority its primary focus. Much like the creation of the Homeland Security Agency after September 11, the mad cow affair led to the creation of new agencies in Germany, France, the UK, and the EU. As Borraz, Besançon, and Clergeau (chapter 6) put it: "After a series of scandals that threatened political authority in France and the EU, governments turned their efforts to the creation of systems capable of protecting them from future crises by turning the public's attention toward independent institutions."

Reforms have also occurred in the private as well as the public sectors. In fact, Steiner (chapter 8) argues that "the heightened incentives for the German food demand chain to implement a large-scale quality assurance scheme after the BSE crisis reflects the shifting balance of regulation, away from publicly mandated food safety regulations, more toward industry-led initiatives." He describes the introduction of an ambitious industry-sponsored quality control system (the QS system) in Germany, which is built around the strategy of industry self-regulation based on the principles of the hazard analysis and critical control point (HAACP) system and a system of certification by independent auditors. While the standards met by the QS system are quite high (higher than public standards in some cases), the system has achieved only limited coverage of the German market. Similarly, Bernauer and Caduff (chapter 4) describe the boost the food safety crisis has given across Europe to the HAACP strategy, but also note that implementation of HAACP is uneven and incomplete.[5] In the French case, Borraz, Besançon, and Clergeau (chapter 6) note the impetus given to the private use of quality labeling and branding strategies by public concerns about food safety.[6] Van Waarden (chapter 2) argues that this increasing reliance on private regulation is related to the squeeze, produced by the internationalization of food markets, between greater demands for risk assurance on the part of consumers and the weakening capacity of national governments to unilaterally regulate food safety.

Although the public sector reforms at the national and EU levels have many similarities, they also differ in interesting respects. Rothstein (chapter 7) provides a good summary of the differences: "The variation among the reformed regimes, however, shows that food safety agencies come in different flavors. In the UK, risk assessment, management, and communication functions were combined within the FSA and kept at arm's length from central government. In France, AFSSA was given responsibilities for risk assessment and communication, but risk management was firmly left in the hands of central government. The German reforms were closer to the French than the British, but involved still other institutional ingredients." In Germany, France, and at the EU level, institutional reform led to a sharp separation between risk management and risk assessment. By contrast, in the UK, risk management, assessment, and communication are brought together.

Although these reforms were conjunctural, they have often responded to issues that had been on the agenda for a long time—notably, longstanding though largely ignored complaints about the legal and institutional fragmentation of food safety authority.[7] In reference to the UK, for instance, Rothstein (chapter 7) argues that the food safety crises were as much the catalyst as the cause of these reforms. The chapters on France, Germany and the EU also suggest that these crises provided a window of opportunity to address long-standing issues of institutional fragmentation, traceability, and liability. Such problems were prior conditions that were easily blamed in the case of crisis. As already noted, the food safety crisis has also fed into a long-term trend toward delegation of regulatory controls to private industry. In part, this is related to the increasingly systemic controls that are needed (HAACP) and to demands for traceability. As Borraz, Besançon, and Clergeau (chapter 6) note: "Hence, standardization made its way in the food industry before the food safety crises, but public authorities found in these further justifications for delegating more controls to the firms, along with greater accountability in case of noncompliance." In addition to these long-standing issues, institutional reform may also interact with parallel but ostensibly unrelated developments in a sector. For example, the quality labeling movement in France was related to finding ways to increase the economic security of small family farmers. However, these labels became attractive to consumers as a certification of food safety. Crisis therefore becomes an opportunity to mobilize support for issues that otherwise have not received public attention or sufficient political backing.

Although the reforms that resulted from the crisis were significant, arguably revolutionary, they did not always make as clear a break with the old regime as it first appears. The reforms all represented various degrees of compromise with preexisting institutions. Institutional adaptations created in the face of contested governance are typically elaborate compromises that do not entirely break with the prior institutional arrangements. The new French agency, AFSSA, provides a good example. Although a new agency was created, it remains dependent on three ministries. Thus, risk assessment has been partially separated from the Ministry of Agriculture, but food safety decisions (risk management) remain firmly within the ministry (though reforms within the ministry do enhance the autonomy of food safety decisions).

Similar compromises occurred at the European level. Both Alemanno (chapter 10) and Buonanno (chapter 11) describe a report by three eminent scientists, commissioned by European policymakers to find a solution to the European food safety crisis, that recommended an independent European agency combining both risk management and assessment. Buonanno captures the revolutionary thrust of the report's conclusions: "They developed a blueprint for a European Food and Public Health Authority (EFPHA), a corporatist-style agency, which they described as a regulatory agency with the combined scope of the U.S. Centers for Disease Control (CDC) and the Food and Drug Administration (FDA). It would be a gross euphemism to describe their proposal as 'nonincremental' because in one bold brush, the commission, the council, and Parliament lost legislative and executive power to a regulatory authority." The scientists report emphatically warned against artificially separating risk management and risk assessment. However, the commission's *White Paper on Food Safety* advised against such a bold move, with concurrence from the both the European Parliament and

Council of Ministers. While a bold departure from past practice as seen from one perspective, EFSA as seen from another was an incremental shift from the institutional status quo. Alemanno also argues that although European reforms have created for the first time a common framework for risk analysis, the new food safety regime is largely a continuation of the mutual recognition principles around which the previous regime was organized.

One irony of the institutional compromises associated with creating new agencies as a response to institutional and legal fragmentation is that the new agencies address some kinds of fragmentation but exacerbate others. This is partly because reform of institutional fragmentation has been only partial in the first place. For example, even in the most extensive case of institutional reform and consolidation—the UK—FSA has limited surveillance and enforcement powers, because these activities remain under the responsibility of local government. All three of our country cases and our analysis of the EU suggest that reforms have only partially reduced institutional fragmentation of food safety and have left opportunities for conflicts to arise between different institutional components of food safety regimes. Whether full consolidation of food safety authority is even desirable remains an important question. It is arguable that the creation of separate risk assessment agencies creates an effective system of checks and balances. Our only point is that we should not become too complacent about the institutional coherence of new food safety regimes.

Institutional reform during a crisis has both advantages and disadvantages. The advantages are that you can sometimes mount enough energy and focus enough attention to make broad-based changes that run against powerful and parochial interests that have previously resisted change. The disadvantage is that the heightened attention can lead to a level of ceremonial adaptation that reestablishes legitimacy without undertaking serious reform. In his study of leadership, Heifitz (1994) has described the general dilemma: the problem with crises is that they lead to a call to decisively reassert authority and authoritative leadership—to resolve the uncertainty of consumers and citizens. Yet the response can introduce more uncertainty and can paper over actual substantive problems. Heifitz argues that uncertainty creates a need for mutual learning processes that can be undermined by (maladaptive) assertions of authority.

The incentives for institutional reform following crisis are sometimes importantly skewed, particularly in cases where there are sharp asymmetries between the routine politics that dominate prior to crises and the heightened issue salience that ensues from crises. Faced with an initial public outcry, experts are very likely to see their role as simply to assuage public outcry and restore trust by reinforcing the logic of the routine, expert system. They will have the tendency to assert their own routines in order to assuage concerns of public trust or legitimacy through impression management techniques. These efforts are likely to be read cynically by the public as attempts to soft-pedal the issue.

The expert's reinforcement of a technocratic solution to risk asymmetries in conjunction with rising concerns about conflicts of interest and none-too-subtle impression management (recall the example of the minister feeding a hamburger to his daughter on national television) can lead to a widening gulf between expert and public opinion. Such has arguably been the case in the mad cow and GMO disputes. This disparity of risk perception on the part of the public and risk management on the part of public and private authorities can prompt a dynamic with important consequences for institutional reform. The early shallowness of the response to heightened issue salience (e.g., the intensification of routine) is likely to be followed in later phases by dramatic attempts to demonstrate that "we've got the message," setting the stage for deeper reforms. These later reforms will be focused on reprioritizing the issue by showing that the salient issue is the overriding priority. (This might even lead to a kind of political one-upmanship to see who can do the most to focus on this issue.)

One consequence of the heightened concerns about conflicts of interest is that institutional reforms in the context of contested governance will tend to focus on independence, transparency, and accountability. This has certainly been true of reforms of food safety governance. The creation of new agencies in Germany, France, the UK, and at the European level all emphasize these qualities. And these efforts were certainly part of a real effort to resolve conflict of interest problems. As Borraz, Besançon, and Clergeau (chapter 6) write: "The creation of

AFSSA was destined to follow the same guiding principles mentioned above and untangle the close relationships between powerful agrobusiness lobbies and state officials." And it is clear that this refocusing of priorities on independence, transparency, and accountability may have important benefits. These same authors argue, for instance, that AFSSA has improved the exercise of expertise.

There is also, however, a potentially more negative side to independence, transparency, and accountability that is partly built into the dynamic of contested governance. Given the deficit of trust and legitimacy characteristic of contested governance, institutional reforms may focus so much attention on transparency, accountability, and independence that the demonstration of these qualities may displace the substantive goal of guaranteeing food safety. Or, alternatively, the need to achieve these goals may create institutional imperatives that enhance conflict itself. Borraz, Besançon, and Clergeau (chapter 6) describe the reputational concerns of AFSSA that have led it to take a strong stand in certain food decisions in order to demonstrate its independence. But AFSSA has also been criticized for unrealistic recommendations. The authors point to Jasanoff's argument that transparency can lead to more adversarial governance and increased focus on rules. It is also possible, they note, that transparency can lead to blame avoidance that undermines the value of openness, which as Rothstein (chapter 7) notes, is highly dependent on local institutional practices and pressures. Steiner (chapter 8), for instance, notes that German reforms have produced only limited transparency.

Van Waarden (chapter 2) concludes his chapter by describing the potential paradox that increased control and accountability may ultimately deepen our distrust: "To every new scandal or crisis, politicians react by adding one more layer of control on top of the already existing levels of controllers. Paradoxically, the more food quality inspectors and tests we have, the more we *can* know about our food quality, the more we *want* to know, the more we feel unsafe, leading to a call for yet another layer of inspectors, controllers and evaluators." This paradox may lie at the heart of many policy sectors characterized by asymmetries of perception and coping: homeland security, child safety, police brutality, nuclear waste disposal.

Multilevel Regulation

We turn now to another theme illustrated by European food safety regulation: the growing importance of multilevel regulatory systems. In this case, the multilevel character of regulation describes not only the relationship between national governments and European governments, but also between Europe and the international food safety regime (WTO, Codex Alimentarius). A potential for conflict is obviously inherent in multilevel systems because they create the possibility for different regulatory standards and decision-making procedures and criteria operating at different levels to come into conflict. Yet these standards probably have the most opportunity for conflict where multilevel systems are early in the process of institutionalization, as they are in the case of the EU and the WTO. Thus, we would argue that it is at least partly the interaction between the public's response to food scares in combination with the creation of a weakly institutionalized, and only partially legitimated, multilevel regulatory system that has in part accentuated the self-sustaining dynamic of contested governance in Europe.

To a large extent, it is the broader institutional imperatives of vertical power sharing inherent in multilevel governance arrangements that constrain and shape the types of criteria that dominate at any particular level. Skogstad (chapter 9) presents this quite clearly in her comparison of European, American, and Canadian policy styles. As she writes: "The institutional framework of food safety regulation in the EU—dispersed policymaking authority across member states and EU institutions as well as unanimnity or supermajority decision-making rules—necessitates a consensual, meditative regulatory policy style. Democratic decision-making procedures are imperative in this 'polity under construction,' which is constantly required to justify the growing authority of EU-level institutions." Consequently, the EU is more sensitive to public opinion than Canadian or American food safety regimes. While the European Commission has obviously been concerned about the scientific basis of its decisions, it has also "reserved the right to take into consideration nonscientific factors, including consumers' expectations." As Alemanno (chapter 10) points out, the commission's authority to take nonscientific factors into consideration remains in place even after the reforms that sought to increase the autonomy of European independent risk assessment and management.

Skogstad (chapter 9) also notes how this greater sensitivity to public opinion (in contrast with the more technocratic styles of Canada and the United States) can interact with the heightened attention to institutional transparency, independence, and accountability: "Food safety risk regulation based on democratic norms and processes goes even further in vesting authority in citizens and their elected governments. Regulatory procedures and outcomes that rely on democratic processes derive their legitimacy from adhering to democratic procedural norms like transparency, public input, and government accountability. In addition, policy outcomes reflect majority preferences, and elected politicians take responsibility for regulatory decisions and are directly accountable to their electorate for risk management." One might also say that concerns about the EU's "democratic deficit" and, consequently, the EU's focus on output legitimacy make it sensitive to building up greater political acceptance of its decisions. It is possible that a slightly different imperative is driving EU decisions. Borraz, Besançon, and Clergeau (chapter 6) argue that "government interventions at the national and European levels aim at preserving the role of the market rather than introduce social or ethical criteria to regulate food safety." Thus, the commission is concerned about achieving defensible common standards that level the playing field (see also chapter 10 on this point).

The institutional reforms described in the previous section can also lead to increased conflict when they come into contact through multilevel governance systems. The creation of independent risk assessment bodies at different levels may increase conflict over scientific advice. For example, the new French agency has opposed the risk assessments of European risk committees. It is possible, however, that independent risk assessment agencies at different levels will also converge in their assessments, creating de facto multilevel alliances. Rothstein (chapter 7) points to still another way in which institutional reforms and multilevel governance may interact: "Regulatory competition between member states and the EC in food safety governance has put member states under additional pressure to beef up their food safety activities if they are to play a senior role in EU decision making."

A third explanation of divergence between national and European-level regulation arises from the different scale of interest representation. Rothstein (chapter 7) argues that it is likely that the EU and UK came to different conclusions about the use of sausage casings made from sheep because the sausage casing industry is more prominent in Europe as a whole than it is in the UK. He further argues that this conflict about BSE in sheep suggests that transparent processes will produce more precautionary outcomes than opaque processes and that the multilevel governance structure therefore moderates the scope for action of national authorities.

A fourth possible source of divergence across decision-making levels results from trading-up dynamics. Multilevel systems accentuate differences in decision-making criteria as they are used by different units horizontally (different European nations in the case of the EU; different nations in the international trading system in the case of the WTO). These differences, however, are politically framed as disputes between vertical levels of government. They create the opportunity structure for higher levels to pressure lower levels to change their standards and for lower-level units to pressure higher-level units to change their standards. As Vogel (1995) has argued and Holmes and Young argue in this volume (chapter 12), such heterogeneity creates the possibilities for trading up to stricter standards.

With respect to food safety, Holmes and Young show that the EU is the source of the majority of food safety disputes at the WTO. These disputes arise because the EU's food safety rules are more risk averse than those of its trading partners. Holmes and Young attribute the stricter standards to the dynamic of trading up. The tendency has been for common European rules to be set at the level of the strictest national rules. Within the context of the international trading regime, they argue that process rules prove to be particularly troublesome:

Within the category of harmonized product regulations, rules that govern how products are produced present particular problems for third-country firms. So-called process regulations do not generally present barriers to trade; however, they can present a problem when the production process is considered to have altered the product. This seems to be a particularly common problem with respect to food safety. The WTO disputes concerning the EU's rules on hormone-treated beef, GM food, and wine making all fit into this category, as do the residual dispute concerning antimicrobial treatments in poultry production, the shelved dispute about rBST milk, and the resolved dispute over the third-country meat directive.

Hence, the setting of higher standards at the EU level can accentuate tensions between nations within the EU and between the EU and its trading partners in the international trading system. With respect to the WTO, however, Holmes and Young argue that these tensions have limits: the EU will have trouble changing rules to bring them in compliance with multilateral obligations, but they will have less trouble designing new rules to be compatible with these obligations. The new risk assessment regime at the EU level is more in line, Holmes and Young argue, with the WTO's SPS Agreement. They argue that conflict between the EU and the WTO is likely to decrease, but that enlargement may increase conflict within the EU. Noiville (chapter 13) similarly argues that there is no inherent contradiction between the European attachment to the precautionary principle and the WTO trading regime. But she remains skeptical that the WTO can accommodate national political choices within its regulatory framework.[8]

A fifth multilevel dynamic, described by Ansell, Maxwell, and Sicurelli (chapter 5), does not so much produce divergence as it guarantees that the different levels of a multilevel governance system will be forced to confront each other. Political mobilization may operate simultaneously at multiple territorial scales—subnational, national, European, and international—and it will attempt to mobilize support of one level to pressure other levels. In the GMO debate, in particular, we have seen the anti-GMO movement skillfully mobilize subnational regions to place pressure on national governments, national governments to influence European decisions, and European policy to shape national positions.

Thus, multilevel governance interacts with the dynamic of contested governance because of the possibility that divergences in standards and decision-making criteria exacerbate conflict. However, we have argued that contested governance represents pervasive conflict, and there is no necessary reason to suggest that multilevel governance leads inherently to pervasive conflict. As Holmes and Young (chapter 12) argue, conflict between levels is mitigated through mutual adjustment. Therefore, we argue that the more important feature of multilevel governance to interact with contested governance is the weak institutionalization of the division of decision-making authority between governance levels. If the relative powers of different levels of a multilevel governance system are themselves disputed, then the types of disputes between science and politics we described earlier are likely to partially be played out as disputes over the legitimate level at which decisions ought to be made. The relative authority of national and European levels of governance is, of course, one of the central disputes of European integration (see chapters 4, 10, and 11). And the authority of the WTO is also only weakly institutionalized. Indeed, prominent food safety cases involving Europe (especially, perhaps, the beef hormone case) represent important steps in the early establishment of decision-making precedent in the WTO system.

In this book, Bernauer and Caduff (chapter 5) take the most decisive stand on the issues of the relative powers of national and European levels. They argue, in effect, that European food safety regulation is unproductively wedged between national regulation and European regulation (a point partially echoed by van Waarden in chapter 2). While recognizing the political reality of the limits on centralization, they argue that the Europeanization of food safety regulation (as detailed in chapters 10 and 11) is more desirable than either renationalization or shared powers. Kjærnes et al. (chapter 3), however, sound a more cautionary note. In their studies of trust in food in European nations, they find that stronger European governance would have to confront the diversity of national food systems: "This presents food agencies on the EU level with a dilemma. On the one hand, the EFSA and its regulations, as well as the systems imposed through the major pan-European retailers, can be expected to be trusted and experienced differently in different countries and different regions. On the other hand, the food scandals in Europe revealed that consumers expect that national (and regional/local) food authorities, supported by civil society actors, have a clear role in regulating actors involved in food production and distribution."

As van Waarden (chapter 2) suggests, national food regulatory systems are founded on different cultural conceptions. "If anything is culture-dependent," he writes, "it is food." The newly reformed European food safety regime, according to Alemanno (chapter 10), remains deeply, if only implicitly, sensitive to the cultural traditions of European member states. Caught between the imperatives of centralization and decentralization, the tensions over who, where, how, and on what basis food safety decisions should be made and implemented are not likely to be easily resolved.

Conclusion

Food safety is not an inherently conflictual policy sector. Indeed, producers and consumers may be bound together by strong mutual interests in guaranteeing trust in the food supply. The contested character of food safety governance in Europe reflects the confluence of several factors: a series of food scares that have heightened the salience of food issues in Europe, European market integration and the project of constructing a European polity, and the creation of a new international trading regime. Other less proximate factors, such as the changing production of food and the globalization of food markets, have also probably contributed to contestation. In this book, we have not only sought to identify the factors that have initially led to contestation, but also sought to understand the institutional and political dynamics that have deepened contestation. We have argued that contested governance can become a self-sustaining dynamic propelled forward by asymmetrical responses to crisis conditions. The result can be a more pervasive sense of distrust of public and private institutions and an expansion of the issues that are contested. However, the book has also examined institutional adaptation to conditions of contested governance. A number of signs suggest that in time, these adaptations may successfully restore trust and legitimacy. Yet it is far from clear that these institutional adaptations have fully resolved nagging issues about the precise relation between science and politics and between market promotion and public health.

Notes

1. Where tensions are asymmetrical but interdependence is low, we should expect public conflicts to lead to balkanization and segmented solutions. For a very similar discussion of the way in which asymmetrical perceptions and coping

strategies contribute to the delegitimation of large technical systems, see La Porte (1994).

2. However, the risks fall unequally across producers at various points in the food production food chain. Among producers, food retailers are generally the most sensitive to consumer preferences.

3. Though as Bernauer and Caduff point out, private firms may also desire stringent public regulation in order to level the playing field among market actors.

4. Schofield and Shaoul (2000) argue that changes in meat production markets contributed to the outbreak of an *E. coli 0157* outbreak in the UK.

5. To characterize HAACP as a system of industry self-regulation, as I have done here, is partially misleading. As Bernauer and Caduff point out, both the EU and national governments have endorsed and supported the HAACP system through directives and other measures. Thus, HAACP is a feature of public regulation.

6. What is common to these findings is that these private forms of regulation became bases of competition within food markets.

7. For more discussion of this point, see the U.S. General Accounting Office report on the consolidation of food safety authority in Canada, Denmark, Ireland, and the UK (1999).

8. She points specifically to the "necessity" and "coherence" tests as sources of future regulatory tension.

References

2003/89/EC Directive of the European Parliament and of the Council of 10 November 2003 amending Directive 2000/13/EC as regards indication of the ingredients present in foodstuffs.

Abergel, Elisabeth, and Barrett, Katherine. 2002. "Putting the Cart before the Horse: A Review of Biotechnology Policy in Canada." *Journal of Canadian Studies* 37, 3:135–161.

Abitbol, William, and Couteaux, Paul-Marie. 1999. "Souverainisme, j'ecris ton nom." *Le Monde*, September 30.

Acemoglu, D., and Johnson, S. 2003. *Unbundling Institutions*. Working paper 3–29, Massachusetts Institute of Technology, Department of Economics, Cambridge, MA.

Aghion, P., and Tirole, J. 1997. "Formal and Real Authority in Organization." *Journal of Political Economy* 105, 1:1–29.

Agrarbericht. 2003. *Ernährungs- und agrarpolitischer Bericht 2003 der Bundesregierung*. Berlin: Federal Ministry of Consumer Protection, Food and Agriculture (BMVEL).

Agrarbericht. 2001. *Ernährungs- und agrarpolitischer Bericht 2001 der Bundesregierung*, Berlin.

Agrar. De. 2003. *Künast kritisiert QS-System und Verbraucher* (Künast criticizes QS scheme and consumers). Rheine, Alfous Deitermann March 13.

Alemanno, Alberto. 2002. "Contentieux, Arrêt 'Commission/France.'" 1 *Revue du droit de l'Union Européenne* 1:159–162.

Albert, M. 1993. *Capitalism against Capitalism*. London: Whurr Publishers.

Allbeury, Kerry, and Truilhé, Eve. 2002. "La preuve dans le réglement des différends à l'OMC. Applications possibles en matière d'OGM?" In J. Bourrinet and S. Maljean-Dubois (eds.), *Le commerce international des organismes génétiquement modifiés*. Paris: La documentation française. Pp. 286–315.

Alleanza Nazionale. 2002. "AG in Piazza: Toleranza ZeroContro gli OGM" Press Release, <http://www.Gioventù Identitaria.Org> December 10.

Almås, R. 1999. "Food Trust, Ethics and Safety in Risk Society." *Sociological Research Online* 4, 3:1–9.

Ancelovici, Marcos. 2002. "Organizing against Globalization: The Case of ATTAC in France." *Politics and Society* 30, 3:427–463.

Andrews N. J., et al. "Deaths from Variant Creutzfeldt-Jakob Disease in the UK." *Lancet* 361:751–752.

Ansa. 1996. "Morbo Mucca Pazza: Italia Sospende Importazioni da Gran Bretagne." "Sportello Europa." <http://www.ansa.it>.

Ansa Ambiente. 2003. "Coldiretti: Vittoria Sicurezza Alimentare; WWF; Sanctito il Principio di Precauzione," <http://www.ansa.it>.

Ansa. 1999. "Cibi Transqenici, a un Passo dalla Moratoria," <http://www.ansa.it/evropa/cercasudea.html>, June 24.

Antle, J. 1995. *Choice and Efficiency in Food Safety Policy*. Washington, D.C.: AEI Press.

Arrow, K., et al. 1996. "Is There a Role for Benefit-Cost Analysis in Environmental, Health and Safety Regulation?" *Science* 272:221–222.

Bardach, Eugene, and Kagan, Robert A. 1982. *Going by the Book: The Problem of Regulatory Unreasonableness*. Philadelphia: Temple University Press.

Barling, David. 1997. "Regulatory Conflict and Marketing of Agricultural Biotechnology in the European Community." In J. Stanyer and G. Stoker (eds.), *Contemporary Political Studies*. Nottingham: Political Studies Association of the U.K. Pp. 1040–1048.

Barling, David. 1996. "Environmental Sustainability or Commercial Viability? The Evolution of the EC Regulation on Genetically Modified Foods." *European Environment* 6:48–54.

Barreto, A. 2000. "Portugal e a Europa: Quatro Décades." In C. Cabral (ed.), *A Situacao Social em Portugal 1960-1999*. Lisbon: Imprensa de Ciencias Sociais. Pp. 37–77.

Barton Hutt, Peter. 1984. "Government Regulation of the Integrity of the Food Supply." *Annual Review of Nutrition*, 4, 1:1–20.

Barton Hutt, Peter, and Merrill, Richard A. 1991. *Food and Drug Law*. 2nd ed. Foundation Press.

BBC News. 2000. "Austrian Chancellor's Doubts over Haider." February 7. <http://news.bbc.co.uk/1/hi/world/europe/646705.stm>.

Beck, Ulrich.1999. *World Risk Society*. Cambridge: Polity Press.

Beck, Ulrich. 1992. *Risk Society*. London: Sage.

Berg, L. 2000a. *Tillit til mat i kugalskapens tid*. [Trust in Food in a Time of Mad Cow Disease]. Report no. 15. Oslo: National Institute for Consumer Research.

Berg, L. 2000b. *Trust in Food in Europe: Focus on Consumer Trust in Norway, England and Belgium*. Working paper no. 15. Lysaker: National Institute for Consumer Research.

Berger, Suzanne. 1995. "Trade and Identity: The Coming Protectionism?" In Gregory Flynn (ed.), *Remaking the Hexagon*. Boulder, Colo.: Westview Press.

Bernauer, Thomas. 2003. *Genes, Trade, and Regulation: The Seeds of Conflict in Food Biotechnology*. Princeton, N.J: Princeton University Press.

Bernauer, Thomas, and Meins, Erika. 2003. "Technological Revolution Meets Policy and the Market: Explaining Cross-National Differences in Agricultural Biotechnology Regulation." *European Journal of Political Research* 42, 5:643–683.

Besançon, Julien. 2003. *Evaluation de l'Agence française de sécurité sanitaire des aliments. Etude auprès des publics et personnels de l'agence*. Paris: Centre de sociologie des organisations.

Besançon, Julien, Borraz, Olivier, and Grandclément-Chaffy, Catherine. 2004. *La sécurité alimentaire en crises. Les crises Coca-Cola et Listeria de 1999–2000*. Paris: L'Harmattan.

BfR. 2005. *Federal Institute for Risk Assessment*. <www.bfr.bund.de>.

BfR. 2003. "Research" *Federal Institute for Risk Assessment*. <www.bfr.bund.de>.

Blau, P. M. 1968. "Social Exchange." In *International Encyclopedia of the Social Sciences*. New York: Macmillan and Free Press. Pp. 452–457.

Böcker, Andreas, and Hanf, Claus-Hennig. 2000. "Confidence Lost and—Partially—Regained: Consumer Response to Food Scares." *Journal of Economic Behavior and Organization* 43:471–485.

Bogdanich, Walt, and Eric Koli. "2 Paths of Bayer Drug in 80's: Riskier One Steered Overseas," *New York Times*, May 22, 2003.

Bonny, Sylvie. 2003. "Why Are Most Europeans Opposed to GMOs? Factors Explaining Rejection in France and Europe." *Electronic Journal of Biotechnology* 6,1. <http://www.ejbiotechnology.info/content/vol6/issue1/full/4/>.

Böge, Remer. 1997. *Report on the European Commission's Follow-up of the Recommendations Made by the Committee of Inquiry into BSE*. Brussels: European Parliament, Temporary Committee on Inquiry into BSE. November 14.

Borraz, Olivier, and d'Arcimoles, Marie. 2003. "Réguler ou qualifier: Le cas des boues d'épuration urbaines." *Sociologie du Travail* 1:45–62.

Borraz, Olivier, d'Arcimoles, Marie, and Salomon, Danielle. 2001. *Les mondes des boues: La difficile institutionnalisation des filières d'épandage des boues d'épuration urbaines en agriculture*. Paris: ADEME-CNRS.

Bové, José, and Dufour, François. 2001. *The World Is Not for Sale: Farmers against Junkfood*. London: Verso.

Bovens, Mark, and 'tHart, Paul. 1996. *Understanding Policy Fiascoes*. New Brunswick, N.J: Transaction Publishers.

Boyd, William. 2003. "Wonderful Potencies? Deep Structure and the Problem of Monopoly in Agricultural Biotechnology." In Rachel Sehurman and Dennis Doyle Takahashi. Kelso (eds.), *Engineering Trouble: Biotechnology and its Discontents*. Berkelen, CA: University of California Press. Pp 24–62.

Bradley, Kieran St. C. 1998. "The GMO-Committee on Transgenic Maize: Alien Corn, or the Transgenic Procedural Maze." In M.P.C.M. Van Schendelen (ed.), *EU Committees as Influential Policy Makers*. Aldershot, U.K.: Ashgate. Pp. 207–222.

Breyer, Stephen. 1993. *Breaking the Vicious Circle*. Cambridge, Mass.: Harvard University Press.

Brinckman, Dirk. 2000. "The Regulation of rBST: The European Case." *AgBioForum* 3(2&3), article 15.

British Nutrition Foundation. 2000. *Preparatory Work on Improving Information in Catering Outlets and for Foods Sold Loose*. London: BNF.

Bunte, F. H. J. 2000. "The Vertical Organization of Food Chains and Health and Safety Efforts." In L. J. Unnevehr (ed.), *The Economics of HACCP*. Eagan Press.

Buonanno, Laurie, and Nugent, Neill. 2002. "Institutional Opportunism: The Case of the European Parliament with Regard to Food Safety Policy." Paper presented at ECSA-Canada, Toronto, May.

Busch, L. 2000. "The Moral Economy of Grades and Standards." *Journal of Rural Studies* 16, 3:273–283.

Buzby, J., Frenzen, P., and B. Rasco. 2001. *Product Liability and Microbial Foodborne Illness*. Agricultural Economic Report No. 799. Washington, DC: ERS.

Buzby, J. C., and Roberts, T. 1996. "Economic Research Service Updates United States Foodborne Disease Costs for Seven Pathogens." *Food Review*, 19:20–25.

Byrne, D. 2004. "The Regulation of Food Safety and the Use of Traceability/Tracing in the EU and USA: Convergence or Divergence?" Speech given at the Food Safety Conference, Washington, D.C., March 19.

Byrne, D. 2002. "EFSA: Excellence, Integrity and Openness." Speech presented at Inaugural Meeting of the Management Board of the European Food Safety Authority, Brussels, September 18.

Cabinet Office (Strategy Unit). 2002. *Risk: Improving Government's Capability to Handle Risk and Uncertainty*. London: UK Cabinet Office.

Caduff, Ladina. 2004. "Vorsorge oder Risiko? Verbraucher- und umweltschutzpolitische Regulierung im europäisch-amerikanishen Vergleich. Eine politökonomische Analyse des Hormonstreits und der Elektronikschrottproblematik" Ph.D. diss., Center for Comparative and International Studies, Zurich.

Cameron, James, and Campbell, Karen. 1998. *Dispute Resolution in the WTO*. London: Cameron May.

Canadian Biotechnology Advisory Committee. 2002. *Improving the Regulation of Genetically Modified Foods and Other Novel Foods in Canada*. <http://cbac-ccab.ca/epic/internet/incbac-cccb.nsf/vwGneratedInterE/ah00186e.html>.

Cantley, Mark F. 1995. "The Regulation of Modern Biotechnology: An Historical and European Perspective." In D. Brauer (ed.), *Biotechnology: Legal, Economic and Ethical Dimensions*. Weinheim: VCH.

Castle, Stephen, and Butler, Katherine. 1999. "The Sourpusses of Strasbourg Fraud Mismanagement and Cronyism Censured in Strasbourg." *Independent*, January 17.

Caswell, J. 1998. "Valuing the Benefits and Costs of Improved Food Safety and Nutrition." *Australian Journal of Agricultural and Resource Economics* 42, 4:409–424.

Caswell, J., Bredahl, M., and N. Hooker. 1998. "How Quality Management Metasystems Are Affecting the Food Industry." *Review of Agricultural Economics* 20, 2:547–557.

Chalmers, Damian. 2003. "'Food for Thought': Reconciling European Risks and Traditional Ways of Life." *Modern Law Review* 66:532, 534.

Chambers, Graham R. 1999a. "The BSE Crisis and the European Parliament." In Christian Joerges and Ellen Vos (eds.), *EU Committees: Social Regulation, Law and Politics*. Oxford: Hart Publishing. Pp. 95–106.

Chambers, Graham R. 1999b. "The BSE Crisis and the European Parliament." In Christian Joerges and Ellen Vos (eds.), *Politics*. Oxford: Hart Publishing. Pp. 5–106.

Chandler, A. 1990. *Scale and Scope: The Dynamics of Industrial Capitalism*. Cambridge, MA: Belknap Press.

Charles, Daniel. 2001. *Lords of the Harvest*. Cambridge, MA: Perseus Publishing.

Cherfas, Jeremy. 1990. "Europe: Bovine Growth Hormone in a Political Maze." *Science*, August 24, 852.

Chmitelin, Isabelle. 2003. "L'analyse du risque aliméntaire au niveau communautaire: Le rôle des Etats Membres dans la sécurité des aliments." In Jacques Bourrinet and Francis Snyder (eds.), *La sécurité aliméntaire dans l'Union européenne* at 95. Brussels: Bruylant.

Christoforou, Théofanis. 2003. "The Precautionary Principle and Democratizing Expertise: A European Legal Perspective." *Science and Public Policy* 30, 3:205–212.

Christoforou, Theofanis. 2002. "Science, Law and Precaution in Dispute Resolution on Health and Environmental Protection: What Role for Scientific Experts?" In J. Bourrinet et S. Maljean-Dubois (dir.), *Le commerce international des organismes génétiquement modifiés*. Paris: La documentation française. Pp. 213–283.

Christophersen, K. A. 2003. *Databehandling og statistisk analyse med SPSS*. Oslo: Unipub forlag.

CIAA. 2003a. "Data and Trends of the Food Drink Industry in the EU." Press release, Brussels, November 28. <http://www.ciaa.be/uk/documents/press/press28-11-03.htm>.

CIAA. 2003b. *CIAA Priorities on the Agenda of the EU Presidency: Proposal for a Regulation on the Hygiene of Foodstuffs*. July. <www.ciaa.be>.

Clergeau, Christophe. 2004. "European Food Safety Policies between Single Market and Political Crisis." In J. Lehto and M. Steffen (eds.), *Europeanisation of Health Policies: Issues, Challenges: Innovations.* London: Routledge.

Clergeau, Christophe. 2003. "La sécurité des aliments entre globalisation et crises politiques." *Revue Politiques et Management Public* 2:103–118.

Clergeau, Christophe. 2000. *Le processus de création de l'Agence française de sécurité sanitaire des aliments: Généalogie, genèse et adoption d'une proposition de loi.* Paris: ENSA Rennes, IEP de Paris.

CNA (Conseil National de l'Alimentation). 2005. *Propositions du CNA pour la mise en place d'une expertise socio-économique dans le cadre de l'analyse des risques alimentaires.* Position 50, adopted February 1.

Coates, Dudley. 1984. "Food Law: Brussels, Whitehall and Town Hall." In David Lewis and Helen Wallace (eds.), *Policies into Practice: National and International Case Studies in Implementation.* London: Heinemann. Pp. 144–160.

Coldiretti. 2003. *La Coldiretti contro gli OGM: siamo per la tolleranza zero.* <http://www.coldiretti.it>.

Coleman, Robert J. 2001. "Communicating Risk to Consumers." Address to the Interim Scientific Advisory Forum, Brussels, October 30. 2001. <http://europa.eu.int/comm/dgs/health_consumer/library/speeches/speech133_en .pdf>.

Colman, Tyler. 2002. "Associational Governance and Production Politics in the French Wine Industry." Ph.D. dissertation. Department of Political Science. Northwestern University.

Committee on Toxicity of Chemicals in Food, Consumer Products and the Environment. 2000. *Adverse Reactions to Food and Food Ingredients.* London: COT.

Committee on Toxicity of Chemicals in Food, Consumer Products and the Environment (COT). 1998. *Report on Peanut Allergy.* London: COT.

Connor, John M. 2003. "The Changing Structure of Global Food Markets: Dimensions, Effects, and Policy Implications." Staff paper no. 03-02, Department of Agricultural Economics, Purdue University.

Copa-Cogeca. 2002. "Position of Copa and Cogeca on the Use of Gene Technology in Agriculture," Press Release, January 21.

Crutchfield, S., and Roberts, T. 2000. "Food Safety Efforts Accelerate in the 90s." *Food Review* 23, 3:44–49.

Defra (Department of Environment Food and Rural Affairs). 2002. "Margaret Beckett Welcomes French Food Standards Agency Report on the Safety of British Beef." September 20. <http://www.defra.gov.uk/news/2002/020920b.htm>.

Dehousse, R. 1997. "Regulation by Networks in the European Community: The Role of European Agencies." *Journal of European Public Policy* 4, 2:246–261.

Die Zeit. 2003. *Künast: "Aktionsplan Verbraucherschutz" noch vor Sommerpause.* Hamburg, December.

DNV Consulting. 2002. *Assessment of the Risk of Exposure to the BSE Agent through the Use of Natural Sausage Casings (for the European Natural Sausage Casings Association).* London: DNV Consulting.

DNV Consulting. 2001. *Risk of Exposure to BSE Infectivity in UK Sheep (for Food Standards Agency).* London: DNV Consulting.

Douglas, Mary, and Wildavsky, Aaron. 1982. *Risk and Culture.* Berkeley: University of California Press.

Dubuisson-Quellier, Sophie. 2003. "Confiance et qualité des produits alimentaires: Une approche par la sociologie des relations marchandes." *Sociologie du Travail* 1:95–111.

Dunleavy, Patrick. 1995. "Policy Disasters: Explaining the UK's Record." *Public Policy and Administration* 10, 2:52–70.

EC—Measures Affecting Meat and Meat Products, Appellate Body Report adopted 13 February 1998, WT/DS26/AB/R ("EC—Hormones"), para. 194 note 12; in a similar vein, see also para. 172 and 213.

Echols, Marsha A. 1998. "Food Safety Regulation in the European Union and the United States: Different Cultures, Different Laws." *Columbia Journal of European Law,* 525–543.

Eden, Karl J. 1993. "History of German Brewing." *zymurgy magazine* 16, 4 [Special issue].

Ehrlich, I., and Becker, G. 1972. "Market Insurance, Self-Insurance and Self-Protection." *Journal of Political Economy* 80, 4:623–648.

Emons, W. 1997. "Credence Goods and Fraudulent Experts." *Rand Journal of Economics* 28, 1:107–119.

Eurobarometer. 2002. *The Attitudes of Europeans towards the Environment.* Directorate-General Environment, No. 58, Brussels: European Commission.

Eurobarometer. 2002. *Europeans and the Common Agricultural Policy.* Brussels: European Commission.

Eurobarometer. 2001. *Europeans, Science and Technology.* Issue 55:2. Brussels: Director-General for Research.

Eurobarometer. 1998. *Public Opinion in the European Union.* DG X, No. 49. Brussels: European Commission.

Eurobarometer. 1991. *Opinions of Europeans on Biotechnology in 1991.* Eurobarometer 35.1.

European Commission. DG Consumer Protection. 2004a. Organisational Chart, DG Health and Consumer Protection. January 19. <http://europa.eu.int/comm/dgs/health_consumer/general_info/organigramme_en.pdf>.

European Commission. 2004b. Commission Regulation (EC) No. 641/2004 on Detailed Rules for the Implementation of Regulation (EC) No. 1829/2003 of the European Parliament and of the Council As Regards the Application for the Authorizations of New Genetically Modified Food and Feed, the Notification of

Existing Products and Adventitious or Technically Unavoidable Presence of Genetically Modified Material Which Has Benefited from a Favourable Risk Evaluation. *Official Journal of the European Union*, April 6.

European Commission. 2004c. Regulation (EC) No. 851/2004 of the European Parliament and of the Council of 21 April 2004 Establishing a European Centre for Disease Prevention and Control, *Official Journal of the European Union*, L142/2, 30.4.2004.

European Commission. 2003a. "Regulation (EC) No. 1830/2003 of the European Parliament and of the Council of 22 September 2003 Concerning the Traceability and Labelling of Genetically Modified Organisms and Amending Directive 2001/18/EC." *Official Journal of the European Union* 46, October 18.

European Commission. 2003b. "Regulation (EC) No. 1829/2003 of the European Parliament and of the Council of 22 September 2003 on Genetically Modified Food and Feed." *Official Journal of the European Union* 46, October 18.

European Commission. 2003c. "General Guidance for Third Country Authorities on the Procedures to Be Followed When Importing Live Animals and Animal Products into the European Union." Health and Consumer Protection Directorate General, September 1.

European Commission. DG Consumer Protection. 2003d.

"EU Enlargement: Questions and Answers on Food Safety Issues." December 5. <http://europa.eu.int/comm/food/food/enlargement/resources/m03_88.en.pdf>.

European Commission. 2002. "Regulation (EC) No. 178/2002 of 28 January 2002 Laying Down the General Principles and Requirements of Food Law, Establishing the European Food Safety Authority and Laying Down Procedures in Matters of Food Safety." *Official Journal of the European Communities*.

European Commission. 2001a. "Amended Proposal for a Regulation of the European Parliament and of the Council Laying Down the General Principles and Requirements of Food Law, Establishing the European Food Authority, and Laying Down Procedures in Matters of Food Safety (Presented by the Commission Pursuant to Article 250 (2) of the EC Treaty)." COM/2001/0475 final, O.J. 2001 (C 304 E), 273–326.

European Commission. 2001b. "Directive 2001/18/EEC of the European Parliament and of the Council of Ministers of 12 March 2001 on the Deliberate Release into the Environment of Genetically Modified Organisms and Repealing Council Directive 90/220/EEC/." *Official Journal of the European Union*, April 17:0001–0039.

European Commission. 2000a. *White Paper on Food Safety*. COM (1999) 719, January 12.

European Commission. 2000b. *Communication from the Commission on the Precautionary Principle*. COM (2000). Brussels, February 2.

European Commission. 2000c. "Proposal for a Regulation of the European Parliament and of the Council Laying Down the General Principles and Requirements of Food law, Establishing the European Food Authority, and Laying Down Procedures in Matters of Food." COM/2000/0716 final, O. J. 2001 (C 96 E), 247–268.

European Commission. 2000d. "Proposal for a Regulation of the European Parliament and of the Council Laying Down the General Principles and Requirements of Food Law, Establishing the European Food Authority, and Laying Down Procedures in Matters of Food Safety." COM (2000) 716. Provisional version. Brussels, November 8.

European Commission. 2000e. "Remarks by David Byrne, European Commissioner for Health and Consumer Protection to the Group of the European People Party and European Democrats in the European Parliament." (EPP/ED). Brussels, September 27. <http://europa.eu.int/comm./dgs/health_consumer/library/speeches/speech57_en.html>.

European Commission. 2000f. Communication from the Commission to the Council, The European Parliament, the Economic and Social Committee, and the Committee of the Regions, Life Sciences and Biotechnology—a Strategy for Europe. COM (2002) 27 Final. Brussels. January 23.

European Commission. 1998. "Proposal for a European Parliament and Council Directive Amending Directive 90/220/EEC on the Deliberate Release into the Environment of Genetically Modified Organisms." COM (1998) 85 final, February 23.

European Commission. 1997a. "The General Principles of Food Law in the European Union-Commission Green Paper." COM (97) 176 final.

European Commission. 1997b. "Communication from the Commission on Consumer Health and Food Safety." COM (97) 183 final.

European Commission. 1997c. "Green Paper: The General Principles of Food Law in the European Union." COM (97) 176 final.

European Commission. 1991. *Consumer Policy in the Single Market*, 2nd ed. Luxembourg: Office for Official Publications of the European Communities.

European Commission. 1990. "Council Directive 90/220/EEC of 23 April 1990 on the Deliberate Release into the Environment of Genetically Modified Organisms." *Official Journal*, L 117, May 8. Pp. 0015–0027.

European Commission. 1985a. "Communication on the Completion of the Internal Market 'New Approach to Technical Harmonisation and Standards.'" COM (85) 19 final.

European Commission. 1985b. "Communication on Community Legislation on Foodstuffs." COM (85) 603 final.

European Commission. 1985c. "Amended Proposal for a Council Directive Amending Directive 1/602/EEC Concerning the Prohibiting of Certain Substances Having Hormonal Action and Any Substance Having a Thryrostatic Action." COM (85) 832, December 18.

European Council. 1999. "Council Resolution of 28 October 1999 on Mutual Recognition." *Official Journal*, C141, May 19, 5.

European Council. 1988. "Council Directive of 7 March 1988 Prohibiting the Use in Livestock Farming of Certain Substances Having a Hormonal Action." EEC, *Official Journal of the European Communities*, L70/16, March 16.

European Court. 1979. "Judgement of 20 February 1979 in Case 120/79 (Cassis de Dijon)." *European Court Reports*, 649.

EUFood. 2001. "EU Unveils GMO Traceability and Labelling Rules." August 1. <http://www.findarticles.com/p/articles/mi_m0DQA/is_2001_August_2/ai_7739 9105>.

European Food Safety Authority. 2004. "B-Brussels: Creation of a Network of Key Sources to Support the Authority in the Identification of Emerging Risks within the Limits of Regulation (EC) No 178/2002 of the European Parliament and the Council." February 10.

European Food Safety Authority. 2003a. <http://efsa.eu.int/task_en.html>.

European Food Safety Authority. 2003b. "EFSA Welcomes Decision on Permanent Location." December 15. <http://www.efsa.eu.int/pdf/press/pressrel_loc_01_en.pdf>.

European Marketing Distribution. 2002. "The Retail Trade: Characterized by Massive Process of Concentration." <http://www.emd-ag.com/e/markt002.shtm>.

European Opinion Research Group 2003. *Consumer Protection in the EU. Special Eurobarometer 59.2*. Special Report 193. Brussels: European Commission.

European Marketing Distribution. 2001. *Globalization—Increasing Trend*. <http://www.emd-ag.com/e/markt001.shtm>.

European Parliament. 2001a. "Legislative Observatory." <http://wwwdb.europarl.eu.int/oeil/oeil_viewdnl.ProcedureView?lang=2&procid=4781>.

European Parliament. 2001b. *Proposal for a Regulation of the European Parliament and of the Council Laying Down the General Principles and Requirements of Food Law, Establishing the European Food Authority, and Laying Down Procedures in the Matter of Food Safety*. May 31.

European Parliament. 2000a. *Draft Opinion of the Committee on Legal Affairs and the Internal Market for the Committee on the Environment, Public Health and Consumer Policy on the White Paper on Food Safety*." June 7.

European Parliament. 2000b. "Draft Report on the Commission White Paper on Food Safety." (COM (1999)719-C5-0136/2000-222/2082(COS)). Committee on the Environment, Public Health and Consumer Policy.

European Parliament. 1997. *Report on Alleged Contraventions or Maladministration in the Implementation of Community Law in Relation to BSE, without Prejudice to the Jurisdiction of the Community and National Courts*." <http://www.europarl.eu.int/conferences/bse/a4002097_en.htm>.

EuroStat INRA (Europe) European Coordination Office. 1998. (for the Commission of the European Communities., DG Health and Consumer Protection). *Eurobarometre 49: La Securite des Produits Alimentaires.* Complete report. September 3. <http://europa.eu.int/comm/dgs/health_consumer/library/surveys/eb49_fr.pdf>.

EuroStat. INRA (Europe) (for Commission of the European Union, DG Health and Consumer Protection). 1999. Eurobarometer 51.5: *Europeans and Consumer Associations.* July 17.

Everson, Michelle, Majone, Giandomenico, Metcalfe, Les, and Schout, Adriaan. 1997. *The Role of Specialized Agencies in Decentralizing EU Governance.* Brussels: European Commission.

Fabi, Randy. 2003. "FDA Cannot Ensure Safety of Biotech Foods—US Group." Reuters online. January 7.

FAO. 1998. *Seafood Safety—Economics of Hazard Analysis and Critical Control Point.* Fisheries Technical Paper 381. Rome: FAO.

FAS Online. 2003. "European Union Moratorium on Biotech Foods: Chronology: Five Years of Patience, Five Years of Delays." U.S. Department of Agriculture. <http://www.fas.usda.gov/itp/wto/eubiotech/chron.htm>.

Fearne, A., Hornibrook, S., and Dedman, S. 2001. "The Management of Perceived Risk in the Food Supply Chain: A Comparative Study of Retailer-Led Beef Quality Assurance Schemes in Germany and Italy." *International Food and Agribusiness Management Review* 4:9–36.

Ferguson, N. M., Ghani, A. C., Donnelly, C. A., Hagenaars, T. J., and Anderson, R. M. 2002. "Estimating the Human Health Risk from Possible BSE Infection of the British Sheep Flock." *Nature* 415:420–424.

"Finns Feel Hard Done by on EU Agency." (2003). *EU Observer*, December 16.

Fisher, Elizabeth. 2002. "Precaution, Precaution Everywhere: Developing a 'Common Understanding' of the Precautionary Principle in the European Community." *Maastricht Journal of European and Comparative Law* 9, 1:7–28.

Fisher, John. 1999. "The Awful Consequences of the CAP." *Policy, The Center for Independent Studies*, Spring issue. <http://www.cis.org.au/Policy/Spr99/polspr99-7.htm>.

Fischler, C. 1988. "Food, Self and Identity." *Social Science Information* 27, 2:275–292.

Food Safety Authority of Ireland. 2001. *Survey of the Implementation of HACCP and Food Hygiene Training in Irish Food Businesses.* Dublin: FSAI, July. <http://www.fsai.ie/publications/other/survey_HACCP_july2001.pdf>.

Food Safety Network (FSnet). 1999. "EU Scientists Say British Beef Is Safe." <http://archives.foodsafetynetwork.ca/fsnet/1999/10-1999/fs-10-29-99-01.txt>.

Food Standards Agency. 2003a. "Muslim, Asian and African-Caribbean Communities Are Briefed on Possible Risk of BSE in Sheep and Goats." *FSA News*, no. 24:5.

Food Standards Agency. 2003b. "Proposed Amendments to EU Regulation 999/2001 on Transmissible Spongiform Encephalopathies." *FSA Consultation Letter* 6, January.

Food Standards Agency. 2003c. *Consumer Attitudes to Food Standards*. London: FSA.

Food Standards Agency. 2003d. *Food Imports*. FSA Paper 01/03. <http://www.food.gov.uk/multimedia/pdfs/fsa010303>.

Food Standards Agency. 2003e. "Food Intolerance, Including Food Allergy." FSA paper 03/02/04. London: FSA, February 13.

FSA. 2003f. "Progress on Agency Plan to Help Food Allergic Consumers." FSA paper 03/09/04. London: FSA, September 11.

Food Standards Agency. 2002a. *Consumer Attitudes to Food Standards*. London: FSA.

Food Standards Agency. 2002b. *BSE and Sheep: Report of the Core Stakeholder Group*. London: FSA.

Food Standards Agency. 2002c. "Agency Takes Further Precautionary Measures on Risk of BSE in Sheep." *BSE Controls Review: Latest News*. London: FSA, June 22.

Food Standards Agency. 2002d. *Report on the Review of Scientific Committees*. London: FSA.

Food Standards Agency. 2002e. *Strategy for Wider Implementation of HACCP*. FSA Paper 01/07. <www.foodstandards.gov.uk/multimedia/pdfs/fsa_01_07_02.pdf>.

Food Standards Agency. 2001. *Strategic Plan 2001–2006: Putting Consumers First*. London: FSA.

Food Standards Agency. 2000. *Statement of General Objectives and Practices*. London: FSA.

Fox, J., and H. Peterson. 2004. "Risks and Implications of Bovine Spongiform Encephalopathy for the United States: Insights from Other Countries." *Food Policy* 29, 1:45–60.

Freidberg, Suzanne. 2004. *French Beans and Food Scares: Culture and Commerce in an Anxious Age*. Oxford: Oxford University Press.

Freeriks, Mark. 2004. "Dutch Animal Feed Regulation." M.A. thesis, University College Utrecht.

Frey, Bruno S. 2001. "Liliput oder Leviathan? Der Staat in der Globalisierten Wirtschaft." Working paper 85. Zurich: Institute for Empirical Research in Economics, University of Zurich.

Frewer, L. J., Howard, C., and Shepherd, R. 1997. "Public Concerns in the United Kingdom about General and Specific Applications of Genetic Engineering: Risk, Benefit, and Ethics." *Science, Technology and Human Values* 22, 1:98–124.

Fukuyama, Francis. 1995. *Trust: The Social Virtues and the Creation of Prosperity*. New York: Free Press.

Garrett, Geoffery, and Tsebelis, George. 1996. "An Institutional Critique of Intergovernmentalism." *International Organization* 50, 2:269–299.

Gaskell, George, Allum, Nick, and Stares, Sally. 2003. *Europeans and Biotechnology in 2002*. Eurobarometer 58.0. Brussels: European Commission.

Gaskell, George, et al. 2001. "Troubled Waters: The Atlantic Divide on Biotechnology Policy." In George Gaskell and Martin W. Bauer (eds.), *Biotechnology 1996–2000*. London: Science Museum, 2001. Pp. 96–115.

Gaskell, George, Bauer, M., Allum, N. C., and Durant, J. 1999. "Worlds Apart? The Reception of Genetically Modified Foods in Europe and the United States." *Science* 285, 5426:384–386.

General Accounting Office. 2002. *Genetically Modified Foods: Experts View Regimen of Safety Tests as Adequate, But FDA's Evaluation Process Could Be Enhanced*. GAO-02-566, Washington, D.C.: Government Printing Office.

General Accounting Office. 1999. *Food Safety: Experiences of Four Countries in Consolidating Their Food Safety Systems*. Washington, D.C.: Government Printing Office.

Gibbons, Ann. 1990. "FDA Publishes Bovine Growth Hormone Data." *Science*, N.S. 249, no. 4971:852–853.

Godard, Olivier. 2001. "Embargo or Not to Embargo?" *La Recherche* 339: 50–55.

Gollier, P. 2001. "Precautionary Principle: The Economic Perspective." *Economic Policy*, October: 302–327.

Gonzalez Vaqué, Luis. 2003. "Objetivo: la seguridad alimentaria en la Union Europea." *Gaceta Jurídica de la UE* 223:59.

Gottweis, Herbert. 1999. "Regulating Genetic Engineering in the European Union." In Beatrice Kohler-Koch and Rainer Eising (eds.), *The Transformation of Governance in the European Union*. London: Routledge.

Graham John D., and Baert Wiener, Jonathan. 1995. *Risk vs. Risk: Tradeoffs in Protecting Health and the Environment*. Cambridge, Mass.: Harvard University Press.

Granovetter, Mark. 1985. "Economic Action and Social Structure: The Problem of Embeddedness." *American Journal of Sociology* 91:481–510.

Greenpeace Italia. 2002. *Greenpeace blocca stabilimento AIA*. <http://ogm.greenpeace.it/>.

Greensite News. N.d. *Mobiltebio non smobilita*. <http://www.greensite.it>.

"Greenpeace Means Business." 1995. *Economist*, August 19.

Greenwood, Justin. 1998. *Collective Action in the European Union*. London: Routledge.

Guseva, A., and Rona-Tas, A. 2001. "Uncertainty, Risk, and Trust: Russian and American Credit Card Markets Compared." *American Sociological Review* 66:623–646.

Hamilton, J., and Viscusi, K. 1999. "Are Risk Regulators Rational? Evidence from Hazardous Waste Cleanup Decisions." *American Economic Review* 89, 4:1010–1027.

Hamm, U., Gronefeld, F., and D. Halpin. 2002. *Analysis of the European Market for Organic Food: Summary.* School of Management and Business, University of Wales, Aberystwyth, Wales.

Hancher, Leigh, and Moran, Michael. 1989. *Capitalism, Culture and Economic Regulation.* Oxford: Clarendon Press.

Haniotis, T. 2000. "Regulating Agri-Food Production in the US and the EU." AgBioForum 3, 2&3:84–86.

Hankin, Robert. 1997. "The Role of Scientific Advice in the Elaboration and Implementation of the Community's Foodstuff Legislation." In Christian Joerges, Karl-Heinz Ladeur, and Ellen Vos (eds.), *Integrating Scientific Expertise into Regulatory Decision-Making.* Baden-Baden: Nomos Verlagsgesellschaft. Pp. 141–167.

Hardin, Russell. 2001. "Distrust." *Boston University Law Review* 81:495–522.

Hardstaff, Peter. 2000. "The Precautionary Principle, Trade and the WTO." Discussion paper for the European Commission Consultation on Trade and Sustainable Development. London: RSPB.

Harrison, Kathryn, and Hoberg, George. 1994. *Risk, Science, and Politics.* Montreal and Kingston: McGill-Queen's University Press.

Havinga, Tetty. 2003. "Private regulering van voedselveiligheid: de supermarkt als regelgever en handhaver." *Recht der Werkelijkheid*, 24, 3 (special issue on self-regulation): 189–212.

Hayek, F. 1945. "The Use of Knowledge in Society." *American Economic Review* 35, 4:519–530.

Heifetz, Ronald. 1994. *Leadership without Easy Answers.* Cambridge, Mass.: Harvard University Press.

Hellström, Tomas, and Jakob, Merle. 2001. *Policy Uncertainty and Risk: Conceptual Developments and Approaches.* Boston: Kluwer.

Henson, Spencer. 2001. "Consumer Perceptions of Food Safety: Survey Research in Economics and Social Psychology." In Peter W. B. Phillips and Robert Wolfe (eds.), *Governing Food: Science, Safety, and Trade.* Montreal: McGill-Queen's University Press.

Henson, Spencer, and Caswell, Julie. 1999. "Food Safety Regulation: An Overview of Contemporary Issues." *Food Policy* 24:589–603.

Hermitte, Marie-Angèle, and Noiville, Christine. 2002. "Marrakech et Carthagène comme figures opposées du commerce international." In J. Bourrinet and S. Maljean-Dubois (eds.), *Le commerce international des organismes génétiquement modifiés*, Paris: La Documentation française. Pp. 317–349.

Heyvaert, Veerle. 1999. "The Changing Role of Science in Environmental Decision-Making in the European Union." *Law and European Affairs* 3 & 4:426–443.

Hirsch, Martin. 2001. "L'expertise scientifique indépendante dans un établissement public: l'exemple de l'Agence française de sécurité sanitaire des aliments." In Conseil d'Etat, *Rapport public 2001*. Paris: La Documentation française.

Hix, Simon. 1999. *The Political System of the European Union*. Basingstoke: Macmillan.

Holmes, Peter, and Young, Alasdair R. 2001. "Emerging Regulatory Challenges to the EU's External Economic Relations." SEI working paper 42. Falmer: Sussex European Institute.

Hollingsworth, J. Rogers, and Robert Boyer. 1997. *Contemporary Capitalism: The Embeddedness of Institutions*. New York: Cambridge University Press.

Hood, Christopher, Rothstein, Henry, and Baldwin, Robert. 2001. *The Government of Risk: Understanding Risk Regulation Regimes*. New York: Oxford University Press.

Hooghe, Liesbet, and Marks, Gary. 2001. *Multi-Level Governance and European Integration*. Lanham, Md.: Rowman and Littlefield.

Hooker, Neal H., Nayga, Rodolfo M., Jr., and Siebert, John W. 2002. "The Impact of HACCP on Costs and Product Exit." *Journal of Agricultural and Applied Economics* 34, 1:165–174.

Hunter, Rod. 1999. "European Regulation of Genetically Modified Organisms." In Julian Morris and Roger Bate (eds.), *Fearing Food: Risk, Health and Environment*. Oxford: Butterworth Heinemann.

Huriet, Claude, and Descours, Charles. 1997. *Renforcer la sécurité sanitaire en France*. Rapport d'information no. 196. Paris: Sénat.

Il Sole 24 Ore. 2000. "Biotechnologie. Verdi all'Attacco di Veronesi," <http://www.ilsole24ore.com>.

Inglehart, R. 1997. "Postmaterialist Values and the Erosion of Institutional Authority." In J. S. Nye Jr., P. D. Zelikow, and D. C. King (eds.), *Why People Don't Ttrust Government*. Cambridge, MA: Harvard University Press. Pp. 217–236.

International Dairy Foods Association v. Amestoy, 92F. 3d 67 (2d Cir. 1996).

Isaac, Grant E. 2002. *Agricultural Biotechnology and Transatlantic Trade: Regulatory Barriers to GM Crops*. Cambridge, Mass.: CABI Publishing.

Isaac, Grant, Banerji, Shondeep, and Woolcock, Stephen. 2000. "International Trade Policy and Food Safety." *Consumer Policy Review* 10, 6:223–233.

James, J. 2001. "Food Allergy and Quality of Life Issues." *Annals of Allergy Asthma and Immunology* 87:443–444.

James, Philip, Kemper, Fritz, and Pascal, Gerard. 1999. *A European Food and Public Health Authority: The Future of Scientific Advice in the EU*. Brussels: European Commission.

Jasanoff, Sheila. 2003. "A Living Legacy: The Precautionary Ideal in American Law." In Joel A. Tickner (ed.), *Precaution, Environmental Science and Preventive Public Policy*. Washington, D.C.: Island Press. Pp. 227–240.

Jasanoff, Sheila. 1997. "Civilization and Madness: The Great BSE Scare of 1996." *Public Understanding of Science* 6:221–232.

Jasanoff, Sheila. 1995. "Product, Process, or Programme: Three Cultures and the Regulation of Biotechnology." In Martin Bauer (ed.), *Resistance to New Technology*. Cambridge: Cambridge University Press. Pp. 311–331.

Jasanoff, Sheila. 1990. *The Fifth Branch: Science Advisers as Policy Makers*. Cambridge, Mass.: Harvard University Press.

Jasanoff, Sheila. 1986. *Risk Management and Political Culture*. New York: Russell Sage Foundation.

Jerardo, Alberto. 2003. *Import Share of U.S. Food Consumption Stable at 11 Percent*. Outlook Report No. FAU7901. Washington, D.C.: Economic Research Service, U.S. Department of Agriculture.

Joerges, Christian. 2001. "Law, Science and the Management of Risks to Health at the National, European and International Level—Stories on Baby Dummies, Mad Cows and Hormones in Beef." *Columbia Journal of European Law* 7:1.

Joerges, Christian. 1999a. "Bureaucratic Nightmare, Technocratic Regime and the Dream of Transnational Governance." In Christian Joerges and Ellen Vos (eds.), *EU Committees: Social Regulation, Law and Politics*. Oxford: Hart Publishing. Pp. 3–17.

Joerges, Christian, and Neyer, Jürgen. 1997a. "From Intergovernmental Bargaining to Deliberative Political Processes: The Constitutionalization of Comitology." *European Law Journal* 3:273–299.

Joerges, Christian, and Neyer, J. 1997b. "Transforming Strategic Interaction into Deliberative Problem-Solving: European Comitology in the Foodstuffs Sector." *Journal of European Public Policy* 4, 4:572–590.

Joly, Pierre-Benoit, Gérald Assouline, Dominique Kréziak, Juhette Lemarié, Claire Marris, and Alexis Roy. 2000. *L'innovation controversée: le débat public sur les OGM en France*. Grenoble: INRA.

Joly, Pierre-Benoit, and Marris, Claire. 2003. "A la recherche d'une 'démocratie technique: Enseignements de la conférence citoyenne sur les OGM en France." *Natures, Sciences et Sociétés* 11, 1:3–15.

Josling, Tim, Roberts, Donna, and Orden, David. 2004. *Food Regulation and Trade: Toward a Safe and Open Global System*. Washington, D.C.: Institute for International Economics.

Judge, David, Earnshaw, David, and Cowan, Ngaire. 1994. "Ripples or Waves: The European Parliament in the European Community Policy Process." *Journal of European Public Policy* 1, 1:27–52.

Just, D., Wolf, S., Wu, S., and D. Zilberman. 2002. "Consumption of Economic Information in Agriculture." *American Journal of Agricultural Economics* 84, 1:39–52.

Kaase, Max. 1999. "Interpersonal Trust, Political Trust and Non-Institutionalised Political Participation in Western Europe." *West European Politics* 22, 3:1–21.

Kagan, Robert A. 1994. "Regulatory Enforcement." In David Roosenbloom and Richard Schwartz (eds.), *Handbook of Administrative Law and Regulation*. New York: Dekker.

Keck, Margaret, and Sikkink, Kathryn. 1998. *Beyond Borders: Activist Networks in International Politics*. Ithaca, N.Y.: Cornell University Press.

Kelly, C. D. 1999. "Education Key to Biotechnology's Future," *The Voice of Agriculture*, November 29. available at www.fb.org/views/focus/fo99/fo1129.html.

Kempf, Hervé. 2003. *La guerre secrète des OGM*. Paris: Seuil.

Kettnaker, Vera. 2001. "The European Conflict over Genetically-Engineered Crops." In Doug Imig and Sidney Tarrow (eds.), *Contentious Europeans*. Lanham, Md.: Rowman and Littlefield.

John Kingdon. 1995. *Agendas, Alternatives, and Public Policies*. New York: Harper Collins College Publishers.

Kjærnes, Unni. 1999. "Food Risks and Trust Relations." *Sosiologisk tidsskrift* 7, 4:265–284.

Koolmees, P., Berends, B., and Tersteeg, M. 2002. "Risk Assessment of the Use of Sheep Natural Casings and Legs of Lamb' Pilot Research for ENSCA, INSCA and NANCA." VVDO Report no. HO2O4 July. Utrecht.

Kourilsky, Philippe, and Viney, Geneviève. 2000. *Le principe de précaution. Rapport au Premier ministre*. Paris: Odile Jacob.

Kreher, Alexander. 1997. "Agencies in the European Community—a Step towards Administrative Integration in Europe." *Journal of European Public Policy* 4, 2:225–245.

Krissoff, Barry, Bohman, Mary, and Caswell, Julie A. 2002. *Global Food Trade and Consumer Demand for Quality*. New York: Kluwer.

Künast, R. 2002. "Rethinking Agriculture and Food." *OECD Observer*, no. 233, August.

La Porte, Todd R. 1994. "Large Technical Systems, Institutional Surprises, and Challenges to Political Legitimacy." *Technology in Society* 16, 3:269–288.

Leitch, Ian, M. Walker, and R. Davey. 2005. "Food Allergy: Gambling Your Life on a Take-Away Meal." *International Journal of Environmental Health Research* 15, 2:79–87.

Leitch, I., Blair, I., and McDowell, D. 2000. "Dealing with Allergy." *Environmental Health Journal*, October.

Lenz, T. 2004. *Consumers First? Shifting Responsibilities in the German Food System in the Light of European Integration and the BSE Crisis.* Trust in Food Working Paper Series no. 8. Karlsruhe: www.trustinfood.org.

Levi, M. 1998. A State of Trust. In V. Braithwaite and M. Levi (eds.), *Trust and Governance*. New York: Russel Sage Foundation. Pp. 77–101.

Libecap, G. 1992. "The Rise of the Chicago Packers and the Origins of Meat Inspection and Antitrust." *Economic Inquiry* 30, 4:242–262.

Lister, Charles. 1992. *Regulation of Food Products by the European Community*. New York: Butterworths.

Listhaug, O., and Wiberg, M. 1995. "Confidence in Political and Private Institutions." In H.-D. Klingemann and D. Fuchs (eds.), *Citizens and the State*. Oxford: Oxford University Press. Pp. 298–322.

Löfstedt, Ragnar E. 2004. "The Swing of the Regulatory Pendulum in the Europe: From Precautionary Principle to Regulatory Impact Analysis." Working paper 04–07. Washington, D.C.: AEI Brookings Joint Center for Regulatory Studies.

Löfstedt, Ragnar, Fischoff, Baruch, and Fischoff, Ilya R. 2002. "Precautionary Principles: General Definitions and Specific Applications to Genetically Modified Organisms." *Journal of Policy Analysis and Management* 21, 3:381–407.

Löfstedt, Ragnar E., and Vogel, David. 2001. "The Changing Character of Regulation: A Comparison of Europe and the United States." *Risk Analysis* 21, 3:399–405.

Louviere, J., Hensher, D., and Swait, J. 2000. *Stated Choice Methods: Analysis and Applications.* Cambridge University Press, Cambridge, UK.

Louviere, J., et al. 1999. "Combining Sources of Preference Data for Modelling Complex Decision Processes." *Marketing Letters* 10, 3:187–204.

Loy, J. P. 1999. "Die Auswirkungen der BSE Krise auf die Verbraucherpreise für Rindfleisch in Deutschland." In E. Berg, W. Henrichsmeyer, and G. Schiefer (eds.), *Agrarwirtschaft in der Informationsgesellschaft*. Pp. 249–256.

Loy, J.-P., and Steiner, B. 2003. "The BSE Scare in Germany: Price Shocks and Pricing Strategies in the Marketing Chain." Mimeo., University of Kiel, Department of Agricultural Economics.

Lugt, Marieke. 1999. *Enforcing European and National Food Law in the Netherlands and England*. The Hague: Koninklijke Vermande.

Luhmann, N. 1979. *Trust and Power: Two Works*. New York: Wiley.

Macdougall, C., Cant, A., and Colver, A. 2002. "How Dangerous Is Food Allergy in Childhood? The Incidence of Severe and Fatal Allergic Reactions across the UK and Ireland." *Archives of Diseases of Childhood* 86:236–239.

Majone, Giandomenico. 2000. "The Credibility Crisis of Community Regulation." *Journal of Common Market Studies* 38, 2:273–302.

Majone, Giandomenico. 1999. "The Regulatory State and Its Legitimacy Problems." *West European Politics* 22, 1:1–13.

Majone, Giandomenico. 1996. *Regulating Europe*. New York: Routledge.

Majone, G., and Everson, M. 2001. "Institutional Reform: Independent Agencies, Oversight, Coordination, and Procedural Control." In O. De Schutter, N. Lebessis, and J. Petterson (eds.), *Governance in the European Union*. Luxemburg: Office for Official Publications of the European Communities.

Marceau, Gabrielle, and Trachtman, Joel-P. 2002. "The Technical Barriers to Trade Agreement, the Sanitary and Phytosanitary Measures Agreement, and the General Agreement on Tariffs and Trade: A Map of the World Trade Organization Law of Domestic Regulation of Goods." *Journal of World Trade* 36, 5:811–881.

March, James, and Olsen, Johan. 1989. *Rediscovering Institutions: The Organizational Basis of Politics*. New York: Free Press.

Maruyama, Warren H. 1998. "A New Pillar of WTO: Sound Science." *International Lawyer* 32, 3:651.

Mattei, Jean-François, and Guilhem, Evelyne. 1997. *De la "vache folle" à la "vache émissaire."* Rapport d'information no. 3291. Paris: Assemblée Nationale.

McNeil, David. 1998. "The First Case under the WTO's SPS Agreement." *Virginia Journal of International Law* 39, 1:89–122.

Medina, Manuel Ortega. 1997. "Report on Alleged Contraventions or Maladministration in the Implementation of Community Law in Relation to BSE, without Prejudice to the Jurisdiction of the Community and National Courts." Brussels: European Parliament, Temporary Committee on Inquiry into BSE. February 7.

Mellon, Margaret. 1994. "Comments to the US Food and Drug Administration Advisory Committee on Genetically Engineered Food." Washington, D.C.: Union of Concerned Scientists.

Meunier, Sophie. 2000. "France, Globalization and Global Protectionism." Working paper series 71, Cambridge, MA: Center for European Studies, Harvard University, February.

Mills, Lisa Nicole. 2002. *Science and Social Context: The Regulation of Recombinant Bovine Growth Hormone in North America*. Montreal and Kingston: McGill-Queen's University Press.

Mishler, W., and Rose, R. 2001. "What Are the Origins of Political Trust? Testing Institutional and Cultural Theories in Post-Communist Societies." *Comparative Political Studies* 34, 1:30–62.

Misztal, B. 1995. *Trust in Modern Societies: The Search for the Bases of Social Order*. Cambridge: Polity Press.

M+MPlanetRetail. 2002. *40% Market Share for Discounters in Germany*. <www.mm-eurodata.com/presse/PressRelease_October2002.pdf>.

M+MEurodata. 2003. *Grocery Retailing in Germany: Discounters and Drug-stores—Once More Increase Market Shares*. <www.mmeurodata.com/presse/PressRelease_March2003.pdf>.

Moe, Terry. 1990. "The Politics of Structural Choice: Toward a Theory of Public Bureaucracy." In Oliver E. Williamson (ed.), *From Chester Barnard to Present and Beyond*. New York: Oxford University Press.

Moore, Elizabeth. 2000. "Science, Internationalization, and Policy Networks: Regulating Genetically-Engineered Food Crops in Canada and the United States, 1973–1998." Ph.D. diss. University of Toronto.

Moravcsik, Andrew. 1993. "Introduction: Integrating International and Domestic Theories of International Bargaining." In Peter B. Evans, Harold. K. Jacobson, and Robert D. Putnam (eds.), *Double-Edged Diplomacy: International Bargaining and Domestic Politics*. Berkeley: University of California Press. Pp. 3–42.

MORI. 2000. *Consumer Information Needs for Food Sold through Catering Outlets and Loose Foods*. London: MORI.

Motavalli, Jim. 1995. "In Harm's Way: Power of Greenpeace's Protests." *E*, 6, 6:28.

National Consumer Council (NCC). 2002. *Involving Consumers in Food Policy*. London: NCC.

National Science Board. 2002. *Science and Engineering Indicators—2002*. Arlington, Va: National Science Foundation.

Nelson, P. 1970. "Information and Consumer Behavior." *Journal of Political Economy* 78:311–329.

Nelson, R., and Sampat, B. 2001. "Making Sense of Institutions as a Factor Shaping Economic Performance." *Journal of Economic Behavior and Organization* 44:31–54. University Press, New York.

Neumann, Jan, and Türk, Elisabeth. 2003. "Necessity Revisited: Proportionality in World Trade Organization Law after *Korea-Beef*, *EC-Asbestos* and *EC-Sardines*." *Journal of World Trade* 37, 1:199–233.

"A New Type of Farming?" 2001. *Economist*, February 3, 50–52.

Nicolas, François, and Valceschini, Egizio (eds.). 1995. *Agro-alimentaire: Une économie de la qualité*. Paris: Inra Editions, Economica.

Nichols, A. 1991. "Comparing Risk Standards: The Superiority of a Benefit-Cost Approach." *Regulation* 14, 4:85–95.

Nielsen, N. 1998. "The Beef Market in the European Union." Working paper no. 51, Aarhus, Denmark: Aarhus School of Business.

Nissen, Jill Lynn. 1997. "Achieving a Balance between Trade and the Environment: The Need to Amend WTO/GATT to Include Multilateral Environmental Agreements." *Law and Policy in International Business* 28, 3:901.

Noiville, Christine. 2003. *Du bon gouvernement des risques. Le droit et la question du "risque acceptable"* Paris: PUF, Les Voies du droit.

Noiville, Christine. 2000a. "Principe de precaution et Organisation mondiale du commerce: Le cas du commerce alimentaire." *Journal du Droit international* 127, 2:263–297.

Noiville, Christine. 2000b. "Principe de précaution et gestion du risque en droit de l'environnement et en droit de la santé." *Les Petites Affiches*, special issue Le principe de précaution. 39–50.

Noiville, Christine, and de Sadeleer, Nicolas. 2001. "La gestion des risques écologiques et sanitaires à l'épreuve des chiffres. Le droit, entre enjeux scientifiques et politiques." *Revue du Droit de l'Union Européenne* 2:389–449.

North, Douglass C. 1991. "Institutions." *Journal of Economic Perspectives* 5, 1:97–112.

North, Douglass C. 1990. *Institutions, Institutional Change and Economic Performance.* Cambridge: Cambridge University Press.

North, Douglass, and Thomas, Paul. 1973. *The Rise of the Western World.* Cambridge: Cambridge University Press.

Nugent, Neill (ed.). 2004. *European Union Enlargement.* New York: Macmillan/Palgrave.

Nugent, Neill. 2003. *Government and Politics in the European Union.* Durham, N.C.: Duke University Press.

Nugent, Neill. 2001. *The European Commission.* New York: Palgrave.

OECD (2000). "Compendium of National Food Safety Systems and Activities." G/ADHOC/FS(2000)5/ANN/FINAL, June 7.

Ollinger, Michael, and Ballenger, Nicole. 2003. *Weighing Incentives for Food Safety in Meat and Poultry.* Washington, D.C.: U.S. Department of Agriculture.

Ollinger, Michael, and Valerie Mueller. 2003. *Managing for Safer Food: The Economics of Sanitation and Process Controls in Meat and Poultry Plants.* USDA, Economic Research Service, www.ers.usda.gov/publications/aer817.

Olson, Mancur. 1971. *The Logic of Collective Action*, 2nd ed. Cambridge, Mass.: Harvard University Press.

Olson, Mancur. 1965. *The Logic of Collective Action: Public Goods and the Theory of Groups.* Cambridge, Mass.: Harvard University Press.

O'Rourke, Raymond. 2001. *European Food Law.* Poole, Dorset: Palladian Law Publishing.

Ouchi, William G. 1980. "Markets, Bureaucracies, and Clans." *Administrative Science Quarterly* 25:129–141.

PABE. 2001. *Public Perception of Agricultural Biotechnologies in Europe.* PABE Research Group. <www.lancs.ac.uk/depts/ieppp/docs/pabe_finalreport.pdf>.

Parker, George, and Dempsey, Judy. 2004. "Europe: Unease over Pace of Reform in New EU States." *Financial Times*, February 23.

Parliamentary Office of Science and Technology. 2000. *The "Great GM Food Debate": A Survey of Media Coverage in the First Half of 1999*. Report 138.

Pascal, Gerhard. 2004. "Curriculum Vitae of Gerhard Pascal." <http://europa .eu.int/comm/food/fs/sc/ssc/cv/cv-pascal.pdf>.

Pauwelyn, Joost. 1998. "Evidence, Proof and Persuasion in WTO Dispute Settlement: Who Bears the Burden?" *Journal of International Economic Law* 1:227–258.

Persson, T., Roland, G., and Tabellini, G. 1997. "Separation of Powers and Political Accountability." *Quarterly Journal of Economics* 112, 4:1163–1202.

Peters, B. Guy. 1994. "Agenda-Setting in the European Community." *Journal of European Public Policy* 1, 1:9–26.

Petersman, Ernst-Ulrich. 1997. *International and European Trade Law after the Uruguay Round*. Dordrecht: Kluwer Law.

Peterson, John. 2002. "The College of Commissioners." In John Peterson and Michael Shackleton (eds.), *The Institutions of the European Union*. Oxford: Oxford University Press. Pp. 71–94.

Peterson, John. 1997. "States, Societies and the European Union." *West European Politics* 20, 4:1–23.

Peterson John, and Bomberg, Elisabeth. 1999. *Decision-Making in the European Union*. London: Macmillan.

Pfizer Animal Health v. Council. 2002. E.C.R. II-3305. Case T-13/99.

Phillips, Peter W. B., and Wolfe, Robert. (eds.). 2001. *Governing Food: Science, Safety and Trade*. Montreal: McGill-Queen's University Press.

Piore, Michael J., and Sabel, Charles. 1984. *The Second Industrial Divide: Possibilities for Prosperity*. New York: Basic Books.

Podger Geoffrey. 2003. "The Role of the European Food Safety Authority." EPC-KBF policy briefing, Oct. 9.

Pollack, Mark. A. 1997. "Representing Diffuse Interests in EC Policy-Making." *Journal of European Public Policy Making* 4, 4:572–590.

Poppe, C., and Kjærnes, U. 2003. *Trust in Food in Europe: A Comparative Analysis*. Oslo: National Institute for Consumer Research.

Porter, Michael. 1990. *The Competitive Advantage of Nations*. New York: Free Press.

Previdi, Ernesto. 1997. "Making and Enforcing Regulatory Policy in the Single Market." In Helen Wallace and Alasdair R. Young (eds.), *Participation and Policy-Making in the European Union*. Oxford: Clarendon Press: Pp. 69–90.

Princen, Sebastiaan, B. M. 2002a. "The California Effect in the Transatlantic Relationship." Ph.D. diss., University of Utrecht.

Princen, Sebastiaan. 2002b. *The California Effect in the External Trade Relations of the European Union*. Deventer: Kluwer.

Prodi, Romano 1999a. Address delivered to Parliament. *Bulletin EU 7/8-1999.* <http://europa.eu.int/abc/doc/off/bull/en/9907/p202001.htm>.

Pumphrey, R. 2000. "Lessons for Management of Anaphylaxis from a Study of Fatal Reactions." *Clinical and Experimental Allergy* 30:1144–1150.

Purdue, Derrick. 2000. *Anti-GenetiX: The Emergence of the Anti-GM Movement.* Aldershot: Ashgate.

Putnam, R. D. 1993. *Making Democracy Work: Civic Traditions in Modern Italy.* Princeton, N.J.: Princeton University Press.

Putnam, Robert D. 1988. "Diplomacy and the Logic of Two-Level Games." *International Organization* 42, 2:427–460.

Putz, U. 2004. "Das QS-Gütesiegel ist eine Verbrauchertäuschung" [The QS label is a consumer deception]." *Der Spiegel*, January 14.

Radaelli, Claudio. 2002. "International Regulatory Competition: Models, Evidence, and Emerging Research Agendas." EUI discussion paper, October 3.

Reisner, Ann Elizabeth. 2001. "Social Movement Organizations' Reactions to Genetic Engineering in Agriculture." *American Behavioral Scientist* 44, 8:1389–1404.

Renn, Ortwin. 1995. "Style of Using Scientific Expertise: A Comparative Framework." *Science and Public Policy* 22, 3:147–156.

Renn, O., and Rohrmann, B. 2000. *Cross-Cultural Risk Perception: A Survey of Empirical Studies.* Drodrecht: Kluwer.

Richardson, Jeremy, Gustafsson, Gunnel, and Jordan, Grant. 1982. "The Concept of Policy Style." In Jeremy Richardson (ed.), *Policy Styles in Western Europe.* London: George Allen & Unwin.

Roberta, Sassatelli, and Alan, Scott. 2001. "Novel Food, New Markets and Trust Regimes: Responses to the Erosion of Consumers' Confidence in Austria, Italy and the UK." *European Societies* 3, 2:313–244.

Ronk, Richard J., et al. 1990. "Governmental Regulatory Issues—Reducing Uncertainties in Food Safety." *HortScience* 25, 12:1482–1484.

Rothstein, B. 2000. "Trust, Social Dilemmas and Collective Memories." *Journal of Theoretical Politics* 12, 4:477–501.

Rothstein, Henry. 2005. "Escaping the Regulatory Net: Why Regulatory Reform Can Fail Consumers." *Law & Policy* 27, 4:520–548.

Rothstein, Henry. 2004. "Precautionary Bans or Sacrificial Lambs? Participative Risk Regulation and the Reform of the UK Food Safety Regime." *Public Administration* 82, 3:857–881.

Rothstein, Henry. 2003. "Neglected Risk Regulation: The Institutional Attenuation Phenomenon." *Health, Risk and Society* 5, 1:85–103.

Rougoor, Carin, van der Weijden, Wouter, and Bol, Pieter. 2003. *Voedselveiligheid tot (w) elke prijs?* The Hague: Stuurgroep Technology Assessment, Ministry of Agriculture.

Royal College of Physicians. 2003. *Containing the Allergy Epidemic*. London: Royal College of Physicians.

Royal Society of Canada. 2001. *Elements of Precaution: Recommendations for the Regulation of Food Biotechnology in Canada*. Ottawa.

"Rural France, Up in Arms." 1999. *Economist*, September 11.

Ruzza, Carlo. 2000. "Anti-Racism in EU Institutions." *Journal of European Integration* 22, 1:145–171.

Sabel, Charles. 1993. "Studied Trust: Building New Forms of Cooperation in a Volatile Economy." *Human Relations* 46, 9:1133–1170.

Sadeleer, Nicolas de. 2002. *Environmental Principles: From Political Slogans to Legal Rules*. Oxford: Oxford University Press.

Sagan, Scott. 1993. *The Limits of Safety: Organizations, Accidents, and Weapons*. Princeton, N.J.: Princeton University Press.

St. Clair Bradley, Kieran. 1999. "Institutional Aspects of Comitology: Scenes from the Cutting Room Floor." In Christian Joerges and Ellen Vos (eds.), *EU Committees: Social Regulation, Law and Politics*. Oxford: Hart Publishing. Pp. 71–91.

Santer Jacques, 1997a. Statement of January 15 to the European Temporary Committee on BSE.

Santer, Jacques. 1997b. Speech, to Parliament on February 18. <http://europa.eu.int/abc/doc/off/bull/en/9701/p203001.htm 1997>.

Sassatelli, R, and Scott, A. 2001. "Novel Food, New Markets, and Trust Regimes: Responses to the Erosion of Consumer Confidence in Austria, Italy, and the UK." *European Societies* 3, 2:213–244.

Saunier, Claude. 2005. *Le renforcement de la veille sanitaire et du contrôle de la sécurité sanitaire des produits destinés à l'homme : application de la loi du 1er juillet 1998*. Rapport no. 2108 de l'Office Parlementaire d'Evaluation des Choix Scientifiques et Techniques. Paris: Assemblée Nationale et Sénat.

Sbragia, Alberta. 1993. "EC Environmental Policy: Atypical Ambitions and Typical Problems?" In Alan W. Cafruny and Glenda G. Rosenthal (eds.), *The State of the European Community*, Vol. 2: *The Maastricht Debates and Beyond*. Boulder, Colo.: Lynne Reinner.

Scharpf, Fritz W. 1996. "Negative and Positive Integration in the Political Economy of European Welfare States." In Gary Marks, Fritz W. Scharpf, and Philippe C. Schmitter (eds.), *Governance in the European Union*. London: Sage.

Schlosser, Erich. 2002. *Fast Food Nation: The Dark Side of the All-American Meal*. New York: Harper Perennial.

Schön, Donald, and Rein, Martin. 1994. *Frame Reflection: Toward Resolution of Intractible Policy Controversies*. New York: Basic Books.

Schofield, Richard, and Shaoul, Jean. 2000. "Food Safety Regulation and the Conflict of Interest: The Case of Meat Safety and E. Coli 0157." *Public Administration* 78, 3:531–554.

Scholderer, J., and Frewer, L. J. 2003. "The Biotechnology Communication Paradox: Experimental Evidence and the Need for a New Strategy." *Journal of Consumer Policy* 26:125–157.

Schurman, Rachel, and Munro, William. 2003. "Making Biotech History: Social Resistance to Agricultural Biotechnology and the Future of the Biotechnology Industry." In Rachel Schurman and Dennis Doyle Takahashi Kelso (Eds.), *Engineering Trouble: Biotechnology and Its Discontents*. Berkeley: University of California Press.

Scientific Steering Committee. 2002a. *Complement to the SSC Opinion of 4–5 April 2002 on Safe Sourcing of Small Ruminant Materials, with Special Reference to the Safety with Regard to BSE Risks of Sheep Intestines and Casings.* Brussels: European Commission, September 12–13.

Scientific Steering Committee. 2002b. *BSE: Result of the Scientific Steering Committee' Press Release, IP/02/1314.* Brussels: European Commission, September 17.

Scott, C. 2003. "Organizational Variety in Regulatory Governance: An Agenda for a Comparative Investigation of OECD Countries." *Public Organization Review: A Global Journal* 3: 301–316.

Scott, Joan, and Vos, Ellen. 2002. "The Juridification of Uncertainty: Observations on the Ambivalence of the Precautionary Principle within the EU and the WTO." In C. Joerges and R. Dehousse (eds.), *Good Governance in Europe's Integrated Market*. Oxford: Oxford University Press. Pp. 253–288.

Seligman, A. B. 1997. *The Problem of Trust*. Princeton, N.J.: Princeton University Press.

Setbon, Michel (ed.). 2004. *Risques, sécurité sanitaire et processus de décision*. Paris: Elsevier.

Shaffer, Gregory C., and Pollack, Marck A. 2003. "Les différentes approches de la sécurité alimentaire." In Jacques Bourrinet and Francis Snyder (eds.), *La sécurité aliméntaire dans l'Union européenne*. Brussels: Bruylant.

Shapiro, S. P. 1987. "The Social Control of Impersonal Trust." *American Journal of Sociology* 93, 3:623–658.

Shavell, S. 1986. "The Judgement Proof Problem." *International Review of Law and Economics* 6:45–58.

Shavell, S. 1984. "Liability for Harm versus Regulation of Safety." *Journal of Legal Studies* 13: 357–374.

Shogren, J., and Crocker T. 1999. "Risk and Its Consequences." *Journal of Environmental Economics and Management* 37:44–51.

Shrybman, Steven. 1999. "The World Trade Organization: A Guide for Environmentalists." <www.wcel.org/wcelpub/1999/12757a.html>.

Sikes, Lucinda. 1998. "FDA's Consideration of Codex Alimentarius Standards." *Food and Drug Law Journal* 53, 2:327–336.

Skogh, G. 1989. "The Combination of Private and Public Regulation of Safety." In M. Faure and R. Van den Bergh (eds.), *Essays in Law and Economics* Antwerp: Maklu. Pp. 87–101.

Skogstad, Grace. Forthcoming. 2005. "Contested Political Authority, Risk Society, and the Transatlantic Divide in Genetic Engineering Regulation." In Edgar Grande and Louis W. Pauly (eds.), *Reconstituting Political Authority: Complex Sovereignty and the Foundations of Global Governance*. Toronto: University of Toronto Press.

Skogstad, Grace. 2003. "Legitimacy and/or Policy Effectiveness? Network Governance and GMO Regulation in the European Union." *Journal of European Public Policy* 10, 3:321–338.

Skogstad, Grace. 2001. "The WTO and Food Safety Regulatory Policy Innovation in the European Union." *Journal of Common Market Studies* 39, 3:485–505.

Skogstad, Grace. 2001. "Internationalization, Democracy, and Food Safety Measures: The (Il)legitimacy of Consumer Preferences." *Global Governance* 7, 3:293–316.

Slotboom, Marco M. 2003. "Do Public Health Measures Receive Similar Treatment in European Community and World Trade Organization Law?" *Journal of World Trade* 37, 3:553–596.

Slovic, P. 1999. "Trust, Emotion, Sex, Politics, and Science: Surveying the Risk-Assessment Battlefield." *Risk Analysis* 19, 4:689–701.

Snyder, Francis. 1993. *A Regulatory Framework for Foodstuffs in the Internal Market*, EUI working papers in law no 94/4. Florence: European University Institute, Department of Law.

Spencer, Leslie. 1991. "The Not So Peaceful World of Greenpeace." *Forbes*, Nov. 11, p. 174.

Stanziani, Alessandro. 2005. *Histoire de la qualité alimentaire (XIXe–XXe siècle)*. Paris: Seuil.

Statutory Instrument No. 780. 2000. The Genetically Modified and Novel Foods (Labelling) (England) Regulations 2000. London: HMSO.

Streeck, Wolfgang, and Philippe Schmitter. 1986. *Private Interest Government: Beyond Market and State*. New York: Sage Publications.

Suchman, Mark C. 1995. "Managing Legitimacy: Strategic and Institutional Approaches." *Academy of Management Review* 20:571–610.

Sunding, D., and Zilberman, D. 1998. "Allocating Product Liability in a Multimarket Setting." *International Review of Law and Economics* 18:1–11.

Sylvander, Bertil. 1995. "Conventions de qualité et institutions: Le cas des produits de qualité spécifique." In François Nicolas and Egizio Valceschini (eds.), *Agro-alimentaire: une économie de la qualité*. Paris: Inra Editions, Economica.

Sztompka, P. 1999. *Trust: A Sociological Theory*. Cambridge: Cambridge University Press.

Tabuteau, Didier. 2002. *La sécurité sanitaire*. Paris: Berger Levrault.

Testori Coggi, Paola. 2003. Speaking notes at the Conference on Risk Perception: Science, Public Debate and Policy Making, Brussels, Dec. <http://europa.eu.int/comm/food/risk_perception /sp/testori_coggi.pdf>.

Thompson, G., Frances, J., Levacic, R., and Mitchell, J. 1991. *Market, Hierarchies and Networks: The Coordination of Social Life*. London: Sage Publishers.

Turner, R. Steven. 2001. "Of Milk and Mandarins: rBST, Mandated Science and the Canadian Regulatory Style." *Journal of Canadian Studies* 36, 3:107–130.

United States. Executive Office of the President. Office of Science and Technology Policy. 1984. "Proposal for a Coordinated Framework for Regulation of Biotechnology." *Federal Register* 49, 50856.

Unnevehr, Laurian J., and Jensen, Helen H. 1999. "The Economic Implications of Using HACCP as a Food Safety Regulatory Standard." *Food Policy* 24:625–635.

Unnevehr, L., and Roberts, T. 1997. "Improving Cost/Benefit Analysis for HACCP and Microbial Food Safety: An Economist's Overview." In J. Caswell and R. W. Cotterill (eds.), *Strategy and Policy in the Food System: Emerging Issues*. Washington, D.C.: Food Marketing Policy Center.

Uslaner, E. M. 1999. "Trust But Verify: Social Capital and Moral Behavior." *Social Science Information* 38, 1:29–55.

USTR. 2004. *European Communities—Measures Affecting the Approval and Marketing of Biotech Products (WT/DS291, 292, and 293): Executive Summary of the First Submission of the United States*. April 30.

USTR. 2002. *National Trade Estimate Report on Foreign Trade Barriers, 2002*. Washington, D.C.: U.S. Trade Representative.

Verdi. 2002. *L'Italia non ceda alle pressioni di Bush*. <http://www.verdi.it>.

Victor, David G. 2000. "The Sanitary and Phytosanitary Agreement of the World Trade Organization: An Assessment after Five Years." *N.Y.U. Journal of International Law and Policy* 32:865–937.

Viscusi, K. 1990. "Sources of Inconsistency in Societal Responses to Health Risk." *American Economic Review* 80, 2:257–261.

Viscusi, K. 1989a. "Toward a Diminished Role for Tort Liability: Social Insurance, Government Regulation and Contemporary Risks to Health and Society." *Yale Journal on Regulation* 6, 1:5–107.

Viscusi, K. 1989b. "Prospective Reference Theory: Toward an Explanation of the Paradoxes." *Journal of Risk and Uncertainty* 2:235–264.

Vogel, David. 2003. "The Hare and the Tortoise Revisited: The New Politics of Consumer and Environmental Regulation in Europe." *British Journal of Political Science* 33, 4:557–580.

Vogel, David. 2001a. *The New Politics of Risk Regulation in Europe*. London: Centre for Analysis of Rick and Regulation at the London School of Economics and Political Science.

Vogel, David. 2001b. "Ships Passing in the Night: The Changing Politics of Risk Regulation in Europe and the United States." RSC working paper 01/16. San Domenico di Fiesole: European University Institute.

Vogel, David. 1997. *Barriers or Benefits: Regulation in Transatlantic Trade*. Washington, D.C.: Brookings Institution.

Vogel, David. 1995. *Trading Up: Consumer and Environmental Regulation in a Global Economy*. Cambridge, Mass.: Harvard University Press.

Vogel, D. 1986. *National Styles of Regulation: Environmental Policy in Great Britain and the United States*. Ithaca, N.Y.: Cornell University Press.

Völker, B., and Flap, H. 2001. "Weak Ties as a Liability: The Case of East Germany." *Rationality and Society* 13, 4:397–428.

von Tunzelmann, N. 2003. "Historical Coevolution of Governance and Technology in the Industrial Revolutions." *Structural Change and Economic Dynamics* 14:365–384.

von Wedel, H. 2001. *Organisation des gesundheitlichen Verbraucherschutzes (Schwerpunkt Lebensmittel): Empfehlungen der Präsidentin des Bundesrechnungshofes als Bundesbeauftragte für Wirtschaftlichkeit in der Verwaltung*, Schriftenreihe der Bundesbeauftragten für Wirtschaftlichkeit in der Verwaltung; Bd. 8, Berlin: Verlag W. Kohlhammer.

Vos, Ellen. 2002. *Institutional Frameworks of Community Health and Safety Regulation*. Cambridge: Hart Publishing.

Vos, Ellen. 2000. "EU Food Safety Regulation in the Aftermath of the BSE Crisis." *Journal of Consumer Policy* 23:227–255.

Waarden, Frans van. 2002. "Market Institutions as Communicating Vessels: Changes between Economic Coordination Principles as a Consequence of Deregulation Policies." In J. Rogers Hollingsworth, Karl H. Mueller, and Ellen Jane Hollingsworth (eds.), *Advancing Socio-Economics. An Institutionalist Perspective*. Lanham, Md.: Rowman and Littlefield. Pp. 171–212

Waarden, Frans van. 1999a. "European Harmonization of National Regulatory Styles?" In John A. E. Vervaele et al. (eds.), *Compliance and Enforcement of European Community Law*. Deventer: Kluwer Law. Pp. 95–124.

Waarden, Frans van. 1999b. "Elk land zijn eigen trant." In Wieger Bakker and Frans van Waarden (eds.), *Ruimte rond regels. Reguleringsstijlen vergeleken*. Amsterdam: Uitgeverij Boom.

Wales, C. 2004. *Country Report: United Kingdom*. Trust in Food Working Paper Series No. 6. Manchester: www.trustinfood.org.

Wales, Corinne, and Gabe Mythen. 2002. Risky Discourses: The Politics of GM Foods." *Environmental Politics* 11, 2:121–144.

Wapner, Paul. 1996. *Environmental Activism and World Civic Politics*. Albany: State University of New York Press.

Webster, Ruth. 1998. "Environmental Collective Action: Stable Patterns of Cooperation and Issue Alliances at the European Level." In Justin Greenwood and Mark Aspinwall (eds.), *Collective Action in the European Union*. London: Routledge. Pp. 176–195.

Weiler, Joseph. 1999. "Epilogue: 'Comitology' as Revolution—Infranationalism, Constitutionalism and Democracy." In Christian Joerges and Ellen Vos (eds.), *EU Committees: Social Regulation, Law and Politics*. Oxford: Hart Publishing. Pp. 339–350.

Werber, D., and Ammon, A. 2000. "Development of a Research Network for Emerging Foodborne Pathogens in Germany." *Euro Surveillance: European Communicable Disease Bulletin* 5, 11:120–123.

Wessels, Wolfgang. 1997. "The Growth and Differentiation of Multi-Level Networks: A Corporatist Mega-Bureaucracy or an Open City." In Helen Wallace and Alasdair R. Young (eds.), *Participation and Policy-Making in the European Union*. New York: Oxford University Press. Pp. 17–44.

Whitehead, Philip. 2004. "Pushing for Parma." *Parliament Magazine*, January, 41–42.

WHO 2002. "Bovine Spongiform Encephalopathy." Fact Sheet no. 113. Geneva: World Health Organization.

Williamson, O. E. 1998. "The Institutions of Governance." *American Economic Review* 88, 2:75–79.

Williamson, O. E. 1996. *The Mechanisms of Governance*. New York: Oxford University Press.

Williamson, O. E. 1979. "Transaction-Cost Economics: The Governance of Contractual Relations." *Journal of Economic Issues* 22:233–261.

Williamson, Oliver E. 1975. *Markets and Hierarchies: Analysis and Anti-Trust Implications: A Study in the Economics of Internal Organization*. New York: Free Press.

Wirth, David A. 1994. "The Role of Science in the Uruguay Round and NAFTA Trade Disciplines." *Cornell International Law Journal* 27:817–859.

Wirz, S. 1996. "Imageanalyse für deutsches Schweinefleisch" (Image analysis for German pork), Master's thesis, University of Bonn.

Woolcock, Stephen. 2002. "The Precautionary Principle in the European Union and Its International Trade Effects." Paper for the Centre for European Policy Studies, February.

WTO. 2004. "Specific Trade Concerns," Committee on Sanitary and Phytosanitary Measures, G/SPS/GEN/204/Rev.4. March 2.

WTO. 1997. "EC Measures Concerning Meat and Meat Products (Hormones): Complaint by the United States: Report of the Panel." DS26, August 18. <www.wto.org/english/tratop_e/dispu_e/dispu_status_e.htm>.

Young, Alasdair R. 2004. "The Incidental Fortress: The Single European Market and World Trade." *Journal of Common Market Studies* 42:4.

Young, Alasdair. 2003. "Political Transfer and 'Trading Up'? Transatlantic Trade in Genetically Modified Food and U.S. Politics." *World Politics* 55:457–484.

Young, Aladair R. 1997. "Consumption without Representation? Consumers in the Single Market?" In Helen Wallace and Alasdair R. Young (eds.), *Participation and Policy-Making in the European Union.* New York: Oxford University Press. Pp. 206–234.

Young, Alasdair R., and Wallace, Helen. 2000. *Regulatory Politics in the European Union: Weighing Civic and Producer Interests.* Manchester: Manchester University Press.

Zechendorf, Berhhard. 1998. "Agricultural Biotechnology: Why Do Europeans Have Difficulty Accepting It?" *AgBioForum* 1, 1:8–13.

Zweifel, Thomas D. 2002. *Democratic Deficit? Institutions and Regulations in the European Union, Switzerland, and the United States in Comparative Perspective.* Lanham, Md.: Lexington Books.

Contributors

Alberto Alemanno, Bocconi University

Christopher Ansell, University of California, Berkeley

Thomas Bernauer, Swiss Federal Institute of Technology, Zurich

Julien Besançon, Center for the Sociology of Organizations, Paris

Olivier Borraz, Center for the Sociology of Organizations, Paris

Laurie Buonanno, State University of New York, College at Fredonia

Ladina Caduff, University of Zurich

Christophe Clergeau, Sciences Po, Paris

Arne Dulsrud, National Institute for Consumer Research, Norway

Peter Holmes, University of Sussex

Unni Kjærnes, National Institute for Consumer Research, Norway

Rahsaan Maxwell, University of California, Berkeley

Christine Noiville, University of Paris 1 Panthéon—Sorbonne

Christian Poppe, National Institute for Consumer Research, Norway

Henry Rothstein, London School of Economics

Grace Skogstad, University of Toronto

Daniela Sicurelli, University of Trento

Bodo Steiner, University of Alberta

David Vogel, University of California, Berkeley

Frans van Waarden, Utrecht University

Alasdair R. Young, University of Glasgow

Index